"All Authority Has Been Given to Me"

"All Authority Has Been Given to Me"

Hearing and Seeing Jesus in the Gospel of Matthew

TIM LEHMAN

RESOURCE *Publications* · Eugene, Oregon

"ALL AUTHORITY HAS BEEN GIVEN TO ME"
Hearing and Seeing Jesus in the Gospel of Matthew

Resource Publications
An Imprint of Wipf and Stock Publishers
199 W. 8th Ave., Suite 3
Eugene, OR 97401

www.wipfandstock.com

PAPERBACK ISBN: 978-1-5326-9486-8
HARDCOVER ISBN: 978-1-5326-9487-5
EBOOK ISBN: 978-1-5326-9488-2

Manufactured in the U.S.A.   OCTOBER 14, 2019

All scripture passages are quoted from the New Revised Standard Version of the Bible, except where altered slightly by the author and indicated as such.

To all who yet long to discover the God of unconditional love.

Contents

PREFACE

Nothing in this life escapes God's view. This is wonderful news, for God is not scary, not angry, not a punishing God, and not someone we need to fear. Any belief that makes God out to be less than unconditional love is of our own creation, formed from personal need—our self-image in self-defense mode.

God would rather we put down our defenses and allow the words and actions—the very life—of Jesus to free us. When they do, the love Jesus taught will overtake in us any impulse to react to the world with violence, any justification of retaliatory, hurtful responses to the hurt the world inflicts on us. In the chapters ahead we will explore many of the words and life examples of Jesus in the Gospel of Matthew. We will be challenged anew by this examination of love incarnate. We will be called to account for anything in our life that is not rooted in and growing out of God's love for us and all the world. This book is a call to all people, but especially to Christians who may have lost their way as they lost sight of Jesus' way.

My hope and prayer is that the chapters that follow will breathe the life of Jesus back into people and situations where love, in a large or a small way, has been lost. Violence, in its many forms and at its many levels, has crippled life in this world—including, often, in the Christian church. But violence will be exorcised and dismissed by the Spirit of God in Christ Jesus. God's good news is intended as good news to *all* people everywhere—no exceptions. Jesus lives in full unity as God and with God, who loves all people unconditionally. Jesus is not a minion of Christianity or the church, to be heeded when it serves us, and to be ignored when following Jesus' life and teachings would impede our leanings toward violence, exclusivism, judgmentalism, and other worldly values. Indeed, as Jesus himself declared, "All authority in heaven and on earth has been given to me" (Matt 28:18). This is good news indeed, because it frees us from feeling compelled to wield such authority.

This book is not exactly a Bible study, a scholarly examination, or an attempt to promote Christianity. Rather, it is an in-depth walk through the life and ministry of Jesus as reported by Matthew. It is an attempt to take *all* of Jesus seriously, and not parse him out in ways that would limit the scope of his message to us today.

Whether you are unfamiliar with Jesus or have followed him all your life, the message of this book may well transform you—not by *my* words, but through your own discovery or rediscovery of Jesus' life within you as, more and more, you have ears to hear his message and eyes to see his living example. My prayer is that what I have written will help you discover the source of all love and life. Together may we discover the joy of living more deeply within the reign of God here on earth, and of knowing that Jesus has total authority over all of life!

ACKNOWLEDGMENTS

I am greatly indebted to many people who have helped me through the personal journey of writing this book. My wife, Susan Gotwals, has supported me throughout the past few years as my writing took much time away from our time together. My daughter, Kristin Grant, has graciously given her time to the cover design of this book. My editor, Heidi Mann, has seriously improved the flow and readability of my writing. Ted Lewis encouraged me and helped prepare my book proposal for Wipf and Stock. My children and grandchildren have inspired me to write as a way of gifting them with an image of the unimaginable love that is God. Through the years of my pastoral work, so many people from the churches I served have given themselves to partnering with me in ministry as we discovered Christ's call to be a faithful community living out the reign of God in the present time. In recent years, I have been challenged and renewed by the fellowship, love, and acceptance of our small Wednesday night church group as we have carefully studied the Gospel of Matthew together.

1 ———————————————————————

THE AMAZING FIRST WORDS

From that time Jesus began to proclaim, "Repent, for the kingdom of heaven has come near."

—MATT 4:17

JESUS' INAUGURAL STATEMENT

With Jesus' opening line in Matthew 4:17, he knocks it out of the park! After about thirty years of preparation, anticipation, and testing, Jesus begins his public ministry like a walk-on baseball player stepping up to the plate for the first time in the Major Leagues and, on the first pitch, hitting a grand slam. No one expects that to happen!

Jesus could have embarked upon his vocation a bit more cautiously—say, with a line like "Please consider what I am about to suggest to you." Or "I'm toying with bringing some new teachings, but I'd like your thoughts on these things first." Or "Would you consider starting to live more like the prophets suggested?" This would have been a walk to the plate and a strike-out with nobody paying much attention and no one feeling either discomfort or excitement.

Instead, Jesus laid it all on the line in his opening declaration. He spoke with authority from the very start. He expected people to respond and react in real time. Surely he knew there would be no turning back once he told people to repent. You can't be God's herald and God's Son and only tentatively proclaim things that will dictate the direction of life from now on. You can't speak for God and then take it back later. This is the big leagues.

I can imagine how people in Galilee hearing Jesus for the first time around AD 30 might have missed the significance of his opening words. I cannot imagine, however, how twenty-first-century disciples of Jesus can miss the power and the life-transforming import of these words for us today. Why would we doubt him? Why would we question his intent? Why would we want to postpone his meaning until a future life? Why would we want just part of him, but not the really profound, albeit challenging, parts?

The importance of what Jesus said not only in his inaugural address but throughout his life of ministry, and the struggle his words present to modern Christians, is what we are about to explore. It will be both exciting and scary. No one, no matter how immersed in Jesus, will go unchallenged, but hopefully also, no one will miss out on being, in the words of C. S. Lewis, "surprised by joy."[1] Jesus' life and words will lead us ever deeper into authentic relationship with God—that is, if we have the courage to allow Jesus' life to invade ours, and his words to truly change us.

DIGGING DEEPER INTO MATTHEW 4:17

Let's look at this foundational verse in segments.

"Repent. . . ."

Repent? How this word has been used and abused. Imagine you walk out your door, meet someone on the sidewalk, and they tell you to repent. I'm willing to bet you would react negatively, perhaps with a few choice words of your own. The word *repent* feels more like a smack to the head than a kiss on the cheek. For most of us, if we were seriously called on to repent, the dark shadows of shame would threaten to swallow us. Let's face it: often the people who claim Jesus hit the hardest.

Read the many commentaries on Matthew, listen to enlightened sermons, study the Greek word *metanoia*, which means "repent." Yet even after doing all this, many of us still feel twinges of shame when confronted with this word. But as we delve into Jesus' teaching, which starts off with this seemingly highly-charged word *repent*, I have a very important message for you:

Know for certain, Jesus is not shaming you with this word—he is freeing you.

The Greek verb form of *metanoia* simply means "to change your mind"; more deeply, it means to reverse the direction of your life. I suppose no one really likes to be told to turn their life around, especially if we believe we have no need for it. But what if the new direction was the most powerful and joyful and freeing path you could ever take? What if your life could become unbelievably more fulfilling, more amazing, and more dynamic? What if you could become more completely your true self? Would you

1. Lewis, *Surprised by Joy.*

be interested? Maybe even intrigued? Perhaps excited? What if you could reverse the course of shame in your life? Reverse the course of hurt, or inadequacy, or addiction, or doubt, or bitterness, or loneliness, or fear, or anger, or all of these and much more? What if your most protected secret darkness could come forward and be released? What if your life could become all about connecting with others in service and love?

Here is where most of us turn to skepticism, and for good reason. So many promises have been broken by Christian apologists, right? Well, this book is no apologetic for Christianity. Rather, this book is about taking Jesus' own words as the true good news. As you continue reading, I will leave it to you to decide if the words and promises of Jesus ring true for you. I do say to you here and now that in this one word, *repent*, Jesus offers us hope beyond any other we could ever have: Jesus offers us hope that is not dependent upon us—not based on the reign of our own self in the world, or even in our life, but on the reign of God. For centuries, Christians and non-Christians alike have chosen not to believe him—at least not to the extent of fully embracing his words and letting his call take hold of their lives. Why is the choice to believe Jesus so difficult? Well, really, who wants to give their life away now if they think they can have heaven later without doing so?

"Repent!" was not a maybe-later or a let's-think-about-it call from Jesus. "Turn your life around!" was not intended as a half-hearted move. Rather, "Turn your life around!" was Jesus' first and foundational proclamation, as Matthew reports it. "Turn your life around!" was and is a commandment based in God's love for us and understanding of our present, self-inflicted, human mess. "Repent!" is a word not for the sake of an afterlife, but for right now. We are urged to choose between a life taught and led by Jesus now, or a hoped-for future heaven but without Jesus in the present. Why on earth (literally) would we want to postpone the joy of living in Christ Jesus *now*?

"From that time Jesus began to proclaim . . ."

Let's back up to the word *proclaim*, which is sometimes translated "preach." The Greek word indicates the type of proclamation as when, in ancient times, a herald would announce the edict of the king. More than half a century ago, Bible scholar William Barclay wrote the following about Matthew 4:17:

> The herald was the man who brought a message direct from the king. . . . The herald had in his voice a note of certainty. He was speaking for the king; he was laying down and announcing the king's law, the king's command, and the king's decision. . . . The herald's message came from a source beyond himself; it came from the king.[2]

Knowing the force of this word, *proclaim*, it would be a huge misreading of scripture, and of Jesus himself, if we were to decide he did not really mean what he said.

2. Barclay, *Matthew*, 1:75–76.

To make this proclamation a half-hearted suggestion would twist the meaning out of Jesus' mouth. The actual gravity of this saying, and what makes it take commandment form, is that the herald is the son of the king, and the king is God. To dismiss this command to repent would be to say, "No, instead of following God's life direction, I want to go my own way."

I make a special point of this command to repent in order to draw a line in the sand, starting from the beginning of Jesus' instructions and the beginning of this book. In fact, Jesus himself drew this line: we either take his words as true and authoritative over our lives, or we don't. On the one hand, it seems so simple. But as we explore Jesus' teachings, it will become clear why it is, on the other hand, so incredibly challenging. It will also then become clear why so many Christians claim Jesus as savior while finding ways to distance themselves from his teachings.

One further note: The phrase "From that time forward" indicates a continuing proclamation. It is clear from this verse and others that Jesus heralded the repentance theme *throughout* his ministry. His life and teachings, and especially his journey to the cross, were all about helping us live the renewed life of the kingdom of God. To live this life that God intends for us, we must hear, understand, and follow Jesus' teachings and his life example. This is what repentance means. It is a glorious alternative to living a life focused on ourselves or a life lived trying to appease other powers that seem to hold sway over our world today. *The incredibly good news here is that, in this proclamation, Jesus is not shaming anyone; instead, he is freeing us to live renewed and transformed lives here and now.*

"... for the kingdom of the heavens is at hand."

Some in Christian circles claim that the kingdom Jesus proclaimed is a future kingdom—either for a future "millennial" rule of Christ or in a future heaven. It takes some serious interpretive gymnastics to get to that view of the kingdom from this verse; indeed, one has to ignore much of what Jesus says and does throughout his ministry to achieve this futuristic view. Let us say outright and with emphasis, there is no happy halfway point between hearing and living out Jesus' words now, and hearing them for a future time in another world. Jesus himself claimed we could not serve two masters. Either we will hear and serve Jesus now, or we will listen to and serve something not of God.

The actual word Jesus speaks in Matthew 4:17 is *heavens*—plural. In the Gospel of Matthew, the Greek word usually translated into English as "heaven" is almost always actually plural. Apparently Matthew and Jesus did not think of heaven and earth as two distinct realms. Maybe this will help us hear just how clear Jesus was in his teaching regarding the present nature of the kingdom of God—in his words, "the kingdom of the heavens."

An understanding of the presence of God's kingdom *now* is paramount to our grasp of *all* Jesus' teachings. If we miss this, we will find myriad ways to disclaim Jesus while continuing to live in our own way, and the wonderful good news of repentance will be lost to us. The whole purpose of Jesus' proclamation to turn our lives around is based on the presence of God's reign in this world, God's reign already come near and experienced in Jesus himself. Jesus makes his stand at the very beginning of his ministry, claiming God's reign and authority within himself. He is saying, "God's kingdom is here in me and my words." Then, the next thing he does is to call his disciples to leave their lives behind and turn and follow him. Oh, that the call could be as clear and as transforming of our present lives as it was for them!

But why did Jesus and Matthew say "heavens"? Think back over all the Bible stories of God's presence. Remember God's Spirit hovering over the waters in Genesis 1. Remember God's leading of Abraham and Sarah, the many visitations of God's angel messengers, God's salvation acts, God's covenant promises, God's presence with Daniel in the lions' den. We could go on and on. It takes a view of God and this world as *not separate* from one another to understand just how closely God walked with those who were open to walking with God. Jesus, of course, is the pinnacle of "God with us" in the Bible.

So, in the world of the first century, a world where Jesus would not have separated God from present life, what did he intend by saying "the kingdom of the heavens"? I love the explanation given by Dallas Willard, writing about Jesus' teaching on anxiety in Matthew 6. As they say, it doesn't get any better than this:

> This bold and slyly humorous assurance about all the basic elements of our existence—food and drink and clothing and other needs of life—can only be supported on a clear-eyed vision that a totally good and competent God is right here with us to look after us. And his presence is precisely what the word *heaven* or, more accurately, *the heavens* in plural, conveys in the biblical record as well as through much of Christian history. The Old Testament experience of God is one of the direct presence of God's person, knowledge, and power to those who trust and serve him. Nothing—no human being or institution, no time, no space, no spiritual being, no event—stands between God and those who trust him. The "heavens" are always there with you no matter what, and the "first heaven," in biblical terms, is precisely the atmosphere of air that surrounds your body . . . it is precisely from the space immediately around us that God watches and God acts.[3]

So, let's note the context for Matthew 4:17. Upon completing his time of testing in the wilderness and then hearing of John the Baptist's arrest, Jesus moves to Capernaum in preparation for his public ministry. This verse then reads, "From that time

3. Willard, *Divine Conspiracy*, 67.

Jesus began to proclaim . . ." Imagine that the herald—indeed, the very Son—of God steps up to the pulpit of his world and opens with this clarion call:

Turn your mind and heart and life around now, because God's ever-present reign is at hand!

If this call to action of heart and mind were not enough, Jesus then calls specific individuals to follow him as his disciples, and he launches his direct-action campaign. Matthew 4:23 states, "Jesus went throughout Galilee, teaching in their synagogues and proclaiming the good news of the kingdom and curing every disease and every sickness among the people."

Given what we have learned so far, and now adding this direct action of Jesus himself, surely it is nearly impossible to take Jesus' call to repent as future tense. Jesus' teaching, God's kingdom, and our own calling as disciples of Jesus are *now*.

GOOD NEWS OF THE KINGDOM—MATTHEW 4:23

Please do not ever think that Jesus was not political. He was, and still is, pivotally political. The politics of Jesus are overarching, hovering over the waters of all human endeavors. As the apostle Paul claimed about Jesus:

> He is the image of the invisible God, the firstborn of all creation; for in him all things in heaven and on earth were created, things visible and invisible, whether thrones or dominions or rulers or powers—all things have been cre-ated through him and for him. He himself is before all things, and in him all things hold together. He is the head of the body, the church; he is the begin-ning, the firstborn from the dead, so that he might come to have first place in everything. For in him all the fullness of God was pleased to dwell, and through him God was pleased to reconcile to himself all things, whether on earth or in heaven, by making peace through the blood of his cross. (Colos-sians 1:15–20)

There is only one Jesus: the Jesus who creates all authority, is before all things, holds all things together. He is the one in whom God is pleased to dwell fully, through whom God reconciles all things, and who makes peace through his cross. This is the same Jesus who tells us to turn our lives around, and the same Jesus who teaches us how to live lives that have been turned around.

My point is this: If we claim to be followers of Jesus and call ourselves Christian, then we have but one authority in this present life. Jesus is the authority above all other authorities in the world—the authority over all aspects of our lives, all our hopes and dreams, all our troubles and fears, all our joys and sorrows, all our comings and go-ings, all our thought and speech and actions, *and surely all our political involvements.*

As followers of Jesus, we must put an end to our confusion about him. Too many people try to retain Jesus as the one they worship and who will get them to heaven, but at the same time, they want to think of him as one who spoke but did not really have the authority to mean what he said. It is crucial that we come to terms with Jesus and his kingdom authority, or we will never be able to take his teachings seriously. If we do not take his teachings seriously, why worship him? In this simple question lies the rise or fall of Christianity.

Speaking still of politics, the good news of the kingdom in first-century Palestine was reserved for the Roman emperor and his latest conquests. The Roman emperor claimed to be God, or the son of God. In that context, consider the opening line of the Gospel of Mark: "The beginning of the good news of Jesus Christ, the Son of God" (1:1). A more political statement does not exist! But before you get excited about your latest cause in life, please know that we cannot equate Jesus' politics with the politics of the world's kingdoms. Politics as we know them—partisan politics—do not exist in God's kingdom. Jesus himself said in John 18:36 that his kingdom is not from this world.

If we seriously submit to Jesus' teachings, we will find that he calls us beyond partisanship and into relationship with God and all humanity. We will also come to realize that any political wrangling is counterproductive and destructive. You don't see Jesus arguing first-century politics. What he did was to live and teach the politics of God's present kingdom-reign on earth. Of course, in teaching and living this way, Jesus challenged all other politics. He, in fact, defeated all other politics. We will come back to this theme in the chapters ahead.

In each of the four gospel accounts, Jesus was opposed by certain people and authorities almost as soon as he started his active public ministry. In Luke 4:18–27 Jesus gave his opening address in the synagogue at Nazareth, and immediately the crowd from the synagogue tried to throw him off a cliff. In Mark, by the beginning of chapter 3, the Pharisees and Herodians were already conspiring to kill him. John 5:16 tells us that the Jewish leaders started persecuting Jesus. Two verses later, John says they were "seeking all the more to kill him." In Matthew's account, the opposition takes a bit longer to heat up, but in chapter 12, verse 14—not even halfway through the book—Matthew reports that "the Pharisees went out and conspired against [Jesus], how to destroy him."

Why the almost immediate move to kill Jesus? Simply put, we humans do not want to give up power and control. In fact, we fear in the depth of our being the loss of power and control. Now as then, we fight Jesus and his way in this world with all the worldly powers we have. It seems to be a duel to the death, for as the gospel accounts tell us, the response to Jesus on the part of those who feared losing power was life-threatening and life-taking. While throngs of needy people crowded around Jesus wherever he went, the religious authorities wanted him dead. Kingdoms clashed from the very beginning of Jesus' ministry, from the moment he opened his mouth in that first call to repent.

It would be too easy to say this was just a clash with the Jewish leaders. In Jesus' day it was only a matter of time until the Roman authorities were brought in for the final kill; then they did it, and thought they had succeeded. They failed, however, for the reign of God has no limits and no end. It stands as all other dominions and powers fall. As the prophet Daniel foretold about the Son of Man: "To him was given dominion and glory and kingship, that all peoples, nations, and languages should serve him. His dominion is an everlasting dominion that shall not pass away, and his kingship is one that shall never be destroyed" (7:14).

It is no accident that Jesus claimed the title "Son of Man." In him was the fulfillment of the Jewish messianic hope. In Jesus, we today find the fulfillment of all longing for peace and justice and love. The dominion and glory of the Son of Man is all around us, as close as the air we breathe. How can this be? It will become clear as we explore his teachings. But for starters, he describes living in a kingdom as entirely different from life under any earthly authorities. The word *kingdom* loses all its negative connotations when we discover how Jesus uses it, and Jesus' kingdom, for us as for the people of Galilee, is really good news!

Modern-day theologian and mystic Richard Rohr writes:

> I am told that there are three kinds of cultures today, each with its own "bottom line": political cultures based on the manipulation of power, economic cultures based on the manipulation of money, and religious cultures based on the manipulation of some theory about God. . . . These are the directions that human culture takes whenever it is left to its own devices. All three are based on some form of violence, although it is usually denied by most participants and hidden from the superficial observer. Evil gains its power from disguise, it seems. It is precisely this darkness and death that God, in Jesus, has come to destroy.[4]

My claim throughout this book, and I believe Jesus' claim throughout his teaching, is that violence does not belong and has no part in God's kingdom. We will explore what that means in the coming pages. It may be difficult for us to imagine a totally nonviolent kingdom here in this world. After all, we are human, and human cultures exist, as Rohr states, through coercion and violence. Without God in Jesus, we will never know another way. I am asking you to trust that there really is another way. I do not ask you to take my word for that. I ask us all to base our trust on Jesus' words.

KINGDOM AS JESUS' CENTRAL THEME

Jesus began his teaching ministry by calling people to repent so they might know that the kingdom of God was as near as the air they breathed. He blessed people with the kingdom. He healed people as signs of the kingdom. He welcomed "sinners" into the kingdom. He said that of all things, we were to seek first this kingdom. He traveled the whole countryside teaching about the kingdom in cities and villages. He sent his disciples out to proclaim the kingdom. He told parable after parable to illustrate the

4. Rohr and Feister, *Jesus' Plan*, 3.

kingdom. He used little children as examples of the kingdom. He warned the rich about how hard it would be for them to enter the kingdom. He claimed that the tax collectors and prostitutes would enter the kingdom ahead of the religious leaders. He talked about kingdom fruits. He warned that the religious leaders were locking others out of the kingdom. He claimed that the good news of the kingdom would be proclaimed throughout the world. When he was not mentioning the kingdom by name, he was talking about it and living it out in other ways.

In Matthew, Jesus talks about the kingdom fifty-four times; in Mark, nineteen times; in Luke, forty-four times; and in John, four times explicitly, but he also uses phrases such as "abundant life" to express the idea of the kingdom. Jesus emphasized no other topic as much as the kingdom of God! In fact, the kingdom was so important to Jesus that all his other teachings can be understood as falling under and within his teaching about the kingdom. His overarching goal was not to get people into an after-life kingdom, but to persuade them to live in, and live out, the present-day kingdom of God.

Think of Jesus' teaching and living like a one-thousand-piece jigsaw puzzle. Every detail he taught and lived was a piece of the big picture, a piece here and a piece there. All the individual pieces are really important, but when we put them together, they become one large and beautiful picture. Jesus' beautiful teaching and the example of his life form a picture of the kingdom of God—or, in Matthew's words, "the kingdom of the heavens." The importance of every piece of the puzzle is both enhanced and superseded when we see and understand the whole.

JESUS AS EMBODIMENT OF THE PRESENT KINGDOM

In the coming chapters we will focus much of our attention on the words and teachings of Jesus. However, if we only focused on his teaching, we would get the head but possibly miss the heart of him. In his actions, his feelings, and his relationships, as well as in his teachings, Jesus embodied the kingdom of which he spoke. We only need to read Philippians 2:5–8 to get Paul's powerful recognition of this, which he turns into an admonition for us all:

> Let the same mind be in you that was in Christ Jesus,
>
> who, though he was in the form of God,
>
> did not regard equality with God
>
> as something to be exploited,
>
> but emptied himself,
>
> taking the form of a slave,
>
> being born in human likeness.
>
> And being found in human form,
>
> he humbled himself

and became obedient to the point of death—
even death on a cross.

I'm a terrible dancer. It was bred out of me by my parents and a community that viewed dancing as sinful. It was only later as an adult that I gave it a try in the form of line dancing. It was a brave move on my part, and it did not go well. I quickly discovered I could learn only so much about line dancing through verbal instructions. In fact, I learned very little that way. What I was mostly able to learn came first from watching people who knew how to line dance. Next, the really big leap of faith came when I walked out onto the dance floor and actually danced. It couldn't have looked good, but I was out there doing it, and the experience became my best teacher.

Consider the importance of all three components of learning to dance, and then applying them to learning to live life as Jesus taught: (1) deeply learning his teaching, (2) closely watching how he lived, and then (3) living it ourselves. We desperately need all three components in order to follow Jesus in this life.

Let's take just one example of Jesus' teaching: the first part of his Sermon on the Mount, known as the beatitudes (Matt 5:3–12). He did not give us these sayings so we could just think about them. He did not just teach ideas; he *lived* these kingdom realities and called us to join him on the dance floor. A great example of Jesus as the very embodiment of the kingdom comes in the form of one of the beatitudes, "Blessed are the peacemakers" (v. 9). Was Jesus a peacemaker? Did he dance the dance of peace and call us to join him on the dance floor? Paul says in Ephesians 2:13–18:

> But now in Christ Jesus you who once were far off have been brought near by the blood of Christ. For he is our peace; in his flesh he has made both groups into one and has broken down the dividing wall, that is, the hostility between us. He has abolished the law with its commandments and ordinances, that he might create in himself one new humanity in place of the two, thus making peace, and might reconcile both groups to God in one body through the cross, thus putting to death that hostility through it. So he came and proclaimed peace to you who were far off and peace to those who were near; for through him both of us have access in one Spirit to the Father.

Jesus did embody peacemaking. Peacemaking was essential to his own calling and to his call to us. The interplay between what Jesus said about peacemaking and how he lived his life "even unto death" provides us today with a seamless example to follow. Even just this one aspect of Jesus clearly illustrates the impossibility of separating his teaching and living from a theology of salvation, yet too often, in regard to our salvation Christians focus only on the cross. The cross provides the most startling and stark example—but surely not the only one—of how Jesus taught and lived out peace, inviting us to join him in that dance.

Flesh and blood are essential to what God was doing, and is still doing, in Jesus Christ. Embodiment is present reality. Without the embodiment of God in Jesus there would be no meaningful Christmas, no Easter, and little in-between. The core of Jesus' embodiment is reported in the four gospels that begin our New Testament and compose approximately 40 percent of it. Surely it is time to return to Christianity the significance of Jesus' heart, mind, and soul—his real presence with us then and now.

TEN TRANSFORMATIONS OF JESUS

Let's return briefly to Matthew 4:17. If Jesus is telling people to turn their lives around, what are they—we—to turn from and to?

One way to understand what Jesus calls us to turn from is to look at how his life and teachings revolutionized and transformed the religion of his day. We need to proceed with sensitivity here. In no way is the following intended as a critique of the Jewish faith. Neither is it a critique of portions of the Old Testament. Jesus was Jewish, and as a Jewish rabbi he taught the Jewish people of his time and place. If anything, the critique here is of pieces of our present *Christian* lives in need of his transformation.

What follows are what I call ten "transformations." Together, these transformations show how Jesus both embraces the Old Testament and moves beyond it—how, in his words, he came "to fulfill" the law and the prophets (Matt 5:17).

Messiah

Jesus was not your "garden variety" messiah—not at all what people of his day were expecting a messiah to be. In today's terminology, we might say Jesus is not what most people expect in a savior. Though sometimes viewed this way, Jesus does not save us from our sins by way of a magical-formula prayer we say. Jesus teaches, lives out, and calls us to join him in God's present-day and future reign. And he does so not in some glorious, triumphal manner, as many expected a messiah to do, nor like a general leading his army against the heathen, as some today expect a savior to do. Rather, Jesus the Messiah came riding on a donkey, embracing humility, not turning from suffering, and offering himself in total sacrifice. To see how Jesus drew on the Old Testament roots of the meaning of *messiah*, we have only to look at the "suffering servant" chapters of Isaiah (generally chapters 42–53, with chapter 53 reaching a climax). For many years Christians have linked these descriptions to Jesus. This is but one example of how Jesus both built upon the foundations of the Old Testament and transformed our understanding of them.

Today, just as two thousand years ago, Jesus' way is love for all humanity: hope, healing, and compassion for outcasts, sinners, and even enemies. He taught non-retaliation in the face of insult, torture, and death. Many people did not want that kind of messiah, just as today many people do not want that kind of savior. But here we glimpse what Jesus asks us to turn from and to: Turn from seeking your life's answers through this world's use of power and control. Stop looking for a messiah/savior God to swoop down and *bam* the bad people, and stop thinking it is God's will that you *bam* the bad people on God's behalf. It is time to let go of the idea of a vengeful and angry God of judgment. It is time to welcome the real God, who comes to us as a suffering servant to heal our need for a false savior who only mimics human power and control. It is time to turn from the fears that keep us desiring a quick-fix, enemy-conquering kind of god. Turn to the one who is pure compassion, the one who invites us into the very depths of God's heart of perfect love.

Kingship

Years before Jesus, Israel's Scriptures recount:

> [It] displeased Samuel when they said, "Give us a king to govern us." Samuel prayed to the Lord, and the Lord said to Samuel, "Listen to the voice of the people in all that they say to you; for they have not rejected you, but they have rejected me from being king over them. Just as they have done to me, from the day I brought them up out of Egypt to this day, forsaking me and serving other gods, so also they are doing to you. Now then, listen to their voice; only—you shall solemnly warn them, and show them the ways of the king who shall reign over them." (1 Samuel 8:6–9)

From there it only gets worse. As God directed, Samuel warns the people about the horrors of an earthly king. In the end they cling to their desire to be like other nations. In this passage, the rejection of God as their king is stark evidence that the people were seeking after idols, and had been doing it a long time. An important lesson we learn from this text is that any form of earthly king in place of God as king is an idol.

If we were to sift through the history of Israel under the rule of earthly kings, we would see time and again how the dire warning of God and Samuel came true. In the end, the kingship years for the early Israelites were pretty much a disaster. Sure, God stuck with them during these years. God worked through prophets, Israel's circumstances, and sometimes the kings themselves. Nevertheless, God's deepest desire was, and is, for people to have a wholly different kind of king. God longs to reign over our individual lives and our corporate life without competition from earthly authorities.

Is it any wonder that Jesus as God's Son takes up the mantle of king?[5] And all of Jesus' talk about the kingdom was more than just talk. Word by word, bit by bit, he was wrenching authority away from earthly powers so he could reclaim what had always been rightfully God's.

Earthly authority has its place in God's design for us, but it must always fall under our allegiance to God in Christ Jesus. All earthly authority is called to govern in the way of God's kingdom taught by Jesus. When earthly authorities take a path other

---

5. For a powerful and insightful study of this theme, I highly recommend two books by N. T. Wright: *Simply Jesus* and *How God Became King*.

than God's way in Jesus, the followers of Jesus must keep to a steady course of following him.

So here we are called to turn from our allegiance to earthly kings—that is, any earthly authority. It is time to let go of our dependence on authority figures that rule with force and human judgment; to release our hold on security-blanket governments that rely on violence rather than on the might of God's love and grace; to cease grasping for security, period. God has greater things in store for us.

Kingdom

While the idea of kingdom overlaps with those of messiah and kingship, it also brings a decidedly unique agenda from which Jesus asks us to turn. Here it will be helpful for us to think really big, to not miss the forest for the trees, so to speak. Would it be possible to turn from our small view of kingdom, such as the kingdoms of this world, countries, borders, racial divides, "us" and "them," partisan politics, our emotionally territorial family feuds, and all the other ways in which we create dividing lines? Are these not all feeble attempts to claim ownership, rule, and authority? Whenever humans put up walls, we define a kingdom ruled by Satan, the accuser who always seeks to divide us from God and others (Gen 3:1-8). As we build dividing walls, we work against God's kingdom, in which all humanity is governed together by God. What a futile and hopeless path we have been on! Jesus calls us to turn from our human attempts to play God. They only lead to heartache.

Rather than dividing people into "us" and "them," imagine instead all peoples of this world living together in God's one and only kingdom. In God's kingdom, countries are intended to become borderless as racial and ethnic divides dissolve, and walls becomes bridges to unite all of us and God. There is and always has been one great big world out there, owned and ruled by God. As Psalm 24:1–2 reads: "The earth is the Lord's and all that is in it, the world, and those who live in it; for he has founded it upon the seas, and established it on the rivers."

Temple

In Jesus' day the temple in Jerusalem was the cultic focal point of all Judaism. The temple was where heaven and earth were understood to meet and where God's presence was most known. The temple was where sacrifices were made and sins forgiven. The temple was the bull's-eye of holy ground, with the space within the temple known as the Holy of Holies being the very center of the bull's-eye. The temple was also where access to God was designated as easier for some, and perhaps even impossible for others, such as women and Gentiles.

Those who have attended a Good Friday worship service or read the gospel accounts of Jesus' death may remember the dramatic occurrence inside the temple. Mark tells us, "The curtain of the temple was torn in two, from top to bottom" (15:38).

This curtain, or "veil," marking the entrance to the Holy of Holies was not torn just a little—it was torn completely apart, symbolizing that whatever would separate humanity from God had been eliminated. In Jesus' life and death, we now have unrestricted access to God. But we still might have a problem.

Think of the countless things that do still separate us from God—how is that? They are human things, of course. God does not re-sew the temple veil; we do. In Matthew 4:17 Jesus declares God's presence in God's kingdom all around us. If we are to experience God's presence as close as the air we breathe, we must turn from the barriers we ourselves have constructed between us and God. I can't possibly list all the barriers people construct, but if I were to list just one, it would be the veil of self-deceit. We imagine there is a veil, a wall between us and God. How could there not be, since we are such a sinful lot? And in mentally building this barrier, we re-enact the garden scene from Genesis 3. Like Adam and Eve, we find ourselves naked and ashamed, believing we need to hide from God. And we do so in a myriad of ways. This is a theme we will take up more fully in chapters to come.

Jesus offers us a way to dismantle—or, better said, to let God dismantle—the barrier of self-deceit. Jesus tells us and shows us how to stop trying to hide from God in the deepest, most personal recesses of our soul. Holy ground is not constrained by geography or limited to any specific place. We can learn to recognize it everywhere, including within ourselves.

Sacrifice

The beginning chapters of Leviticus describe in detail the various offerings and sacrifices expected of the Israelites. Some of this can be interpreted as heavy on guilt and sin. Some of it is about worship and thanksgiving. We know that even in Jesus' day, a heavy expectation lay on the people to journey to the temple in Jerusalem to offer sacrifices. It is thought that in Jesus' time, a majority of the commerce in Jerusalem was centered on the sacrifice of animals on the temple altar. It would have included, among other things, buying and selling animals, transportation and housing animals, and disposing of animal parts. This was big business, never mind the clear message of the Old Testament prophets about God's true desires regarding sin and restitution. For example:

> "With what shall I come before the Lord, and bow myself before God on high? Shall I come before him with burnt offerings, with calves a year old? Will the Lord be pleased with thousands of rams, with ten thousands of rivers of oil? Shall I give my firstborn for my transgression, the fruit of my body for the sin of my soul?" He has told you, O mortal, what is good; and what does the Lord require of you but to do justice, and to love kindness, and to walk humbly with your God?

Once again, we see in the Old Testament the roots of the direction Jesus would take regarding outward and inward expressions of penitence. Instead of temple sacrifice, Jesus offers another pathway to the heart of God. Throughout his teaching ministry and his living example, Jesus expanded on Micah's call to justice, mercy, and a humble walk with God.

So what is the modern equivalent of blood sacrifice from which we are to turn? It might mean turning from defining the problem and the solution as something "out there." Turning away from projecting our guilt and shame onto persons or problems outside ourselves. Turning from making excuses for the trouble in our own souls. We may need to stop running from the emptiness or the anger or the fear that lurks within us. And surely we must turn from thinking that something *we* do or say can magically make things right between us and God; turn from thinking it is or ever was up to *us* to set things straight with God. The harder we try to fix others or ourselves, the deeper we gouge the gap between our need and God's healing. Later, we will see how God invites us not into a self-help program, but into a *relationship*.

Law

Both Leviticus 20:10 and Deuteronomy 22:22 say a man and a woman caught in adultery should be put to death. In John 8:1-11 Jesus releases the woman caught in adultery, saying, "Neither do I condemn you."

In Matthew 5:17 Jesus says, "Do not think that I have come to abolish the law or the prophets; I have come not to abolish but to fulfill." He then goes on to say that nothing will pass away from the law, and he warns against breaking the "least of these commandments." Jesus then provides six couplet sayings, in each case declaring what the law says and how he now fulfills it by going further. What's more, in Matthew 22:37–40, Jesus teaches that the greatest commandment is to love God with every part of ourselves, and that the second-greatest is to love our neighbor as ourselves. He then says, "On these two commandments hang all the law and the prophets."

What are we to make of all this? For now, let's take Jesus at his word and say that in his authoritative teaching, and in his living example, he has indeed fulfilled the law. In him, love of God and of all humanity is the very essence of the law. In the chapters ahead we will learn about this love through multiple examples in Jesus' own life and teaching.

So, in calling for our repentance in Matthew 4:17, might Jesus be telling us to turn away from a life focused on anything but love of God and all people? Might he be telling us to turn from making anyone into an enemy (Matt 5:44), for true love of an enemy defeats the hurtful power of anger, hate, bitterness, revenge, grudge-holding, and violence? Might he be saying the only way to find release from our inner darkness is to stop giving hurt and anger a place to live? Might Jesus be telling us to allow God to take total hold of us so that our heart reflects the very heart of God? In all of these ways, the true meaning of God's law is recognized as beauty and freedom and forgiveness unbounded.

Consider the possibility of living ledger-free—with self-incrimination a thing of the past, judgment of others no longer taking up space in our heart; we simply don't keep track of these things anymore. Only by turning from them can we allow God's heart to fully invade our daily living. The men in John 8 who silently left Jesus alone with the woman caught in adultery were caught in their own inner turmoil of self-incrimination and judgment of the woman. I imagine they left bewildered: What to make of a kingdom of God so close as to reveal the darkness in their hearts, while not condemning the woman? In Jesus, the law became a mirror of God's heart. Hopefully our hearts will come to reflect God's heart too.

Sabbath

Keeping the Sabbath was, of course, a key element within the law. As Jesus' ministry progressed, it became a major point of conflict between him and the religious leaders. There is perhaps no more practical disagreement than the one between Jesus' message on Sabbath and how the scribes and Pharisees interpreted the meaning and keeping of Sabbath. Consider the various stories of Jesus healing on the Sabbath. Add to this the story of his allowing his disciples to pick and eat grain from a field on the Sabbath (Matthew 12:1-8).

The Pharisees had many laws governing what was and was not lawful to do on the Sabbath. They were attempting to be holy and to regulate the holiness of others by keeping a strict regimen of behavior. Jesus had a different agenda altogether. Jesus cared about what people had going on in their hearts. Jesus ministered to people's needs: sickness, demon possession, various forms of captivity and oppression. In living and teaching God's love, Jesus was all about showing us and welcoming us into the kingdom of God, where God's love reigns in all things. Indeed, Jesus was all about relationship with God, not about doing right by the law. For Jesus, this meant fulfilling the law in the way God always intended.

Leviticus 25, about the Sabbatical year and the year of Jubilee, is helpful context for understanding Jesus' teachings on Sabbath. Once the Israelites had entered the Promised Land, every seventh year was to be a Sabbath year, when the land itself would be given a rest. Imagine the rest this also gave to all who labored in an agrarian society—no sowing, pruning, gathering, etc. Furthermore, every seventh Sabbath year was to be a year of Jubilee. In this fiftieth year all property was to be returned to its original owners, relieving the inequities of a landed society. There would also be the same rest for the land and the laborers as in a normal Sabbath year, and indentured servants were to be freed from their obligations.

Leviticus 25 is all about justice for the land, for laborers and servants, and in terms of land ownership. Rest and renewal, justice for the poor, and return to a fair and caring way of living in the land of promise: all of this is bound up in the meaning of Sabbath. Rest, of course, was not merely a cessation of work; it was an opportunity to thrive together within a God-led community of people, a way of declaring oneself a person of God, trusting in the providence of God, and living in gratitude to God.

So regarding Sabbath, from what might Jesus be asking us to turn? He calls us to turn from a rest-less life. To turn from a drive to accumulate that which takes advantage of the poor and needy among us. To remember that God will take care of us. To be as non-anxious as the lilies of the field (Matt 6:25-34). In Matthew 12:11–12, Jesus uses the image of a sheep that has fallen into a pit on the Sabbath, and asks what shepherd would not run to the rescue immediately. Imagine that you are that sheep. Surely you have fallen, as we have all fallen in various ways. But Jesus calls people to let go of a God who has rules against pulling you out of that pit and saving you; to let go of a God not altogether ready and willing to lift you, heal you, forgive and love you. In Jesus' ministry there are no Sabbath rules limiting God's mercy.

War

This is a tough topic; let's not try to smooth over the difficulties. Read the history of the Israelite conquest of the Promised Land. Read the history of the Israelite kings. Anytime anyone suggests that Jesus had something to say about peace and love for enemies, someone else reminds them about holy war in the Old Testament. That said, those who would remind us of holy war seem able to accept most or all of the other ways in which Jesus transformed ancient ideas. Why not this one?

We live in a militarized country and world. From birth to death, we exist in a society replete with scapegoating and making others into our enemies, whether on a person-to-person or country-to-country level. It's like constantly inhaling and exhaling a smog of violence. We know no other reality. We are helplessly and hopelessly caught in the cycle of violence. Hosea 4:2 says, "Bloodshed follows bloodshed." And for those of us in the United States, we happen to live in the wealthiest, most powerful, and most militarized country in the world. Our militarized life goes unquestioned, even for the most part in Christian churches and from Christian pulpits. In fact, in a great many US Christian churches, the militarization of our country is openly supported.

If this were not a difficult enough environment in which to hear Jesus, we also live in a society, country, and world locked in fear. Fear fuels all violence. Whether of a personal or national nature, our need for security is based on fear.

Much of our fear comes from the threat of the powers all around us. If we were to actually live and teach others all that Jesus has commanded us, we, like Jesus, would be attacked by a variety of authorities in our world. In the book *Kingdom Ethics: Following Jesus in a Contemporary Context*, David P. Gushee and Glen H. Stassen write, "To proclaim a just reign of God is to attack unjust power structures in God's name, and thus to bring the wrath of those powers on one's head."[6] Imagine living, teaching, and proclaiming God's unconditional love, peace, justice, and forgiveness for all and in all situations. We would slam up against a wall of resistance attempting to limit those same things.

Another difficulty is our lack of full trust in God. I'm reminded of the story of Jesus and the disciples crossing the Sea of Galilee, when suddenly, a storm blew up. The disciples panicked until Jesus calmed the storm. After things settled down, Jesus said, "Why are you afraid? Have you still no faith?" (Mark 4:40)? Well, of course they were afraid! They thought they were going to die out there!—just as we fear we will die in a terrorist attack, or from a bomb launched by China or Russia. Fear and danger are real, no doubt about it.

So, based on (1) only knowing a violent culture and solutions involving violence, (2) living in constant fear, and (3) failing to trust fully in God's deliverance, what choice do we have but to arm ourselves? It is only too clear why Christians and non-Christians alike choose to follow in the footsteps of Israel's militaristic conquest of the Promised Land and the Israelite kings' countless wars. The only problem we Christians have, though, is that Jesus taught, lived, and died a wholly different reality. In fact, he launched a wholly different kind of kingdom. He had the audacity to teach and live as if this really was *God's* world and *God* was in control.

Jesus modeled humility, servanthood unto death, mercy, unconditional love, peacemaking, turning the other cheek, love of enemies, meekness, justice, giving up one's life, and even taking up one's cross. He didn't merely teach these things verbally; he lived them out—so fully that his living led to his dying. To avoid the deep truth of how Jesus responds to violence, how Jesus practices peace, how Jesus treats his enemies, we have to avoid his teaching altogether. How true, then, is our claim to be his followers?

Like I said, Jesus' transformation of holy war is a tough one. To obey Jesus means to turn from everything in our hearts, minds, and lives that contributes to anger, fear, mistrust, and violence on all levels. Let's admit it: most of us are not ready to make that kind of commitment. Most people do not truly want God's kingdom to come on earth, God's will to be done on earth, if it means we can't have *our* security *our* way.

But just because we don't want it, that doesn't mean Jesus simply goes away. We can take his teachings out of our creeds. We can take his living example out of our Bible studies. We can take him out of our sermons. We can take him out of our politics. We can relegate him to a "worship him only" religion. Yet none of these denials changes God's rule of this life and the next in the manner Jesus modeled. God invites us to participate in this kingdom that is "not from this world" (John 18:36), but it is up to us to decide whether we want to dance alongside Jesus.

---

6. Gushee and Stassen, *Kingdom Ethics*, 15.

I'm convinced that God's kingdom rules, period. What we see of violence in our world today is a temporal, feeble, misguided grasping at things other than what Jesus declared to be the power of God's rule of love.

So, what is Jesus asking us to turn from and leave behind? Fear—pure and simple. Fear of losing our life or some part of it is probably the most deeply ingrained human reaction to any threat. Humans instinctively respond to threat in fear and self-defense. Folks who study how the human brain functions tell us that this self-defense reaction is automatic and natural. Self-defense comes from the most primal core of our brain, sometimes called the "reptilian brain." Next time you react in self-defense, remember, you are thinking and acting like a crocodile!

Jesus asks us to leave behind that which is naturally a part of our human brain. How can he expect that? Perhaps he is offering us something better, a God-sized transformation. We will explore this in depth in the coming pages.

Covenant

Covenant in the Bible is much more than a promise. Covenant is God's doing, through and through. Human agreements are great when they are honored, but human agreements depend on human will and circumstances that can change. By contrast, in Genesis 15, God made a covenant with Abram while Abram slept. It was *God's* will and commitment—Abram made no promises whatsoever; he literally slept through it all! Even so, throughout the Old Testament centuries, people often believed it was largely up to *them* to "keep covenant" with God. When they failed, they believed it was their responsibility to set things right by performing the right sacrifices—the carefully prescribed spilling of an animal's blood for the sake of atonement and reestablishment of covenant.

The transformation in biblical covenant brought by Jesus, however, was written in *his* life blood. Talk about a God-sized guarantee! At the last supper Jesus and his disciples shared before his death, after they had eaten, he took the cup and said, "Drink from it, all of you; for this is my blood of the covenant, which is poured out for many for the forgiveness of sins" (Matt 26:27–28).

This covenant was for the forgiveness of all our misdeeds and our failures to love. Jesus did not mean that from now on we would never sin. He meant that in God's kingdom, and with this new covenant, forgiveness was granted, and never again would there be a need to meet evil with evil or violence with violence. Jesus offers us absolute forgiveness, brings us into the bosom of intimacy with God. And in that sacred, secure place, the cross of Christ puts an end to all retaliation and accusation. God in Christ Jesus makes covenant personal, intimate, and absolute, both on an individual level and on the level of all humanity.

With this new covenant, Jesus invites us to turn from and leave behind the prison cell where we have been locked for so long. That prison's name is "unforgiven." But the door of that cell now stands wide open—indeed, it has been torn off its hinges and thrown away! Jesus calls us to turn away from our doubts about our worthiness, for life is not and never has been about our worthiness. Life is about God's covenant guarantee that God will never leave or forsake us: "And remember, I am with you always, to the end of the age" (Matt 28:20).

Jesus also asks us to turn from our unwillingness to forgive others. Surely our own unforgiving attitude has been part of the prison bars keeping us locked in a cycle of self-centered doubt and fear. Imagine the joy of being set free from any need for shame of self and blame of others. This freedom is offered us through the new covenant in Jesus' blood. Remember, God is the covenant maker, and God's covenant is forever and totally assured.

Circumcision

Genesis 17:9–14 gives Abraham instructions about circumcision. Circumcision was meant as a sign throughout generations to come of the covenant between God and the people. God declares, "So shall my covenant be in your flesh an everlasting covenant" (v. 13).

Jesus never specifically speaks against circumcision. Yet he speaks clearly about the importance of obedience that comes from the heart and goes beyond a literal interpretation of the law. While the apostle Paul does expressly teach about circumcision, his understanding of it echoes Jesus: "Real circumcision is a matter of the heart—it is spiritual and not literal" (Rom 2:29). Paul states that what is truly important is obeying God (1 Cor 7:18–20), "faith working through love" (Gal 5:6), and being a new creation through the cross of Christ (Gal 6:14–15); it has nothing to do with bodily circumcision.

In Acts 7:51 Stephen accuses those about to stone him of being "uncircumcised in heart and ears." When some of the Pharisees claim that Gentiles must be circumcised in order to keep the law of Moses, Peter declares, "On the contrary, we believe that we will be saved through the grace of the Lord Jesus, just as [the Gentiles] will" (Acts 15:11).

It seems quite evident that Jesus' emphasis on heart-and-soul commitment to God and God's kingdom was taken up by his followers. For Jesus, Stephen, Peter, and Paul, true circumcision was not an outward sign but an inward submission to the will and way of God.

In this way of the heart, from what does Jesus tell us to turn? Likely, he is asking us to let go of any spiritual crutch we have used to show ourselves to be good Christians. It is possible to go to church, read the Bible, give money to missions, treat people fairly, pray, even go to weekly Bible study while all these things serve only as spiritual crutches. We can do all these things and more without fully giving our heart to God. Good Christian behavior can be as meaningless as bodily circumcision. I'm not saying we are to stop doing those faith practices, but rather, stop relying on outward signs of faith to make ourselves appear steady and well balanced as Christians. Instead, let's ready ourselves for how Jesus will fill us on the inside.

SUMMARY OF THE TEN TRANSFORMATIONS

Each of these ten transformations is important in itself, but taken together, they embody a "complete makeover" of human life and identity. *We might say Jesus takes us beyond religion and into a dynamic, self-emptying relationship with the one true God of love.* This, then, is both an actualization of the repentance Jesus calls for in Matthew 4:17, and an open doorway into Jesus' teaching and living out of the kingdom of the heavens in the rest of Matthew.

JESUS AS PRIMARY BIBLICAL TEXT

Before we delve further into Jesus' teachings in Matthew, we need to be honest about what importance and authority we have given him. When issues of life and faith clash with culture and society, where in scripture do we first turn? To Jesus, or to Old Testament texts, or to Paul or Peter?

The best way to challenge any other authority that might be used to preempt Jesus' life and teachings is to examine a few representative texts from Jesus himself and various New Testament writers.

Words of Jesus

"All authority in heaven and on earth has been given to me. Go therefore and make disciples of all nations, baptizing them in the name of the Father and of the Son and of the Holy Spirit, and teaching them to obey everything that I have commanded you" (Matt 28:18–20).

"Thus it is written, that the Messiah is to suffer and to rise from the dead on the third day, and that repentance and forgiveness of sins is to be proclaimed in his name to all nations, beginning from Jerusalem. You are witnesses of these things" (Luke 24:46–48).

"Very truly, I tell you, the Son can do nothing on his own, but only what he sees the Father doing; for whatever the Father does, the Son does likewise" (John 5:19).

"Very truly, I tell you, anyone who hears my word and believes him who sent me has eternal life, and does not come under judgment, but has passed from death to life" (John 5:24).

"I am the light of the world. Whoever follows me will never walk in darkness but will have the light of life" (John 8:12).

Words of Others

From John's prologue to his gospel:

> In the beginning was the Word, and the Word was with God, and the Word was God. He was in the beginning with God. All things came into being through him, and without him not one thing came into being. What has come into being in him was life, and the life was the light of all people. The light shines in the darkness, and the darkness did not overcome it. (John 1:1–5)

From the writer of the New Testament letter to the Hebrews:

> Long ago God spoke to our ancestors in many and various ways by the prophets, but in these last days he has spoken to us by a Son, whom he appointed heir of all things, through whom he also created the worlds. He is the reflection of God's glory and the exact imprint of God's very being, and he sustains all things by his powerful word. (Heb 1:1–3)

From the book of Revelation:

> . . . from Jesus Christ, the faithful witness, the firstborn of the dead, and the ruler of the kings of the earth. (Rev 1:5)

And from Paul, in Colossians:

> He is the image of the invisible God, the firstborn of all creation; for in him all things in heaven and on earth were created, things visible and invisible, whether thrones or dominions or rulers or powers—all things have been created through him and for him. He himself is before all things, and in him all things hold together. He is the head of the body, the church; he is the beginning, the firstborn from the dead, so that he might come to have first place in everything. For in him all the fullness of God was pleased to dwell, and through him God was pleased to reconcile to himself all things, whether on earth or in heaven, by making peace through the blood of his cross. (Col 1:15–20)

Through these and other New Testament texts, Jesus' role as absolute authority over any other authority is clear. The statements above affirm Jesus as God's Word made flesh, the exact image of God in human likeness. These descriptions are powerful expressions of Jesus' place above anything and everything else, which certainly includes other passages of scripture.

This does not mean that other scripture is unimportant. It does mean that for Christians, other scripture serves in a supportive role to Jesus and gets its fullest interpretation through him. The overarching significance of scripture that reveals Jesus within all other scripture is sometimes referred to as "the canon within the canon."

It is important when studying any portion of the Bible to allow each text to speak clearly from its own context. Whether it is Old Testament law or Paul on justification and grace or any other passage, all scripture deserves to stand on its own and be allowed to speak powerfully into our lives. That said, if indeed the above descriptions of Jesus are the truth about him, all other scripture will find its fullest meaning through an understanding of Jesus.

How can Christians possibly reconcile some of the differences between Jesus and other scripture? Here are a few key ways, and the sequence is very important:

1. Start by submitting to and knowing all you can about Jesus' life and teachings, and about the meaning of his death within that context. The Sermon on the Mount may be the best place to start with this, but all of Jesus' teachings and actions are important to understand full knowledge of him—at least as full as the Bible has to offer us. It is extremely important that we start with Jesus and not from a bias we might have from Paul's writings or the Old Testament or any other New Testament text. For the time being, let go of what you think you know of Jesus from other scriptures.

2. Commit to allowing Jesus to be your teacher and guide for living. This is essential, and will be transformational on a personal level. In applying Jesus' life and teachings to your own life, give him the same preeminence the New Testament writers quoted above gave him. Place his words and actions at the forefront of your mind and heart. Do not shrink back from him when he challenges your previously held assumptions about how to live in this world.

3. Once you are thoroughly grounded in Jesus, both in your knowledge of him and your commitment to follow him, you are ready to hear all other biblical texts, both from within their own context and from the perspective of Jesus.

4. Resist every temptation to understand Jesus *from* Paul (or other scriptures). Always understand all other scriptures from your understanding of Jesus. Remember always the preeminence the New Testament writers gave to Jesus, and relentlessly apply this to your interpretation of other biblical texts.

5. Finally, put all of this in the context of community and world. Let go of your previous notion of personal salvation, and replace it with a heart for the salvation of all humanity. Jesus is the savior of *the world*, not your personal ticket to heaven.

Once we have followed these steps, the supposed disagreements between Jesus and other parts of scripture will start to fall away. Take, for example, the list of Jesus' transformations outlined earlier. With a thorough understanding of Jesus and how his life and teachings are a fulfillment of what has gone before him in scripture, we have opened a whole new biblical understanding. We will begin to see how all of scripture is integrated in ways we could not have seen before giving Jesus first place in all things, including biblical interpretation.

MORE ON PAUL'S PLACE IN SCRIPTURE

It has been my experience that many Christians, including many Christian leaders, teach and preach Paul more than Jesus. In fact, these same folks seem to take their core Christian theology from Paul and not Jesus. Issues of faith and life are too often given over to a study of Paul and his thought instead of the thought and action of Jesus. If we were to take a sampling of texts studied in Christian Bible studies, I believe we would find a significant disproportion of Paul over Jesus. This has been a problem for many generations. If we start with Paul, we risk misunderstanding Jesus or, worse, disregarding Jesus. Paul himself would be horrified at this.

I love Paul's writings. I have quoted him in this chapter as a strong support for what I am saying about Jesus. Paul was all about being and living "in Christ." He, above all people, would want us to understand his words only through our full and primary commitment to Jesus. It just can't work the other way unless we are prepared to say that Paul is Lord, or that Paul is the exact imprint of God. This sounds ridiculous, but by taking our life and theology more from Paul than Jesus, are we not in effect saying just that? Paul's own words call out the lie in the way we have placed him first: "Was Paul crucified for you? Or were you baptized in the name of Paul?" (1 Cor 1:13). The obvious point of his rhetoric is "Of course not."

When we place Jesus first, we will see that there is no contradiction between Paul and Jesus. We will see that Paul is doing his very best to understand, live, and teach Jesus. We will see Paul's ministry within the context of everything Jesus. If you have put Jesus first and continue to see contradictions between Paul and Jesus, then I suggest you are misunderstanding one or both. The way through this misunderstanding is to go back to Jesus and recommit to giving him lordship of your life through his specific teachings. Then start reading Paul again in the understanding that Paul has made Jesus Lord of his life. You just might start seeing Paul's meaning in a different light!

WISE OR FOOLISH BUILDER?

In addition to placing Jesus first in our scriptural interpretation, we need to remember the importance of really hearing and living out his teachings. For example, before we push aside the Sermon on the Mount as concerning an other-worldly kingdom or dismiss the hard sayings of Jesus as not actually intended for our daily living, we must carefully consider Matthew 7:21–27. Here Jesus makes it clear that even if we say and do some awesome deeds, if we do not do the will of the Father, Jesus will not know us.

He goes on to tell a parable about wise and foolish builders. The wise builder, says Jesus, is the person who "hears these words of mine and acts on them" (v. 24). And the foolish builder is the one who "hears these words of mine and does not act on them" (v. 26). As the premier authority over all things, including scripture, Jesus is our premier teacher. It makes no sense—indeed, it's foolish—to call him Lord and Savior while disobeying his teachings.

THE CHOICE WE MUST MAKE

Jesus said in Matthew 11:30, "My yoke is easy and my burden is light." I believe this is true, but only after we truly submit to his teaching and to God's will on earth as in heaven. Only after we submit will we understand what Jesus means by "easy" and "light" because we will have reached a new level of living and breathing the kingdom. It will become life giving in unbelievable ways. Yet submission often seems nearly impossible. Few of us want to give up full control of our lives, so instead, we keep making life more difficult and more painful than God ever intended it to be. If we try to take Jesus' teachings as easy and light without submitting to them fully, we dumb Jesus down according to our own comforts and desires. We take life easy and seek to keep things light and *say* we are following him, even as we ignore some of the most important things he has told us and shown us. In the end, this always backfires and puts us right back on the pathway of fulfilling ourselves—which is a dead end both figuratively and literally.

If you want to follow Jesus, claim his way as your way, seek God's will on earth as it is in heaven, and realize daily the kingdom of the heavens as close as the very air you breathe, you will need to choose his teaching over any other. You will need to choose obedience not just to what you perceive as easy and light, but also to what you recognize as difficult and challenging. As we look more closely at Jesus' teachings, how he lived them, and how he calls us to live them, you may find your life under the microscope of Jesus' words. You may find yourself challenged more than ever before. But I trust you will also find "rest for your soul" (Matt 11:29).

2

Joyfully Salt and Light

"You are the salt of the earth. . . . You are the light of the world."

—Matt 5:13–14

THE SERMON ON THE MOUNT—AND OUR DISCONNECT

In the Sermon on the Mount, Matthew 5–7, Jesus tells us who we truly are. He reveals God's plan for our lives and seeks to draw us back to living out of the image of God in which we are made. In his teachings we learn the purpose for which we were created.

"This classic Sermon," states Philip K. Clemens, ". . . appears to be the best-known and least-obeyed teaching of Jesus."[1] And in apparent agreement, David P. Gushee and Glen H. Stassen declare, "We believe that Jesus meant what he said. And so it is no overstatement to claim that the evasion of the teachings of Jesus constitutes a crisis of Christian identity and raises the question of who exactly is functioning as the Lord of the church."[2] The evasion of Jesus' teachings from these chapters has been going on for many years and has taken many forms.[3]

The trouble is not with the Sermon on the Mount. No, the trouble is with us. This trouble is especially acute for those of us who have only known a culture of dominance

---

1. Clemens, *Beyond the Law*, 14.

2. Gushee and Stassen, *Kingdom Ethics*, xi.

3. A thorough review of the many ways the Sermon on the Mount has been interpreted is provided in Bauman, *Sermon on the Mount*.

from the side of acquisition and privilege. Our trouble is the disconnect between our lives and Jesus' life and teaching. This is both tragic and illogical: tragic because we have lost our true identity and are left with false gods; illogical because we call Jesus "Lord" and sing his praises, but disobey him at the same time.

Our human spirit as designed by God and created in God's image (Gen 1:27) has suffered much over many generations. We all have our demons, false gods we allow to fill our souls. We are demon possessed in a very real sense of the term: satanic forces thrive in our personal hell of fear, bitterness, and pain. This may sound extreme, and most of us would not think of things this way. But many people—Christians and non-Christians alike—have not allowed Jesus close enough to reveal the truth in their souls. The truth is that many people desperately need enemies, people they can use to redirect the hurt in their own lives. At times all of us rely on scapegoats. Who among us has looked close enough within themselves to see what is beneath the anger and bitterness? How many people can honestly say they have embraced their deepest, wounded spirit? Do we understand the source of our self-doubt, and have we embraced it? Who among us has been courageous enough to plumb the depths of their loneliness and depression? What of the self-hatred we sometimes face at night or in an embarrassing moment? Who lives fear-free? How many have considered the rootedness of their own agony within generational cycles of pain inflicted and suffered? Who is gutsy enough to link their own suffering with the suffering of the world, understanding that all humanity suffers together?

My point is this: Jesus teaches us to live out the very image of God buried deep under the rubble of all the hell our souls endure in this life. With Jesus guiding and empowering us, this Godly image can reemerge from deep within us as God's all-powerful love casts out our demons.

In John 5:6 Jesus asks a man who has been paralyzed for thirty-eight years if he wants to get well. What an odd question! Who in such a circumstance would *not* want to get well? But I could ask the same of all of us: Who among us would *not* want to be healed from our deep soul wounds? Many Bible stories of Jesus show him healing body and soul. He is available to heal us too, if we will only let him. If we will submit to his teachings, our road to soul-healing can begin today.

But if we are brutally honest, we recognize that in many ways we would rather remain possessed by the demons of fear, bitterness, and personal suffering than be freed of them because this condition is all we know. We live in the hopelessness of our captivity and have constructed an intricate system of defenses and excuses to convince ourselves we are okay. If we were to accept Jesus' call to live again in God's image, we would have to accept that we are *not* okay; indeed, we have not been okay for a long time.

James Finley writes about the lofty quest attempted by so many religious people. Though we look for God on the mountaintop, it is in the valley of our own pain where we discover God's healing love. It is in the moments of our own embrace by God that we learn to look out at the world with this same love. Finley concludes:

> God loves and is one with the communal preciousness of all that is lost and broken in everyone. So, too, you begin to realize that you are falling in love with each and every person in the world. As you go on in this love for others, you fail again and again. This is no obstacle so long as you see your failure to be compassionate as just another opportunity to renew your faith in God's compassionate love for you and for all of us in the midst of our wayward ways.[4]

How many of us can say we have left the lofty quest for Godliness in order to embrace the wounds of our soul? Many people I know have chosen the lofty quest, for it helps them have a sense of self-confidence, or even holiness. But it is a *false* sense. In fact, they know no other holiness. They believe theirs is the only holiness quest available. To take that quest away from them would be cruel. To help them encounter Jesus anew so that he might show them the path down the mountain and into their pain, guide them through their pain and into his heart of mercy—this would be a profound task. My hope in writing this book is to lead us into just such a new encounter with Jesus.

If we allow the words of Jesus in Matthew 5:1–16 to become our truth, God will heal us and shape in us a new identity. We will explore how this can be and how we then can become "salt and light" to the world, doing good works so that people around us will praise God because of us (Matt 5:16).

LAW OR GRACE OR WHAT?

The Sermon on the Mount has for too long been something of a battleground between folks who love ethical teachings and those who would rather avoid them altogether. The arguments about how seriously Christians ought to take these chapters have left many tired. Compared to the "law" feel of the Sermon on the Mount (at least at first blush), Paul, with his emphasis on grace, just seems the easier route to God's will for our lives. But it's a false dichotomy. Law and grace, as Jesus taught, are *both* fully anchored and connected in God's love for all humanity.

It is sad to think we have not figured out the faulty logic of the law/grace battle. Every time I think maybe we are past it and my hope builds, I hear another version of that age-old debate. I look out over the landscape of the twenty-first-century church and see the law/grace battle thinly veiled and continually reenacted. You hear it in the words we use to describe ourselves or others: *conservatives, liberals, evangelicals, progressives, the Christian right, the Christian left,* those embracing *cheap grace,* those relying on *works righteousness,* and so on and so on. Why don't we just call ourselves "followers of Jesus, our teacher and Lord"?

4. Finley, "Dreaming Compassion."

If you were to sample Christian preaching across the spectrum of theologies, I believe you would discover just how much theological identity is wrapped up in defense against the "other side" of the battle. As I suggested in chapter 1, if we would first and fully understand Jesus and his teachings as our ground of knowledge, then Paul and the theology he brings, especially in Romans, would fit together with Jesus like a glove to a hand. Neither Jesus nor Paul in their (correctly understood) teachings embraced a battle between law and grace. So why do we?

SOCIAL AND THEOLOGICAL TRIANGLES

This is not the place to go into a lengthy explanation of the dynamics of social "triangles," but a quick look will pinpoint why the law/grace battle never gets resolved. A triangle forms in human relationships whenever anxiety emerges between two people. This happens almost all the time. The anxiety can come in the form of disagreement, hurt feelings, suspicion, jealousy, and much more. Probably the least understood yet most pervasive root form of anxiety is our deep fear of and resistance to intimacy, because the more intimate our relationship with another, the more vulnerable we are. When humans feel vulnerable, they typically feel a deep-seated fear—maybe even terror. When we experience this vulnerability and fear of intimacy, we react by "triangling" a third person into the relationship. This usually results in the subtle, or not-so-subtle, aligning of two people against one, which somewhat relieves the burden of intimacy/vulnerability for the one who aligns with a third party. However, the "triangling" process doesn't actually relieve the problem of anxiety; it just spreads it out in a more complex way within the "system" of, now, multiple relationships. The anxiety becomes ingrained within this set of relationships, and it is much more difficult to reverse.

Admittedly, the above explanation understates the complexities of relationship triangles, but it gives us a template to talk about our relationships with other people and with God. Relationship triangles can be as simple as three people, but often they involve many. In addition, God gets triangled regularly by religious people who seek solace in the midst of their disagreements. By *solace* I mean relief from the threat of intimacy. For any person on either side of the theological argument of law/grace, to honestly and openly engage the other side would mean leaving their beliefs that feel safe and becoming vulnerable to the person or people on the other side. It is much easier and seemingly safer to stay locked up on our side of things. When religious people stay locked up on either of the opposing sides of this battle, they inevitably believe they have God on their side and use God in a triangle against the other. It becomes a "me and God, against you" triangle. And this is not the worst of it.

The "me and God, against you" triangle pretty much destroys any hope of loving intimacy between Christian sisters and brothers, but worse, it also destroys the possibility of loving intimacy between me and God. The reason for this destruction of our relationship with God is that in this type of triangle, we are using God for our purposes. It is not God's desire that we remain at odds with our brothers and sisters. It is God's desire that we love them to the extent that love between humans is possible—loving our neighbor as ourselves (Matt 22:39). Using God will never bring us close to God. Though it may feel like closeness, it only builds a wall of defense around us that keeps others and God out. In this using of God, we always end up feeling close to a god we have created in our own mind, and the tragedy is that the more we do this, the more we lose faith in and relationship with the true God.

This is the heart of the matter: our broken intimacy with God. To be intimate with God would leave us completely vulnerable, and we are not ready to be face-to-face with God and lose ourselves in the heart of God.

But when at last we are able to come face-to-face with God without creating a triangle with others or with God, without using God for our purposes, we will discover that the God of covenant faithfulness takes away our fear of intimacy and replaces it with love. Then, we will be able to rest in God's loving embrace. As the author of 1 John says, "There is no fear in love, but perfect love casts out fear" (4:18). When this starts to happen, we will not need our defenses or the battle anymore because we will be caught up in a new sense of freedom and the joy of intimacy with God.

PREPARING TO HEAR THE BEATITUDES WITH AUTHENTICITY

This brings us to where I hope we can discover an authentic way of hearing the beatitudes—Jesus' paradoxical statements recorded in Matthew 5:1–12—and our calling to be salt and light for the world (Matt 5:13–16). The first sixteen verses of Matthew 5 are not rigid law or easy grace. Rather, Jesus is sharing his heart—God's heart—with us. He is training us to recognize the reality of God living in us and us living in God. Jesus calls this the kingdom of the heavens. In effect, he walks right up to us, face-to-face, and calls us into a relationship of full intimacy with God. He bypasses any triangle we might try to set up. Many years ago, Martin Buber called this the "I/Thou" relationship,[5] to express the essential place from which all authentic relationship flows.

The beatitudes go beyond any theological debate. They go beyond any question of whether Jesus intended us to live them out in this present life. With or without our submission to his will and way, Jesus is inaugurating the truth of life in God's world. This is what humanity is and always has been meant to be and do. As the Gospel of John tells us, Jesus is the living Word of God. Jesus brings all things to life! In the first twelve verses of Matthew 5, the opening lines of Jesus' teaching, he calls us to life in God, resulting in God's heart implanted within us. Here, there is nothing to debate,

5. Buber, *I and Thou*.

nothing to battle over. There is only the question of our willingness to be vulnerable in the presence of God and allow Jesus to mold our heart into the shape of his own.

We are going to look at Matthew 5:1–16, starting from the end, verse 16, in order to be perfectly clear that life in God's kingdom of the heavens flows *from* God, *through* us, and *into* the world. The beatitudes are pass-through traits, God-like characteristics shaping us, and therefore shaping the world around us. They reverse our being shaped in the *world's* image and reinstate the eternally proper order of our identity being shaped in *God's* image.

At verse 16 Jesus says, "Let your light shine before others, so that they may see your good works and give glory to your Father in heaven." Don't get this wrong: It does not say we are blessed *so that* we will do good works or that we *should do* good works (either one would tend to view his words as legalistic law). Rather, the blessings of the beatitudes are God's descriptions of *who we are and what we do as children of God*, born and reborn into God's image. Hear this in resonance with John 3:7, where Jesus tells Nicodemus he must be born again (the Greek actually says "born from above"). How could we have missed, at the heart of God's instructional beatitudes, the importance of being born again within God's kingdom? Yet, we *have* missed this key connection! On the other hand, if we think of being born again as another way of saying "poor in spirit," we begin to see it.

The link between the beatitudes in Matthew and Jesus' and Nicodemus's conversation in John 3 continues as Jesus talks about the light of the world and the darkness of the world (3:17–21). Again, we have an important parallel. John emphasizes Jesus as our spiritual source of light and how separate this light is from the world's darkness. With Jesus as our source of light, our deeds will be deeds of light, coming directly from God.

I have never heard a Christian orator or writer link Matthew 5:1–16 and John chapter 3. What rich blessings we miss by not understanding *true* born-again spirituality! The beatitudes are the reality of our existence as we live with God's heart beating within us. This is who God's children are and how they live. In the kingdom of the heavens there can be no distinction between being and doing. These are inseparable parts of a whole life in God. Jesus simply tells us to allow this light to shine for others to see, to let the ocean of God's love flow out of us so that all may swim in its "wetness." What could be more natural than to let loose what is crying out from within us? What joy flows with this most natural spill-over of God's light, love, and life from within us? We are tiny containers—thimbles, really—with the ocean of God's love poured into us, resulting in a dam-break overflow of waters! When Jesus tells us in verse 16 to let the light of God shine—or, using our other metaphor, to let the waters of God flow—he is naming the most natural thing we could ever do and be. Think of the tragic waste of spiritual energy when we use a negative spirit to stop the overflow of God's love. The negative spirit that blocks God's love is the truly *unnatural* spirit, yet so many Christians have turned this upside down. Once again, we learn what to turn from and what to turn to in Jesus' instructions to us.

My wife and I have a dining room table made of wood, but that is not its purpose. Its purpose is to provide a platform for dining, but that is not what it is made of. I believe Jesus is saying we are *made of* these beatitudes, which includes living them. They are not our *purpose*, but they describe who we are meant to *be* in God's kingdom, created in God's image. We can't seriously deny that the table is made of wood, just like we can't deny that in God's kingdom people are made of the being and doing of these beatitudes.

Our wood, our substance, is essential to God's kingdom purpose, but *we are not* the kingdom purpose. The overall purpose is not about us; it is much bigger than us. But we can be partners with what God is doing in the world by letting our light shine so that people can see God, who is transforming all human culture into kingdom culture. Jesus is telling us to live our part in revealing God to the world. In living the beatitudes, we help draw all the world to God.

If we do not allow our light to shine and live the beatitudes, we are simply being wood with a misguided purpose. I live in the North Woods of Minnesota. We have a lot of wood growing in the forests around us. Wood can serve many purposes; in fact, most wood does *not* provide a platform for dining. The wood in our dining room table was shaped for a specific purpose, just as God wants to shape all people for a specific purpose. God has shaped us for a purpose beyond ourselves. Jesus, in his teaching in these sixteen verses, is remolding us for God's purpose.

Hopefully we are now ready to hear the beatitudes with open minds and hearts, silencing the voices that are too narrow or negative, while amplifying the voices that call for the expansive purpose of God's kingdom of the heavens come to earth. This new hearing will require our face-to-face vulnerability in God's presence.

EXPERIENCING GOD'S JOY—MATTHEW 5:1–12

Show me a person without joy, and I'll show you someone who has been unable to discover the meaning of the beatitudes for their life. Each beatitude begins with the word *blessed*. Each beatitude is in present tense. In each beatitude Jesus describes a present reality which we are either coming to realize within the fabric of our lives, or finding confusing and distasteful. These blessings of God's joy are the "standard" human experience for beings created in God's image from the beginning. As such, this joy lives in the heart and soul of every person. It gets buried by the weight of life, but in the beatitudes, Jesus removes the weight and unveils the joy.

The joy unveiled in the beatitudes is not mere surface-level happiness. It is not based on emotions. This joy is discovered in our being reunited with our creator. Joy in the sense of these beatitudes can be described as a deep, inner realization of being heart-to-heart in the presence of God. This joy comes from knowing we are living out of the heart of God. Part of knowing this joy is knowing release from any expectations other than what God has created in us. We no longer live under the weight of any standard other than God's acceptance and love. It may be hard to imagine, but God's joy, deeply rooted in our oneness with God, will set our hearts burning as we live the life God has ascribed to us.

Consider God's heart of love. God is the very source of love infusing us with mercy and grace in every vulnerable moment we allow. Have you ever experienced unconditional love without simultaneously experiencing a deeply felt joy, a oneness with the one who loves you? God's unconditional love fills our hearts with joy to the point of overflowing! Unconditional love and deep joy are inseparable. But our vulnerability is key. How are we to become vulnerable in God's presence in order to access the fullness of God's love and joy? The beatitudes name the reality of our vulnerability, and with these beatitudes Jesus draws us into greater and greater vulnerability before God.

A DESCRIPTION OF YOU?

A cursory reading of the beatitudes leaves most people scratching their heads and wondering how these things could possibly describe them. Oh, many people will latch on to one or two of the beatitudes. We can all identify with "Blessed are those who mourn" when a loved one dies. We like to think God will reward us when we feel persecuted by friends or enemies. These seemingly natural attachments to one or two of the beatitudes are fine but come nowhere near the depth of meaning Jesus has in mind for us.

Think back to Jesus' call to repentance in Matthew 4:17. He calls us to turn our lives around. This is not possible while we hold on to the very things that protect us from vulnerability before God. The words from Genesis 3:9–10 come immediately to mind where God calls out to Adam, "Where are you?" Adam replied, "I heard the sound of you in the garden, and I was afraid, because I was naked; and I hid myself." Simply substitute the word *vulnerable* for *naked* and you begin to understand where all the trouble with our vulnerability before God began. In Jesus' call to repentance, he urges us into a way that is opposite of and at odds with every hurtful, harmful, and defeating message the world has ever given us. No lie of the *satan* (Hebrew for "adversary" or "accuser") is exempted. None of these negative messages bring us joy, though we too often are lured by their shiny appeal. We will need to turn from them in order to experience God's joy.

As we delve more deeply into the beatitudes, please guard against the temptation to limit any one or all of them to applying only to certain times, places, or people. If indeed Jesus is telling us the truth about our identity in God's kingdom come, then God's kingdom-of-the-heavens joy is offered to everyone, everywhere, all the time. This is precisely the point of the beatitudes. Jesus wants to re-wet the world with God's ocean of pure love and joy through every disciple willing to heed Jesus' call. Some people, because of circumstance, may more easily receive at least some of these blessings of God's joy than other people are able to. Those who are poor, those brought low by suffering, those living day to day under the injustice and unrighteousness of the world's powers, and all in general who are outcasts, as well as people already on a path of letting go their own willfulness and those ill-suited for the world's way of getting on top, may at least initially find Jesus' call an attractive summons. Or they may not. Life is not so simple as to allow us to categorize people so easily. Plenty of destitute people turn to other gods for solace, just as plenty of sexy, wealthy, powerful people are satisfied with the gods they already possess. Jesus wants the ocean of God's love and joy to flow anew to us all!

Quite possibly the biggest challenge of these blessings of God's joy comes in the form of our excuses: Jesus meant *this* for me, but not *that*. Jesus must not really understand my situation, or he would not have called me in this way. Jesus must not have understood the present-day world balance of power, so he surely was not speaking to politics today. These are just a few excuses Christians make. When we make any excuse about the application of these blessings to our lives, we are in effect saying that Jesus did not know what he was talking about, or that Jesus did not know about the world of the future, or that Jesus simply is not God. To whatever extent we limit Jesus, we cut ourselves off from his blessings of joy. In the following exploration of the beatitudes, let us resist any attempt to wiggle our way out of Jesus' challenge. Let us embrace his joy.

While there is value in treating each beatitude separately, the real transformative power comes when we experience the overwhelming cumulative effect of all the beatitudes on our discovery of vulnerability and joy. With Jesus as our guide, let's hear a brief explanation of each beatitude, but as we go through them, keep in mind the profound human transformation that comes as they are added together.

THE BLESSINGS PARAPHRASED AND BRIEFLY EXPLAINED

In this section, I introduce each of the beatitudes, or blessings, first in the words of the NRSV Bible, and then in a paraphrase of my own, before taking up a bit of explanation.

"Blessed are the poor in spirit, for theirs is the kingdom of heaven" (5:3).

Or: *Blessed with God's joy are those who embrace their own poverty of spirit. They know and discover just how comprehensively destitute they are (whether spiritually or physically) as they enter the living presence of God. They learn their true identity as God's image on earth, which transforms earth into the kingdom of the heavens.*

Having served as a pastor for thirty years, I can say that this beatitude especially needs to include the poverty of spirit of the clergy and other church leaders. Any person in church leadership must constantly acknowledge their own immense spiritual need. Each of us in church leadership is just as spiritually destitute as anyone else. The spiritual authority with which we lead in the church must come from our deep admission of total dependence on God's Spirit as it reshapes us into God's image.

There is no limit to who Jesus calls into this blessing. No amount of material resources or lack thereof can change the truth of our complete dependence on God. This blessing is experienced by all willing to turn from the world's messages of self-reliance, self-dependence, self-attention, self-assurance, or anything self-bolstering. *The real joy of this blessing is in our discovery of our utter lack of need for a self that is separate from God's self.* This discovery is a lifelong learning process, ever deepening and broadening our capacity to reach out to the world with God's kingdom message.

Here we have Jesus' welcome into the unconditional loving presence of God where only true spirit resides. This blessing call is addressed to us today just as it has been addressed to humanity from the moment Jesus spoke these words. Today, as we find ourselves in God's presence, we also know that without God's unconditional love gracing our every moment of life, we die spiritually and emotionally. In this state of total vulnerability before God, our hearts are filled to overflowing with love and joy. This is what the kingdom of the heavens is all about. We now live within and out of God's reign of love and joy on a daily basis. This love and joy of God's Spirit encompasses our lives, while in this love and joy of God we experience that which we then pass on to all the world. This is all we know and this capacity for love and joy is all we now have to share. In the words of 1 John 4:13–16:

> By this we know that we abide in him and he in us, because he has given us of his Spirit. And we have seen and do testify that the Father has sent his Son as the Savior of the world. God abides in those who confess that Jesus is the Son of God, and they abide in God. So we have known and believe the love that God has for us. God is love, and those who abide in love abide in God, and God abides in them.

These verses leave no doubt as to the divine role of Jesus for the salvation of the world. These words welcome us into his saving work. These verses make clear the connection between God's Spirit and God's love. They are really two sides of the same coin, the coin from which our joy comes. It becomes our experience of heaven on earth, a blessing like no other. And it is ours if only we will accept it. We can probably say that for every beatitude-blessing, but surely for this first one: accepting this welcome, this call to spiritual poverty, is crucial to all other teachings of Jesus. If we miss this one, we risk misinterpreting or misappropriating everything else he said in the rest of the Sermon on the Mount.

"Blessed are those who mourn, for they will be comforted" (5:4).

Or: *Blessed with God's joy are those who mourn over their own brokenness and the brokenness of the world. Within the very process of mourning these things, they are comforted as their hearts are both broken by and opened to the compassion of God's heart.*

We might say this is a process of being broken and blessed all in one or all at the same time. Remember, these blessing-beatitudes are Jesus' call to enter God's presence and allow God to return us to who God created us to be. As we enter the space of God's heart, many things in this life bring us into a state of mourning. With this reference to mourning, Jesus is describing the sense of deep sorrow over what is not right in the world. Death, destruction, injustice, disaster, and violence—all are certain to be experienced personally and are inevitable in our broken world.

But Jesus is also addressing that which is not right *within* me—all that I have become, apart from God's love and grace. The world as we know it will continue to suffer brokenness. Similarly, in this present life, I will never be perfectly face-to-face with God. On both counts—the world's brokenness and my own—mourning is an ongoing reality. It doesn't make sense that we would be blessed in mourning either the world's tragedy or our own, but not both.

It is when we come before God in deep sorrow over what is broken both within ourselves and within the world that we are enabled to lay these things down, give them to God, and allow God to comfort us. None of this is possible when we take our deep sorrow somewhere else, like turning it into anger or accusations or denial. Over and over again, we witness how people respond to the world in anger rather than recognizing their own deep sorrow for what it truly is: a doorway by which God can enter us with grace and forgiveness.

Every time we are wounded by the world and respond with accusation, we turn our pain away from the source of healing and comfort. We forget, time and time again, that our pain *is* the world's pain and the world's pain *is* our pain. Any attempt to separate ourselves from the world's pain is a denial of our own, and we will never find comfort and healing in anything but God's love, unconditional acceptance, and forgiveness. Whatever the world can do, God can forgive and redeem. In the brutal murder of Jesus, God's Son, the world did its absolute worst and God turned it into resurrection and life everlasting. In response to the worst the world could ever do, God did the best that could ever be done.

How much more assurance and comfort do we need? God's love in Jesus can and will redeem all pain and suffering, and not just at some later time. God's love in us now will redeem the pain and suffering we experience in life *now*, but only when we bring our broken hearts to Jesus and allow him to heal us. Once that happens, we will have the love and joy it takes to start healing the world around us. If our healing is the real thing accomplished by God's grace and forgiveness, then out of what God has done in us will come our own quest to heal the deep sorrow of others. Show me someone who is transforming the world with God's love, grace, and forgiveness, and I'll show you someone who has submitted their broken heart to this beatitude of Jesus whether they are Christian or not.

"Blessed are the meek, for they will inherit the earth" (5:5).

Or: *Blessed with God's joy are those who humbly give their will over to God's will. They will find all the treasures of earth already available to them in God's wonderful creation.*

The joy of this blessing comes when people completely give up their status in life in order to let God work fully in and through them. This does not mean they resign their position of leadership or purposefully become unpopular. It means they become God's kingdom agents, living lives fully pliable to God's will and purpose in this world. Paul's words about Jesus in Philippians 2:5–8 must be the best-written description of this kind of meekness:

> Let the same mind be in you that was in Christ Jesus, who, though he was in the form of God, did not regard equality with God as something to be exploited, but emptied himself, taking the form of a slave, being born in human likeness. And being found in human form, he humbled himself and became obedient to the point of death—even death on a cross.

This is not the meekness we typically think of when we say the word. We tend to think *meek* describes someone who is quiet, soft-spoken, rarely noticed in a crowd—maybe even a "doormat" who lets people "walk all over them." While this sometimes describes the actions or attitudes of a meek person, being meek as Jesus uses the word in this blessing is another thing altogether. If the first beatitude focused on our need for God's Spirit and the second focused on God's healing love, this third beatitude focuses on God's will—specifically, God's will directing and guiding our will. Understood in this way, the meaning of *meekness* here is certainly not "weakness."

When Jesus invites us to meekness, we might be surprised to realize he is actually speaking of a *powerful* attribute, one fully guided by God. Because of our humble willingness to submit fully to God, God will accomplish amazing things through us. This meekness in us becomes a force as powerful as God is powerful. This meekness unleashes God's will into the world, transforming present pain into the reality of kingdom living. We discover all the earth to be our home because now God's will is done on earth just as in the heavens.

The great thing here is how meekness sneaks up on people. Jesus did not conduct his teaching and healing ministry as a direct confrontation with established religious power, and certainly not with the power of Rome. God does not ever need to stoop so low as to fight against the powers of this world *with* the power of this world. Rather, God in Christ Jesus knew it was time to establish a kingdom of love, forgiveness, and healing regardless of what the powers-that-be thought about it. Jesus reclaimed true humanity not in competition with any worldly view of humanity, but as the true replacement for anything other than God's will for us in this life. As such, Jesus' meekness is an attitude out of which God's love, forgiveness, and healing always grows. It is never forced but always offered. It comes as a quiet revelation, not a direct challenge.

It does not play by *our* rules but sets a whole different standard by which our rules are judged.

In the end, meekness, as Jesus lived and taught meekness, always threatens wills that are not connected with God's will. Powers that do not look, feel, or act like God's love, forgiveness, grace, and joy are revealed to not be powers at all. They are ultimately unmasked, and the people caught up in them become very upset by Jesus' teachings and by the followers of Jesus' teachings.

As Gregory Boyd says in *The Myth of a Christian Nation*, God's power of love will always look like the cross.[6] God's power always takes the form of love and service willing even to suffer death on a cross. In Matthew 20:25–28, Jesus instructs his disciples in the ways of meekness as they consider what it means to be great in the kingdom of God:

> You know that the rulers of the Gentiles lord it over them, and their great ones are tyrants over them. It will not be so among you; but whoever wishes to be great among you must be your servant, and whoever wishes to be first among you must be your slave; just as the Son of Man came not to be served but to serve, and to give his life a ransom for many.

Jesus frees us from the world's power-grabbing ways. Power in God's kingdom is nothing to be grabbed because it is freely given. This free power is what God shares with us as we enter this third blessing. We become amazingly empowered, but it comes in the form of Jesus' life and teachings lived through us. The power of this blessing only comes through transformation in God's presence as we let go of any so-called power we think we own. It is a joy-filled experience when we realize the extent of God's power available to and through us! Then we can wield the power of love from a joyful and grateful heart. It is experienced as a power altogether different than any form of coercive power.

So, what does it mean that these blessed ones will inherit the earth? If our energies are now turned from grabbing coercive power over people and things in this life, we are left with an awareness of the gifts of life God has already given. We have no need to strive after things, but can experience the inheritance already given us. Unlike the prodigal son, we realize we are already living the inheritance of our father. We do not have to seek it on our own—we will never find it on our own anyway. This changes the whole focus of our life from anxiously making our own way to calmly and meekly living God's way. It is truly a joy to now focus on blessing others instead of self-advancement.

6. Boyd, *Myth of a Christian Nation*, 33.

"Blessed are those who hunger and thirst for righteousness, for they will be filled" (5:6).

Or: *Blessed with God's joy are those who thoroughly and desperately long for God's right justice in all relationships. Their lives will be filled with the realization of right justice.*

A dear friend of mine fell and broke her leg last winter. She needed surgery, which included anesthesia, of course, and then pain medications afterward. The accumulation of these medicines left her vomiting and seriously dehydrated. This continued for days while she could barely eat or keep food down. I recently asked her what it was like to not be able to eat for that period of time. She described how desperately hungry she was and how she constantly thought about food. Her mind was consumed by the images of food and by her hunger.

Her story has become a lens through which I now look deeply into the meaning of this beatitude. My friend's body was cut off from the sustenance it needed, so it responded by constantly crying out for food. *From the beginning of creation, God in Christ Jesus formed our hearts, souls, and spirits to thrive on righteousness as much as our bodies need food.* If denied righteousness, our hearts, souls, and spirits crave it, for righteousness represents a wholeness within all our relationships with people, the earth, and, most importantly, God. Given this truth, it is time to confront a most uncomfortable question: What has gone so wrong with the human heart, soul, and spirit that our craving for righteousness is now dumbed down, or even nonexistent?

If we hope to truly answer that question, we first need to understand the meaning of *righteousness* as Jesus used the word. While this exploration could take an entire book, we will look at only a few of the most important points regarding its meaning in Matthew 5:6.

Biblical scholars widely agree that the prophet Isaiah is an important source for Jesus' teaching; he quotes Isaiah often. Scholars also agree that Isaiah 61 is particularly important in Jesus' teaching of the beatitudes and, I would add, especially in this teaching about righteousness. In Isaiah 61:1–4, 8–11 we read:

> The spirit of the Lord God is upon me, because the Lord has anointed me; he has sent me to bring good news to the oppressed, to bind up the broken-hearted, to proclaim liberty to the captives, and release to the prisoners; to proclaim the year of the Lord's favor, and the day of vengeance of our God; to comfort all who mourn; to provide for those who mourn in Zion—to give them a garland instead of ashes, the oil of gladness instead of mourning, the mantle of praise instead of a faint spirit. They will be called oaks of righteousness, the planting of the Lord, to display his glory. They shall build up the ancient ruins, they shall raise up the former devastations of many generations. . . . For I the Lord love justice, I hate robbery and wrongdoing; I will faithfully give them their recompense, and I will make an everlasting covenant with them. Their descendants shall be known among the nations, and their offspring among the peoples; all who see them shall acknowledge that they

are a people whom the Lord has blessed. I will greatly rejoice in the Lord, my whole being shall exult in my God; for he has clothed me with the garments of salvation, he has covered me with the robe of righteousness, as a bridegroom decks himself with a garland, and as a bride adorns herself with her jewels. For as the earth brings forth its shoots, and as a garden causes what is sown in it to spring up, so the Lord God will cause righteousness and praise to spring up before all the nations.

Jesus took this Isaiah text as his own. He began his ministry quoting from it in Luke 4:18–19 and referencing it in Matthew 5:3–6. In adopting this text to declare his mission in first-century Palestine, he left no doubt that he was taking upon himself the mantle and meaning of Isaiah the prophet. Anyone at that time who knew the scriptures would have understood what Isaiah said about righteousness, and they would have understood what Jesus meant when he used this word. There remains no excuse for us present-day Christians to mix up Jesus' meaning of *righteousness* and what we have come to know today as piety.

Read through Isaiah 61 and from that context define the word *righteousness*. Let's simply list some of the related words and phrases here: "good news to the oppressed," "bind up the brokenhearted," "proclaim liberty to the captives," "release to the prisoners," "comfort all who mourn," "they will be called oaks of righteousness," "for I the Lord love justice," "I hate robbery and wrongdoing," "they are a people whom the Lord has blessed," "the Lord God will cause righteousness and praise to spring up before all the nations."

Let's simplify this by only using some of the words associated with righteousness: *good news, binding up, proclaiming liberty, release, comfort, love for justice, hate wrongdoing, blessing,* etc. We now start to see the tremendous importance of righteousness for all relationships on earth and in the heavens. If we take this list of words and add them together, we get a whole lot of very good news. Righteousness restores relationships on all levels. Righteousness is who God is and how God acts. What comes from this righteousness? Isaiah 61 says many wonderful things come from righteousness, but the sum of it all seems clear in verse 7: "everlasting joy."

Nowhere in the text of Isaiah 61 do we find the words *personal piety*, or *prayer*, or *the reading of scripture*, or *attending synagogue* (or *church*); nor do we find any rules against personal habits like smoking or drinking. This does not mean these things hold no importance, but it does indicate that God's righteousness, and therefore our own righteousness, means something else altogether. Jesus knew this well, as he knew the scriptures better than anyone.

To go a bit deeper and add an even stronger emphasis, we find in Isaiah, other prophets, and the Psalms that the word *righteousness* has a companion word: *justice*. Many readings include both words, dovetailing their meanings. This is why I paraphrased this beatitude with the words "right justice." Glen Stassen writes in *Living the Sermon on the Mount*:

The reign-of-God passages in Isaiah often place the two words *justice* and *righteousness* in parallel because they are meant to translate crucially important Hebrew words that mean almost the same thing. . . . The first is *mishpat*, justice in the sense of decisions of the authorities and practices of the markets that are fair to the poor and the powerless. . . . The other word is *tsedaqah*, which means the kind of justice that delivers from slavery and from oppression and restores community relationships. Most translations render *tsedaqah* as "righteousness."[7]

Given this background for the meaning of *righteousness* as Jesus used it in this blessing, we can now elaborate on Matthew 5:6. Blessed with God's joy are those who desperately long for an end to oppression in any form, who crave restorative justice for all people, who seek an end to poverty and abuse of power, who hunger and thirst for these things for all peoples of the earth regardless of country, ethnicity, or religion. This last part—regarding all peoples, countries, ethnicities, and religions—has its roots in Isaiah 61:11, "so the Lord God will cause righteousness and praise to spring up before all the nations." There was not and is not a biblical basis for righteousness that is *self*-righteous. From the beginning of God's call to Abram (Abraham) and Sarai (Sarah), the blessing of God was given so that "all the families of the earth shall be blessed" (Gen 12:3).

A crystal-clear and fundamental principle to gain from this beatitude on righteousness is that our right relationship with God is integrally wedded to justice for all who share this planet with us. I do not mean punitive justice, like what is so predominant in the US Department of Justice and our court system; this is not biblical justice in the least! Biblical justice is restorative justice that offers forgiveness and second (third, fourth, . . .) chances, helps people grow into healthier ways of living, lifts people from poverty, shelters the homeless, feeds the hungry, comforts the mourners, resists oppression in all its forms, welcomes the stranger, offers asylum for the persecuted, builds bridges, and tears down walls. According to Isaiah and Jesus, restorative justice is what God does and what God gives and who God is. To borrow a word from Luke 6, "woe" to all who do not heed this call to right justice.

If you are a Christian leader, then you, like me, must take this "woe" very seriously. Remember that in Jesus' day, the religious leaders did not possess the righteousness needed to enter the kingdom of the heavens. "For I tell you," said Jesus, "unless your righteousness exceeds that of the scribes and Pharisees, you will never enter the kingdom of heaven" (Matt 5:20). As my father liked to say, "Never is a long time." He was telling me not to use the word *never* lightly. "Never" is forever, and Jesus says that right justice is nonnegotiable for being a part of the kingdom of the heavens. I can only hope that Christian leaders everywhere would take this to heart as they proclaim the Gospel of Jesus to their parishioners and the world. Of all people, leaders who call themselves Christ's followers need to understand right justice, teach it, and lead with

7. Stassen, *Living the Sermon*, 33–34.

it, living at the forefront of restitution, reconciliation, and forgiveness for all people. This is not a "social gospel." Right justice is the Gospel of Jesus Christ.

We are now back to our question "What has gone so wrong with the human heart, soul, and spirit that our craving for right justice is now dumbed down, or even nonexistent?" It will help if we go back to the beginning, about how God in Christ Jesus created us in God's image, which includes an essential hunger and thirst for right justice. This deep longing for right justice is ingrained in our human nature. We were created for right relationships. But for many people, including many Christians, this craving seems to have been lost. Actually, I don't think we have lost the craving for right justice. I believe that craving has gotten buried under other cravings alien to our essential human nature as created by God.

The heart is still the heart of the problem. If indeed God is the source and sustenance of all right justice, then abiding in God in Christ Jesus is paramount. Any alternative to abiding in Jesus will lead us into some form of *self*-abiding. Self-abiding always leads to addiction—dependency on dehumanizing substances. There are as many forms of addiction as the legion of demons in Mark 5:9. These self-serving behaviors are addictions because they never really satisfy, they never really bring us God's joy, they only make us crave them more, and they only leave us empty in the end. Our addiction to self-*anything* can be compared to physical drug addiction. As the addict needs progressively more drugs, their desire for anything else, from food to friendship to love, is buried. The drug takes over their life. Any type of addiction to self instead of God, and God's right justice, can do the same thing to us spiritually.

To recognize our own self-addictions, we only need to honestly explore what stops us from living lives of right justice. What stops us from confronting the powers of this world who wield injustice? What stops us from believing in the God of right justice? Why are the inequalities of the world okay with us? Why have we settled for personal piety instead of caring for the suffering of the world?

If we won't honestly ask these questions and others like them, I believe it is because we lack the courage to face our own addictions. Instead, we live in some form of denial: I'm powerless against the injustice, I'm not called to right justice, Jesus didn't mean to call people like me, I don't believe what the guy in this book is writing. We will bolster our denial by twisting the statements of Jesus to fit our need for self-justification—another self-addiction. We will convince ourselves of all the things we are doing and earning and giving up for our salvation. We will resign Jesus to the cross, grave, and Sunday praise. We will also convince ourselves that Jesus and politics should not mix. We will make Christ's gospel a gospel of the future, absolving us of any responsibility for the heartache in this world. In all this we will miss our chance in this life on earth to live as created in God's image, stewarding all things around us on God's behalf. And we will miss God's blessing, God's joy.

This beatitude about right justice assures us that as we hunger and thirst, we will be filled. It is interesting that Jesus does not say *God* will fill us, just that we will *be* filled. So, let's not take too simplistic a view of what it means to be filled. I suggest that Jesus is saying we will be filled through the ever-renewing and ever-deepening right relationship we experience within our dependence on God alone. We will be filled by knowing God, whose being and doing is right justice itself. We will be filled as we live free of addictions and free to embrace all forms of justice in this life. We will be filled with the joys of reconnecting the dots of formerly broken human relationships—ours and whatever of the world's relationships God gives us power to influence. We will be filled with God's joy, and it will be made complete in oneness with the triune God, other people, and the world.

"Blessed are the merciful, for they will receive mercy" (5:7).

Or: *Blessed with God's joy are those who live lives of compassionate action. They will receive the results of their own compassionate action, which will include God's compassionate action toward them.*

Mercy—what I call "compassionate action"—comes in many forms. It is not always easily discerned or enacted. Let's also not take a simplistic view here. To grasp this beatitude more fully, let's take a stroll through Matthew 9, where Jesus practices compassionate action in several important ways. He also gives us examples of seeing into the heart of the matter as he assesses each situation and need and discerns what to do. Here we find five examples of Jesus healing people.

In the cases of the paralyzed man (9:2–8) and the woman who suffered from hemorrhaging (9:20–22), Jesus told them, "Take heart." Jesus knew the heartlessness of their condition and the years of toll it had taken on them. They needed healing not just in body but in heart and soul. They needed hope and encouragement. They needed to know they were forgiven and healed in terms of their relationship with God. They needed to know that in God's eyes, their condition was not punishment for sins. In God's eyes, they were not alienated or ostracized as they were by human society; rather, they were precious and loved. Physical healing by Jesus was a clear and practical sign of God's love and acceptance.

In these two cases (and many others), Jesus acted with compassion by healing physically, mentally, emotionally, spiritually, and socially. We should not underestimate the *multiple* needs Jesus meets. Let's also not miss the importance of these healings as Jesus confronted unfair social stigma and society's ignorance of who God is and how God acts toward us. We see here how Jesus' compassionate action addresses all the needs blocking people from wholeness with God and others.

In the case of the two blind men (9:27–31), they are following Jesus as he walks along. When they cry out to him, "Have mercy on us, Son of David," the word *mercy* is from the same Greek word translated as *merciful* in our fifth beatitude. Some have translated this Greek word as "pity," but *pity* is not the right word. These blind men did not want pity; they wanted compassionate action. Our English word *pity* does not carry the active meaning implied by what these two men needed. To be merciful, on the other hand, is to respond to human need with direct action, whatever form the need may take.

In the privacy of the house, Jesus asks about the two men's faith. This is an important question; once again, he is not just interested in their physical condition. Jesus always cares about spiritual healing too. Once Jesus has discerned their spiritual state, he immediately heals them. He does not hesitate—his mercy translates into immediate action. We see in his example both the importance of his merciful heart and of the action it produces. With the remainder of the healings in this chapter, and the many other healings throughout Jesus' ministry, we always see God's compassionate action. The inner being and the outer action are one and the same.

Backing up to Matthew 9:13, Jesus makes a very curious statement: "Go and learn what this means, 'I desire mercy, not sacrifice.'" And yes, this is the same Greek word for *mercy*. Jesus is quoting Hosea 6:6. Here is the expanded passage:

> What shall I do with you, O Ephraim? What shall I do with you, O Judah? Your love is like a morning cloud, like the dew that goes away early. Therefore I have hewn them by the prophets, I have killed them by the words of my mouth, and my judgment goes forth as the light. For I desire steadfast love and not sacrifice, the knowledge of God rather than burnt offerings. (Hosea 6:4–6)

Let's take Jesus seriously and learn what this means. What stands out in this text from the prophet Hosea are the words "steadfast love" and "knowledge of God." These are parallel phrases, which indicates that Hosea believes they are closely linked and, for all practical purposes, are one and the same. Think of these two phrases as verbs because, in the reality of God's kingdom of the heavens, they are actions. *Steadfast love/knowledge of God* translates here in Matthew 9:9–13 as compassionate action, illustrated by Jesus' intimate association with "tax collectors and sinners" (vv. 10, 11). Jesus is sitting down at table with people considered bad and unclean. Various religious rules were being broken, upsetting the religious leaders. But far above the importance of religious rules is God's rule of compassionate action. No, Jesus is not healing the sick here in a literal sense, but he is welcoming and healing spiritually the outcast and the unclean, those who otherwise might never experience the "steadfast love" and "the knowledge of God" (Hos 6:6).

In this brief story we learn from Jesus two essential things about compassionate action: (1) It is especially important that we be merciful to people who otherwise have been overlooked, underappreciated, devalued, rejected, or denounced. The immense blessing of God's joy awaits us in ways we cannot imagine until we do this. (2) No amount of religious piety or rule-keeping will satisfy either our own hearts or the heart-desires of God. Rather, compassion for the marginalized of society, shown to them through active love and acceptance, is what God desires of us.

Mercy—compassionate action—can be accurately described as "knowledge of God," as sharing God's "steadfast love." Just ask Hosea, who also tells us that when compassionate action is lacking on our part, God's judgment against us is sure.

Before we leave this beatitude, and its connection to Matthew 9, we need to look at how the latter concludes:

> Then Jesus went about all the cities and villages, teaching in their synagogues, and proclaiming the good news of the kingdom, and curing every disease and every sickness. When he saw the crowds, he had compassion for them, because they were harassed and helpless, like sheep without a shepherd. Then he said to his disciples, "The harvest is plentiful, but the laborers are few; therefore ask the Lord of the harvest to send out laborers into his harvest." (Matthew 9:35–38)

This is a great summary statement! Jesus went to all the cities and villages teaching and proclaiming the good news of the kingdom of the heavens. This is his mission everywhere. Everywhere, he is curing diseases and illnesses, having *compassion* for the crowds because he saw them in dire need, "harassed and helpless, like sheep without a shepherd." Going everywhere, seeing every need, Jesus models for us the necessity of compassionate action in all situations. This is, in fact, the good news of the kingdom of the heavens. Teaching, proclaiming good news, and providing compassionate action—together, these actions are the kingdom come.

One more thing: So often the lines here in Matthew 9:37–38 concerning the harvest are used to help reproduce missionary zeal in the hearts of Christians gathered for praise and worship. This is a good thing, but most of the time we miss what the zeal should truly be about. I hope, as we read this text in the context of the whole of chapter 9 and the present study, we will begin to understand that Jesus is giving instruction here on the worldwide need for compassionate action. Compassionate action *is* the mission, and the laborers seem to be few. Now maybe we understand the importance of this beatitude on mercy.

"Blessed are the pure in heart, for they will see God" (5:8).

Or: *Blessed with God's joy are those whose hearts are singularly opened to God. They will clearly see and know God.*

This just might be the pivot point in these eight beatitudes. I say that because to be pure of heart, singular of heart, focused only on being in communion with the one true God, brings all the beatitudes into a seeing/knowing-God orbit. To devote one's heart to God's heart without the impurities of focusing on other agendas or alliances would surely mean a gathering of all the blessings into one. What a joy that would be!

This idea of singularity of heart and seeing God is directly related to Matthew 6:19–24. Here Jesus uses the word *healthy*, *whole*, or *single*, depending on your translation. He is describing the idea of singleness of purpose. The following quote from my book *Seeking the Wilderness: A Spiritual Journey* is apropos:

> In Matthew 6 Jesus speaks in favor of the single eye—the whole body depends on it. The Greek word for *single* carries the English meaning of a sincere simplicity, a singleness of sight and mind. . . . Our word *simple* finds its roots in the Greek word *plex*, meaning "fold." Thus, in straightforward usage, simplicity is the concept of being in a spread-out state, without folds ("Unfolded and Enfolded by Mercy" by Elaine Prevallet in *Weavings*, vol. V, no. 3, May/June 1990, p. 8). I liken this concept to that of a tablecloth spread out without wrinkles, awaiting the table setting.
>
> If we place the Greek and English meanings together, our understanding of the simple adventure becomes clear. We discover a dynamic metaphor for life in the unfolding process. I use *unfolding* in the sense that we choose not to continue being folded up into ourselves, layered no more with our ever-multiplying self-desires. Instead, we are freed from the many things that would keep us from fully entering God's presence. This is the process of opening ourselves completely to God's world, for it is God's world and God's realm of activity with us. We become the tablecloth spread smoothly, prepared to accept God's china. This represents an end to all deception, where our lives become truthful again, and where distances can be crossed without the maze of self-enfolding.[8]

Whether our vision, or purity, is torn by treasures on earth (vv. 19–21) or by fears for our security or by any other distractions, Jesus says we cannot serve two masters (v. 24), let alone multiple masters. We cannot open our heart in purity before God while being folded up in ourselves. Most of us—perhaps all of us—fall far short of singleness of heart in God's presence. Yet Jesus is telling us that when we do make God the sole focus of our heart, instead of being distracted by other concerns, we will find ourselves filled with joy!.

"Blessed are the peacemakers, for they will be called children of God" (5:9).

Or: *Blessed with God's joy are those who create peace with all and with everything around them, for they will be called children of God.*

This is an action-focused blessing. It clearly points us toward God being active as supreme peacemaker. Why else would those who create peace be called the children of God? We have already partially addressed this beatitude in chapter 1 as we looked at Ephesians 2:13–18, which declares that Jesus is our peace. Jesus embodies this beatitude about peacemaking, just as he does the others. His birth was welcomed by the angels' words, ". . . on earth peace . . ." (Luke 2:14). And in 2 Corinthians 5:19, Paul states,

8. Lehman, *Seeking the Wilderness*, 111.

"In Christ God was reconciling the world to himself." The New Testament writers are clear that the work of God, and the work of God in Christ Jesus, is peacemaking.

In the New Testament, peacemaking and reconciliation are parallel concepts. "To reconcile" means to restore relationships. To be a peace-creator, we go about life in such a way as to unite people with one another and with God, to restore these relationships. This is an all-inclusive instruction, just as when Jesus tells us to love or to show mercy. Whom should we *not* restore to another? To whom should we *not* show mercy? Who is undeserving of God's love and ours? Is there anyone with whom God does *not* want us to create peace? No! In this blessing of Jesus, peacemaking becomes our full-time vocation.

There can be no true way to create peace and show mercy without God's love at its core. A companion passage to this beatitude is Matthew 5:43–48, where Jesus says, "Love your enemies . . . so that you may be children of your Father in heaven." How is this possible? First, God makes peace with—pours out love to—us. Then we are empowered to make peace with—to love—others: "All this is from God, who reconciled us to himself through Christ, and has given us the ministry of reconciliation" (2 Cor 5:18). We could never face the world as peace-creators unless we ourselves were first reconciled through God's love. But when the love and grace of God in Christ Jesus transform us into God's likeness, when we experience God's love reconciling us to God, we are moved to take up the ministry of reconciling—of peace-creating—with others.

Throughout my life I have noticed Christians distinguishing between God's grace, love, and salvation on the one hand, and a lifestyle of actively creating peace on the other. They have tried to do the impossible. God's love, grace, and salvation are inseparable from God's reconciling peace-creating. The very cross of Jesus is at the heart and center of peace-creating. Through Jesus, God reconciled all things—everybody—"by making peace through the blood of his cross" (Col 1:20). How dare we call ourselves sons or daughters of God if we have not joined in God's work of reconciling the world? God would leave no one out; nor should we. William Barclay says it well in his commentary on Matthew:

> The Authorized Version says that the peace-makers shall be called the *children of God*; the Greek more literally is that the peace-makers will be called the *sons* (*huioi*) of God. This is a typical Hebrew way of expression. Hebrew is not rich in adjectives, and often when Hebrew wishes to describe something, it uses, not an adjective, but the phrase *son of* . . . plus an abstract noun. Hence a man may be called *a son of peace* instead of *a peaceful man*. Barnabas is called *a son of consolation* instead of *a consoling and comforting man*. This beatitude says: Blessed are the peace-makers, for they shall be called the sons of God; what it means is: Blessed are the peace-makers, for they shall be doing a

God-like work. The man who makes peace is engaged on the very work which the God of peace is doing.[9]

This is why the blessing includes our being called "children of God," because when we engage in peace-creating, we are doing the very work of God. Paul's letters often conclude with a blessing to his readers, which begins with something like this: "The God of peace be with all of you" (Rom 15:33). Oh that we Christians would be called by all the world around us "the children of peace." There could be no higher compliment. But, by and large, the world has not witnessed us being peace-creators.

We must make an important note here that our blessing says "peacemakers," not "peacekeepers." We are to create something new, not maintain something old. Peace-making comes from the infinitely creative heart of God; thus, it is alive with hope and possibility and new revelation. The peace the world tries to maintain is a dead thing, for it cycles and recycles forms of violence incapable of even maintaining peace, let alone creating peace. This dead thing is certainly incapable of creating anything *new*. But in all the places we humans think peace impossible, God is already at work creating peace, bringing people together, reconciling the world to God's self. When Christians fail to create peace or to act as peacemakers, it is almost always because of a lack of faith in the God of peace.

"Blessed are those who are persecuted for righteousness' sake, for theirs is the kingdom of heaven" (5:10).

Or: *Blessed with God's joy are those who are persecuted because they live right justice, for theirs is the kingdom of the heavens.*

It is obvious from this final beatitude that to "hunger and thirst for righteousness" in an earlier beatitude (v. 6) does not mean to have an inward attitude without outward action. In this final beatitude, Jesus implies that we will be persecuted because we are *living* right justice. This beatitude is expanded and given special emphasis in verses 11–12. As the prophets were persecuted, we will be persecuted. Jesus even elaborates on the blessing of joy: "Rejoice and be glad, for your reward is great in heaven."

In verse 11, persecution is expanded to include being reviled and having evil things said against us falsely. The long history of persecution against Christians demonstrates that the persecution Jesus was talking about could run the spectrum from name-calling to slander to murder. Persecution takes many forms, all painful and scary. No one I know wants to be persecuted, including me. So how can being persecuted possibly be a blessing of God's joy?

First, as we learned from the beatitude about hungering and thirsting for right justice, we will be filled. We find joy in the experience of communion with God as partners in God's work of justice. No amount of suffering in this life can take away this joyful communion. Though it may come as a surprise, persecution itself draws

9. Barclay, *Matthew*, 1:109.

us into God's blessing. God will not leave us alone in our suffering. Jesus tells us in Matthew 28:20, "Remember, I am with you always, to the end of the age." Persecution will potentially include experiencing many or all of the beatitudes: poverty of spirit, mourning, meekness, hunger and thirst for right justice, purity of heart. But all the blessings of God's joy will accompany these beatitudes: you will be comforted, you will be filled, you will see God. The trials of persecution will strengthen us in our image-of-God identity, and God will draw us ever closer in communion of heart and mind. God reminds us in Hebrews 13:5, "I will never leave you or forsake you." And in the following verse the writer quotes Psalm 118: "The Lord is my helper; I will not be afraid. What harm can anyone do to me?" Remember these things.

Second, Jesus is clear that it is not just *any* suffering, but suffering *for his sake*, that brings God's joy. If we are living the beatitudes of Jesus and this brings persecution, we can know beyond doubt that we suffer for all the right reasons. We will also come to know an even deeper communion with our Lord and Savior. Aligned with him in being and doing, in substance and purpose, and in his mission, in the end we will also share in his triumph.

Third, not only are we aligned with Jesus; we are aligned with the prophets who were persecuted in the same way. There can be no greater biblical alliance than with Jesus and the prophets. Think of the generations and generations of faithful witness the prophets and Jesus represent. If we suffer persecution on account of Jesus, we join the ranks of the most faithful people on biblical record. What assurance we have! What accumulated wisdom, courage, and commitment we share!

Fourth, there is something of extreme importance for us to do in any time of persecution: Jesus tells us in Matthew 5:44 to pray for our persecutors. I know this is hard to imagine, but God gives us the strength to do this. Jesus did this from the cross. The first Christian martyr, Stephen, did this as he was being stoned. As they were dying, they both prayed that God would forgive their persecutors. To be able to pray genuinely that God would forgive the very ones tormenting us, torturing us, ridiculing us, blaming us, ostracizing us, laughing at us, imprisoning us, firing us, humiliating us, terrorizing us, and possibly killing us—this takes a person who has lived and is living the beatitudes of Jesus. It takes a person whose heart has become God's heart. It takes a person who truly knows the joy found only in the heart of God, because only there will we ever find love's source. Only from God's heart can love flow to us and through us, even to our persecutors.

SALT AND LIGHT FOR THE WORLD

We now circle back to Matthew 5:13–16, where Jesus names us the salt and light of the world. The beatitudes of verses 1–12 show us a life beyond what we have known, in which the meaning of our individual lives takes on a significance far exceeding our previous focus. As we now discover ourselves created in God's image, we are enabled in our daily lives to be co-creators with God. In other words, we live the blessed life of God each day and thus help create this blessed life for the world around us. Just as both salt and light permeate their surroundings, the joyful blessings of God in us permeate the lives of all we meet. The world around us becomes a significantly more blessed place for all.

Any *one* of the beatitudes might cause us to wonder at the mystery of God at work in the world—how what at first seems like weakness or insignificance is really power beyond measure. Any *one* of these beatitudes contains the DNA of God's living being. What of all eight? What of living and breathing the kingdom of the heavens through *all* these blessings of Jesus? What of living and breathing the kingdom of the heavens in and through the community of believers who follow Jesus together in all these ways? We would surely see the fulfillment of Psalm 46:6–11:

> The nations are in an uproar, the kingdoms totter; he utters his voice, the earth melts. The Lord of hosts is with us; the God of Jacob is our refuge. Come, behold the works of the Lord; see what desolations he has brought on the earth. He makes wars cease to the end of the earth; he breaks the bow, and shatters the spear; he burns the shields with fire. "Be still, and know that I am God! I am exalted among the nations, I am exalted in the earth." The Lord of hosts is with us; the God of Jacob is our refuge. (Psalm 46:6–11)

3

Bringing the Beatitudes to Life

Blessed are the poor in spirit, for theirs is the kingdom of heaven. Blessed are those who mourn, for they will be comforted. Blessed are the meek, for they will inherit the earth. Blessed are those who hunger and thirst for righteousness, for they will be filled. Blessed are the merciful, for they will receive mercy. Blessed are the pure in heart, for they will see God. Blessed are the peacemakers, for they will be called children of God. Blessed are those who are persecuted for righteousness' sake, for theirs is the kingdom of heaven. Blessed are you when people revile you and persecute you and utter all kinds of evil against you falsely on my account. Rejoice and be glad, for your reward is great in heaven, for in the same way they persecuted the prophets who were before you.

—Matt 5:3–12

The beatitudes are God-given blessings. In them we find Jesus' call to live as the image of God within the kingdom of the heavens here on earth. If we make them out to be something else, we lose their intention altogether. If we try to live differently from these blessings, we lose God's desired influence on our daily lives, on our hearts and minds, and on our words and actions. If we do not find a way to live these blessings, we risk being cut off from God's power and purpose for us. If we are cut off from God's power and purpose, what is the point in calling ourselves Christian?

Because the beatitudes are God-given blessings, they are available to everyone who wants to live them. Contrary to some popular opinions, these blessings are not out of reach for everyday people; indeed, they are not impossible requirements of perfection. They are quite attainable *especially* for everyday people. Jesus was not addressing the religious elite, the wealthy, or the powerful here. He was talking to people like the guys who threw nets in the lake so they could catch fish. He was addressing the deepest needs and desires of normal human beings, which is precisely the point of his teaching—to bring the kingdom of the heavens into reach for us all.

This attainability for everyone is why these blessings are such good news, why there is such true joy in living the beatitudes. But motivation is important: we need a reason to live one way and not another. I am not going to give up my hold on life as I know it unless I have something clearly better to grab onto. So, what motivation does Jesus offer us for living these beatitudes? If we back up and read them again (go ahead—they're at the top of this chapter) we see that Jesus offers more motivation than we could ask for. He offers us nothing less than life with him in God's holy presence right now. Lack of motivation is not the problem.

At least part of our problem if we are not living the beatitudes is that we don't *believe* Jesus. As mentioned in chapter 2, there is a big pile of life's rubble—all the hell our souls endure—riding on our human spirit. Many people I know do not believe that Jesus offers to unload the rubble by giving these blessings. To live the beatitudes takes a lot of faith. The irony is that many people say they believe that Jesus takes away our sins, giving us a pass into heaven when we die, but they do not believe him when he tells us how to live heaven now.

There must be a way to help people see and believe the incredibly good and joyful news in the beatitudes. The world within and beyond Christianity depends on this, but before we proceed, let me again define the word *joy*. As discussed in chapter 2, joy is not gleeful celebration, or situational happiness. Joy is not an emotional high, and it is not founded in or dependent upon our experiences of the world around us. Joy, as we are defining it here, is knowing the certainty of our existence within the existence of God. Joy is that spiritual space where God's presence fills us and lives through us. Joy is knowing and living God's love for us and the world. Joy flows from our receiving and returning God's love, because we are created for this connection.

LIVING LIKE A GARDEN HOSE

I love to grow vegetables. The soil, the sun, the rain, some sweat, dirty hands, and the watching—this is the stuff of gardening. Sometimes the sun is too hot and the rain doesn't come in time. Then I hook up the garden hose to the faucet, turn on the tap, and open the nozzle at the end of the hose. Life-giving water flows to the growing plants.

The joy of living the beatitudes functions like that garden hose. God created you and me to be conduits for the flow of God's blessings; this is part of what it means to be made in God's image. Our purpose in this life is to receive and distribute God's blessings. We are like the garden hose with God's blessings flowing through us. God, like the tap to which the hose is connected, is the source of all blessing.

Note how crucial it is when watering a garden to hook up the hose to the faucet and turn on the water at its source. Nothing else works if you don't do this. But *only* hooking up to the faucet and turning it on does not make anything happen. Little or no water flows because air or stagnant water is trapped in the hose. Pressure builds up, but nothing good comes from it. What's wrong? Why doesn't the water flow? The source is there and pushing. The hose is intact and ready.

You know the answer as well as I do: If water is to flow from the source into the hose, through the hose, and to the garden, one must open the nozzle on the garden end of the hose. There must be a pressurized source with an open valve, a hose, *and* an open nozzle for the water to flow.

In the beatitudes, Jesus is saying that you and I must be "hooked up" to God, the source of all blessing. God's blessings are present and ready to flow, just like pressurized water is. We are conduits available for the flow of blessings. But it only works when we also open the valve at our end, allowing the blessings to flow into us and then out of us. No matter how great a conduit we think we are, without the *flowing* water of God's blessings pouring through us, we are simply a container for stagnant water that becomes useless and lifeless. When we close our end of the conduit, God's blessings cannot flow *into* our lives and cannot flow *out of* our lives. There is no God-like joy in stagnant water.

Let's explore how the flow of joy-filled blessing works by considering the first beatitude: "Blessed are the poor in spirit, for theirs is the kingdom of the heavens" (Matt 5:3, my adaptation). Without God's joy pouring into me, I am a container for my own stagnant spirit dependent on my own neediness, the lures of life around me, and a false understanding of who God is and how God works. My life's hose is either empty or partially filled with stagnant spirituality that becomes increasingly lifeless as time goes on. This seems to be the situation for many people—Christians and non-Christians. These folks may even be convinced they are conduits of God's blessings, but if examined closely, it's apparent that the water—the spirit they have and share—is either lifeless or, worse, life-destroying. They are not functioning as God's conduit of blessings to the world, for they are not living out the beatitudes of Jesus.

Almost anywhere you look, almost anytime you turn on the news, almost anytime political discourse takes place on any level within our so-called Christian society, we see examples of thinly disguised but stagnant spirituality. Many people try to persuade us to think and act according to standards that do not align with Jesus' beatitudes. In our present situation in the United States, many of these alternate voices call themselves Christian and pretend toward that banner. But look at the garden end of their life and their views: Are the blessings of Jesus flowing out of their life, or are they missing?

In this first beatitude, Jesus tells us we must be connected to the source of God's Spirit; furthermore, he tells us how this takes place: by consciously acknowledging that our spirit alone is inadequate to give life. Jesus says we must recognize our total poverty of spirit apart from God's Spirit. Why would I hook up the garden hose at the house faucet if I believed my hose contained its own flowing water? If I had a hose like that, I could make millions by marketing it as a self-generating water source! In admitting our extreme poverty of spirit, (1) we recognize deep inside our soul just how totally dependent we are on God's Spirit, (2) we come into God's presence with an open heart and a submissive spirit, and (3) we allow God to connect with us, giving us full access to the Holy Spirit's flow. This is the first part of the beatitude: "Blessed are the poor in spirit."

Each of the beatitudes includes an essential second part; in this first one Jesus declares, ". . . for theirs is the kingdom of the heavens." Resist thinking of this kingdom as a static entity; rather, think of it as flowing, living, breathing reality. This second part of the beatitude emphasizes how we must open our end of the hose to let God's life-giving Spirit flow into and through us. Jesus tells us that through God's Holy Spirit, we can live within God's kingdom right here on earth in our day-to-day lives. Imagine all the fruits of God's Spirit ("love, joy, peace, patience, kindness, generosity, faithfulness, gentleness, and self-control" [Gal 5:22–23]) continually flowing into us, through us, and out of us! This is precisely what Jesus is naming for us and inviting us to experience in the first beatitude, and it is how he describes living the present reign of God. This description of how the flow of God's Spirit works is a universal concept, but one we too easily miss in our own spiritual lives.

We have been created to be conduits of God's loving, creating power as it blesses all the world around us; therefore, we must do our part. Our part is not that complicated: to come fully into the presence of God, our source of blessing, then to open our end of the hose and allow God to use us to bless the world. In this is joy unspeakable, and it is guaranteed. Think of a time when you were excited about and joyfully experiencing God's goodness. Remember how, at that time, you were acting as a conduit for God, fully open to the flow on both ends of the hose. Now think of times in your life when the spiritual excitement was missing. What was obstructing the flow of God either into you, through you, or out of you?

Think about the flow process this way: When we demonstrate love in any way in a relationship, that is God's love flowing to us, and through us to the world. In the process, we benefit, and all those we love benefit. The joy spreads around most naturally. But when we withhold love in any way, God's love does not flow to us or to anyone else. In the process, we lose out on God's love, as does the world. The joy stops in us first, and then it stops in our relationships with others. It is as simple as the garden-hose metaphor.

It's important to note that God is always faithful. God constantly and for eternity provides pressurized water. God will never fail to provide all the blessings we can handle: the water pressure is always on, and the faucet is always open. The only thing that can keep the blessings from flowing is if we don't have our end of the hose turned on. If you are not experiencing God's blessings of love and grace and so much more, try turning on the love and grace from your end. How? By loving and cherishing the people around you. God will be faithful, and joy will follow.

It is powerfully encouraging to know we can normally and naturally live the flow of these beatitudes. Don't get trapped in believing anything less. Carefully test all the voices that would tell you how to live, vote, or think. Believing voices other than that of Jesus and his beatitudes has meant spiritual death for too many people past and present. There is no God-infused joy in the souls of those who fail to believe and live these beatitudes.

The spiritual state Jesus describes in the first beatitude is one where God's Holy Spirit flows fully through us. This is the most natural spiritual space we could ever find ourselves in since the beatitudes are the very purpose for which God created us. Consider what it would be like to have all the fruits of the Spirit freely flowing into us and out of us. In the spiritual state of the first beatitude, we do have God's love flowing freely into and out of us. We do have God's joy, peace, patience, kindness, generosity, faithfulness, gentleness, and self-control flowing freely into us and out of us. And what God-like joy when we totally function as unobstructed conduits of God's Spirit-fruit! Add to this then the result of living not just one but *all* the beatitudes! Together, the joy filled blessings are nearly beyond imagination!

If we Christians miss the significance of the beatitudes as our spiritual reality, present and accounted for daily, it is a terrible loss to both us and the world. These beatitudes are spiritually foundational for every part of our existence. I am convinced we will never know God's joy until we learn from Jesus the blessed meaning of living our lives in God's life, the present kingdom of the heavens. With the beatitudes ingrained in us and throughout our lives, God's joy will become as natural to us as breathing God's air. This is the purpose for which we were created.

NOT CREATED TO BE . . .

Considering the alternatives to living the beatitudes, we get a good idea of what we were *not* created to be and what will *not* bring us joy. These are the things Jesus would tell us to turn from, things we will need to leave behind to live within God's present kingdom of the heavens. Now we get to a big reason many Christians and non-Christians alike reject Jesus' teaching. Let's look again at only the first beatitude to illustrate the point.

As we have already seen, we are created to be fully dependent on God's Holy Spirit. In this mode of full dependency, our spirit finds its true experience and expression as it is fully infused by God's Spirit. Remember again Paul's list of the fruits of God's Spirit, which helps us understand how God's Spirit works in this world. As fruit, the attributes of love, joy, peace, patience, and the others grow directly from God's being; they express the normal and natural outcome of a life lived in God and for God.

Once we grasp the significance of God's spiritual fruit, it becomes much easier to name things that are not the fruit of God's Spirit. Many varieties of fruit do not come from God's tree, but to put it briefly, whatever we think, do, or say that is not loving is not from God; whatever we think, do, or say that is not joyful is not from God; whatever we think, do, or say that is not peace-creating is not from God; whatever we think, do, or say that is not patient, kind, generous, faithful, gentle, and self-controlling is not from God.

By now, some of us will be back to thinking it is impossible to so fully live the fruits of God's Spirit. But it is not. You and I will never do this *perfectly*, but that is not and never was the point. The point of what Jesus teaches in the beatitudes is for us to know we have totally free access to God, the source of all blessings. With each and all of the beatitudes, Jesus invites us into a way of thinking, being, and doing that will help us remain in God's presence and keep us hooked up to God's pressurized faucet of all blessings. Jesus says to all willing to hear the wonderful news that it is indeed safe to be this vulnerable and this face-to-face with God. Jesus is saying, Come as you are into the intimate presence of God and allow God to fill you and flow through you. Stay connected to the one and only source of all blessing, and stay open on your end to allow God's blessing to flow through you. Stay connected to God, not some other source of (rotten) fruit. It's not about striving for perfection; it's about striving to stay open at both ends of your life's garden hose.

We need to be discerning of the difference between God's Spirit-fruit and fruit from other trees. Fruits God did *not* create us for include any form of violence, hate, bitterness, or ongoing anger; any form of selfishness or rudeness, envy or coveting, faithlessness, divisiveness, conceit, idolatry; any form of sexism or racism or any other "ism" that seeks to set self above others. We could name other such "false fruits," but this is a fairly comprehensive start. There is no excuse for us to be in denial about these things; they are visible wherever we look. But in the beatitudes, Jesus provides us a way to deal honestly with our struggles with these harmful things and to lay them down at the throne of God. Jesus enables us to say no to these "rotten fruits" as we become aware of their false power over us. Jesus heals our desperate and restless spirits with God's Spirit.

Let's be honest: any time we make an excuse for not being loving, kind, patient, peace-creating, etc., we are withdrawing from God and God's purpose for us. We are leaving the presence of God because we think we and God together cannot handle the truth of what is in our hearts or the agony of the world. When we back away and make excuses, we take ourselves out of the very place where God's truth could have healed us. We declare God's power insufficient to mold us in God's image. As soon as we start with the excuses, we shut off our end of the garden hose. It would be so freeing to just stop making excuses for why we cannot allow ourselves to be fully blessed by God.

One additional point: The more we realize the depth of what Jesus teaches in the beatitudes, the more our personal spiritual lives will blossom. We will grow in God's

Spirit and will recognize those things for which we were not created. Yet *personal* spiritual growth is never enough. Life does not revolve around your life or mine. Jesus' beatitudes are intended to change the *world*.

An essential element in true spiritual growth toward living the beatitudes is learning to recognize and resist the things aimed to un-create what God is creating, and the voices that champion all the rotten fruits listed above (violence, hatred, and so on). If these evil things are present in someone's words, actions, viewpoints, beliefs, or attempts to persuade others, we must resist them—but with every ounce of *love* that God implants within us. We resist, we name, we stand against the evil of the world around us. We accomplish this resistance with the same love Jesus showed us as he went to the cross. We do not compromise what God is creating in us by keeping silent in the face of evil, nor by opposing evil with evil.

THE BEATITUDES AS ONE BRAIDED ROPE

It is tempting to separate the beatitudes into single strands instead of understanding them as one braided rope. If a person feels comfortable with their spiritual life because they are meek or because they work to create peace, then maybe they don't worry that they are not poor in spirit or merciful. If we can feel righteous because we are out on the picket lines of life fighting against injustice, it is likely easier to skip being pure in heart and meek.

We all have a natural bent toward one or more of the beatitudes but not all of them. Meanwhile, Jesus does not ask for *partial* submission. He knows better than to simply encourage us toward the path that comes easy to us, the one we are already on. Jesus is aware of the human heart's holistic need for God's will to be done fully in us. Jesus knows that with just one or a few of these beatitudes in our spiritual rope, we are weak and will fail when the weight of life pulls hardest against us. Jesus also knows we need all strands of these beatitudes to keep the rot of alien strands from invading the few good strands we do have.

Jesus knows false spirituality when he sees it—just read the passages in Matthew where he names the weakness and rot of the religious leaders of his day. When we try to live our lives omitting one or more of the beatitudes, we deny ourselves the part of God's will and way that we most need to be in us, and we become falsely spiritual.

So here is the challenge: Pick the one beatitude you have the most difficulty believing and living fully. This is likely the weakest strand of your spiritual rope. I might choose the challenge to be merciful. Oh, I have no trouble being merciful if I can pick and choose when and with whom to be merciful! My problem comes when I am called by Jesus to be merciful at *all* times and with *all* people. My merciless spirit shows up when I witness Christian people not living some or all of these beatitudes. I easily slip into a judgmental mode, my anger rises, and I want to say, "How could you?" or "How could you not?" Using my own weak spiritual strand as an example, let's look at the serious problems we face as a result within ourselves and within our relationships with others and God.

First, when I judge others and how they are or are not living as Christians should, I am living in denial of my own need for full submission to God's merciful Spirit. I have the capacity to go through my life believing I am right—even righteous—while I surely am not righteous when I look down on others. Second, by closing my end of the garden hose by not showing mercy to all and in all situations, I have cut myself off from God's mercy. Is there any wonder I find these times a spiritual struggle? Third, without realizing it, I believe myself to be merciful by my own power, and I fail miserably in my relationships with the people I have judged. I have forgotten that without God's mercy flowing in and through me, I am powerless to show real mercy. Fourth, in withholding mercy, I have shut down God's peace-creating with the very people with whom I most need to create peace. I have restricted God's flow of meekness so that Jesus' mind is no longer in control of me. I have certainly lost my sense of the desperate poverty of my own spirit. In other words, *all the beatitudes in me lose power when I shut off just one.*

If, like me, you have trouble picking just one beatitude as your weakest strand, it's because all of them make up God's nature and are therefore intended to make up ours. We see this divine wholeness in Jesus, who lived each and all of the beatitudes fully. When we try to separate one or more beatitudes out of our life, since they are intertwined, we cut at and weaken the whole rope, resulting in joyless living.

Far too many folks have not experienced the joys of the beatitudes because they have limited the flow of God's blessings when they deny their need to live one or more of the beatitudes. By way of example, the righteously zealous worker for justice who cannot or will not balance this work with a truly submissive spirit or a genuinely pure heart will always find their work hard, exhausting, and ultimately depressing. They experience this because they are not being renewed in spirit and purity of heart by God. They may continue in their work despite their struggles, but they will not experience joy in it. And their work will have nowhere near the positive impact on the world that it could have. Their own spirit and heart are simply not magnanimous enough to significantly change themselves or the world. We could use any one of the beatitudes to illustrate this point. Without the whole rope, the power and joy will be lacking.

With which beatitudes do you struggle most? These are the locus of your greatest need for spiritual growth, balance, and maturity.

THE BEATITUDES HELP US UNDERSTAND SIN

Sin is a word used often by some people and adamantly avoided by others. Christians have spent much time and focus on sin, often with more attention to sin (especially the sin of others) than to the health and wholeness we were created to enjoy and to live. The fallen lives of the sinful have sometimes drawn us away from keeping our own eyes on Jesus. We might be surprised to learn how varied and numerous the definitions of sin are.

Anytime people fall into legalistic thinking, they have misunderstood sin. Anytime Christians ignore their need to do good works (Matt 5:16), they have misunderstood sin. These two misunderstandings, and the many variations of these, are not opposing forces as if one were good and the other bad. Rather, they equally misdirect us from a life lived in God's kingdom of the heavens.

Sin and our attempts to understand sin have rightly been important concepts in helping define the bounds of Christianity. We have correctly emphasized the importance of sin and turning from it in many biblical texts from Leviticus through Paul's letters. Where much of Christianity has gone wrong about sin is in the understanding of what sin is. Sin in biblical terms cannot be reduced to a list of bad things, which then provides us the right to define certain people as "bad." Sin is not a yardstick by which to measure ourselves or others in order to punish or reward. So, what is sin, and how do the beatitudes help us understand it?

As I have already said in various ways, the beatitudes show us who we were created to be as God's images here on earth. We can also claim the beatitudes as clear indicators of God's mind and heart—who God is as source and sustenance for our living of all these beatitudes. Jesus, in being "the reflection of God's glory and the exact imprint of God's very being" (Heb 1:3), teaches us in the beatitudes how to live like God's images (reflections, imprints) in God's presence now. While Jesus has plenty more to say about God and God's way in this world, his beatitudes are a wonderful initial description. Hold on to this concept.

The literal meaning of the Greek word for sin, *hamartia*, is "error." In verb form, the Greek word, *hamartano*, means "to miss the mark." Likewise, the most commonly used Hebrew root word for sin is illustrated by the Hebrew noun *chet*, which means "error" or "failure." The verb form, *chata*, means (as in Greek) "to miss the mark." While the literal meanings don't do justice to all the Hebrew and Greek nuances of sin as concept or action, they do provide a helpful guide to understanding a basic meaning of sin in the Old and New Testaments. Simply put, sin is missing the mark.

What is the mark? The mark is our life lived in God's image. Missing the mark is falling short of living according to God's character and will for us on earth as in the heavens. For the purpose of this chapter, I wish only to point out this simple meaning of sin and explain it. Since I have a very good friend who is an archer, teaches archery, and is an avid bow hunter, I draw from his expertise for the analogy of an archer aiming for the bull's-eye of a target.

A serious archer spends hours patiently practicing their stance, aim, and release. They strive to get better and better at hitting the center of the target. All effort is for the sake of hitting the bull's-eye as often as possible. They shoot many, many arrows always working to better their aim so as not to miss the mark with each next shot. Their long-term goal is to hit the bull's-eye every time, even though they will never reach that level of perfection. Not reaching perfection does not discourage the serious archer; rather, it motivates them to keep striving.

No serious archer would purposely miss the mark, for that would be alien to all they strive for. No serious archer would mistake another target for theirs, for their whole focus is given to the right target. No serious archer would miss their target and wave it off as "no big deal." They know that if hitting the target becomes unimportant to them, then being an archer has become unimportant as well. No serious archer quits the competition with the excuse that the target is too hard to hit. They just keep doing their best to hit the mark assigned them. Would that we could all learn the archer's discipline, commitment, and focus and apply these to living our faith.

A few very basic things keep us mired in sin. (1) Sometimes we miss the mark because we shoot at the wrong target because we don't actually know the right one. It is hard to hit the mark if we're not even shooting at it. (2) Sometimes we sin because we consciously choose the wrong mark. Obviously, when shooting at the wrong target, we will miss the mark every time. (3) Finally, like the serious archer, even when shooting at the right target, we all miss some of the time. In this case we sin not for lack of trying, but due to an imperfect aim.

In the beatitudes, Jesus says, in effect, "Let's get you fully focused on the right target." The right target is not a negative concept like carefully avoiding the bad things in life. The right target is not making the world more righteous through our constant strivings. The right target is not perfecting ourselves so we can go to heaven. The right target is not simply saying the "sinner's prayer." The right target is not understanding atonement theory correctly. *The right target is not anything we can do or say in this life. The right target is purely and simply not about us at all.*

As long as the things just named, or others like them, form the basis of our understanding of sin, we will miss the mark of what God wants for us and through us in this life; in fact, we will actually be shooting at the wrong target altogether. Believe it or not, this is great news.

While sin is an important concept, it is a terrible thing to focus on or use as a way of directing our aim. This was the downfall of the scribes and Pharisees of Jesus' day. It remains the downfall of all rule-based Christianity and all legalistic thinking. Jesus taught "archery" in a totally different way. Jesus took a positive and joyful approach with the beatitudes to help us fully focus on the right target. So, what then is the right target?

If we listen carefully to Jesus, our master teacher, we hear in the beatitudes a call to aim toward living life as God's image here on earth, right now. That means aiming to reflect God's own character and God's will for us and the world. This is an encouraging, exciting, and motivating invitation! As we come to understand this right mark to aim for, our understanding of sin changes dramatically.

To not seriously aim at living the beatitudes is an automatic zero at hitting the mark because we are not even shooting at the right target. My entire point regarding sin is this: When we take our focus off living these beatitudes in full, we miss the mark entirely. It becomes impossible for us to not sin because we aren't even shooting in the right direction. This flips on its head the whole reasoning of not living the beatitudes because they are impossible ideals. When we do not strive to live all the beatitudes as a serious archer would strive to hit their bull's-eye, we make it impossible to *not* sin. Sin becomes automatic when we focus on living something other than the beatitudes, something other than the life God prepared for us from "the foundation of the world" (Matt 25:34).

So why is this such great news? (1) If we open our hearts to this new way of understanding sin, it helps us aim for the right target and keeps us from hopelessly sinning our way through life. (2) It puts an entirely hopeful, joyful, and blessed aiming process in place rather than the negative alternatives of focusing on sin or sinful objectives. Even though we will still miss the mark at times, at least now we know what to aim for, and we will know when we miss. Most important of all, (3) it puts us directly in a position to allow God to fundamentally change our hearts and minds so that the joyful existence intended for us is in reach. This new joyful existence now becomes a most natural pathway out of our sinful nature. This change of our heart and mind is the only answer to the destruction and pain of sin in our lives. Now, sin is not our focus at all, and the sin of others is not our focus either.

Once more we come squarely up against the quandary of all those who do not take God in Christ Jesus seriously as master teacher. Jesus was and always will be the definitive authority pointing us toward the right target for our lives. Don't take my word for this; take Jesus' words and the apostle Paul's words, Isaiah's words and the words of 1 John. Only Jesus can say what the right target is for our lives. He is saying exactly this in the beatitudes. What a joy to find in Jesus the best of all instructors for living in God's kingdom of the heavens!

Finally, we can begin to see past the extremely negative way in which many have used the word *sin*. In most circles I know, if you start to talk about sin, people fade from the conversation. Some people actually walk away. Any focus on sin seems to draw us all into a semi-depressed state of mind deeply attached to unresolved personal issues. Next time the family gathers around the holiday table, try discussing sin—good luck! What if, instead, you chose to talk about the joy of living as God's image? With joy as your focus, sin, evil, and the ugliness in the world, while not ignored, lose their power and influence.

THE HOPE OF ALL THE WORLD—GOD'S KINGDOM OF THE HEAVENS AS REALITY

Joy cannot be contained. It will always spill out of us into the world. This is because God is the source of our joy and God wants us to spill goodness into all the world. We were made for this spilling, so if we live the beatitudes, they will spill out. Though the beatitudes are very personal, face-to-face encounters with God, they are never private. Personal and shared, they become the perfect balance of the heart of God living in me, and my sharing the heart of God with others. If the beatitudes are not lived out in a communal way, they are not lived out at all. In fact, living the beatitudes creates community. I am convinced that healthy churches that thrive over time are founded in some significant way on the beatitudes.

Healthy churches do not need evangelism programs; they focus on helping people live all the beatitudes. Consider how wherever Jesus went, the crowds followed. People saw the beatitudes alive in him and wanted what he had. Living the beatitudes grows God's community of followers organically. In living the beatitudes, we become parts of a movement bringing the reality of God's will and way into all the world. This is where the world finds hope.

Again, let's take just one beatitude as an example: "Blessed are the pure in heart, for they will see God" (Matt 5:8). To be pure in heart means to be fully focused on living with God's heart, in the kingdom of the heavens here on earth. As we live with pure hearts, the reality of God's kingdom spreads to others around us, creating a new reality where only shadows of truth existed before. Pretty soon more and more people cease to live fake lives based in fear, violence, or pain.

This leads us to the point of "realizing"—bringing to reality—a true experience of community; that is, collectively we live the God-image that we were created to be as people together in this world. This real community naturally reflects what Jesus, in the Gospel of Matthew, repeatedly calls the kingdom of the heavens.

This also means that whenever we are together as Christians and are *not* living the beatitudes, not living the kingdom of the heavens, we are living a false reality. Think of the many experiences in society, politics, and human relationships that we once thought were real in the sense of being final and unchanging. But if something is not of God's heart and will for us, it is a "false reality"—an oxymoron that cannot hold; not only *can* it be changed, but it *must* be changed.

If people believe the story line of dominant culture and that they are living within a complex social network that is the only reality available, they will find it difficult to believe what Jesus teaches. Most people I know, both Christian and non-Christian, believe the dominant culture. They have been immersed in this culture from birth such that it is all they know. We might even say most people, including most Christians, *believe in* the dominant culture—rely on it, trust in it, ground their lives in it. Since Constantine and the Edict of Milan in 312 AD, the movement of Christianity has fought for a way to believe in both dominant culture and Jesus. The result is a precarious, deeply flawed melding of two opposing systems. What is lost in the melding is the truth of what Jesus lived, taught, died for, and rose for.

What if Christians could wrap their hearts and minds around the possibility that Jesus spoke the truth and that we have instead believed a big lie? What if we could erase dominant culture from our hearts and minds and start over with hearing, first, the truth Jesus speaks? What if we could allow Jesus' proclamation about turning our lives around to settle afresh into our very depths?

It is time for all of us to start over, especially all who would follow Jesus. It is time to say yes to the little child claiming that the emperor has no clothes. It is time to speak the truth, for instance, that no form of retaliation ever brings reconciliation. Dominant culture has fed us the lie of retaliation since at least 1,700 years ago, when Emperor Constantine experienced the epiphany that prompted his conversion to Christianity while at war; thus, the marriage of church and state was directly founded upon the lie of retaliation and violence.

Enough is enough. As I look around at the world's dependence on dominant power, fear, and false hope, all I see is conflict, or attempts to smooth over conflict with subtler forms of dominance. The subtle forms of dominance always lead to continuing conflict in the end.

The time is way overdue for us to acknowledge Jesus as the only truth-teller, the only one who will ever reveal divinely created reality for us as persons and as a people. Any part of our experience that does not square with Jesus and his claim to truth is false. Any way in which we have tried to live other than how Jesus tells us to live is not real. Whenever we live falsely, we self-destruct.

In the Gospel of Matthew, in Jesus' opening teaching of the beatitudes, he does nothing less than take away our false identification with worldly culture. He rips the veil of the temple figuratively even before it is torn literally at his death, and so reveals the nakedness of our dependencies and idolatries. In these beatitudes Jesus profoundly instructs us in the reality of life as God has ordained it. Stay with these beatitudes. Allow these teachings to invade your heart. Let go of any preconceived ideas that might keep you from believing Jesus, and thus from truly *believing in* him.

Discovering truth as Jesus teaches it is a lifelong process. We are all like alcoholics who, though they may never drink again, are always recovering alcoholics. We will be recovering from the world's dominant culture always. So, expect it to take time, but I urge you: Don't fear Jesus' truth, don't fight it, don't become discouraged even when it seems a far reach from all you have known. Begin living reality as God defines it, and more and more you will discover freedom from the false teachings all around you.

To begin to comprehend the extent of the falsehood under which we have lived is like a blind person beginning to see for the first time, or like a deaf person beginning to hear for the first time. Is it any wonder Jesus so often told his listeners to have ears that hear and eyes that see? Take these beatitudes as your life's truth, and more and more you will have the ears to hear and the eyes to see Jesus. The world's supposed reality will fool you less and less. You will be growing pure in heart, and you will see God.

Finally, the freedom and joy of this new reality will flow from you to all the people around you. You will discover the freedom and joy of real community. The kingdom of the heavens will open to you in ways you could not have imagined earlier.

The kingdom of the heavens will become for you the reality in which all your relationships are embedded. The kingdom of the heavens will in fact become unbounded for you because any previously unreconciled relationships you had will now be fully open to reconciliation because, no matter what has gone before, you will become, in your real nature, a reconciling presence. Through you and through others who have opened themselves to God's reality, the hope of the whole world will become realized, one relationship at a time and one community of faith at a time.

HEAVEN CAN'T WAIT

The 1978 movie *Heaven Can Wait*[1] tells the story of an NFL quarterback prematurely taken to heaven because his guardian angel believed he had been killed in a bicycle–car crash. The quarterback, Joe Pendleton, who was not actually killed in the crash, pleads his case in heaven for more time back on earth so he can play in the upcoming Super Bowl. The movie is obviously fiction and an entertaining comedy of circumstance. In the end, after going through a great deal of trouble and two separate incarnations in other people's bodies, Joe finally gets his wish to continue his life on earth and play in the Super Bowl.

While the movie is light-hearted and not intended as serous viewing, I find a subtle message here for all Christians with their eyes on the afterlife. We might learn a lot from Joe Pendleton, who desperately longed for an extended life on earth rather than a quick exit to heaven. Joe had important things he wanted to do with his life on earth. He had a dream to pursue. He had unfinished business that charged his imagination and his emotions. He anticipated great things to come in this present life.

What about the followers of Jesus? Most of us have far more exciting things ahead of us on earth than playing in the Super Bowl. Most of us have the opportunities of a lifetime waiting for our imaginations to catch up. We could be living the full capacity of our richest dreams as God's conduits of love, peace, joy, and grace. In Jesus' own words as he speaks the beatitudes, heaven begins *now* as we recognize him as our teacher, our Lord, and our Savior.

The beatitudes are bookended by Jesus saying, ". . . for theirs *is* the kingdom of the heavens" (Matt 5:3, 10). These present-tense statements leave no doubt that Jesus was teaching a present reality. In fact, all the beatitudes are in present tense—aspects of living a present kingdom of God. We have already seen in chapter 1 that "the kingdom of the heavens" denotes the ongoing presence of God here on earth. For those prepared to live with God living through them now, any future notion of heaven can wait.

Think of one small act of love or grace or forgiveness—just one small act. Any of us can do this one small act. Maybe we think it is insignificant, but even one small act of love or grace or forgiveness can change a life, including maybe our own. Now

1. Beatty, May, and Towne, *Heaven Can Wait*.

multiply this one small act times many years of small acts, and maybe even some larger acts. None of us knows the potential impact our lives can and will make in this world. None of us can imagine what God will do through us as we fully live the beatitudes of Jesus. Is it so difficult to imagine God at work transforming the world through us right now and every day we have left on this planet? In living the beatitudes, we are God's garden hose nourishing the garden of the world.

As more and more we understand the beatitudes to be present-life, God-sized blessings, how could we wish to withhold them from a pained, fearful, and suffering world? How could we not feel excitement about rising to the challenge? Not to quarterback in the Super Bowl, for that is way too small a dream. Jesus gives us a God-sized dream as he speaks of the joy in store for us and the world when we help to "realize" heaven on earth, now. Yes, any future heaven can wait, but the present heaven cannot.

HOW TO SEASON AND LIGHT THE WORLD

Jesus says that just as salt flavors the whole soup and light brightens the whole room, the life to which Jesus calls us is to be a visible demonstration of God's glory for the world to see. This does not mean we go around telling the world we are Christians, preaching shame-based sermons, handing out tracts on street corners, or proving our righteousness by our upright lifestyles. Instead, Jesus says that as we live out the beatitudes in everyday life, we will show the world the goodness of God. By the witness of how we live, we will draw others to the God of love, grace, and peace. This is one reason it is so important that we live the beatitudes in the present: *we, in essence, become the living gospel of Jesus Christ.* Were the world to not see this good news lived out in us, what would prompt it to believe in a future version of good news for the life to come?

Living the beatitudes, being salt and light for the world, is our calling as Christians. So, how do we season and light the world? We will approach this from three areas of influence: within the relationships closest to us, within the community of faith, and within the realm of public policy and politics.

OUR PERSONAL AREA OF INFLUENCE

It all starts in our heart. Any beatitudes flowing out of us must come from the transformation God is enacting within us right now. Note that this is a present occurrence, not something that happened last year or last night. Living the beatitudes is always *now*, just as the kingdom of the heavens is always *now*. We make a terrible mistake when we treat the beatitudes like a bank account, thinking we have built up a reserve so we are okay spiritually and can slack off a bit. Remember, we are created to be conduits of God's blessings, and when we close off the flow on our end, God's flow into us is closed off too. It is all-important that we give ourselves fully and in an ongoing way to every one of these beatitudes. In so doing, we commit ourselves wholly to Jesus Christ and to his heart's instruction to us, moment by moment.

Remember where we began in chapter 1, with Jesus calling people to repent, to turn their lives around. To live the beatitudes within our personal sphere of influence, we must be ready to let go of some things that have been precious to us. Let's take *pride* as an example. However it manifests, we must name and release our self-pride. In living the beatitudes, there is no longer anything for us to gain, no weakness to hide, and no accomplishment of which to boast. Whatever amount of us pride has captured over the years, we can now be freed from its prison. If we are experiencing God's blessings in the beatitudes, we will know we have nothing more to lose or win. We will have found our worth in God's embrace, and it will be enough. We will know for certain that we are okay. And because pride and the struggle for self-worth are fused, we will finally be at peace with ourselves. How radically this will change all our relationships!

Is there anyone in your life with whom you find yourself in competition? How many expectations—your own or placed on you by others—are you attempting to live up to? How many of your "hot buttons" connect directly to threats to your self-esteem? Who are you trying to impress? Do you find yourself dominating discussions, needing the last word, regularly telling others of your accomplishments, or vying for attention? Are you looking to the people around you to boost your struggling self-worth in any of these ways?

On the other hand, by taking personal pride and feelings of lack of self-worth out of the equation, we will have energy to encourage and support others instead of competing with them. Someone else's accomplishment no longer places pressure on us—indeed, it does not reflect on us in any way. We get to celebrate with others fully and without hesitation. Mutual appreciation grows naturally. We find ourselves liking and loving friends and family more than ever. Suddenly we realize that love and joy in life are not zero-sum games. Worthiness is God-given, no exceptions. The blessing of worthiness then flows through us to those around us. As we treat others as valuable, value increases in all our relationships and in the world. We find, more and more, just how faithfully God holds and molds us, as well as the people around us.

This change begins in our own heart and mind as we acknowledge the value of replacing pride with celebration of others. Now it is a matter of changing how we speak to and respond to our friends and family. We need both the will to start and a place to start, so begin with offering others words of encouragement. It's that simple! Make it a regular habit in all your close relationships. Soon you will find that your focus is no longer on yourself, and your neediness is lessened. You will enjoy your close relationships more. In this simple way, you will bless others as God has blessed you through the beatitudes. You will share the joy of the beatitudes with your loved ones. People's defenses will crumble. The living out of God's blessings always changes us *and* those around us.

This example of replacing self-pride with encouragement of others can serve as a template for applying the beatitudes to all relationships, and it demonstrates how one small but significant change in us leads to further blessings. In replacing self-pride with encouragement of others, we naturally stop judging ourselves and others. It is difficult to focus on a friend's faults if we are genuinely appreciating and encouraging them. The more we appreciate and encourage others, the less we will find reason to complain, blame, and judge them. As we make progress in appreciating and encouraging others, our own pride will no longer be our focus, and we will enjoy life more fully as a result.

One thing leads to another: Focusing on appreciation and encouragement while losing our need to judge will knock directly on the door of that room in our heart where we hide our shame. I know this from personal experience. For most of my life I lived in the shadow of a person who never encouraged me with words of appreciation or with affirmations of any sort. Remember again how when you pour God's blessings on the world, God's healing blessings flow into you. As you pour out words and actions that heal others' shame, God will heal yours.

It is also important to examine how our hurt feelings, resentment, anger, and revenge come from wounds deep inside us. Our most natural reaction to hurt is to focus on the problem outside ourselves (usually other people) while avoiding the depth of our own pain. As we live the beatitudes, we will face our own wounded self through our encounter with God. We will discover a path to healing instead of avoiding our pain. We will also discover that we have less and less need to project our pain onto others, blaming them for our wounded heart. In ceasing to blame others, we will experience the diminishment of our anger and resentment. Now we will be free to share our kindness, mercy, love, and joy with the very people we formerly judged.

This last section is not intended as therapy or pop psychology. We must not treat lightly things like clinical depression or bipolar disorder. That said, living out the beatitudes within our everyday personal relationships will transform us and those around us. If you live with mental illness, I urge you to get the clinical care you need; alongside therapy or other forms of treatment, to the extent you can live the beatitudes, you will also experience the blessings of God as you share them with others.

OUR AREA OF INFLUENCE WITH THE CHURCH OR OTHER COMMUNITIES OF FAITH

> For I tell you, unless your righteousness exceeds that of the scribes and Pharisees, you will never enter the kingdom of the heavens. (Matt 5:20)

The religious establishment of Jesus' day did not "get" the beatitudes. It would be fair to say this failure also holds true, at least in part, for much of the present-day religious establishment. I'm not trying to overblow this to make a point. Think about how many church meetings you have been in where one or all the beatitudes were lacking. How did church leadership respond? Were the leaders the problem? Were they silent in the face of the problem? Did they respond by living out the beatitudes and calling others to do the same?

How many times have you participated in church endeavors where it was more about the planning and programming than about living beatitude lives? How many sermons have you heard in which shaming and blaming tactics drowned out joy and love? When is the last time you witnessed a church leader filled with poverty of their own spirit? When has judgment held sway over mercy in the lives of church leaders, even as they shepherded others in the path of mercy? Is creative peacemaking taught and led in your congregation? Does your church regularly mourn the injustices in the world? Do you witness clear servant leadership, of the sort Jesus meekly lived, in the lives of pastors, elders, Sunday school teachers, rabbis, priests, and others? Where are the religious leaders who hunger and thirst for right justice? Is it easy for you to see that your leaders see God with singularly focused hearts?

Hopefully these questions reveal how crucial the beatitudes are to healthy leadership in our congregations. Christian leaders must be leaders of character fashioned after God's own character as taught by Jesus in the beatitudes. Whether or not you are in a position of leadership in a church, there are many practical things you can do and say to bring the beatitudes to life in your church and, thus, influence your faith community's life and health.

If you found the questions about leadership in your congregation depressing, and if they seem to confirm the failure of leaders to live beatitude lives, take heart. Jesus did not say all was lost in the face of unhealthy leadership. He told his followers that their righteousness was not dependent on the righteousness of their leaders. You are not dependent on whether you see the beatitudes lived by others. Dallas Willard states, "Going to the source of action is a major part of what he (Jesus) has in mind by saying that one must 'go beyond the goodness of scribes and Pharisees.' One must surpass humanly contrived religious respectability 'if one is to mesh their life with the flow of the kingdom of the heavens'" (5:20).[2]

Whenever and wherever you see one or more of the beatitudes lacking, don't point a judgmental finger. Instead, offer a healthy dose of the beatitude that is lacking, drawing from your own storehouse of God's blessings. Here are a few practical suggestions:

1. Put a guard around your own judgmental spirit. Don't criticize or blame others, no matter what. Rather, use the wisdom you are learning from the beatitudes to focus your attention on being a living example of the very beatitudes you see lacking around you. The more darkness in the room, the more your light will brighten the whole space.

2. Willard, *Divine Conspiracy*, 139.

2. Don't simply accept the fate of beatitude-less leaders. Carefully confront beatitude-less leaders by forging a clear path of leadership for yourself based on Jesus' blessings. In whatever position you find yourself, you can answer Jesus' call to live the beatitudes and exemplify the joyful blessings of God. For example, if your congregation lacks leadership in creating peace, then it is up to you to lead the way of peace-creating. Peace-creating will always be needed on every level of human relationship, so your opportunities for peace-creating are endless.

3. Where you see dysfunctional church organization, you will often find dysfunctional leadership. This does not mean there are bad people in leadership. Again, rather than judging, offer to help. If you have the capabilities to see the dysfunction, you can also see at least the beginnings of a healthy alternative. No step toward health is too small. If you find yourself doubtful that your concerns will be heard, join the club, but do not be defeated by these concerns. Always help from the position of living the beatitudes healthily yourself.

4. List all eight beatitudes on a large piece of paper. Leave plenty of space between them. Now prayerfully consider and write down the ways your faith community is living or not living each beatitude. Refrain from judging. Once you believe you have a fair assessment of your faith group for all the beatitudes, take out another piece of paper. Again list the beatitudes with space in between them. Under each beatitude, write the positive ways you *personally* can affirm, encourage, and participate in the ways your church is already living that beatitude. Also write down the positive ways you can shine your living light where that beatitude is lacking. Now focus all your attention on doing positive things and none of your attention on the negatives.

5. We should note that there are situations in community where dysfunction becomes so overwhelming it is beyond the scope of our personal influence to effect positive change. Both good leaders and followers may face a dysfunctional wall that is simply too high. As a last resort, it may be necessary to withdraw from the dysfunctional relationships and seek a different community of faith.

Before we move on from pondering our influence within the life of our faith community, we should recognize an "elephant in the room." Where the beatitudes are lacking, there is a grave problem with theology. Any organized denomination or other type of church group that does not consistently profess, teach, and live the beatitudes is not listening to Jesus. They are instead listening to a different lord. I believe it is reasonable to use the beatitudes of Jesus as a litmus test to determine whether a congregation or a church denomination is listening to Jesus at all. I do not mean this as a harsh judgment but as an invitation to confession.

If you find yourself in a church or group of churches ignoring the teachings of Jesus, I hope this chapter will be a clarion call to embark on your prophetic ministry.

If you believe you have no influence in this situation, you are wrong. You have a voice, and your voice is desperately needed. By living the beatitudes you bring a deep poverty of spirit, a heart for mourning, a bold meekness, a hunger and thirst for right justice, a merciful life, a heart singularly focused on God, an ability to create peace, and resilience to persecution. These traits are God's blessings within your life, and they are powerful. With these blessings of God, you have more authority and influence than you can imagine. Don't hold back, or you will lose them! God's blessings flow to and through you when you live them.

I can't tell you how long I have grieved the denial of Jesus by so many Christian people and groups. I look out over the Christian landscape of my country and see countless examples of those who say they believe *in Jesus* but clearly do not *believe him*, for they do not take his teachings as words to live by. The evidence of this is all around the Christian church in the form of lack of mercy, right justice, peace, and all the other beatitudes. This leads us into our final section on our influence.

OUR INFLUENCE IN PUBLIC POLICY AND POLITICS

Just the mention of this section may have raised your blood pressure. Or maybe you have waded through three chapters of this book just to get to a rant on your favorite political issues. Or you may suddenly fear the words to come and the gut-wrenching disagreements to follow. Such is life in the kingdoms of this world. The battles over policies and politics never end. But these battles *could* end, and they could end for *you* right now.

I hope by now you are learning how much your inward thoughts and feelings change through living the beatitudes. If you have stayed with me this far and the beatitudes are already changing you—or you are grasping how they can change you—deep within, I believe you will find the following words incredibly freeing. At least this has been my experience.

I said in chapter 1 that partisan politics do not exist in the kingdom of the heavens, God's kingdom on earth. We Christians pray for this every time we recite the Lord's Prayer, "Thy kingdom come, thy will be done. . . ." Whatever your political flavor, it would be hard not to agree that partisan politics are often dysfunctional; the tactics used on both (all) sides divide and polarize. I am presently writing during the beginnings of the Trump presidency. If you live in the United States, every single day you awake, as do I, to the political news of new arguments, new accusations, and increasing animosity. I am guessing we are all wondering what the coming years will hold for a country seemingly at war with itself. If you live outside the United States, you likely find at least some of the same problems in your own country.

To whatever extent any person or group becomes enmeshed in political wrangling, they have lost sight of Jesus and his instruction in the beatitudes. It simply is not possible to remain in poverty of spirit, mourning, meekness, mercy, hunger and thirst for right justice, purity of heart, and the act of peace-creating while lobbing accusations toward and clinging to resentments of the other side. Oh, I know you can take hungering and thirsting for right justice and claim the political high ground, but you cannot live the other beatitudes while doing this. Once again, if you try to live just one or a couple of the beatitudes, and not all of them, you will sever the braided rope Jesus offers us as a lifeline for living in this world.

Here is my personal confession: Following a year and a half of a mean and nasty US political process where any sense of civility seemed lost, in November 2016 I sat up through a sleepless presidential-election night. By late that evening I was shocked and angry over the results, and I was wrong and in sin to respond this way. My anger and depression lasted for weeks. I was living with resentment toward those who voted for Trump. I could not see that my struggle was not "out there" with other people, but was an inward one, for I had lost sight of Jesus and his braided lifeline offered to me in the beatitudes. Altogether it took me three months to come to terms with my own sin, my misplaced anger and resentment. I knew I could not begin writing this book until I regained my focus on Jesus and the mark I had not been shooting toward—God's image intended for me to live out, here on earth.

I still have twinges of anger—I'm no more perfect than anyone else—but I have a peace now that I have never known before. I have found a sense of spiritual and political *home* in Christ Jesus that I formerly thought impossible. For months now I have done what I could to live and breathe all of the beatitudes. This process has been for me like the slow healing of a wound I previously thought could not be healed.

A few paragraphs back I said that the battle over policies and politics could end for you. I know this because it has ended for me. Today I live mostly free from the never-ending ugly news cycle. I am free from fearing the next policy decision and how my inner wound might reopen or be rubbed raw by some injustice. I am mostly free from anger that formerly disabled my peace-creating, God-given nature, which is so needed now as I act to heal strained relationships in my life. I am free from the need to be proven right, to live the moral high ground, to be a better Christ-follower than other people I know. In my experience, this is nothing short of amazing. I feel like a lifetime of pain has been lifted from me.

We will soon discuss what this means in terms of our personal influence in politics, but we first need to hear from Jesus in scripture. In a fascinating exchange between Jesus and the Roman governor, Pilate (John 18:33–38), three times Jesus declares that his kingdom is not *from* this world. He does not say his kingdom is not *in* this world, but that it does not *originate* here. Jesus' kingdom is the kingdom of the heavens that we have been discussing. The kingdom of the heavens is God's kingdom where God's will is done. Wherever God's will is done, God's kingdom is realized on earth as in the heavens.

Pilate then asks if Jesus is a king. Jesus' answer is nothing short of revolutionary politics. He avoids answering Pilate's question. Rather, he says, "For this I was born, and for this I came into the world, to testify to the truth. Everyone who belongs to the truth listens to my voice." Pilate's response is to say, "What is truth?"

From the standpoint of earthly authority and political wrangling, Pilate gets it exactly right. He knows no clear truth. He knows no clear moral authority. Politics then and now is like a school yard full of children at recess fighting over the rules of a game. All sides claim the truth, and who is to say, finally, what is right and wrong? In the political wrangling of this world, everyone thinks their side has the truth. Everyone is wrong. *Our political process is completely unable to determine truth.*

In this passage from John, Jesus proclaims that *he* (his life, his teaching) is testimony to the truth. Jesus' truth does not come from any earthly political party or platform, for his kingdom is not *from* this world. If only all Christians involved in politics or political debate could understand that their only truth will come from listening to Jesus. In his words, "Everyone who belongs to the truth listens to my voice." This is monumental, for it covers all areas of political life—and all areas of life in this world are political.

For Christians, all areas of this earthly life are intended to fall under the jurisdiction of the truth Jesus speaks. We are to belong to the truth. In other words, we are not the masters of truth via our own version of truth, but we are to give ourselves over to be owned by God's will and way as described by Jesus himself. To belong to God's truth in Jesus is to find our very political identity in him. This is not just about what we are to say or how we are to act in a political world. This is about the core identity we discover, perhaps for the first time, when we submit fully to Jesus and his way, truth, and life (John 14:6). If we belong to God's truth, Jesus is then first our master teacher, then our Lord, and in living this renewed life we experience him as our Savior. Jesus is the one speaking the truth, and the beatitudes are primary in his truth-telling ministry.

This passage in John 18 comes at the culmination of Jesus' life and ministry. Jesus' words here declare a truth capable of staring down any earthly threat of violence and/or death. This truth that Jesus claims is offered for us in the most radical demonstration we could possibly imagine: his cruel torture and death on the cross. This same truth of Christ is confirmed in the most unimaginable way as God raises Jesus from death to life. Here then, the atonement so many Christians like to speak of is no longer a "theory"; instead, it reveals who God is and how God brings salvation to a world imprisoned in its own violent ways. We now find our identity in the words and way of Jesus. We become beatitude people, and this directs our every political thought and move.

Perhaps we should nurture a sense of compassion for Pilate and his disturbing dilemma, for he was caught in the middle of dispensing a form of truly unjust justice. He knew of nothing better than being on the side of power wielded in a supreme effort to control others by force and threat. Even if he contemplated a response of fairness and compassion for Jesus, he really had no choice but to crucify someone.

Someone needed to be scapegoated for the sake of "peace" and the "well-being" of the whole people. Pilate never knew the real truth of which Jesus spoke, the truth Jesus lived. Pilate died a pawn in the power struggle of the world, having lived his life in a meaningless effort to preserve a system of injustice and violence. On the other hand, Jesus died innocent and suffering under the full weight of injustice and violence. Jesus showed us a way out of all destructive politics. Instead of dying a meaningless death, Jesus gave dying its only true meaning.

All human politics ultimately blames someone else or some other group. Sooner or later we always project our pain onto the other, unless we learn and live the life and teachings of Jesus. Before we leap to the conclusion that we now know better than Pilate how to dispense justice, we must acknowledge that we *are* Pilate; we *are* the religious leaders and the crowds calling for Jesus' crucifixion. We are complicit and emotionally enmeshed in scapegoating. We too will die meaningless deaths in service to the blaming gods of our violent human egos unless we find a way out of the cycle of blame. To the extent that you and I have entered negatively into the political struggles of our day, we are enmeshed and hopelessly foundering in the muck of it all. This is where I personally spent the weeks following the 2016 US presidential election. This is where I am tempted too often to return. As long as we focus our attention on what is wrong in our world, we miss the mark; we miss the call of Jesus on our lives. Until we give ourselves over fully to the constant pressurized flow of God's beatitudes, we will never withstand the constant pressurized flow of negative politics.

So, whose flow are you passing on—this world's negative politics or the flow of Jesus' life and teachings that come from God's world? Perhaps a simple way to ask this is: *In everything, are you blessing this world as Jesus blesses you?*

Back in October 2016, I was visiting one of our daughters and her family. My oldest granddaughter was upstairs watching a presidential debate. Soon after the debate began, she came downstairs and said in a pained and surprised way, "Mom, Dad, they are being *mean* to each other!" It was a sad moment for me as I reflected on what a rude introduction this was for her to the world's politics. Before that debate, she thought people from different political parties would be nice to each other. If only that were so. But it is not, and it only seems to be worsening.

You and I cannot deny that we are a part of the political system of arguing, blaming, accusing, back-biting, and unceasing hostility. Even when we try not to take sides, the forces of society pull us in or push us away. If you have ever been with a group of people gathered and lathered against the "other" side while you tried to remain neutral, you know the pressures of anger and self-righteousness. When two sides gather against each other, no one listens to anything that would challenge their deeply inset, emotionally arrested, self-righteous identity. I say "identity" because that is what the political wrangling becomes—an attack on or a defense of our identity. Most of us are that deeply enmeshed, and as such, we have lost our sense of identity in the truth of God in Christ Jesus.

Don't be fooled: any Christian group that sounds like and acts like a partisan political group *is* one. I'm purposely not pointing left or right. I am trying to bring honest reflection to all our political methods and motives as Christian people. Wherever you find yourself on the political spectrum, if you are focused on and arguing for or against a policy or an issue, you are likely stuck. No matter how worthy the cause, if you are participating in partisan politics where there will always be winners and losers, right and wrong, good and bad, then you are stuck. It is almost impossible to stay out of this political fray. I, personally, find it difficult, and I know few people who have succeeded in doing so without resorting to apathy and withdrawal.

This chapter is not the place to cover all possible political discourse and divide. We will take just one example: the fight over abortion. While Christians and others fight over *Roe v. Wade*, who is acknowledging the economic disparity, racism, sexism, and violence that run rampant throughout our country and the world? Who will work for life and justice, peace and prosperity for the unborn *and* the born? Who will stop the arguments long enough to admit the limits of our legal system's ability to heal these societal "diseases"? Who will be courageous enough to admit we are striving for the wrong things in the wrong ways? Who will start asking why none of the wrangling ever brings peace, joy, and love into the human relational system?

I am convinced that our wrangling over political issues conveniently protects us from needing to live into the pain and lament of our real diseases. To do so, we as a people would have to face our desperate need for repentance and fundamental change. Again, I'll give just one example from the abortion issue to illustrate my point.

Within our society, so much needs healing in terms of how we live together as women and men: how we raise and educate our boys and girls; how we teach and model love, respect, and equal treatment; how we help our children grow into adults repulsed by society's treatment of all people (but especially women) as sex objects. We could go on and on about the rampant sexism that exists in the fabric of our society, oozes from the media and the internet, and plays out in dirty jokes, sexual insults, physical and emotional abuse.

Even in Christian churches we often still treat women as less than men while denying our complicity in the disease of sexism and its ugly contribution to abortion. In any form it takes, treating women as less than men is sexism, and it is wrong. Yet even in our churches, we easily succumb to the quick fix and the easy cure. Like putting a band-aid on skin cancer, we would like to not think about the malignancy below the surface of our life together. For many Christians, it is easier to throw our weight into overturning or supporting *Roe v. Wade* than to face our own guilt over the systemic causes of abortion.

We can point our finger at insensitive and abusive men, at promiscuous women, at any other causes, but if we truly want to make a lasting difference for the life of unborn babies, we have to see a larger picture of life—what gives life and what takes life in our world. We ourselves will have to change how we deal with our own sexual insecurities and pain. We will need to stand firm against anything in our culture, society, and church that belittles women (and therefore men) in any way. If we ourselves cannot find freedom in Jesus' truth, healing for our sexual identity, and release to fully love, respect, and offer grace to one another across gender lines, then our work to uphold or repeal *Roe v. Wade* will be shown to be the meaningless self-righteous band-aid that it is.

The God-like joy of the beatitudes offers us a way out of all our political strife—not just in the abortion issue, but in all issues. Imagine responding to any ideological struggle from your own deeply abiding identity fully immersed in Jesus' first beatitude. Remember that it is here that Jesus says you belong; you belong to this truth! You are not the possessor but the possessed—in a positive way! You are loved, held, protected, safe. God claims you and gives you roots as you submit to the truth of spiritual poverty and embrace God's own Spirit-fruit. In this truth you no longer have worry about being right. No longer is there anything to battle over. You no longer find yourself in an adversarial role. In fact, you discover that in this space God simply grants you the grace to shower the world with that same grace.

Instead of being drawn into negative thoughts and partisan words, you are now free to offer true Spirit-fruit from God's overflowing storehouse. Imagine the possibilities for expressing real love, joy, peace, patience, kindness, generosity, faithfulness, gentleness, and self-control. In the midst of seemingly intractable ideological struggle, the fruits of God's Spirit are most urgently needed, and God can dispense them through your life. But remember, you cannot dispense God's Spirit unless it already owns you.

About eight years ago I was tired of being questioned about this or that political hot-button issue. It seemed everyone in the congregation wanted me, their pastor, to be on their side. So I adopted a response to this form of political side-picking that I continue to use to this day. My response managed to subvert all side-taking and usually ended the conversation altogether. It also relieved any pressure I felt to say the right thing or take the right position. Here is a brief story of one such time this happened.

I was between pastoral assignments. Following a phone interview I had with a church's board of elders, they paid for my wife and me to fly out to spend a weekend with them so we and they could further discern the call. After being together for a few days, all things seemed to be leading toward a positive outcome. On the last night of our stay, the board chair, her husband, my wife, and I were enjoying a casual conversation when the husband of the board chair started a brief political rant and attempted to engage me in his way of thinking. As he was talking, I noticed that his wife had a pained—even frightened—look on her face. She wanted to stop him but did not know how.

I waited until he finished his rant. As he turned it over to me to respond, I assured him of two things. First, I said I loved to talk politics and would be glad to spend as much time as he wanted on the subjects in which he wanted to engage me. Second, I said the only politics I would discuss were the politics of Jesus. As soon as I concluded this double statement, all tension left the room and he no longer had any interest in engaging me in political dialogue. Most importantly, the board chair relaxed. In the end we worked together to lead that congregation in an awesome, Spirit-led revitalization over the next two years.

I have been surprised over and over at just how little interest lifelong Christians have in discussing the politics of Jesus. By "the politics of Jesus," I simply mean taking what Jesus said and how he lived as our true guide for living in a political world. You may remember the WWJD bracelets popular some years ago that posed the question "What would Jesus do?" With my response to people wishing to engage me in political discussion, I am essentially asking two questions: "What did Jesus teach and live?" and "How can I learn from him and live it too?"

Now at the end of this section, if you are disappointed because I have not laid out a political agenda, take heart. I joyfully ask you to answer these same two questions: "What did Jesus teach and live?" and "How will you learn from him and live it too?" If you are seeking help in directing your thoughts and actions regarding policy and politics, I would simply ask you to submit your political identity to the truth Jesus taught. Possibly the best place to begin is where Jesus himself began in his teaching in Matthew, with the beatitudes. I am not asking you only to *learn* what he *said*. I am inviting you to *submit your very being* to the will and way of God that these beatitudes describe. I hope you will discover that it is actually not me making this invitation, but Jesus. I hope you will discover your true identity living as the image of God you were created to be.

SUMMING UP LIVING THE BEATITUDES

Recently, I enjoyed reading a murder mystery series written by William Kent Krueger. These books are set in the Minnesota North Woods near where I live, which is one of the reasons I was hooked. In two of the books, one of Krueger's characters recounts a commonly told story that I offer as a closing parable for chapters 2 and 3, this discussion of the beatitudes. The main character of the books is Cork O'Conner. Another character is a wise Native American sage named Henry Meloux. Cork has followed Henry's instruction to spend a sleepless solo night in the woods, simply watching and waiting. The next morning, this conversation takes place:

> Henry asks Cork, "What did you see?"
> Cork says he saw two wolves fighting in an open meadow. Cork asks, "What does it mean?"
> Henry explains that every person has two wolves doing battle inside them. One wolf is love and the other wolf is fear.
> Cork asks, "Which wolf wins?"

Henry answers, "The one you feed."[3]

Whether we live out of our God-given identity as salt and light for the world, sharing love and all the other fruits of the Spirit, or live out of fear, acting and reacting in violence, hatred, bitterness, and retaliation, will depend on which identity we opt to "feed"—to engage, to practice, to cultivate, to let "own" us. We can live according to the world, or we can live according to Jesus and the beatitudes he taught. One choice will bring us heartache and the other will bring us lasting hope and joy.

3. Krueger, *Vermillion Drift*, 269, 297.

4

God's Grace and the Law of Love

THE SEEMING IMPOSSIBILITY OF GRACE

We probably all underestimate the possibility of living fully within God's grace. The moment we start to "get" it, we seem to lose it again. Grace, by definition, is free. God's grace is a totally unrestricted and unbounded gift, ever present and unavoidable. It is there in the air we breathe. It is there in the first and last light of every day. The expanse and extent of God's grace personally imparted to us seems unbelievable to the human heart and mind. In my best moments, I do believe in God's grace, maybe even with all my heart.

Our struggle with grace comes naturally. In every aspect of life on this planet, we learn to be someone, do something, make a difference, turn things around, accomplish, run and hide, be right, look good, behave, get over it, make money, survive, protect and defend, provide, nurture, love, be generous, be joyful, or myriad combinations of the above. We are hard-wired to perform from womb to tomb. It seems impossible not to judge ourselves and others according to this script. In this drive to self-generate, even for God-believing people, our personal ego-needs too often crowd out the relevance of God incarnate and available to us moment by moment throughout life.

Everything is potential fuel for the fire of the times we withhold grace from others and ourselves. For Christians, any Bible verse is malleable material for our self-defense. Nothing in Scripture or church life is beyond the reach of our use of it. Often, Christian churches have been and continue to be hotbeds for the misusing of Scripture, the misusing of so-called righteousness, the misusing of so much good in the service of so much self-protection. It does not matter what flavor of theology or biblical interpretation we favor; the seeming impossibility of living within God's grace is a challenge for every Christian, every church, and every human being. If we could successfully and continually experience the depth of God's grace, any sense that we need to judge ourselves or others would fall away.

But it's as if we fear grace becoming an epidemic and infecting everyone—even people we don't think deserve it. And as long as we cling to an attitude of right versus wrong, we will inoculate the world to any threat of the real, Jesus-revealed, God-given epidemic of grace—which is actually not an epidemic, but a medicine desperately needed by everyone today. There must be another way to understand and live the gospel of Jesus Christ. How do we get beyond pitting one person against another, and the incessant need to self-justify?

TRYING TO BE RIGHTEOUS

I fear that many—or even most—Christians often live the righteousness of the scribes and Pharisees. Jesus says, "For I tell you, unless your righteousness exceeds that of the scribes and Pharisees, you will never enter the kingdom of heaven" (Matt 5:20).

Each of us, somewhere in the depth of our soul's emptiness, feels the need to justify ourselves. We feel an insatiable need to protect our own agenda, our religious turf, our way of life. To the extent we bow to this need, we live a never-ending search for a righteousness that is not of God. As Jesus states outright, this is not a righteousness that will ever gain us entry into God's kingdom. I would add: Neither in this world or the next.

So where does the seeming impossibility of living within God's grace leave us? If we have the nerve and the conviction to acknowledge our inability to fully live from within God's grace; if we could learn how to never again need to be right about anything; if we could find the release from any self-imposed goal to be righteous; if . . . then we would literally discover hope beyond imagination.

We will explore in this chapter how the human need to be right is indeed the opposition to the righteousness of which Jesus speaks. We will also explore what Jesus offers us in place of the need to be right, keep the law and commandments as measures of personal worth, thereby "qualifying" for entrance into God's kingdom. We will explore the unspeakable hope Jesus gives us and how he invites us into his kingdom. The righteousness to which Jesus calls us is different from—indeed, alien to—how we typically think of rightness. It is so different that religious seekers throughout the centuries have often missed it.

Matthew 5:17–48 might seem like an odd scripture passage to use to explore God's grace. So often these verses have either been understood as some new, impossible form of law or as new ways to prove our own righteousness. What if we approached them from an entirely different angle, one that is not about us at all? What if having absolutely *nothing* to prove was the key to entering God's kingdom? What if these verses were the complete opposite of any form of legalism? What if these verses formed the very definition of God's grace that goes far beyond our previous notions? Could we learn to live in this world in such a way as to embody God's grace for all, instead of worrying about proving anything about ourselves? Let's allow Jesus to teach us the answers to these questions.

BIBLICAL LAW IS NOT A LIST OF REQUIREMENTS BASED ON PUNISHMENT

Exodus 31:12–17 reads:

> The Lord said to Moses: You yourself are to speak to the Israelites: "You shall keep my sabbaths, for this is a sign between me and you throughout your generations, given in order that you may know that I, the Lord, sanctify you. You shall keep the sabbath, because it is holy for you; everyone who profanes it shall be put to death; whoever does any work on it shall be cut off from among the people. Six days shall work be done, but the seventh day is a sabbath of solemn rest, holy to the Lord; whoever does any work on the sabbath day shall be put to death. Therefore the Israelites shall keep the sabbath, observing the sabbath throughout their generations, as a perpetual covenant. It is a sign forever between me and the people of Israel that in six days the Lord made heaven and earth, and on the seventh day he rested, and was refreshed."

This passage is just one example of many from the early giving of the law in Exodus, Leviticus, and Deuteronomy. Many dos and don'ts are listed, along with varying degrees of punishment for failing to obey. Some of the most extreme consequences are for eyes and teeth to be removed, and for people to be stoned for this or that. Exodus 32 tells the story of the Israelites making and worshiping a golden calf. Just as Moses descends the mountain of the Lord, he comes upon the people in the very act of dancing and worshiping the human-made sculpture. In response, he throws down the tablets of the law and commands the sons of Levi to take up their swords and kill their family members throughout the camp. Three thousand are reported to have been killed that day for worshiping an idol.

There is no easy way to temper this account and other Old Testament texts where murder and mayhem reign among the people of God, even among God's chosen leaders in their understanding of religious law. It would be easy for us, as the civil people we are, to judge those times and peoples as crude and cruel beyond our more reasonable sensibilities. It would also be well for us to remember the inhumane cruelties of modern warfare, the deaths of innocent people all over the world—the born and the unborn—sacrificed, still, for senseless reasons.

Yet an Old Testament light shines through the darkness of this night. Leviticus 19 lists the aspects of holiness to which the people are called based on God's holiness. From this text we begin to see the intent of the law—to turn people toward the holiness of God, which includes love of neighbor, justice for all, and love for people from other lands. Other passages in Leviticus also instruct the people toward a holiness reflective of God's holiness. For example, Leviticus 25 details instructions for sabbath and Jubilee. God has a purpose in the law beyond punishment—a purpose that ends with justice and shalom (peace, wholeness, well-being) for all peoples, animals, and the earth. In these passages we are reminded of the covenant God made with Noah and all the earth in Genesis 9, following the flood. God's covenant of reconciliation promises to put an end to destruction for all humans, all creatures, and the earth.

So, in Matthew 5:17–20, when Jesus declares in all sincerity the importance of every bit of the law and prophets (meaning all Scripture[1]), is he condemning us all to death? Who among us has not worked on the sabbath? Who among us has not worshiped an idol?

When our daughter was three years old, she had it in mind that hiding from her parents was a fun game. This presented no problems at home, but out in public places things could get tense. We tried to warn her of the dangers of her little game. One day while we were visiting a zoo, she got away from us even though we thought we were being vigilant. In a panic we searched and searched. We finally found her safe but completely ignorant of the danger in which she had placed herself. In response, I walked her to the parking lot and spanked her. That was the first and last time I punished her physically. I was desperate to find a way to convince her of the danger she had put herself in. I was desperate to find a way to safeguard her from being lost to us forever.

There are good reasons for a loving parent—or a loving God—to say no to ways we cause hurt and pain to ourselves and others. There are wonderful reasons for warnings and restrictions. There is ample cause for God's will for us to be spelled out clearly as the way to life, and for that which is not God's will for us to be spelled out as the way to death.

I do not tell this story to make excuse for the severe punishments detailed in some Old Testament texts, just as I can never make an excuse for wars in the Old Testament or, for that matter, in the twenty-first century. What I am saying is that, already in God's early covenants with people, we see God's intention, not of punishment, but toward redemption and abundant life. We then have the many positive passages, like those in Leviticus, many of the psalms, and much in the prophets. It is important to know that the Old Testament punishment texts were an early way the people understood God, but they were already losing their grip and being replaced by new understandings long before Jesus came on the scene.

Lest any uncertainty remain, however, with the Sermon on the Mount, and especially the text we are exploring in this chapter, Jesus puts an end to interpretations of scripture that do not include redemption, reconciliation, and love. After all, as he says in Matthew 12:8, "For the Son of Man is lord of the Sabbath." This is but one example of how Jesus is the only lord and interpreter of the true law of God. And through Jesus,

1. Osborne, *Matthew*, 181.

we see that the real purpose of Old Testament law was to protect and guard people against pain, suffering, and death—as my purpose was to keep my daughter safe. The real purpose of the law was not to produce pain, suffering, and death, but to ensure life and well-being.

THIS PASSAGE IS NOT ABOUT LAW AS WE KNOW IT

> Do not think that I have come to abolish the law or the prophets; I have come not to abolish but to fulfill. For truly I tell you, until heaven and earth pass away, not one letter, not one stroke of a letter, will pass from the law until all is accomplished. Therefore, whoever breaks one of the least of these commandments, and teaches others to do the same, will be called least in the kingdom of heaven; but whoever does them and teaches them will be called great in the kingdom of heaven. For I tell you, unless your righteousness exceeds that of the scribes and Pharisees, you will never enter the kingdom of heaven. (Matt 5:17–20)

This teaching of Jesus may seem confusing. On the surface it seems to be all about obeying the law and Jesus' new version of every exacting part of the law. It is only natural that we would think this, given the way most of our lives center on doing right or being right—some version of legalism.

Like it or not, rules govern our lives more often than we care to admit: both formal and informal rules, some acknowledged, others subconscious. An acknowledged rule can be anything from a speed-limit sign to how you place the silverware for dinner. A subconscious rule might be an automatic action you do to protect your ego, or a script taught long ago by your parents and that you follow even now for how to be good. We are all programmed throughout life to live within boundaries set up either for us or by us: to do one thing and not the other, act one way and not the other, be someone and not another.

A clear-cut list of laws or rules to live by is actually a gift because, otherwise, most of us would wallow in a confusion of conscious and subconscious messages flooding our brains. A code to live by is a benefit. In fact, a code to live by gives most of us a sense of purpose and identity. Whether the rules are a part of our church or family, our workplace or school, the government or military, we find ourselves living accordingly. Often, we become so dependent on these rules that if they were taken away, we would feel lost.

Jesus understood our human need for laws to guide us, protect us, and give us identity. Biblical scholars tell us that Matthew was written for a Jewish audience, and surely Old Testament scripture (what Jesus here calls the law and the prophets) was the code followed by those hearing his teaching. Jesus knew better than to take this code away from a people dependent on it, and he knew the many positive truths and life-changing instructions of scripture.

Let's think of laws or rules as establishing a baseline. Rules that are given us, and rules that we adopt on our own, are necessary for us to form a solid sense of self. Assuming these rules are helpful ones, we have a healthy baseline—a starting point from which to mature emotionally and spiritually. Jesus affirms this in verses 17–18.

But Jesus also knows how easy it is for us to fall prey to a tyranny of rules, which only embeds us in a rule-keeping, score-keeping identity. Our dependence on rules too easily moves from a helpful baseline to an end goal where our identity is overly wrapped up in keeping the rules. When this happens, we become spiritually stunted, wooden, and dead. When we remain at the starting point and make rules our lifelong guide, we sacrifice emotional creativity, spiritual maturity, and relational blessings both human and divine.

If we cling to our rules, they become our security and, eventually, our surrogate god. For Bible-based people, we can then become self-righteous judges dependent on our own interpretations of scriptural "rules." As an example, I cringe inwardly when Christians say something like, "The Bible says . . ." The conclusion of this statement is almost always a rule-based use of scripture which ends all creative exploration into the truth of God incarnate moving and shaking our fragile worldview.

So, rather than falling into a legalistic pit, let's dig deeper into the meaning of Jesus' teaching here. The most important word to understand in verses 17–18 is "fulfill." This word is the key to what Jesus teaches next, about the fulfilled law. We might even conclude that Jesus himself is the embodied fulfillment of the law, with this embodiment being his ministry's primary purpose.

The Greek word used in verse 17 is the past active infinitive of the Greek verb meaning "to fulfill." This word conveys the meaning "to fulfill *totally* or *completely*." For example, Acts 2:2 reads, "And suddenly from heaven there came a sound like the rush of a violent wind, and it filled [same Greek root word] the entire house where they were sitting." The word here means "filled the house *completely*." In Philippians 4:18, Paul uses this word to describe how he has been paid *in full*, has *more than enough*, and is *completely* satisfied with the gifts sent to him. Colossians 1:9–10 reads: "For this reason, since the day we heard it, we have not ceased praying for you and asking that you may be filled [same Greek root] with the knowledge of God's will in all spiritual wisdom and understanding, so that you may lead lives worthy of the Lord, fully pleasing to him, as you bear fruit in every good work and as you grow in the knowledge of God."

"There is in the term a strong element of exclusiveness or totality. The joy, knowledge, etc. which fill the Christian shapes his [*sic*] whole existence and imperiously claims his whole being."[2]

In addition, when specifically connected with Jesus, this term carries even greater weight to its use in Matthew 5:17. We see a prime example in Colossians 2:8–10:

2. Kittel, *Theological Dictionary*, 6:291.

> See to it that no one takes you captive through philosophy and empty deceit, according to human tradition, according to the elemental spirits of the universe, and not according to Christ. For in him the whole fullness [same Greek root] of deity dwells bodily, and you have come to fullness [same Greek root] in him, who is the head of every ruler and authority.

Now, let's look at this word in Matthew 5:17. First, it comes at the beginning of Jesus' teaching on law. It designates that he is now explaining the law as it is *fulfilled* in him and in his teachings. Second, this word makes clear that the law and the prophets, indeed the entire Old Testament, is *completely* and *absolutely fulfilled* in Jesus' ministry and teachings. Third, the remainder of the New Testament bears witness to the fact that Jesus has the authority to do this.

> The goal of the mission of Jesus is fulfilment (Matthew 1:17b); according to Matthew 5:17a this is primarily fulfilment of the Law and the prophets, i.e., of the whole of the Old Testament as a declaration of the will of God. Jesus does not merely affirm that He will maintain them. As He sees it, His task is to actualize the will of God made known in the Old Testament. He has come in order that God's Word may be completely fulfilled, in order that the full measure appointed by God Himself may be reached in Him.[3]

Noting the context of these verses within Jesus' teaching ministry, either directly or indirectly following the beatitudes, we discover how important he believed his teaching was for those who would listen. This *fulfilled law* will never pass away "until all is accomplished" (Matt 5:18), said Jesus. In verse 19 he takes the importance of his teaching of the fulfilled law even further: "Therefore, whoever breaks one of the least of these commandments, and teaches others to do the same will be called least in the kingdom of heaven; but whoever does them and teaches them will be called great in the kingdom of heaven."

My daughter who ran away from us at the zoo is now thirty-eight years old, and I cannot remember a time when I last felt it necessary to warn her of the danger of running away. We would do as well if we were to heed Jesus' warning here. Living life in God's kingdom on earth is dependent on hearing Jesus' teachings as the complete fulfillment of not only Old Testament scripture but New Testament scripture as well. Paul makes this clear in Colossians 2:9–10: "For in him the whole fullness of deity dwells bodily, and you have come to fullness in him, who is the head of every ruler and authority." Jesus' teaching authority should be just as essential for his followers today.

---

3. Kittel, *Theological Dictionary*, 6:294.

RIGHTEOUSNESS IS THE KEY TO FULFILLING THE LAW OF LOVE

Why does Jesus say in Matthew 5:20, "For I tell you, unless your righteousness exceeds that of the scribes and Pharisees, you will never enter the kingdom of heaven"? Were the scribes and Pharisees bad people? Where they purposely leading others astray? I doubt it.

In Jesus' day the scribes and Pharisees were focused on the right keeping of the law as they best understood its meaning from Old Testament scripture and tradition. The scribes were the specialists in understanding religious law, somewhat like how we think of lawyers for civil and criminal law today. The Pharisees were the keepers of the law like how we think of present-day religious leaders with power and authority to influence their parishioners, or the clergy of their jurisdiction, with regard to religious behavior. Much of the work of the scribes and Pharisees was good and helpful. We err greatly if we blame them as being bad people or accuse them of killing Jesus.

The task of interpreting, keeping, and enforcing the law was the life work, and seemingly had become the end goal, of the scribes and Pharisees. Sadly, their greatest gift to the world became their greatest sin (missing the mark). The law was never intended to be an end in itself, never a means by which people were to find the meaning of life or reconciliation with God and the world. The law was intended as a help to safely guard people on their journey toward loving God with all their heart, soul, and might. Hear these words from Moses in Deuteronomy 6:1–5:

> Now this is the commandment—the statutes and the ordinances—that the Lord your God charged me to teach you to observe in the land that you are about to cross into and occupy, so that you and your children and your children's children may fear the Lord your God all the days of your life, and keep all his decrees and his commandments that I am commanding you, so that your days may be long. Hear therefore, O Israel, and observe them diligently, so that it may go well with you, and so that you may multiply greatly in a land flowing with milk and honey, as the Lord, the God of your ancestors, has promised you.
>
> Hear, O Israel: the Lord is our God, the Lord alone. You shall love the Lord your God with all your heart, and with all your soul, and with all your might.

If one takes the last sentence out of this instruction from Moses, one is left without the meaning of life on earth as intended by God. Without this last sentence, this instruction simply says, in effect, keep the law and things will go well for you. The object is self! And the only formula for things to go well is to keep the law. The danger of this understanding is that the object of life becomes self-preservation, and legalism becomes the means to this end.

Let's not miss the subtlety of this mistake—that of law becoming the means to the end that is self. I doubt there is a person alive who does not make this mistake regularly. It simply makes no sense to blame the scribes and Pharisees and not examine our own personal motives and sense of the meaning of life. Any amount of blaming would mask our own life's motive of self-interest. In Matthew 7, Jesus likens this to seeing a speck of sawdust in our neighbor's eye while missing the log in our own eye.

Note that Moses states with an air of command, "Hear, O Israel: the Lord is our God, the Lord alone" (Deut. 6:4). This statement, as well as others like it, is the basis for monotheism in the Old Testament. Without this statement, a centrally defining commitment of the law and prophets would be lost, and the very heart of the gospel message in both Old and New Testament scriptures would fall apart. In other words, placing the object of life on ourselves bolstered by legalism is a terrible mistake we too regularly make. That the Lord our God is to be God alone is echoed in Matthew 5 as Jesus reclaims the purpose of the law. We are not to be self-centered, but God-centered.

Like all human beings, the scribes and Pharisees were vulnerable to a self-righteousness never intended by God nor taught by Moses. As long as we or the scribes and Pharisees use the law toward our own end, no matter how subtly, we will as Jesus says, "never enter the kingdom of heaven."

Where, then, is our hope? Where is the true and only meaning of life? How might we discover the true righteousness Jesus indelibly links to the kingdom? How indeed might our righteousness exceed that of the scribes and Pharisees?

Moses had the answer, which God had given him. He states it clearly in Deuteronomy 6:5—love God completely with everything you've got. Jesus offers us crucial help in discovering the path to this complete love in the beatitudes. We simply cannot love God completely by living the beatitudes if we retain our need for self-justification.

I'd like to offer a paraphrase of Matthew 5:17–20, in light of our reflections thus far:

> Jesus says: Don't be mistaken, thinking that I have come to do away with the Old Testament scriptures. Rather, I have come to fully complete them so that you might know their meaning and intent. This is what my presence and my teaching represent—a fulfilling revelation aligning God's original intent for the law with present instruction so you might understand how to live out God's law of love in your everyday lives. I have come to teach and embody what it means to love God completely and how that love, in turn, will reveal God to the world around you. Don't dare think that any of this law of love I am bringing will ever pass away until all of God's plan for this world is accomplished.
>
> So, because of this, if anyone takes away even the least of the commandments I am bringing you and teaches others to do the same, that person will become the most insignificant person in the present and future kingdom of the heavens. On the other hand, the person who follows my commandments

and teaches others to do the same will become known as great in the present and future kingdom of the heavens.

Pay careful attention and know this: Unless your righteousness is based firmly on your love of God, and unless you have given yourselves over to my commandments (the beatitudes as prime example, plus more to come in the following verses) as the way for God's love to flow through you to the world, you will never know the joy of living in God's kingdom here on earth as in the heavens. For you to enter my kingdom now and my kingdom yet to come, you will need to move beyond any legalistic notion of righteousness that is separate from a fully devoted and loving relationship with God in the present. The righteousness I bring represents a reordering of all your relationships so that God's loving justice (refer to chapter 2) will be accomplished through you, and begins and ends with your complete love of God. This is what so many religious leaders and people in general miss.

THE INCOMPREHENSIBLE GRACE AND LOVE OF GOD

As we prepare to examine Matthew 5:21–48, a glance at the book of Leviticus will help us ponder the richness of Jesus' teaching beyond the legalistic traps of the human mind. Leviticus represents a time in the life of the Israelites after the tabernacle was built and arranged. The conclusion of Exodus, in particular Exodus 40, grounds us in the specifics of how the tabernacle was set up. Leviticus picks up the story of Israel after Moses has come down from meeting God on Mount Sinai and after the people have built the tabernacle. At the beginning of Leviticus, God's presence now dwells in the tabernacle, located just outside the Israelite camp. In essence, God has come near, to be present to the people. Perry B. Yoder says the following about Leviticus 1:1:

> God summons Moses to the tent of meeting. God will no longer speak to Moses on Mount Sinai: the cloud of God's presence has come down from the mountain and taken up residence in the tent of meeting. God now speaks to Moses from the tent and in full view of the people.
>
> The coming of God to God's people is a revolutionary development. God is no longer out there on top of a mountain, hidden by a cloud. God is present just outside the camp. God's new location necessitates the central question of Leviticus: How do God's people live in the light of God's presence?[4]

This same question could well form the basis of our study of Matthew 5:21–48: *How do God's people live, now that God is present to us in Christ Jesus?*

In Ephesians 3:14–19, Paul writes about God's profound presence with us:

> For this reason I bow my knees before the Father, from whom every family in heaven and on earth takes its name. I pray that, according to the riches of his glory, he may grant that you may be strengthened in your inner being with

4. Yoder, *Leviticus*, 42.

power through his Spirit, and that Christ may dwell in your hearts through faith as you are being rooted and grounded in love. I pray that you may have the power to comprehend, with all the saints, what is the breadth and length and height and depth, and to know the love of Christ that surpasses knowledge, so that you may be filled with all the fullness of God.

Paul is describing God in Christ Jesus as a God of incomprehensible, yet accessible, love, present and available to us in our inner beings. Paul envisions us as people filled with God's love to the absolute limits of time and space. This love exceeds the bounds of our knowledge; it can only be known through Jesus Christ dwelling in our hearts, in our inner being.

This is the indwelling to which Jesus invites us in Matthew. In the final section of Matthew 5, which we will explore shortly, Jesus cuts across any human-made barriers to uncover the brilliance of God's loving presence. God has come near, and not just to the outskirts of the Israelite camp. Jesus himself is now the presence of the one and only God whose indwelling love will wash away any pretense of love that is less than God's.

In Jesus, God offers us grace, forgiveness, and love unbounded! But to learn to live with the indwelling presence of God, we will need to let go of self-righteousness and instead believe Jesus. So, what if we put away our need for an external law? What if we could forget the hurtful lessons of this life that have taught us to hide in the supposed safety of rules? What if you and I could find freedom in knowing a God of infinite grace and forgiveness? If we can be open to knowing God as fully gracious, loving, and forgiving, it will transform our understanding of Jesus' meaning when he declares six times over in Matthew 5:21–48, "But I say unto you . . ."

GOD'S RIGHTEOUSNESS IMPARTED TO US/KINGDOM LOVING OUTLINED—MATTHEW 5:21–48

In these twenty-eight verses, Jesus takes six examples of teachings based in Old Testament scripture and teaches what it will look like to fulfill them completely. With these examples, he clearly illustrates what we must never allow to "pass away" from his law of grace and love. Jesus is teaching us what God's righteousness is and how it is intended as grace and love, first embedded in us, and then shared with the world. At the same time, he is showing us the great gulf between human-based righteousness (that of religious rule-keepers) and God's righteousness. He is clear and emphatic about how to live beyond simplistic or legalistic attempts to be righteous according to external law. With these teachings it becomes clear that the hard work of letting go of self-righteousness has been the spiritual dark shadow avoided by far too many religious people.

The six sayings of Jesus that we will explore in detail momentarily are important examples of how our lives are to be reordered from the inside out. They illustrate a pattern of submitting heart, mind, and soul to God within the practicalities of life as we move forward believing Jesus instead of any other gods. To submit so completely is to discover that the fulfillment Jesus offers at Matthew 5:17 is actually a fulfillment of the heart—his heart embedded in the cavity vacated by our self-righteousness! Now maybe we can begin to see how keeping the law in any humanly generated way is alien to everything Jesus proposes. As we start to understand the significance of Jesus' heart in us, we will better grasp how these sayings are anything *but* a new rule book.

In Jesus and his teachings, God has come to dwell among us and in us! No longer does God speak from the tabernacle on the edge of camp. God now speaks to and within our very hearts! To recognize the impact of Jesus' six sayings is to discover the answer to the question mentioned earlier: How are we to live, now that God is present among us in Jesus?—or now that "the kingdom of heaven has come near" (Matt 4:17)?

THE SUM OF THE SIX SAYINGS

Rather than working through all six sayings in verses 21–48, we'll look carefully at the sixth one, verses 43–48. Practically speaking, to carefully examine all six sayings would take time and space beyond the scope of this chapter. Interpretively, I believe we will find the examination of the sixth saying fully sufficient to illustrate the depth of Jesus' "fulfillment" of the law intended to take place within our hearts.

This sixth saying also serves to summarize—add up and examine as a total sum of—Jesus' teachings in Matthew 5. Jesus says in verse 48, "Be perfect, therefore, as your heavenly Father is perfect." Think in terms of a completed sum of what Jesus intends God's indwelling to be and to accomplish in our hearts and in our daily lives. Think in terms of the Lord's Prayer: "Thy kingdom come; thy will be done on earth as it is in heaven." This would be perfection in the sense of "completeness."

POTENTIALLY THE MOST TRANSFORMATIVE TEACHING OF JESUS—LOVING ENEMIES

> [Jesus said,] "You have heard that it was said, 'You shall love your neighbor and hate your enemy.' But I say to you, Love your enemies and pray for those who persecute you, so that you may be children of your Father in heaven; for he makes his sun rise on the evil and on the good, and sends rain on the righteous and on the unrighteous. For if you love those who love you, what reward do you have? Do not even the tax collectors do the same? And if you greet only your brothers and sisters, what more are you doing than others? Do not even the Gentiles do the same? Be perfect, therefore, as your heavenly Father is perfect." (Matt 5:43–48)

If Christians around the world would truly love their enemies, they would soon find they had no enemies! These same Christians would alter the course of history, moving peoples and nations, families and churches, acquaintances and intimate relationships toward reconciliation and healing. Human history would undergo a transformation like has never been seen or imagined.

You are probably saying that such a worldwide transformation will never happen. You may be correct. But what *can* happen is that the world in which you and I live every day can be transformed, and will be, if we learn to love our enemies. You and I can participate in this transformation as we are transformed from the inside out by God in Christ Jesus dwelling within us. For to love our enemies puts an end to the very idea of *enemy*. To love our former enemies will mean a completed (perfect) love of God and self as well. But this will only happen through the presence of the God who came down the mountain to dwell at the edge of camp, and who now in Christ Jesus has come to dwell in our hearts.

To love our enemies and pray for those who persecute us would mean we take Jesus seriously and actually believe him, allowing him to take over our inner being. It would also mean disbelieving much of what our world teaches us about enemies, and no longer allowing the world's teaching to control our inner being. It's about time.

It is important that we both carefully examine this text and the context of Christianity's denial of this text. To do this well, we need to submit heart, mind, and soul to God's heart, mind, and soul of love, for no human power or will can make enemies disappear. That is God's job, and in Christ Jesus, God wants to accomplish it in and through us.

In the remainder of this chapter we will examine the concept of dismantling and loving enemies in this order: (1) We will examine the text on loving enemies; (2) we will examine how and why Christians who say they follow Jesus deny his teaching here; and (3) we will ask ourselves how we can personally believe Jesus, love enemies, and become, as he says, "perfect . . . as [our] heavenly Father is perfect" (Matt 5:48).

1. Jesus Teaches Us to Love Our Enemies—the Text

Take a moment to look back at the beginning of the previous section to reread Matthew 5:43–48.

This teaching on love of enemies comes in the context of Jesus' accumulated teaching in Matthew 5. It is a powerful example of what Jesus intended when he began his teaching ministry by calling people to repent, turn their lives around, and discover the joy of living in the kingdom of the heavens now (Matt 4:17).

I doubt it would be possible to even come close to understanding this text on loving enemies if we isolated it from what Jesus has said up to this point. But in context, it makes perfect sense and speaks truth to us, captivating us in the bosom and character of God. In order to know the love of enemies as our truth, we must believe Jesus each step of the way he has led us so far. This is why chapters 2 and 3 of this book have preceded our look at Jesus' teaching on loving enemies. Let me add up what we have learned so far in preparation for loving enemies:

A. In turning our lives around, we rest at the pivot point of our lives, ready to let Jesus guide us forward into new life. (Matt 4:17)

B. This new life is our freshly discovered truth that we are created in God's image, as described by Jesus in the beatitudes. (Matt 5:3–12)

C. As we live the beatitudes, we live in the image of God, and therefore, the world sees God's glory because we reflect God's image. (Matt 5:13–16)

Hold these three points together carefully. They are foundational, but Jesus is not done yet. He makes three more points to solidify this first triad. If we are to understand the six sayings to come, and especially the one on love of enemies, we will need to absorb all six points Jesus has made thus far.

D. Jesus tells us his teaching is a complete fulfillment of scripture. He sternly cautions us not to believe that one tiny bit of his teaching will ever "pass away." Jesus alone has the authority to claim this, as many New Testament texts proclaim. What he has taught so far, and what he is about to teach, is God's truth, and it is forever! (Matt 5:17–18)

E. We must not disobey any of these teachings, nor teach others to disobey them. The six new sayings—and in particular the sixth one, on loving enemies—are certainly included in this warning. Our status in living the kingdom of God is dependent on our obedience and our teaching this obedience to others. (Matt 5:19)

F. The result of our repentance, living the beatitudes, and obeying all Jesus' teachings is a life of living out God's righteousness now. In this righteous living, we experience what it is like to joyfully live in the kingdom of God even in the midst of the swirl of daily life. (Matt 5:20)

Jesus' six sayings, which follow these six points, are what Jesus teaches as real-life application of God's righteousness and of living in the kingdom.

Hearing the Truth of God within Us

> You have heard that it was said, "You shall love your neighbor and hate your enemy." But I say to you, Love your enemies and pray for those who persecute you. . . . (Matt 5:43–44)

In Matthew 5:21–48, Jesus says six times, "You have heard it said . . ." and then presents his interpretation of the law: "But I say . . ." Jesus' teachings here come with the weight of new commandments. While that might sound like we now have a serious list of new rules, Jesus is speaking in light of the six points listed above. He is speaking into the reality of life surrendered to God's will and way in the world, God's kingdom come on earth.

Therefore, these statements are not new commandments so much as declarations of how God's grace and love flow from God, into us, and from us as God's reflections. These new declarations clarify the importance of God's grace and love as the ruling factor in every human transaction. If we were to try to make new rules out of these, we would be dumbing them down beyond recognition and making them the opposite of God's intent. For example, the commandment to love our enemies is not a new rule we must strive to live by. Rather, it declares God's love and grace for everyone regardless of deserving. You and I are intended to live as God's image on earth with God's heart implanted in us; therefore, what Jesus is commanding is actually the most natural, God-given act of love, grace, and forgiveness we can imagine. In a powerful sense, Jesus is saying, "This is how it is and is to be in God's present and future kingdom." This is what it is like for God's love to direct your life!

With the full authority of God now dwelling among us, Jesus speaks the truth of God into a world mostly lacking God's love-of-enemy truth. It is scary to think that so many of Jesus' would-be followers have placed this truth on a dusty back shelf. But God's truth is not dependent on our obedience. Rather, our status in the kingdom is dependent on our obedience. Jesus makes this utterly clear.

Jesus' truth-telling about loving enemies, compared to any other possible ways to handle enemies, is a radical new reality not only taught, but lived, by Jesus. He takes this personally. He claims it as his truth: "But *I* say to you . . ." We should not be too surprised that when God becomes so present as to live within us, when God takes human life on this earth this personally, our own former ideas about enemies must fundamentally change. *To love our enemy is not a mere command; it is the truth of God within us.*

In verse 44, Jesus tells us not only to love our enemies but to pray for them. Think about how this eliminates so many other possible responses to enemies! This certainly covers not being angry, or not taking retaliation, which Jesus mentions earlier in Matthew 5. It also eliminates ignoring, resenting, being unforgiving, keeping score, defending against, reacting badly, labeling, bombing, shooting, killing, or any form of not loving and praying for our enemies.

Love and *pray* are action words. Jesus is not speaking theoretically. Think about how you treat someone you really love. Your heart goes out to them. You long for their best interests. You want to lavish them with your open and generous care. If you are a spiritual person, to pray for them is one of the most natural things you do. In praying, you speak your longing to God, and in the sense that God hears our prayers, you engage God in the act of loving.

To love the person or group of people you find the most difficult to love is a divine imperative in that it is God's choice to act in you and through you. This love comes from God, creating something new in your heart, melting it, molding it, and reshaping it. This love is not idealistic but practical, as practiced by God and through God's image, which is you. This love originates from God's original act of love toward all creation. As you surrender your heart to God, God creates within you a oneness both human and divine. *When you act out your (God's) love toward an enemy, you become one with God. This is the supreme indwelling divine experience, and it is available in every moment of life on this earth.* Nothing could be more practical or more truly human than to choose to love enemies. The world as a whole and far too many Christians miss this divine opportunity, misjudging the immense power of God's love available to and through them. Think of the million miracles we have missed.

So, how do we allow God's love of enemies to invade us? First, we realize that we have been separated from God in ways we did not even realize. In a real sense, we have been enemies of God. Second, God's love seeps into the parts of our heart we formerly held back from any divine touch. God's love replaces the anxieties we have held in the inner depths of our hearts. God cleans house, so to speak, removing the dirt and clutter that have kept us afraid of God. We no longer need a "safe" distance from God as we discover that God uses only grace and love with which to overpower our fears.

It is paramount in this experience of God that our concept of God at a deeply personal level becomes an experience of pure grace. As Ephesians 2:4–7 claims:

> But God, who is rich in mercy, out of the great love with which he loved us even when we were dead through our trespasses, made us alive together with Christ—by grace you have been saved—and raised us up with him and seated us with him in the heavenly places in Christ Jesus, so that in the ages to come he might show the immeasurable riches of his grace in kindness toward us in Christ Jesus.

Once we personally experience God's presence as pure grace, our entire concept of God and God's role in this universe will change. We will no longer be capable of thinking of God as a vengeful and punishing presence. We will realize just the opposite! Our view of God and this world we live in will take on a new understanding. We will begin to experience grace everywhere. We will now know we are held in God's loving embrace all the time and in every wonderful or painful experience of life.

The third part of our coming to love our enemies is in the form of God's compassion for hurting and troubled people. It is not possible to blame someone for "persecuting" us when we live in the experience of God's love showered on us without blame. If, as Ephesians says, we are saved by God's grace and made "alive together" with Jesus, then we share in Jesus' prayer from the cross, "Father, forgive them for they do not know what they are doing" (Luke 23:34). Jesus was not making an excuse for the horrible things people had done to him; rather, he was acknowledging how lost they all were within the sinful violence and power struggles of this world. Jesus could share God's compassion for his torturers because the love of God within him was far greater than the hurt and the hate of the world. His prayer from the cross reveals the supreme power of God's kingdom of love flowing from Jesus' heart and now also available from ours.

In the process of loving enemies, we find ourselves left with no one to blame for the hurt and the pain and the violence and the death this world endures, not because the other did nothing wrong, but because God's love in us leaves no room for judgment except the judgment of love. You may think that somehow this judgment of love allows for evil to flourish. To the contrary, there is no greater condemnation of evil than love. There is no greater destroyer of evil than love. There is no greater power in all the universe than the love of God in Jesus Christ and in us.

When we are left with no need to blame, we are truly free to love both the best and the worst that humanity has to offer. This love of God is the only real salvation for the world. *In the command to love and pray for enemies, Jesus makes clear to his followers that the choice to experience God's salvation is a choice to love our enemies.*

How to Become Children of God—Matthew 5:45–47

> . . . so that you may be children of your Father in heaven; for he makes his sun rise on the evil and on the good, and sends rain on the righteous and on the unrighteous. For if you love those who love you, what reward do you have? Do not even the tax collectors do the same? And if you greet only your brothers and sisters,[a] what more are you doing than others? Do not even the Gentiles do the same? (Matt 5:45–47)

Let's remember what is at stake in Jesus' teaching so far: Lives fully turned around. Lives transformed into the image of God, and God then displayed to all the world. God's righteousness lived in us, and the kingdom of the heavens becoming real present-day reality. Hearts full of love, and relationships renewed.

Within the context of everything happening through Jesus' teaching, it is especially intriguing that he says we *become* children of God through the process of loving and praying for enemies. As we live the beatitudes, are we not children of God? As we act out the righteousness of peace and justice, are we not children of God? In fact, at Matthew 5:9, Jesus said the peacemakers would be "called children of God." And as we let go of our anger and reconcile with our brothers and sisters, are we not children of God? Yet here, in the call to love and pray for enemies, Jesus says, more specifically than before, "so that you may be children of your Father in the heavens." He follows this statement with examples of how God blesses all people regardless of whether they are good or bad, worthy or unworthy. Additionally, he makes the point that we don't demonstrate God's love by showing love only to those who love us back. There is little or no reward in this kind of quid-pro-quo exchange of love for love.

Like Jesus' listeners of old, we may find it hard to believe all this. Perhaps such disbelief is why Jesus goes into a detailed description of how this love does and does not work, and how it defines the process of becoming a child of God. Perhaps a simple way to say what Jesus means here is that through the process of loving and praying for enemies, we embrace what it means to be children of God. This does not diminish his earlier teachings, but it suggests that we must love and pray for our enemies if we are to love as God loves.

Let's take a deeper look at how we become children of God. The Greek text actually says "sons of your Father in the heavens." I have been using the more inclusive word *children* instead of *sons*, but it may be helpful to examine this idea of sonship more closely. The most important example of sonship we have in the New Testament is that of Jesus' identification as the Son of God. For Jesus there is a oneness with God, a shared divinity, a complete identification. Though we will never be children of God in the exact same way Jesus is God's Son, it will help us take this passage more seriously if we think in terms of how loving and praying for our enemies likely gets us as close as possible to how Jesus is a son of God.

Another angle from which to pursue this concept of being sons and daughters of God is to consider the idea of being "born again." This phrase is used in some Christian circles as a way to describe being "saved." It implies a spiritual rebirth and connotes now being a son or daughter of God. The term *born again* comes from John 3, where Jesus tells Nicodemus that he must be born from above (which can also be translated "born anew" or "born again"). It would be nothing short of amazing if Christians, especially evangelical Christians, could see a way clear to link this concept of being born again with loving enemies. I suggest that the process of discovering God's grace and love in the depths of our hearts, and in turn realizing the strength of this love extended to our enemies, is the very process of being spiritually born again. Indeed, there is no way humanly possible to love and pray for our enemies without being born again. The next time you hear the phrase "born again" or think in terms of being born again, understand that Jesus claims love of and prayer for enemies as distinguishing marks of this aspect of one's life.

Jesus knew that the salvation of the world depended upon God's unbounded love come into the world through him and his followers (John 3:16). The world in which we live is utterly dependent on the hope and dream of God's children loving others unconditionally despite the worst realities of hurt and despair. This explains why Jesus culminates his six sayings with a description of God's love embodied (literally) in his followers sharing God's love in this world. Imagine if we all modeled Jesus' sonship by loving enemies to the very end, just as he did.

Summing It All Up

Be perfect, therefore, as your heavenly Father is perfect. (Matt 5:48)

"Therefore": in other words, "taking into consideration all that has just been said, let's sum up this teaching on love and prayer for enemies by saying . . ."

It is easy to see how Jesus' teaching here could be taken as a call to perfectionism if we were to read this verse in isolation from its context. Who could possibly be perfect as God is perfect? If we are looking for an excuse to not obey Jesus' command to love and pray for enemies, here it is. But to use this verse in this way is called proof-texting. In other words, it is taking a Bible verse or saying out of context and using it to "prove" our own preferred interpretation.

The real problem for us is this: If we are to justify ourselves and not believe Jesus' command to love and pray for enemies, we need to be consistent and also deny his other teachings, including the previous five sayings in chapter 5. We will need to discount his call to repentance, his call to a greater righteousness, his warning not to discount the smallest part of his new teaching on the law; even the beatitudes we most love, such as "Blessed are those who mourn. . . ."

Dallas Willard says this about Jesus' teaching in the Sermon on the Mount:

> Remarkably, almost one sixth of the entire Discourse (fifteen of ninety-two verses) is devoted to emphasizing the importance of actually doing what it says. Doing and not just hearing and talking about it is how we know the reality of the kingdom and integrate our life into it.[5]

Further on, Willard states this about disobedient proof-texting:

> We have heard. For almost two millennia we have heard him, as already noted. But we have chosen to not do what he said. He warned that this would make us "like a silly man who built his house on a sand foundation. The rain poured down, and the rivers and winds beat upon that house, and it collapsed into a total disaster" (Matthew 7:26–27). We today stand in the midst of precisely the disaster he foretold, "flying upside down" but satisfied to be stoutly preaching against "works" righteousness.[6]

I have been claiming all along in the opening chapters of this book that Jesus was not promoting a new legalism, nor a perfectionistic way to live. The context of his words "Be perfect . . . as your heavenly Father is perfect" must be taken in context as the result of his eight beatitudes that we are learning to accept and live. The person whose heart, mind, and spirit are transformed into God's earthly image through those eight blessings will know beyond a doubt that loving and praying for enemies is the most natural outcome of a life attuned to Jesus' dwelling within us. What is inside us will be what comes out of us. It is the only way the heart can operate. To quote Willard one more time:

> The various scenes and situations that Jesus discusses in his Discourse on the Hill are actually stages in a progression toward a life of agape love. They progressively presuppose that we know where our well-being really lies, that we

5. Willard, *Divine Conspiracy*, 137.

6. Willard, *Divine Conspiracy*, 140.

have laid aside anger and obsessive desire, that we do not try to mislead people to get our way, and so on. Then loving and helping those who hurt us and hate us, for example, will come as a natural progression. Doing so will seem quite right, and we will be able to do so.[7]

It will help us here to understand that the Greek word for "perfect" in Matthew 5:48 conveys the meaning of completeness. It does not mean "flawless." In addition, it will help to refer to the parallel passage in Luke 6:36, "Be merciful, just as your Father is merciful." Instead of the word *perfect*, Luke uses the Greek word for "mercy," or perhaps more strongly, "compassion." *Perfect* here conveys a sense of rounding out, making whole or complete. Then, adding Luke's sense of compassion and putting it all together, we have Jesus summing up his command to love and pray for enemies by again telling us that life in this world for those who would follow him is intended to be completely lived out of the love of God in us. This love of God comes from the heart of God and infuses us with the life-energy of God. God's unbounded love and compassion are to flow through us in a complete manner, inclusive of all our dealings with both the good and the bad in this world.

Finally, we are ready to add even more importance to Jesus' command to love and pray for our enemies. This sixth saying obviously comes at the end of a list of sayings. With its emphasis on loving in perhaps the most difficult of life's situations, this saying of Jesus may now be understood as the pinnacle of the six. It is both the final one sequentially and the finale of how Jesus applies the law of love to daily life. In particular, the idea of being complete in love, as God is complete in love, sums up all the law Jesus teaches in Matthew 5:21–48.

Verse 48, then, is not unlike Jesus' declaration in Matthew 22:37–40, where he makes perhaps his most stunning of all statements about the law of love. In answer to the question about which commandment is the greatest, Jesus says:

> "You shall love the Lord your God with all your heart, and with all your soul, and with all your mind." This is the greatest and first commandment. And a second is like it: "You shall love your neighbor as yourself." On these two commandments hang all the law and the prophets.

If today's followers of Jesus miss the all-important message of his command to love and pray for enemies, we have missed the cornerstone of his message about how to live in the kingdom of the heavens. That cornerstone is love—complete love—not as we would love out of our own life experience and our own will, but God's complete love offered to us as God's lavish grace, which we receive as we submit to this love and its power. This love's power is the only power able to overcome the worst animosities this world inflicts. This is the power of love as best shown us by Jesus on the cross. Living in the completeness of God's love is a wonderful way to understand the salvation Jesus offers through his teachings, his kingdom invitation, and, indeed, his ultimate

7. Willard, *Divine Conspiracy*, 139.

act on the cross. Love, including and especially love of enemies, does indeed sum up not only Matthew 5, but also, as Jesus says, "all the law and the prophets" (Matt 22:40)—all of scripture!

2. How and Why Christians Deny This Teaching of Jesus

Let's lay down any and all presumptions and assumptions even a little bit void of love. Let's think of love in this way: Love is compassion in action. It is God's most all-encompassing way to confront and to reconcile, to admonish and to heal. It is the thing most needed in every situation known to humanity. So, let's confront and reconcile. Let's admonish and heal.

The following is a list of some of the reasons those who identify themselves as Christian do not take seriously Jesus' teaching on love of enemies. Each of the following realities calls for confrontation and admonishment, but it must be through a compassionate process of reconciliation and healing. It is quite interesting to note how these following seven reasons are almost entirely unrelated to careful biblical interpretation of Jesus and his teaching. Understanding this should help us realize the depth of human pain that causes our divergence from believing Jesus. Too much of the struggle over biblical interpretation has taken the form of arguing over the meaning of certain texts instead of examining the depth of pain in our hearts. It is time we looked deeply into the pain that keeps us from believing Jesus.

A. Like everyone else, we are wounded. Christians in general have just as much unresolved hurt as the non-Christians sitting beside us on the bus of life. We also have the same reasons to nurse this pain instead of letting it go. Often, it seems, our very belief system bolsters our resistance to healing. In our faith and the faith communities with which we associate, it is common to gloss over the real burdens we carry, the ones we are not prepared to lay down. This is perhaps our most frequent form of denial—to pretend we are okay, free of damaging passions and lasting injuries. We Christians do not want to think of ourselves as hypocrites, yet the true sense of this word is "pretender," and we are pretenders. Most Christian communities I have experienced are to some extent self-supporting environs for pretense. I do not mean this in a judgmental way, but simply as a sad truth about our human sense that we need to protect ourselves.

B. In part because of our woundedness, we are eager to follow a leader, teacher, or preacher who espouses a certain doctrine instead of encouraging us to have an honest and vulnerable heart. Our worst fear is vulnerability. A strong and sure doctrine claimed by an authority figure is a wondrous solution to what otherwise might become a spiritual journey to that vulnerable part of us we hide from others, from God, and from ourselves. As we latch on to the strong doctrinal leader, a clear doctrinal theology, or both, the next step is small and easy. We move away from Jesus and from believing him.

Jesus is anything *but* a strong doctrinal leader. Instead he teaches us the way of God's heart, and it is all about messy compassion for the messy, hurting interior lives from which we live. Jesus requires honesty from us before the searing love of God. Perhaps that sounds frightening—even painful. But if we had the courage to stand before this searing love, it would cauterize our wounds and leave us gasping for more vulnerability and compassion. Once seared, we would not—could not—go back to pretense. By following a leader other than Jesus, we ensure that we won't stand full in the presence of God's searing love, and in this we fail to understand that it will not harm us but save us.

C. We have made peace with the way of the world, as have most of our leaders. As long as Jesus doesn't challenge the fundamental way of life we have established, we'll let him be our God. As long as we can keep Jesus separate from the tough realities of our world, we will claim to follow him. It makes for a neat and concise theological package to put Jesus and his cross on a pedestal separate from real-life violence, greed, and desire. This separate pedestal is ensconced in concepts we glibly toss around, like salvation and heaven and hell and rapture and predestination, among others. I'm not saying these concepts aren't important, but their importance can only be known after we have recognized and confessed our idolatry and the idolatry of our world.

More simply put, *any* form of violence, from the least to the greatest, is opposite to the love of God. It makes no difference how we rationalize it. It makes no difference how much we have suffered; any violent response on our part is opposite to the love of God.

D. Love is the way and the will of God. Yet so many Christians around the world continue to live and spout violence, even while praying, "Thy kingdom come, thy will be done, on earth as it is in heaven."

E. We are victims of our own insecurities, which flourish amid the conflicting judgments we place upon ourselves. We gather these judgments from the world around us, from what people think of us, from what we think is the proper way to look or act, and from the accumulated inner messages that declare us unworthy. The best proof of our insecurities is when we feel the need to be right, and act on that need. This need to be right leads us away from the way of Jesus. It is frightening to consider this in light of how so many Christian leaders lead. If we will allow it, Jesus will instead lead us in the way of vulnerability, humility, and gracious response to both our friends and our enemies. Jesus will lead us in the way of the cross—his and ours.

F. We seek to protect our own ego. This, of course, goes hand in hand with our insecurities but discloses our neediness from a different angle. Here the angle is the false self we have built up to shield us from admitting we are wrong, "less than," or inadequate. Our ego forms an obstacle to God's love and vastly limits our capacity to let God love us. It is like Jesus saying, "If you only love those who love you, what good is it?" It is as if we believe that God can and will love only the lovely parts of us. The truth is that *we* cannot love the unlovely parts of us, so we don't believe God does either; moreover, we won't *allow* God to do so. And in this mess of unloving, we surely cannot love the unlovely parts of someone else. Love of enemies becomes impossible, but only because we have been protecting our own ego.

G. We are just plain afraid. No one wants to lose their secure lifestyle, especially western Christians who have one. No one wants to risk persecution, pain, or death. Let's be honest: the fear of this kind of serious loss clouds our ability to trust God's providence and to believe Jesus. It would be dishonest for us not to confess this level of fear. If we were to love and pray for our enemies, this surely would eliminate any form of defense or retaliation, from within personal relationships to participation in the military-industrial complex of whatever country we live in. Few are prepared to do this.

H. *Therefore, we are inoculated against the boundless love of God.* The accumulation of the above explanations, and probably others we have not covered, securely establishes a threshold within us beyond which God's love and grace cannot pass. This does not mean we cannot *experience* God's love and grace. It just means that our capacity to receive God's love and grace is much lower than God's capacity to give. So, when Jesus commands us to love and pray for enemies, most Christians, like most people in general, have no capacity—or even the concept of a capacity—for this kind of love. *It is because of our limited capacity to receive God's love for us that we also lack the capacity to love in God's boundless way.*

The tragedy of having a threshold that limits our receiving and giving of God's love is revealed in scary fashion by the way this threshold leaves many Christians with a certain conviction: that the extent to which *they* possess and understand God's love is the true capacity of *God's* love. Too many Christians, when it comes to loving and praying for enemies in any real-world, down-and-dirty way, are convinced they cannot love to this extent because (they believe) they know the limits of God's love and of God's expectation for how they should love. Rather than allowing themselves to fall down at the throne of eternal love in confession of their weakness and sin, they choose to remain "holy" in love at a level not much different than that of the non-Christian world.

Again, I need to name an uncomfortable truth: The seven realities listed above have little or nothing to do with Bible study, careful reading of the text, or discernment of what Jesus said and meant when he said it. Great amounts of time and energy have been spent debating over the Sermon on the Mount, Matthew 5–7. I refer again to Clarence Bauman's telling book *The Sermon on the Mount: The Modern Quest for Its*

Meaning, in which he diligently describes the various ways scholars have struggled to explain away these teachings of Jesus.

Our quest for the meaning of Jesus' words might actually succeed if we were all to look into the causes of the limitations of our own hearts. The actual messages of Jesus in Matthew 5, including his command to love and pray for enemies, are quite easy to comprehend aside from the darkness that remains protected deep inside us.

3. How Can We Believe Jesus and Love Our Enemies?

The first thing that must be said here is that it is entirely possible for us human beings to love and pray for our enemies rather than defend ourselves against them or fight them. This is true both on a personal scale and on an international scale. We have undeniable historical examples to support this. To say Jesus is asking something impossible or overly hard of us would be a lie. When we claim this, it is because we simply don't want to believe him and to live differently than we have been living.

Not only is it possible for us to love our enemies; it is imperative if the human cycle of violence is ever to end. In *The Gift of Love*, Dr. Martin Luther King Jr. wrote:

> Upheaval after upheaval has reminded us that modern man is traveling along a road called hate, in a journey that will bring us to destruction and damnation. Far from being the pious injunction of a Utopian dreamer, the command to love one's enemy is an absolute necessity for our survival. Love even for enemies is the key to the solution of the problems of our world. Jesus is not an impractical idealist: he is the practical realist.[8]

In the same book, King went on to say:

> Hate multiplies hate, violence multiplies violence, and toughness multiplies toughness in a descending spiral of destruction. So when Jesus says "Love your enemies," he is setting forth a profound and ultimately inescapable admonition.[9]

The second thing to be said here is a plea for compassion. If we wish to end the cycles of violence in this world, we must start with ourselves—in this case, with our attitude toward those who do not believe Jesus the way we do. Whether or not you agree with the direction this chapter and this book are going, know this: God counts you worthy; loves, accepts, and forgives you; and forever offers you grace through our Lord Jesus Christ.

There must be no judgment here but that of love. God's compassion toward you does not depend on you getting it right when it comes to loving enemies—or any other matter. I pray that God's compassion is also apparent in me. We will proceed

8. King, *Gift of Love*, 45–46.

9. King, *Gift of Love*, 49.

toward the end of this chapter by lifting up compassion as the beginning and the ending of any treatise on Jesus' teaching.

On the cross, in the midst of violence, suffering, and death, Jesus gave himself completely (in perfect love, like our Father in heaven). The immediate recipients of his love were his tormentors, even though they would not accept it. In the wake of his suffering and death, the unconditional love of God was and still is broadcast to the entire world, even though so many still do not accept it. The most profound thing I can hope for at the end of this chapter is that anyone reading these words would find it in their heart to accept the full scope of Jesus' love for them demonstrated on the cross.

No dark shadow in the heart, no devilish desire, no hate-filled action can separate us from the love of God in Christ Jesus (Romans 8:38–39). God's love is inescapable! It is the alpha and omega (the Greek letters at the beginning and end of the alphabet— thus, he is the beginning and the end of all things).

The unbounded love of God as demonstrated on the cross of Jesus Christ creates two unalterable truths which in turn forever answer the plea of the human heart. The first is this: The complete and perfect love of God is available to us—in fact, is pressing us toward accepting it. God is, and for all our lives will be, in relentless pursuit of our hearts. Sometimes I wonder if anyone—myself included—can ever really understand this. It seems everyone has something in their shadowy past that they use to block the relentless love of the cross. John's story is a good example:

Decades ago, while in my early years as a pastor, I found myself relating to a man named John, who had recently begun attending our church. John was rough-cut, not the typical cherub-like parishioner. We struck up a friendship and John began to seek me out for spiritual counsel. He was sincerely interested in following Jesus, but he was also troubled by things about which I could only guess. I clearly remember the day John sat in my office and confessed he had killed a man. I did my best to keep the shock out of my voice as I asked him about the details.

John had struggled with alcohol. He was not drinking at the time I knew him, but at a time in his past when he was drunk and driving, he ran over and killed a man. John did not share this confession with me to obtain forgiveness. Rather, he shared it to maintain his guilt and shame, to prove himself unworthy. It did not matter at all that I was eager to help him understand God's love and forgiveness. He had decided he was unforgivable long before he met me.

There is some of John's unforgivable spirit in each one of us. Consciously or unconsciously we hold on to the darkness and believe it is the truth about us. This may be the single most destructive obstacle we face in the process of loving enemies outside of us or inside ourselves. *How could a holy God ever wish to reside in loving relationship with the darkness of me?* Some form of self-hate always precedes and spawns any other hate. Our unforgiving attitude toward others grows out of our inward and unresolved struggle for—and against—forgiveness of ourselves. *To whatever extent you or I are unable to love enemies, we are first unable to experience God's complete love of us.* The greatest need of every human being is to fully know God's complete love for them. Our experience of the love Christ demonstrated from the cross is the only thing that can transform our hearts in the way of God's heart.

The journey toward loving and praying for enemies begins with confession. It comes back to that process of spiritual poverty from the first beatitude, "Blessed are the poor in spirit, for theirs is the kingdom of the heavens" (Matt 5:3). It continues through all the beatitudes. The end of Matthew 5 is closely tied to its beginning. Every time we judge harshly or withhold forgiveness or blame someone, this is our time to confess our spiritual poverty, our need and desire for God's forgiveness poured into us. We might start by visualizing God suffering and dying out of extreme love for us, including any unloveliness that is a part of us. We can pray for the persecutor within us and ask for the overpowering love of Jesus to fill our darkness. Then we can rest in that place of confession, allowing God's love time to do its work of lifting our burden of guilt and shame.

It has been said that the opposite of love is not hate but fear. The writer of 1 John understood the power of God's love as a stronger force than all the fear in the world, and all the fear in our heart. "There is no fear in love," he wrote, "but perfect love casts out fear; for fear has to do with punishment, and whoever fears has not reached perfection in love" (1 John 4:18). In our confession, as our guilt and shame are overpowered by God's love, so is our fear. Fear of our enemies, or fear of loving our enemies, will be debilitating unless and until we enter this place of confession and allow God to infuse our heart with love.

The second unalterable truth is this: Every enemy and every persecutor desperately needs to know they are completely loved by God. The very fact that they are acting cruelly in any way is an indication that their hearts are dark and desperate for the compassion and grace only God in Christ Jesus can give. If we could remain firm in this knowledge, it would be much more difficult to justify a response of self-defense or retaliation. Loving an enemy would be so much easier if we stayed focused on their desperation as they try to cope with life without any real recognition of God's love. Any person or nation of people controlling, bullying, or destroying another person or people reveals the hopelessness in the bully's own soul. What they have inside them from which they can draw is anything but the life-giving, living water of which Jesus speaks in the Gospel of John. Of all people in this world, one would think that Jesus' own followers would recognize the black hole in the soul of a persecutor.

Once again, Dr. Martin Luther King Jr. speaks from the struggles of extreme racism and violence which gripped our nation in the 1960s and still does so today:

> To our most bitter opponents we say: "We shall match your capacity to inflict suffering by our capacity to endure suffering. We shall meet your physical force with soul force. Do to us what you will, and we shall continue to love you. We cannot in all good conscience obey your unjust laws, because noncooperation with evil is as much a moral obligation as is cooperation with good. Throw us

in jail, and we shall still love you. Send your hooded perpetrators of violence into our community at the midnight hour and beat us and leave us half dead, and we shall still love you."[10]

There is surely tragedy when Christians choose not to respond to enemies in love. When followers of Jesus refuse to love and pray for enemies, or simply find they are unable to love and pray for enemies, millions of people around the world are denied a chance to see God's love for them in action. We may not want to admit it, but in this process, we write off literally millions of people as evil and unworthy of God's love. When we, Jesus' followers, deny God's love to the masses of the world, we in effect support, condone, and affirm the cycle of violence in which the masses live. We confirm to the enemy his or her justification of evil. We submit to the power of evil and its endless cycle of violence. We give up in defeat, believing that Jesus' love on the cross has become weak and unable to redeem the power of violence in our world. In our submission to evil in this way, the reality of Jesus' kingdom of the heavens and God's will done on earth is compromised beyond recognition.

The tragedy of tragedies comes into play as we watch some Christians across the generations seek to save the lost of the world while doing an end run around God's complete compassion for the world. They read and apply John 3:16 in theory, but they withhold the impact and intent of this text from their enemies. This, of course, makes any witness about Jesus to the world ineffectual. No wonder so little of the evil in the world has changed since Jesus' time; if this is our witness, we have very little to offer the world that is not already there in the darkness.

Of course, this can't be the end of the story. The message of God's complete love still rings from the words of Jesus in Matthew 5. No matter how much we try to hide from it, Jesus' call to love and pray for enemies will always convey the two unalterable truths I named above:

A. The complete and perfect love of God is available to us—in fact, is pressing us toward accepting it.

B. Every enemy and every persecutor desperately needs to know they are completely loved by God.

As I write the last lines of this chapter in the fall of 2017, national headlines announce that the US Congress has passed this year's $692 billion defense budget. Another $65.7 billion will go to a war fund known as the Overseas Contingency Operations account. In all, $757.7 billion is our country's current price tag for our fears, our ego needs, our wounded spirits, our desire for leaders other than Jesus, and our uneasy pact with violence. These monetary costs are a drop in the bucket compared to the time, energy, emotion, and spiritual loss we suffer.

---

10. King, *Gift of Love*, 53.

The country I love and in which I live massively perpetrates the very cycle of violence Jesus came to end. I don't say this out of anger or frustration. I say it in the name of God's unbounded love and grace. My heart, and I believe God's heart, hungers and thirsts for all hearts in our land and all lands to know the love of Jesus and his redemptive peacemaking on the cross.

It is time for all followers of Jesus to admit our own fears, our ego needs, our wounded spirits, our desire for leaders other than Jesus, and our uneasy pact with violence. God wants to do a new work in us and in the world. It is time for all followers of Jesus to say no to the perpetrators of violence, and indeed it is time for us to end our participation in this violence. What we can do and what Jesus calls us to do is to love and pray for all who remain stuck in the downward spiral of violence.

A STORY OF MODEST HOPE

About a year and a half ago I was on a wilderness canoe trip with three Christian friends. Our last evening out, we began talking about gun violence. One friend admitted he carries a hand gun with which to protect himself. No one chastised him. None of us tried to talk him out of it. Of his own accord, he said he understood he was wrong to carry. He said he knew that Jesus taught nonviolence and that he agreed with Jesus. He also said he simply lived in fear of being shot by a gunman in a Walmart store or out on the street. The taste of my friend's honesty and of his fear has stayed with me. It is what drives my compassion for him and for all of us caught in the cycle of violence.

So I conclude this chapter on a note of enduring, if modest, hope. If you are reading these words and feeling a sense of hopelessness, take heart. Loving and praying for enemies is a very hopeful action to take. It is a radical demonstration of God's extreme love for you and the world. The act of loving and praying for enemies proves you have found the power of God's love redeeming your heart and mind. You are forever changed from the inside out, and the painful actions of this world cannot match God's awesome love and grace that now sear your soul. You and I are now free to honestly name the violence within us and outside of us. We can decry every dollar spent on hurt, pain, and war while we speak and act in love, grace, and forgiveness toward all.

In the act of loving and praying for enemies, we discover the deepest part of God's completeness. Herein is the truth to which Jesus calls us: being perfect, like our heavenly Father.

5

Seeking First the Kingdom of God

But strive first for the kingdom of God and his righteousness, and all these things will be given to you as well.

—Matt 6:33

Would it not send a chill down your back and put a permanent smile on your face to know for certain that the God of pure love is Lord of all life on planet earth? Would it not forever warm your heart to know that this same God constantly lives and reigns within your heart, mind, and soul? Would your confidence not swell to overflowing if you could trust this God's present rule in you and everything else, regardless of what good or evil transpired in the world?

This is the stuff for which so many Christians hope and dream. It is what we often claim we believe, yet it has for so many become like a distant mirage fading in the face of present adversity. It is difficult to trust a mirage. In the face of life around us, it is near impossible to experience our hopes and dreams about a God of pure love as *reality*.

The goal of this chapter is to help us all, Christians and non-Christians alike, take Jesus seriously as he invites us into living the reign of God on earth. As I discuss the reign of God in this chapter, I'm not talking about dreams and hopes in a distant mirage. Jesus invites us into real everyday living. In the following pages we will describe our dreams come true in bold and practical ways. We will be challenged to let go of fuzzy-headed, comfort-food type of thoughts about God. We will allow ourselves to encounter God's pure love in action as it transforms our world.

TWO PRIMARY CONCEPTS: KINGDOM AND RIGHTEOUSNESS

God's Kingdom: A Summary

We have already considered the importance of the kingdom of God. In this chapter we will dig deeper into the meaning and practical outcomes of kingdom living. Before we do so, let's briefly review what we have learned so far.

A. The presence of the kingdom is cause for turning our lives around. (Matt 4:17)

B. Through his teaching and healing ministry, Jesus proclaimed the present reality of the kingdom wherever he went. (Matt 4:23)

C. The gospels of Matthew, Mark, and Luke are saturated with Jesus' teaching and living the kingdom. The kingdom of God is Jesus' central life focus and teaching theme. (chapter 1)

D. In the Gospel of Matthew, Jesus predominantly uses the phrase *kingdom of the heavens* when referring to the kingdom of God. This plural form of *heavens* implies multiple layers of God's reigning activity, with clear emphasis on heaven being present now and in every moment of our present lives. (chapter 1)

E. This present kingdom of God is good news! It is all about the political reality of God's reign. All earthly politics are to be subject to the politics of Jesus and the kingdom of God. (chapters 1 and 3)

F. The kingdom is the overarching and central concept Jesus uses to describe God's present reign on earth. (chapter 1)

G. Jesus himself, in his words and actions, embodies the kingdom; thus, we see in him the reality of God's presence intended for us also to embody. (chapter 1)

H. Jesus asks us to turn from the ways of earthly kingdoms to live out his kingdom. (chapter 1)

I. To live the kingdom in this present life, we will need to hear and submit to Jesus' teaching. (chapter 1)

J. The beatitudes (Matt 5:3–12) describe our identity as God's image living the kingdom now. (chapters 2 and 3)

K. The righteousness of the kingdom is far beyond any form of self-righteousness. We must get beyond self-righteousness if we are to enter the kingdom of God. Kingdom righteousness is the actual indwelling of Jesus Christ in us. (chapter 4)

As we move forward now to add teachings from Matthew 6 onto the above understandings about God's kingdom, we will discover a new way to live in this present world, no longer controlled by the many negative and debilitating messages and pressures each day seems to bring.

Kingdom Roots from the Old to the New Testament

In Genesis 1–2, the creation accounts claim humans as made in God's image. From the first stories of Abram and Sarai in Genesis 12, God's people were to be a blessing to all the world. From the earliest accounts of sin (e.g., Gen 3, 4, 11), we witness the heartbreak of God. From the slavery of the Israelites in Egypt and their liberation at the hand of God (Exo 1–15), we learn the early episodes of God's salvation story. From the giving of the law (e.g., Exo 20), the people were to learn what was required to live in the presence of a holy God. From the repeated breaking of the covenant by the early Israelites, we learn of God's mercy, forgiveness, and faithfulness to the people and to God's covenant with them. From the Bible's wisdom stories, we glimpse the interplay of God and faithful individuals like Job. From Israel's desire for earthly kings, we witness the destruction caused when we idolize human institutions. From the Psalms, we learn the poetry of worship, longing, and hope. From the prophets, we learn the deeper meanings in all of the above. From Isaiah 42 and 52–53 in particular, we learn about a nonviolent, suffering servant-messiah.

In Jesus, we learn the culmination of all the scriptures, and for those with ears to hear him, of all the hopes and dreams of Israel. Jesus' kingdom is not *from* this world; it is unlike any form of earthly, human-designed kingdom. Whether or not we believe Jesus, the New Testament witness is clear about Jesus being the complete fulfillment of all the hopes and longings of the faithful in the Old Testament. Jesus is the living Word, the cornerstone, the Savior, the light of the world, the Lord of all.

We read about this witness to Jesus in Matthew 1:21, where the angel says to Joseph, "[Mary] will bear a son, and you are to name him Jesus, for he will save his people from their sins." Matthew 2 retells the old story of the clash of kingdoms erupting again, even before Jesus' birth. King Herod is simply a stand-in for the entire history of human rejection of God. These are just two examples from the beginning of Matthew's gospel that clearly place Jesus as preeminent within the beginning and the ending of God's reign in human history. He indeed is "the Alpha and the Omega, the beginning and the end" (Rev 21:6).

An Unaccepted King

In Jesus' day, much anticipation remained for a coming messiah who would save the Jewish people from Roman oppression. This messiah, the people understood from their scriptures, would be God's own representative, for God alone was to be the savior of remnant Israel and the world.

> How beautiful upon the mountains are the feet of the messenger who announces peace, who brings good news, who announces salvation, who says to Zion, "Your God reigns." Listen! Your sentinels lift up their voices, together they sing for joy; for in plain sight they see the return of the Lord to Zion. Break forth together into singing, you ruins of Jerusalem; for the Lord has

comforted his people, he has redeemed Jerusalem. The Lord has bared his holy
arm before the eyes of all the nations; and all the ends of the earth shall see the
salvation of our God. (Isa 52:7–10)

While Jesus himself and the four gospel writers understood that he was the climax of God's covenant with Israel and the whole world, Jesus was not the kind of
messiah most of the people were expecting. The "Walk to Emmaus" story, about two
disciples encountering the resurrected Jesus but not recognizing him at first, provides
one of the best narratives about this discrepancy of understanding (Luke 24:13–35):

Then [Jesus] said to them, "Oh, how foolish you are, and how slow of heart
to believe all that the prophets have declared! Was it not necessary that the
Messiah should suffer these things and then enter into his glory?" Then beginning with Moses and all the prophets, he interpreted to them the things about
himself in all the scriptures. (Luke 24:25–27)

Had the people missed—or, as we often do, chosen to ignore—the portions of
their scriptures that would have given them a clearer understanding of what their
messiah would be like? Isaiah 42 and 52–53 speak of a suffering servant, an anticipated messiah—one who would suffer on behalf of the people. These texts represent a
new work that God is doing for and among the peoples and on display to the nations
of the world. Importantly, these chapters affirm that salvation does not come by the
might of earthly kings. Instead, salvation comes through God in humble form, willing
to suffer and speaking peace and justice to the nation and the world.

Yet, like the people of old, we set our sights on earthly and human "saviors." We
would do well to remember God's words to Samuel when the early Israelites clamored
for an earthly king because they wanted to be like the nations around them:

The Lord said to Samuel, "Listen to the voice of the people in all that they say
to you; for they have not rejected you, but they have rejected me from being
king over them. Just as they have done to me, from the day I brought them up
out of Egypt to this day, forsaking me and serving other gods, so also they are
doing to you. Now then listen to their voice; only—you shall solemnly warn
them, and show them the ways of the king who shall reign over them." (1 Sam
8:7–9)

Following this heartbreaking word from God, Samuel warns the people about all
the ways an earthly king will oppress and use them. The people nevertheless choose
the way of earthly kings. In the generations that follow, God's warning comes true
again and again. For the Israelites, the tale of earthly kingship and kingdoms is one of
tragedy, death, and destruction with very few exceptions.

The people's call for an earthly king and kingdom is a continuation of the human history of idol-worship. Looking to earthly authorities instead of to God as king
and Lord was a clear example of early Israel's choice for other gods. Far too many

Christians around the world, and in particular within the United States, continue to pin their hopes and dreams and allegiances on king-like political systems instead of on God. It would seem clear from Old Testament scripture that any king or political system that we put before God in any way is an idol, and to choose any idol is to reject God.

Now we get a better glimpse of why the rejection of Jesus was so immediate and thorough. Jesus claimed a kingdom wholly different than any earthly one. He taught us to pray according to this kingdom, to live this way, and to turn our lives around in this way. Jesus represented God's move to retake the hearts and minds of people everywhere. Jesus called for them and us to stop rejecting God and to listen anew to God as revealed in him—in Jesus. For all of human history following his first words, Jesus claimed the kingdom of God come, and he became the king in God's kingdom, God incarnate right here on earth, right now!

For the many years since Jesus, millions have claimed him as Savior, but not in any real way as king and ruler over their present lives. Today as I look around my world at Christians and Christian churches, I hear the "Savior" language, but I don't often witness a full recognition of Jesus as king and lord *first*, over all aspects of people's lives. Instead, what I see around me time and time again is a rejection of Jesus' words and commands. Most Christians seem unwilling to put Jesus and God's kingdom first, before their own political, social, and spiritual desires. For so many Christians, Jesus' words about seeking *first* the kingdom of God and God's righteousness mean little in the face of present-day politics, whether local or national. We place first our wealth, our desire for earthly security, the resources that assure our power and privilege in society, and in so doing, we miss the significance of Matthew 6:33.

It is two weeks before Christmas as I write these words, and I have to say, King Herod from Matthew 2 just might have had a better understanding of the threat of Jesus than do many Christians today. Herod seems to have known somewhere deep down that he was the impostor, and that if his kingdom was to remain, he had to destroy any notion that God would become king. We present-day Christians, for the most part, celebrate Christmas not even realizing that the Christ-child is a real threat to our current way of life. So much of Christianity remains an idealized fantasy of what we already have and hope to hold onto. For this fantasy to continue, we must choose not to believe Jesus' teachings. To believe Jesus, we would need to put him, his words, his righteousness, and his kingdom first. Everything else about our present lives would then have to conform to God's will and way in the world. Indeed, "all these things will be given to you as well" (Matt 6:33).

This concept of kingdom, or the reign of God, is witnessed and realized in Jesus throughout New Testament scripture whether or not we believe it. If Christians today are to understand Jesus enough so they can authentically accept him or not, we will need to come to terms with the overarching, all-consuming truth of the Lord's Prayer: "thy kingdom come, thy will be done on earth as it is in heaven" (Matt 6:10).

This prayer that Jesus taught us claims that God's kingdom, God's present reign, has authority over all life in this world. This prayer helps lay the foundation for the summation we find at the end of Matthew 6—Jesus' command to seek *first* God's kingdom.

Righteousness Inseparable from Kingdom Living

> But strive first for the kingdom of God and his righteousness. (Matt 6:33)

God's kingdom and God's righteousness belong together forever. Jesus knew this and combined them in this statement. He did not say "kingdom *or* righteousness." Rather, these two *together*—the reality of Jesus as the ruling king, and Jesus' teachings and actions—form our way of life under the rule of God.

Our understanding of God's righteousness now becomes crucial for our deepening grasp of God's kingdom. Let's again do a quick review, this time of what we have established as the meaning of God's righteousness.

A. God's righteousness is something we are to desperately hunger and thirst for. (Matt 5:6)

B. Isaiah 61 is a key Old Testament text that provides the most direct background to Jesus' use of the word *righteousness* in Matthew 5:6 and its sense in Luke 4:18–19. The term *righteousness* gets its fundamental meaning in phrases from Isaiah 61:1–2 such as "good news to the oppressed," "bind up the brokenhearted," "proclaim liberty to the captives," "release to the prisoners," "proclaim the year of the Lord's favor," and "comfort all who mourn." (chapter 2)

C. God's righteousness and God's justice are two sides of the same coin. These terms must remain together if we are to know and live the righteousness of God. (Isa 61; chapter 2)

D. Righteousness restores relationships on all levels—with God, among humanity, and with creation (chapter 2). We are created precisely for these relationships of right-justice because we were made in God's image. (Gen 1–2)

E. What keeps us from living lives of righteousness and justice is our own self-addictions. (chapter 2)

F. To live righteousness and justice means, in part, that we will be persecuted as a result. Lives of righteousness and justice are lives lived actively in opposition to unrighteousness and injustice. (Matt 5:10; chapter 2)

G. Any form of self-justification (attempts at self-righteousness) will lead us away from God's righteousness and justice. (chapter 4)

H. God's righteousness goes far beyond any form of legalistic thinking. (Matt 5:17–20; chapter 4).

I. Righteousness describes the truth of how people are to live in the very presence of God now and daily. Jesus is this indwelling, personal, and ongoing presence of God. (chapter 4)

J. The law of love is the way of living the righteousness and justice of God. (Matt 5:21–48; chapter 4)

K. Love of enemies is the sum of the law of love. This is the most complete form of righteousness (Matt 5:43–48; chapter 4)

GOD'S WILL AND GOD'S WAY

As we now see, there is a lot to consider when we try to understand God's kingdom and God's righteousness. It does not help that these terms, *kingdom* and *righteousness*, are somewhat foreign to our twenty-first-century vocabulary. Furthermore, so much biblical background, emphasis, and significance can get confusing. So, let's sift our way to the core meaning of these terms without dumbing them down. In the following pages, when we talk of kingdom and righteousness (unless otherwise noted), we will be talking about the biblical understanding of God's kingdom and God's righteousness—God's present reign in our lives. Jesus' life and teachings form the primary example and core meaning for both terms.

A simple and direct way to speak of kingdom and righteousness would be with the terms *God's will* and *God's way.*

The Kingdom as God's Will

Remember the line in the Lord's Prayer that says, "Thy kingdom come, thy will be done on earth as it is in heaven." In the kingdom, God's reign is realized when God's will is *done.* God's reign means nothing if it is not *realized*—that is, made real. In this part of Jesus' prayer, which he gave us to pray and live, the kingdom is not something theoretical, a safe way for us to feel comfortable with a cool idea about how God is running things. If we do not enact God's will, we render it meaningless within the sphere of our earthly lives. Without God's will being *done,* we are not in any practical way living in God's kingdom. Rather, in the real-life kingdom of God, the will of God is constantly moving and shaking, upsetting and dislodging, uncovering and exposing, renewing and redeeming. Nothing goes unnoticed or forgotten; nothing is without significance and eternal meaning. For those who would live in God's kingdom come, nothing is secular; everything is holy. All the moments of our days now hold God-ripened, transformative power like fruit that must be picked before it rots.

God's kingdom is the realm wherein God's will is actualized. The will of God is the kingdom lived in every practiced aspect of life. It is nice to feel compassion for someone, but this is not the kingdom realized or the will of God. The kingdom of God is realized in the *act* of compassion. I can have all the good will humanly possible, but that is not how Jesus taught us to pray. In good will alone, nothing actually gets done. It is in the giving *act* that God's transformation of life takes place. It is in the continual giving act that God's kingdom takes over my life.

This is not about doing as opposed to being. It is in the compassionate doing that our being becomes God's will invested and transacted. It is in the ongoing compassionate doing that God's being within us generates *more* doing. This is not a chicken-or-egg question, unless the answer is simply yes! In the case of being and doing, the chicken and the egg become one reality most accurately understood as the expression of God's active love in us and through us. Daily active and lived compassion is the reality of God's kingdom and God's will for us on earth.

In the most practical sense, being and doing are fully intertwined, just as God in us must burst forth without a thought of containment. We are meant to be conduits, not mere receptacles of God's kingdom. In fact, to be God's mere receptacle is not even possible; it's an oxymoron. God's kingdom and God's will cannot be stagnated; rather, they are the very definition of creative movement.

Think of it this way: For much of my early life I was a swimmer. I loved water, and swimming in it was a great pleasure. By my thirties, I had taken six courses in lifeguard training. Part of the training was to swim a mile without stopping. I found this distance swimming to be a fun challenge. I certainly identified myself as a swimmer. I was confident in my swimming and my ability to swim to the rescue of anyone in need. I regularly and willingly got wet and swam to my heart's content.

Today I am older and my love of swimming has diminished. These days I live in a part of the country where the water is forever cold. I hate getting in cold water. Occasionally, on a hot day I will "rinse off" in a lake while canoeing. One could hardly call this swimming. The point is, I still think of myself as a swimmer, but I am not. A swimmer is someone who swims, not someone who thinks about swimming. To be in God's kingdom means "swimming" in God's will—not simply "rinsing off" in it once in a while!

Let's summarize the kingdom this way then: God's kingdom is the inward and outward arena where, because we have been transformed by the law of God's love, we obediently live out (in our being and our doing) the will of God. This living out of God's will is made possible in and through us by God's overpowering love and the Holy Spirit's guidance at work in our hearts and through our hands. In doing God's will here on earth, we are co-creators with God; with God dwelling in us, we make visible the truth and presence of God's reign. In this way, the kingdom of God is simultaneously God's will being done, and God's realized realm of influence—God's kingdom come.

Praying as Jesus taught us in the Lord's Prayer, Christians so often say they *want* God's kingdom to come and the will of God to be realized on this earth now. Let's continue to explore how we move from mere praying into living.

Righteousness as God's Way

Remembering that God's kingdom and God's righteousness can be referred to as *God's will* and *God's way*, if God's will enacted on earth describes the kingdom, God's way clarifies the pathway for doing God's will and actively living within the dynamic reign of God.

In other words, we need some careful instruction on how to live out God's will here on earth, how to live God's righteousness in practical ways. Perhaps it will help to state this in the form of a question: How can we truly live the will of God in our daily lives? God's kingdom and God's righteousness must coexist within our everyday lives. With God's kingdom/will as the "what," God's righteousness/way is the "how."

Consider the following Old Testament texts as we explore the pathway of doing God's will—living the kingdom by way of God's righteousness:

> [Job said,] "I delivered the poor who cried, and the orphan who had no helper. The blessing of the wretched came upon me, and I caused the widow's heart to sing for joy. I put on righteousness, and it clothed me; my justice was like a robe and a turban. I was eyes to the blind, and feet to the lame. I was father to the needy, and I championed the cause of the stranger. I broke the fangs of the unrighteous, and made them drop their prey from their teeth." (Job 29:12–17)

> The Lord is my shepherd, I shall not want. He makes me lie down in green pastures; he leads me beside still waters; he restores my soul. He leads me in right paths (paths of righteousness) for his name's sake. (Ps 23:1–3)

> Give the king your justice, O God, and your righteousness to a king's son. May he judge your people with righteousness, and your poor with justice. May the mountains yield prosperity for the people, and the hills, in righteousness. May he defend the cause of the poor of the people, give deliverance to the needy, and crush the oppressor. . . . For he delivers the needy when they call, the poor and those who have no helper. He has pity on the weak and the needy, and saves the lives of the needy. From oppression and violence he redeems their life; and precious is their blood in his sight. (Ps 72:1–4, 12–14)

> I hate, I despise your festivals, and I take no delight in your solemn assemblies. Even though you offer me your burnt offerings and grain offerings, I will not accept them; and the offerings of well-being of your fatted animals I will not look upon. Take away from me the noise of your songs; I will not listen to the melody of your harps. But let justice roll down like waters, and righteousness like an ever-flowing stream. (Amos 5:21–24)

> With what shall I come before the Lord, and bow myself before God on high? Shall I come before him with burnt offerings, with calves a year old? Will the Lord be pleased with thousands of rams, with ten thousands of rivers of oil? Shall I give my firstborn for my transgression, the fruit of my body for the sin of my soul? He has told you, O mortal, what is good; and what does the Lord

require of you but to do justice, and to love kindness, and to walk humbly with your God? (Mic 6:6–8)

And once more, as this text is the foundation for Jesus' use of the word *righteousness* in Matthew 5 and 6, and in his opening lines in Luke 4:18–19:

> The spirit of the Lord God is upon me, because the Lord has anointed me; he has sent me to bring good news to the oppressed, to bind up the brokenhearted, to proclaim liberty to the captives, and release to the prisoners; to proclaim the year of the Lord's favor, and the day of vengeance of our God; to comfort all who mourn; to provide for those who mourn in Zion—to give them a garland instead of ashes, the oil of gladness instead of mourning, the mantle of praise instead of a faint spirit. They will be called oaks of righteousness, the planting of the Lord, to display his glory. . . . For I the Lord love justice, I hate robbery and wrongdoing. (Isa 61:1–3, 8)

The above texts are but a sampling of the Old Testament's witness to the meaning and the importance of the word *righteousness*. It is obvious from these texts that righteousness is a fundamental attribute of God and intended to be the same for us. In addition, Psalm 89:14–16 declares the wonders of God, along with the importance of our role in righteousness:

> Righteousness and justice are the foundation of your throne; steadfast love and faithfulness go before you. Happy are the people who know the festal shout, who walk, O Lord, in the light of your countenance; they exult in your name all day long, and extol your righteousness.

Psalm 82 declares God's judgment against any gods who do not carry out justice (righteousness). Remember that righteousness and justice are companion words in scripture and are often used together or interchangeably.

> God has taken his place in the divine council; in the midst of the gods he holds judgment: "How long will you judge unjustly and show partiality to the wicked? Give justice to the weak and the orphan; maintain the right of the lowly and the destitute. Rescue the weak and the needy; deliver them from the hand of the wicked." They have neither knowledge nor understanding, they walk around in darkness; all the foundations of the earth are shaken. I say, "You are gods, children of the Most High, all of you; nevertheless, you shall die like mortals, and fall like any prince." Rise up, O God, judge the earth; for all the nations belong to you!

Perry B. Yoder sums up this psalm: "For biblical faith, the doing of justice was essential to the nature and being of God and for the actions and purposes of God on earth in history."[1] Please don't miss the importance of the last line in this psalm,

---

1. Yoder, *Shalom*, 28.

which makes clear that the nations of the world belong to the God of righteousness and justice.

Based on the texts above, and many more we could have examined, the *way* of righteousness looks like this:

A. Taking care of the needs of the poor, the orphan, the widow, and the wretched. Caring for any in society with serious need of our help—those who have no other recourse or resource.

B. Being eyes to the blind, feet to the lame, and parents to the needy. Standing in for those who cannot manage at least some of life for themselves.

C. Championing the cause of the stranger. Standing up for those who for whatever reason are not from the "in" crowd—people who otherwise would be left out of anything from friendship circles to asylum in our land.

D. Crushing the oppressors. Confronting injustice, no matter where we see it and no matter who we see doing the oppressing.

E. Seeing that rulers take care of the needy, help the poor, and save them. We have a biblical mandate to call our leaders to the task of providing justice for anyone who is oppressed, left out, and forgotten.

F. Stopping our participation in empty worship, which results from not doing justice and righteousness—essentially, praising God without taking up the cause of the poor, the needy, strangers, and those who are otherwise vulnerable.

G. Caring for those who mourn.

H. Claiming liberty for captives and prisoners. This includes all the ways we might speak to and show mercy and justice to anyone held captive by their pain and addictions. How might we proclaim the liberty of God's love and justice to the imprisoned?

I. Declaring the year of jubilee—a time of rest and restoration of all people and all relationships with people, God, and creation. In everything, seeking this all-inclusive shalom/peace taught to us in scripture.

At a minimum, these nine actions form the basis for Jesus' call to righteousness. Is it any wonder then that he healed the sick, cast out demons, confronted the religious authorities, taught the masses, and commanded that we practice God's radical, unconditional love for all people, even our enemies? In his life and teaching, Jesus completely fulfilled the righteousness of God and exemplifies that way of righteousness for us. Once again, we see the all-importance of receiving Jesus as our master-teacher and guide through life.

What we have in Old Testament scripture is a very clear description of doing righteousness. It is God's justice, grace, love, and loving judgment for all, with special care given to anyone in need. To whatever extent we need even more specific instruction on the *way* of righteousness and kingdom living, all we need do is believe Jesus, know his teachings and life example, and commit our own lives to following his.

In case this still sounds theoretical and impractical, consider this challenge: In our daily lives we often meet people with needs unmet. In our ongoing relationships with friends and family, we are in contact with people struggling for whatever reason. At school or work we rub shoulders with hurting people. If we are willing, there are countless ways to join forces with others in caring for the outcast and oppressed in our community, country, and world. How are we living God's will and way daily? If there is a need, we can respond. We can bring mercy, companionship, love, financial help, or other caring responses. We can challenge unjust authorities and systems on people's behalf if they are not able to stand up to them on their own, or if broader resistance is needed. We can be the truth-telling voice for the voiceless, or for those whose voice has been ignored. Where do we see injustice in the world, and how will we confront it?

The challenge of God's will and way is real because we are conduits, not mere receptacles, of God's love. If we don't get this truth, we will never know the joy of following Jesus. If we call ourselves Christian and do not live the kingdom and God's righteousness, the will and the way of God, we show the world a deformed and debased, counterfeit version of God, God's character, and God's reign. I fear there are too many "praise Jesus" songs and too few honest commitments to love like Jesus loved while living on this earth.

THE AMAZING FAST

I'm tempted at this point to include the words of the Hollies' song "He Ain't Heavy, He's My Brother," but instead, I'll suggest that you might want to look them up if you can't call them to mind. What I will do here is share the dialogue that is taking place inside of me right now—I'm guessing it goes on inside of you sometimes too:

First me: Wow, all this talk of the will and the way seems so heavy and complicated. It just seems like such a burden. Is the Christian life supposed to be so hard and joyless?

Second me: Are you kidding? The will and the way of God is the best good news you will ever hear and ever be a part of! Sharing God's radical love with all people can only bring you and others joy!

First me: But I don't get all this talk about justice. How do I know what people really need or why they think they need it? What does this have to do with being a Christian? I'm a good person. I go to church, I put money in the offering plate. I just can't be bothered with *all* the hardships in the world. It's not my fault—why is it somehow my responsibility?

Second me: Listen to you. Do you hear the whining? Do you realize you are just concerned with *yourself*? Where in your heart are you asking God to fill you with compassion? Where in your heart are you submitting to the call of Christ? When will you trust the love of God to flow to you and out of you? When will you get it that God is not as small as your projection of God?

First me: Don't blame me! I'm in this whole Christian thing with tons of other people. Surely you can't think we are *all* wrong. I mean, we have a right to defend ourselves. We have a right to say this is my job, or this is my country, or this is my money. Justice is about me and ours. I've earned everything I've got, so leave me alone. Stop talking about God's kingdom coming to earth through me. I'm not God, and I believe God's judgment will be swift and sure in the end of time. Everybody will then get what they deserve. Thank goodness for that!

Second me: I think I hear Jesus weeping over Jerusalem.

Perhaps religious piety has gotten a bad rap. Maybe the problem has never been with piety, such as going to church and putting money in the offering plate, but with *false* piety. Let's take fasting as an example of piety. What is the purpose of fasting? How might one go about fasting in a meaningful way? Usually fasting has to do with denying ourselves something so that we might grow spiritually. That is good, right? Or does that maybe sound like it is all about us?

Let's examine these words from Isaiah:

[God says,] "Shout out, do not hold back! Lift up your voice like a trumpet! Announce to my people their rebellion, to the house of Jacob their sins. Yet day after day they seek me and delight to know my ways, as if they were a nation that practiced righteousness and did not forsake the ordinance of their God; they ask of me righteous judgments, they delight to draw near to God. [The people say,] 'Why do we fast, but you do not see? Why humble ourselves, but you do not notice?' [God says,] Look, you serve your own interest on your fast day, and oppress all your workers. Look, you fast only to quarrel and to fight and to strike with a wicked fist. Such fasting as you do today will not make your voice heard on high. Is such the fast that I choose, a day to humble oneself? Is it to bow down the head like a bulrush, and to lie in sackcloth and ashes? Will you call this a fast, a day acceptable to the Lord? Is not this the fast that I choose: to loose the bonds of injustice, to undo the thongs of the yoke, to let the oppressed go free, and to break every yoke? Is it not to share your bread with the hungry, and bring the homeless poor into your house; when you see the naked to cover them, and not to hide yourself from your own kin? Then your light shall break forth like the dawn, and your healing shall spring up quickly; your vindicator shall go before you, the glory of the Lord shall be your rear guard. Then you shall call, and the Lord will answer; you shall cry for help, and he will say, Here I am." (Isa 58:1–9)

This is a shock. The fast that God wants is righteous living?—for us to care for the needy? God wants righteous living?—not self-imposed, temporary sacrifices done to get a reward from God? Think how the truth in this passage might upend many of our religious acts. Let's say I skip a meal, hold off on chocolate throughout Lent, or resist eating meat one day a week. Do I really think this is what God wants to accomplish in this world through me? Is this God's will actualized, God's will being done? Probably not. Let's say I believe all the right things. Is *this* God's will being done? Probably not.

So where does this leave us? What is left of the Christianity we have known? Why is fasting quite possibly an amazing thing?

This last set of questions is answered by Jesus as he takes up the mantle of kingly authority over life in this world and establishes his kingdom come. In the strong and shocking tradition of the Old Testament texts on righteousness, Jesus launches his ministry, calling people to turn from false piety. He calls people to turn to full submission to God, letting go of anger as it arises, letting go of lust, retaliation and the keeping of enemies. He calls us to love in action. He demonstrates this love in action time and again. Once he launches his ministry, his entire life is carried out in service to God and all in need of his teaching and his healing touch.

Jesus teaches us the absolute importance of righteousness—feeding and clothing, caring for and helping, reaching out and doing for others, naming oppression and challenging oppressors, seeking and doing justice. This is what we are to hunger and thirst for (Matt 5:6). This is what we must do instead of some falsely pietistic form of righteousness (Matt 5:20). This is what we are to seek first in this life (Matt 6:33). This is the way of the kingdom being established by God though Christ Jesus in this world now. This is the fast God wants from us!

IS THERE A PLACE FOR REWARD?

Starting with verse 8 of Isaiah 58, there is incredibly good news about how God's light will break forth like the dawn. Our healing will come, we will be vindicated, God will answer our call, and much more. Is this some other roundabout way in which we finally get our reward for being good? The simple answer is no. God does not have a reward system in place whereby we can pull the puppet strings to get what we want.

What is in place is a God full of love and mercy and grace who offers these exact same things to us through a relationship in which our hard hearts are melted down and softened in order to receive them. Nothing in God or from God is pretend. Everything is true and real. Love really is love, and it overcomes us and engulfs us and moves through us; therefore, we become love in action, as God is love in action. This is not a reward; it is true self-giving, unconditional love originating from the very heart of God. There is no vindication, light breaking forth, healing, or answered prayer so great as the experience of receiving and giving God's love in action.

OUR GREAT NEED TO LET GO OF THE LIFE WE HAVE FORGED

In God's care, we already have all we need. There is no work we need to do to gain God's benevolent attention, for God is and has always been attentive toward us. We are already cared for beyond what we can know. The will of God's kingdom and the way of God's righteousness are all about the active, loving people we become when we allow God's complete generosity to overtake our lives. It is noteworthy that Jesus' call to seek first God's kingdom and righteousness follows on the heels of his admonition to not be anxious (Matt 6:25–32). Living the will and following the way of God are predicated on the guidance to "not worry about your life . . ." (Matt 6:25).

It makes sense that to whatever extent our worry and concern are wrapped up in ourselves (security, future, resources, etc.), we will be restricted in our ability to live God's kingdom and righteousness. If we were to backtrack through Matthew 6 from verse 25, we would find examples of human anxiety and its symptoms. Jesus names these as the false righteousness of showing off piety and storing up treasures on earth while serving wealth instead of God. Every human alive struggles with anxiety about something: money, power, security, recognition, or something else. We strive for these things, but Jesus says these are false emblems of security, false saviors, false gods. Jesus is saying that we strive after these false things out of anxiety.

All the while, there is an alternative way of life waiting for us based on abundance, the bounty of God's blessings. In Matthew 6, Jesus teaches an essential sequence that leads to righteous living in God's kingdom. To stop trying to forge our own way in life, we need to follow the sequence Jesus teaches: (1) Allow God's blessings to overwhelm you. (2) Strive *first* for God's will and way. (3) Trust God to meet all of life's needs. Let's examine this sequence and the way God's bounty sustains us in all three steps.

1. Allow God's Blessings to Overwhelm You.

No one I know—including me—allows themselves to be overwhelmed by God's blessings in an ongoing way. Life is simply too distracting. The car breaks down. You wake up with a headache. The dog chews up you shoe. You don't get that promotion. It rains or it is too hot. Your child doesn't make the team. Money is tight. There is unresolved anger, hurt, disappointment, and one hundred things to worry about. This is just one day or one week, and then life gets *more* complicated.

It is mostly the little things that sink our hopes and dreams. We just get worn down. We end up in a place where we must fight to hold our own, to hold our head up, to stay positive for the whole day. I'm not talking about being medically depressed or greatly upset over a crisis. I'm talking about the ongoing need to manage our emotions, and being constantly aware of the risk of failing at that responsibility. We end up halfway happy about our life and just as much suspicious of its worth. Joy is something we can't ever quite grasp.

Somewhere in the middle years perhaps we accept the mediocrity of our life. I suppose it is not so much hopelessness as resignation. The companion to our resignation is a deeply set determination to at least hold on to what we have, which in turn tempers any generosity of spirit we have had toward others. Sum all this up and we get the opposite of the life Jesus would have us live. When Jesus instructs us to lose our life so we can find it (Matt 16:24–26), he is talking about losing our *sheltered* life, our *protected* life, our *mediocre* life, and our *false understanding* of life's possibilities. He is talking about letting go of a life full of ongoing anger and resentment, the nursing of our pain, unresolved conflict, enemies, negative energy spent holding on to small but debilitating distractions. This "losing" of life as we know it is possible because we have a resource beyond ourselves. We are not limited to our own strivings. We have so much more to experience beyond the calamities of life. We are not destined to trudge through life, because authentic life is about *love* given and received.

I challenge you this very moment to pause and consider: The air you breathe is given to you in love. The light by which you see is a pure gift from God's heart. The strength in your body is sourced from love's will for you. Whatever goodness you have in you is but a whisper of the grand declaration of God's compassion hurtling toward you at light speed.

On what do you focus your waking hours? Be honest. How much of your typical day is spent rejoicing in the compassionate care you receive from God, and how much on personal concerns, responsibilities, and discomforts? I would be surprised if anyone could say that 10 percent of their thoughts each day focus on God's loving care for them. Even if we spent 10 percent of our day focused on God's loving care, that would leave 90 percent of our focus on ourselves and our concerns. That would be 90 percent of our time disbelieving and/or disobeying Jesus' teaching to let go of worry because God will care for us completely (Matt 6:25–32).

If this lopsided focus on life's challenges even comes close to representing our daily life, how could we possibility think we can take and accept Jesus' command to strive first for God's kingdom and righteousness? For this reason, we need to come to terms with our anxieties about life before we can claim God's will and way as our first priority.

A big part of the human dilemma, in terms of experiencing the full love and care of God, is our misunderstanding of power and control in relationships. The common descriptions of God—all-powerful, all-knowing, ever-present, unchanging, incomprehensible—do not help us here. All they do is solidify our sense that God is beyond us, so terribly much greater than us, powerful and controlling. But in Jesus' life and teachings, God comes to us in the most personal and accessible way possible. God comes to us from outside the realm of power by which our world functions. In Jesus, we experience God as, and in, a wholly other kind of relationship. God wants to love us, not control us. This God relationship comes not from *our* world, but from *God's* world. God enters into relationship with us on God's terms, not ours. God's terms have nothing to do with a balance or imbalance of power and authority such as what we experience in our world. God's terms are centered on one thing: unconditional love. God's unconditional love for us is totally independent of anything we do, which is almost impossible for us to accept because it is so alien to our mental constructs and our ego needs.

In order to more fully experience God's unconditional loving care, we will need to get past our own defenses. We might think it would be easy to accept God's unconditional love. What could be the downside? The downside is how tough it is to let go of our ego's dependence on power and control. If we are to allow God to love us unconditionally, we also need to let God make us into beings who love unconditionally. Transitioning from the world's way of power and control to the wholly uncontrolling realm of God's unconditional love will be an identity crisis. But then it will be an identity transformation!

When we begin to live in God's realm of unconditional loving care, we will start to recognize this love everywhere, in all things, and with all people regardless of how nasty they are. We will experience the kind of God-care Jesus tells us about as he compares us to the lilies and the grasses of the field: How much more will God take care of us (Matt 6:28–30)? Even the air we breathe will become a moment-by-moment exchange of love from God's heart to ours. Here indeed is the potential for God's blessings to overwhelm us so we can, at least to a greater degree than we have before, let go of the anxieties of our lives.

2. Strive First for God's Will and God's Way.

To strive first for God's kingdom and righteousness is the alternative to carrying our anxiety through life (Matt 6:32). So, even with the command to "strive," this word from Jesus is joyous news!

Jesus does not tell us in Matthew 6:33 to automatically become cherub-like angels of God's love. He says to "strive" for it. Lean into it with your life's purpose and intent. Make God's will and way your goal, your prize. To strive for these things means to focus our attention on the objects of God's focus and attention. There is no magic formula, no special prayer or words by which this happens. It's not merely a feeling or a mental process. To strive for God's kingdom and righteousness is to live it wherever and whenever we can, and the transforming, unconditional love of God in us is what makes our striving possible, real, and effective.

Some English translations use the word *seek* instead of *strive*. Whether you are seeking something or striving for it, you certainly give it your attention. Something that happens around our house now and then is seeking and striving to find the car keys. This might sound a little silly, but when you are late for an important appointment and need to run out the door, start the car, and go, the car keys take on great significance. Not being able to find the keys now becomes a frantic search. During the frantic searching we don't consider which items we need to add to the grocery list. We don't discuss politics. We don't contemplate the nuances of atonement theories. We first seek and strive until we find the keys. The goal of finding the keys gets all our attention. Likewise, Jesus is telling us to fully focus our attention on the goal of kingdom living.

But there is also this important word *first*, which qualifies the verb *strive* and gives additional emphasis to the command. *First* can mean "top priority" or it can refer to sequence, as in first in the lunch line or first to cross the finish line. It can also mean that it puts everything else in its proper place. Top priority, first before anything else, and putting all other things in their place—all three senses are combined in Jesus' command here. How could we strive first for God's things but take care of our things first? Clearly, we can't!

Many Christians have demonstrated for years that God's will and way were not first in their lives. If God's will and way were first, then love for enemies, compassion in action for anyone in need, justice for the oppressed of this world, full forgiveness in all relationships, cessation of judgment, submission to God's Holy Spirit, finding joy in all God's blessings, unconditional love for all, and adherence to all Jesus' teachings would be their top priorities. Things like arguing over issues of life and faith, divisions among Christians, judgment of others, false concepts about God, holding grudges or anger or resentment, and violence in any form would fade away.

I don't think Jesus expected any of us to make a total transformation overnight. Consider again how, under the pressure of being late for an important appointment, we fully focus on finding those lost car keys. From the time we realize the keys are missing until we find them, we go about urgently hunting. We may enlist other family members to help. While hunting, we do not allow distractions. In fact, if we are asked to answer a question or take up another activity, we most likely get irritated. The keys are our first—indeed, our only—priority until they are found, for without them we cannot go about the pressing business of our day.

Finding the car keys makes the remainder of our day's agenda possible. Likewise, seeking first God's will and way makes the remainder of our life's agenda possible. In fact, this is how the rest of our life is empowered to flow with God's agenda.

3. Trust God to Meet All of Life's Needs.

The text of Matthew 6:33 ends with the phrase "and all these things will be given to you as well."

This does not refer to a roundabout way for us to still get whatever we want out of life. It can't possibly work to both find fulfillment in receiving and sharing God's unconditional love *and* continue to seek our own agenda. It will help us to look carefully at what Jesus means when he uses the word *things*. Here are the verses that come immediately before his instruction to seek first God's will and way:

> But if God so clothes the grass of the field, which is alive today and tomorrow is thrown into the oven, will he not much more clothe you—you of little faith? Therefore do not worry, saying, "What will we eat?" or "What will we drink?" or "What will we wear?" For it is the Gentiles who strive for all these things; and indeed your heavenly Father knows that you need all these things. (Matt 6:30–32)

In this context, *things* refers to the necessities of life that God will provide. Specifically, *things* refers to food ("What will we eat?"), drink ("What will we drink?"), and clothing ("What will we wear?"). More generally, it would be appropriate to think in terms of other necessities as well, such as shelter and safety. *Things* does not refer to wealth that can be stored up, any kind of earthly treasures, or spiritual blessings supposedly given for false piety.

We know that not all faithful followers of Jesus have literally all necessities of life provided to them. Human greed and violence intervene against God's will and way in too many ways in this world. Natural disasters take lives and cause destruction. Jesus is not providing a guarantee as a reward for seeking the right things. He is making a more general statement. He is urging us, instead of worrying and focusing on the things of this life, to make it our top priority to do all we can to live into the reality of God's will and way. And when we do God's will and follow God's way, all other things in life take their rightful place. Everything else finds its appropriate context. Our greediness for the treasures of this world will certainly fall away and cease to have a hold on us. Our need for personal acclaim through acts of false devotion will vanish. Worry over our personal needs or the needs of our loved ones will turn into praise for all that God has already done for us.

What's more, we will now have time, energy, and enthusiasm for a wholly other kind of lifelong agenda. We will now see with different eyes and hear with different ears, for everything we experience in life will be interpreted through unconditional love exchanged continually within our sphere of influence. We will know and understand from the perspective of God's pure and loving heart. Even in the face of tragedy, God's presence and care for us will be enough, for we will know the things of this world through the eyes of a deep and everlasting faith. We will know God and life itself to be love unbounded by any circumstance in this present life.

Paul has said this so much better than I can:

> Who will separate us from the love of Christ? Will hardship, or distress, or persecution, or famine, or nakedness, or peril, or sword? . . . No, in all these things we are more than conquerors through him who loved us. For I am convinced that neither death, nor life, nor angels, nor rulers, nor things present, nor things to come, nor powers, nor height, nor depth, nor anything else

in all creation, will be able to separate us from the love of God in Christ Jesus our Lord. (Rom 8:35–39)

I find words inadequate for sharing the meaning of the out-of-this-world love of God that comes through Jesus' teachings and ministry touching and changing our hearts through the Holy Spirit. Just a bit further in the book of Matthew, Jesus tells us that if we ask, it will be given; if we seek, we will find; if we knock, the door will be opened (Matt 7:7). God's kingdom and righteousness, God's will and way, are *that close* to our grasp. Nothing in this world of ours compares even remotely to what God wants to give us. The kingdom and righteousness of God, more than anything else, have to do with the transformation of the human heart and mind, yours and mine. This goes far beyond any agenda we might have, for it is not our will and way, but God's.

In the end, even the kingdom and the righteousness—perhaps especially these— are pure gift and grace. We may be asked to seek, but it is no burden to do so. Even the command to seek is an act of God's unconditional love for us—that which transforms our focus of life on earth to "as it is in heaven."

HOW TO LIVE GOD'S WILL AND WAY FIRST: FIVE EXAMPLES

In *The Great Spiritual Migration: How the World's Largest Religion Is Seeking a Better Way to Be Christian*, Brian McLaren asks:

> Could Christians migrate from defining their faith as a system of beliefs to expressing it as a loving way of life? Could Christian faith lose the bitter taste of colonialism, exclusion, judgment, hypocrisy, and oppression, and regain the sweet and nourishing flavor of justice, joy, and peace?[2]

These questions seem similar to the matters we've been examining—living God's kingdom and righteousness as opposed to practicing false piety. Following are five case-study-type examples of what this might look like in practical, day-to-day life.

Right Action, Not Right Belief

Right beliefs are simply not what Jesus taught or lived. Right beliefs are not why he gave his life. Right beliefs have little to do with God's raising Jesus to life on the third day. Jesus did not teach us to pray, "Our Father in the heavens, holy is your name. Your kingdom come, your will be *believed*." So why have Christians across the world often created a system of beliefs instead of following all of Jesus' teachings?

If we are serious about doing God's will and following God's way, we will need to release our grip on the importance of right beliefs. An easy way to know if you are stuck on right beliefs instead of living God's will and way is to ask yourself whether

2. McLaren, *Spiritual Migration*, 2.

disagreements about religious beliefs have come between you and others. Are you spending any time or energy judging others because of what they believe? And the answer to that question is, Of course you are! Human beings do this frequently, and no matter how "Christian" you want to be, you are still human.

One of the strongest examples of Christians judging other Christians is the matter of homosexuality. In the past few decades, this issue has probably caused more pain and division within the Christian church than any other. You may be asking where this train of thought is leading. I'll tell you up front that where I am going is back to Jesus and his call for us to seek first his kingdom and his righteousness. I propose that getting back to Jesus is the only key that can open the door to a world where disagreements over homosexuality no longer divide us.

This is not the place to delve deeply into an understanding of homosexuality and how to surmount our disagreements. That said, in Jesus we do find a way to end this war once and for all. This will sound too simple at first, but the answer is to believe Jesus and focus first and primarily on God's will and way. This is what we have been learning together throughout this chapter.

Believe Jesus; follow him; do what he says—it is that straightforward. Too often, Christians have done the opposite, especially with divisions over a difficult issue like homosexuality. The battle over homosexuality has shown Christians to be judgmental, angry, falsely pious, and willing to sever relationships with sisters and brothers in the faith (and in their family). The battle over homosexuality lays bare the truth that many Christians seek other things *before* the truth of Jesus. In general, many Christians have placed first their need to be right, their need to draw a line whereby some are in and some are out, their belief system, their understanding of scripture, their need for purity (a false piety), and their own fears of alternative ways to live as Christians. As a result, the world often sees the church as divided and mean-spirited—the very opposite of what Jesus calls us to give witness to in Matthew 5:16, when he says, "In the same way, let your light shine before others, so that they may see your good works and give glory to your Father in heaven."

For those of us caught up in divisions or painful disagreements, the first practical and life-changing thing we can do is to lay down our battle gear. We must surrender our conviction that right beliefs are somehow the same as God's righteousness. Jesus teaches absolutely nothing about believing rightly as a way to live God's will and way.

Here is the key question: Why do we feel the need to be right and to judge others as wrong? Our need to be right runs deep and is connected to the parts of us not yet surrendered to God's unconditional love. When we fully surrender our heart and soul to God's love, we give up all attempts to be right, think right, and act right. The core of our being is found in God's all-consuming love. Human rightness doesn't apply.

What happens when we live out of our inner core now created and sustained in God's all-consuming love? It's almost too obvious. The all-consuming love of God flows out of us and into all our relationships. Having surrendered to God's all-consuming love, having let go of our need to be right about anything, we are completely free to spread God's love, acceptance, mercy, forgiveness, and grace to everyone, no matter where they stand in the struggle over homosexuality (or anything else). We no longer have a need to treat anyone as "in" or "out." Our judgmental spirits and attitudes are gone forever! We can now love all people as God loves them—unconditionally. We are forever released from the job of being gatekeepers to the church or to God's kingdom. We were never actually assigned the job in the first place, never commissioned as God's purity police.

Whatever your understanding or experience of homosexuality, you have nothing to defend, nothing to lose, nothing to gain, and nothing to do but love the people with whom you find yourself in relationship. It doesn't matter if they agree or disagree with you. It doesn't matter if they are gay or straight. It doesn't matter if they are nice or unkind, angry or joyful, or if they meet or do not meet some standards of conduct set by someone who is not Jesus.

If we still feel the need to hold on to some form of right belief, some gauge of holiness, some Godly ledger, Jesus offers exactly what we need and the most practical calling imaginable: Live the love and justice he teaches. Jesus says we should keep our eyes, our focus on him, on his words, and on his example, and not look anywhere else. The rightness Jesus gives us is the only rightness we need. Loving, not judging; reaching out, not creating distance; fellowship, not rejection; inclusion, not exclusion—these will be your way of being right. By acting on and living out Jesus' teaching, we indeed live God's will and way. *If there is any call for you to extend instruction to a brother or sister, let it be the same invitation Jesus has given you: to focus first and foremost on the kingdom and righteousness of God.*

Whose World Is It?

In Matthew 6:19–21 Jesus says:

> Do not store up for yourselves treasures on earth, where moth and rust consume and where thieves break in and steal; but store up for yourselves treasures in heaven, where neither moth nor rust consumes and where thieves do not break in and steal. For where your treasure is, there your heart will be also.

It is normal to hold on to what we have. To be caretakers of what God has given us is a good thing. However, to place this normal and good holding and caretaking first, instead of placing the will and way of God first, is a problem; it misses the mark God wants us to aim for.

Part of what Jesus is teaching earlier in Matthew 6 is that God's will and way are the opposite of our "storing up treasures" here on earth. This includes anything we hold on to in this life that keeps us from first doing God's will and way. God's kingdom and righteousness are the reign of God actualized here on earth through people doing God's will in loving acts of mercy, peace, and justice for all in need.

Whenever I have something and will not share it, I run opposite of God's will and way. My own possessiveness counters the idea that everything in this life is God's and not mine. Psalm 24:1–2 proclaims, "The earth is the Lord's and all that is in it, the world and those who live in it; for he has founded it upon the seas and established it on the rivers." This is a clarion call for all of us to stop "storing up treasures" here in this life.

The challenge for us to share what we have with those in need cuts quite a swath through our personal and corporate lives. Many areas of our lives call for generosity, kindness, and mercy. Each of these areas could be the focus of our need to re-examine our priorities. I hope that in looking at just one area we might learn lessons of generosity, kindness, and mercy in other areas as well. Because of the present global issues of displacement and inequity among peoples, it makes sense to consider the plight of refugees and laws of immigration. Given today's political climate in the United States and the world, we are faced daily with the question "What do I consider mine and refuse to share with others in need?"

Borders between countries serve good purposes, including defining where one government's laws end and another's begin, helping to keep peace between nations. But borders between countries do nothing to stave off gross inequities of wealth. Borders between countries sometimes promote hoarding instead of generosity, cruel indifference instead of kindness, and injustice instead of mercy. Any time borders preclude generosity, kindness, and mercy, they divert the will and way of God.

Of course, the problem does not lie so much with borders themselves as with the laws that govern them. There are laws that are just and laws that are unjust. No country on earth can be expected to fully reflect the righteousness of God's kingdom. Where laws concerning borders, refugees, and immigration obstruct God's compassion, mercy, peace, and justice, what are Christians to do? How might Christians bring healing and hope to counter the unjust laws pertaining to borders? Jesus' teachings, our commitment to follow him first, and our inner renewal based on God's overwhelming love serve as our guide.

The following principles are part of Jesus' guidance in the Gospel of Matthew, and especially in Matthew 6:33.

A. Respect the government and laws of the country in which you live. Jesus was not a rabble-rousing, anti-Roman radical.

B. Commit your life and the resources you manage to doing God's will and way as the first and most important part of how you live. Unconditional love and loving beyond all boundaries are the foundation of God's will and way.

C. Always place God's loving will and way before any government's will and way that is less than God's loving justice. Do not get caught up in a sense of obligation to the government's will and way when this clashes with God's.

D. Keep in mind that any limitation on God's love for people in need is a human construction. Nothing in Jesus' teaching, ministry, or especially the sacrifice of his life on the cross would suggest we should put ourselves first in a world of need; in fact, he taught just the opposite.

If we apply these four principles to the controversies over border security and immigration, we will discover many ways to share God's love with all concerned. We will also hold on to our only true compass for charting our journey through these complexities: remaining true to God's will and way. We will help display the reign of God and the justice-way of living within it. The following are a few possible ways to actively live God's love for all.

A. Let go of your need to ensure your own security. Trust the love and generosity of God. Remember that it is God's world, not yours. Everything you have and hold on to is God's, and is a potential way for God to bless people in need. In God's world there are no borders or boundaries to love and generosity. Borders and boundaries are a human invention. In God's world, my job, my property, my country, my things are not really mine. *You and I are only stewards of God, which means we use what we have for God's will and way.*

B. Offer your time, energy, and resources to refugees, to people seeking a better life for themselves and their families, and to people who for whatever reason are less fortunate than you. In God's world, no human law has the authority to stop you from doing these things. Let God's unconditional love be your only true guide.

C. Open your eyes and ears to the cries of people suffering from injustice. Allow God's love to melt and mold your heart, to sensitize you to the inequalities and unfair practices that abound in our world. Know that injustice is one of the cruelest evils of earthly kingdoms. Any unjust policy is foreign to God's will and way.

D. In love, speak truth to power whenever you can. You have a vote. Vote for the love and care of neighbors from other countries, religions, races, and backgrounds. Say no to walls and yes to bridges, no to fear and yes to hospitality, no to apathy and yes to welcome.

E. Love your country and your government officials. Treat them with respect. Even as you go the way of Jesus, know that in all things God would have you show the way of love to the world. During his trial and suffering, Jesus both confronted Pilate and treated him with respect (John 18:33–38). We never know when the love of God through us, and the respect we offer, might bring at least some small aspect of healing and hope to those in government.

F. Bask in the luxurious flow of God's blessings. Freedom to live God's unbounded love is one of the most precious aspects of God's grace to us. This unbounded love reaches our innermost being and opens us to God's blessings. To live in the flow of God's blessings makes fear of scarcity a distant memory.

Living out the above principles and practical suggestions will surely pit us against much of the world's treatment of people in need. People will oppose what I have said above in many ways. But my response and my final suggestion regarding borders and immigration take us once more to the heart of the matter: In God's love there is no one for us to be against. God's love frees us from being on any "side" of things. It is as if we are floating in a river of love flowing through the heart of the human experience. Jesus said there would be persecution, and he was right. But whatever resistance we experience is simply an opportunity to love like God loves. *To be grounded in, surrendered to, and lost within God's love is to know no other response to the world but this same love.*

Knowing the Voice of Jesus

Jesus says in John 10:27, "My sheep hear my voice. I know them, and they follow me." Is this true of Christians today? Is this true of you and me? Can we discern Jesus' voice amid all the other voices we hear in this world?

Let's assume we want to hear Jesus' voice over all others. So here are a few questions to consider: How do you respond when a respected Christian leader supports our country's military defense buildup? What do you do when either local leaders or national figures call you to policies that support racism? What do you do when a Christian preacher tells you to vote for a politician who clearly does not espouse the teachings of Jesus?

The basic question is this: Do you recognize Jesus' voice and place it first? And then: Have you immersed yourself enough in Jesus to know his teachings, his life of ministry, and his way of the cross? In light of this knowing, have you given your life to following him first? Can you say that Jesus is Lord as Paul does in Philippians 2:9–11?

> Therefore God also highly exalted him and gave him the name that is above every name, so that at the name of Jesus every knee should bend, in heaven and on earth and under the earth, and every tongue should confess that Jesus Christ is Lord, to the glory of God the Father.

In your life, is Jesus the name and the voice above every other? If so, Jesus' voice will trump all others, and you will not relegate his voice to a future time and place removed from the present hurt and pain in this world. Jesus' prayer in Matthew 6 is for God's kingdom to come now and God's will to be done now on earth as in heaven.

I know that for many people, following a respected leader is important. I am claiming that as a Christian, the leader you respect and follow needs to be Jesus. I am saying that any other leader you follow needs to be, themselves, following Jesus first. Where and when you hear or see a discrepancy between Jesus and another leader, follow Jesus every time. This advice includes anything in this book. If in your best intention to listen to Jesus' voice and follow him you hear anything different said in these pages, then please disregard the voice here and follow Jesus.

If you are still wondering how to hear Jesus' voice instead of other voices, listen to what Jesus himself says:

> Beware of false prophets, who come to you in sheep's clothing but inwardly are ravenous wolves. You will know them by their fruits. Are grapes gathered from thorns, or figs from thistles? In the same way, every good tree bears good fruit, but the bad tree bears bad fruit. A good tree cannot bear bad fruit, nor a bad tree bear good fruit. Every tree that does not bear good fruit is cut down and thrown into the fire. Thus you will know them by their fruits. Not everyone who says to me, "Lord, Lord," will enter the kingdom of heaven, but only the one who does the will of my Father in heaven. (Matthew 7:15–21)

In response to this scripture, I offer two points that I hope will help us distinguish the voice of Jesus from other voices. The first point is Jesus' emphasis on fruit. What is inside a person is what sooner or later comes out of them, though it may not come out in the words they use. Too often words are cheap, and the character of a person can be wholly other than the words they say. Always ask yourself, Is this person whom I respect and follow living the fruit of God's Spirit? Are they embodying God's love, joy, peace, patience, kindness, generosity, faithfulness, gentleness, and self-control? If they are not embodying these Spirit-fruits, don't listen and don't follow.

The second point is Jesus' emphasis on doing God's will. Always ask yourself, Is this person whom I respect and follow living in a way that shows they are doing the things Jesus has taught us to do? Are they actively living a Christ-like life? If not, don't listen and don't follow.

Be Careful Who You Worship

I'm one of those people who likes both old hymns and contemporary music. My first choice in worship music is a blend. But there are plenty of old hymns and contemporary songs that say little to nothing about what Jesus said or how he lived. These songs often claim his death and resurrection without linking them in any way to his life on earth and his call on our lives. If our worship songs do not echo the teachings and ministry of Jesus, we are back to listening to other voices.

I want to be careful to say that there are powerful and accurate songs, both old and new, about Jesus, his teachings, and his ministry. We have the choice to worship God and Jesus with singing that reminds us of Jesus' teachings and his call to us. It is up to us to choose what voice we listen to and what voice we echo in praise.

Worship is important—so important that we must not worship a god who is other than God in Christ Jesus. Any form of worship in song, dance, or the spoken word that does not give praise for, celebrate, and goad us toward God's kingdom come and will being done here on earth is worship of a false god. Any worship that does not help us put God's kingdom and righteousness first in our present lives is likely helping us put the things of this world first.

I realize there is an important place to purely express our love and praise to God, recognizing God's majesty, thankful for God's saving grace and Jesus' sacrifice. This is a very personal and heartfelt cry in many worship songs. Yet as I pore over many of the contemporary Christian worship songs and older hymns alike, I believe we face a challenge in worship singing to move beyond simple praise and devotion to God. The prophet Amos said this better than I can. Here he conveys the words of God:

> I hate, I despise your festivals, and I take no delight in your solemn assemblies. Even though you offer me your burnt offerings and grain offerings, I will not accept them; and the offerings of well-being of your fatted animals I will not look upon. Take away from me the noise of your songs; I will not listen to the melody of your harps. But let justice roll down like waters, and righteousness like an ever-flowing stream. (Amos 5:21–24)

In this text, God is not saying worship is wrong or unimportant. God is telling us that love is a whole, not a part. Yes, we are to love God completely, but we cannot do this without fully loving God's people—all people, and especially those in need of justice. Remember, Jesus never told us to worship him, yet of course we do this a lot. Jesus did say, "Follow me"; he said to make disciples and teach them all that he commanded; he told us and showed us how to love. These things too, in addition to his death and resurrection, must be reflected in our praise and worship. Are we not grateful for his words of wisdom and his examples of healing? Is Jesus not praiseworthy for showing us how to live, how to love, and how to experience God's reign in our lives?

In closing this section, I encourage you to go online and listen to a song called "The Potter's Hand," by Darlene Zschech.[3] Surely there are other fine examples, but this is one I have found particularly meaningful as a way to hear, echo, and worship God in Christ Jesus. Without prescribing specific ways to do so, this song encourages us to be in God's full will and way. I hope we can all strive to sing praises both to God's majesty and to Jesus' calling to follow.

Just Say No to Taking Any Side but That of Jesus

We are not talking about a pick-up basketball game. We are talking about all the ways people choose sides on issues instead of living God's will and way. I live outside a town in northern Minnesota where iron mining has a long and honored history. Iron mining has helped keep the economy going in this area for decades. The area where I live is also a gateway to the Boundary Waters Canoe Area Wilderness (BWCAW), about a million acres of pristine forests and waterways. Presently, a battle is raging over the proposed mining of copper and nickel just a few miles from the BWCAW—a different

---

3. Zschech, "Potter's Hand."

type of mining from that of iron, and involving different impacts to the environment and to the health of those who live nearby. Millions of dollars and many jobs are at stake, as well as the pristine forests and waterways.

I moved to this area because of its proximity to the BWCAW. I find my spiritual home amid the forests and on the waters. I count myself an environmentalist because this world is God's and I am called to be a good steward of it on God's behalf. I also care about people who struggle to find work and who need jobs that pay a living wage. I love this community and want our economy to flourish.

I have friends on both sides of the mining issue. As a follower of Jesus, what should I do? What side should I take? I ask myself, What side would Jesus take? I don't mean this in a simplistic way; rather, I think of Jesus' deep love for people, his role in creation, his journey to the cross on behalf of the cosmos—remember the wording "God so loved the *world*" (John 3:16; italics mine). I think of how Jesus demonstrated the compassion of God's very heart. Surely the God who sees the sparrow fall cares about pristine waters and forests, *and* of course the welfare of all people.

It seems most people I know have approached this issue as if there were only two choices—two distinct sides—mining *or* the environment. This has led many to a need-to-win attitude and vilification of the other side. The longer the battle goes (and it's been over a decade now), the more people become entrenched. In all of this, my question is, Who is listening to the concerns of everyone involved? Who is listening long and hard enough to know the heartaches and fears, the hopes and dreams of those for and those opposed to the proposed mining projects?

I believe that to live out God's reign amid controversy is to resist the temptation to take one side or the other, and that God's will and way are best demonstrated by clear-headed, one-choice followers of Jesus. As followers of Jesus, we have only one choice in any controversy: to love unconditionally everyone on both sides. Again, I don't intend this as a simplistic solution. To love as Jesus has shown us to love is to let go of our personal needs and take up our cross daily—which means to follow in Jesus' footsteps of sacrificial love. We can and must allow God's love to be the medium of our active engagement with persons caught in the whole right-vs.-wrong, us-vs.-them struggle of any controversial matter.

What would it look like to live God's will and way in the battle over mining in my community? I suggest this sequence:

1. Listen as deeply as you can.

2. Get to the heart of the matter.

3. Walk along with both sides.

4. Bring God's love to bear in all you do and say.

5. Let no injustice go unchallenged regardless of the side.

6. Put loving relationships first before "right" solutions, understanding that the process of loving *is* the solution.

7. Regardless of the outcome, continue loving all parties.

Notice that this sequence has no final, secure, and right answer. *If there is a "right" answer, it will only be discovered by those living out the process of loving all involved.*

A HUMBLE SUMMARY

I find it hard to bring this chapter to a close. There are just too many important aspects of God's will and way begging to be explored. I hope that looking at two words (in a sense, actually just one word) and the contrast in how they are used can serve as a humble, yet helpful, summary.

Matthew 6:31–33 reads:

> Therefore do not worry, saying, "What will we eat?" or "What will we drink?" or "What will we wear?" For it is the Gentiles who strive for all these things; and indeed your heavenly Father knows that you need all these things. But strive first for the kingdom of God and his righteousness, and all these things will be given to you as well.

The verses above point to two contrasting things people can strive for: (1) our own security (food, drink, clothing, and whatever else we need or think we need), and (2) the kingdom and righteousness of God. Jesus says the Gentiles (the Greek word is actually "nations") strive for the first. On the other hand, Jesus calls his followers to strive first and foremost for the other—God's will and way—and assures us that what we need will be provided.

The importance of accepting Jesus as the authority over our lives is an ongoing theme of this book. Despite all the talk of God's will and way, it still comes down to our choice to believe Jesus or not. He has laid out the two contrasting things for which we can strive. One is not the other, and we must not make the mistake of blending the two. One is the way of people and the systems of this world bent on self-reliance, and with it comes great anxiety. The other is the way of God and freedom from our anxieties. The way of God is the way to which Jesus calls us.

6

IS JESUS THE ONE?

Controversy followed Jesus wherever he went. Ever since the beginning of his ministry, throughout human history Jesus has parted the waters of public and private opinion. Where he does not part these waters, people don't take him seriously.

Jesus asks for things we don't easily give up. He claims things we don't easily believe. He lives things we don't easily choose to live. Jesus knows all this and refuses to pander to public opinion. As stated in chapter 5, Jesus taught and lived God's kingdom and God's righteousness first; no opposition could throw him off course. He knew his teaching and ministry would take him to the cross, the worst form of torture and suffering the Romans could devise. His mental, emotional, and physical suffering could not have been greater, yet he loved and taught love, healed and raised the dead, faced off against demons and powerful religious leaders. He lived a consistent challenge to anyone not yet ready to hear and practice his message of mercy, grace, forgiveness, peace, and love.

Was Jesus crazy, or was he really the Son of God? People have been asking this since he began his ministry. The question itself points to the confusion initially caused by his life and teachings. Similar confusion follows him today. The question also indicates resistance to his life and teachings—maybe he was crazy, or maybe he is not the Son of God. Doubts seem to swirl endlessly about his identity, authority, and sanity.

I prefer the honesty of doubts. Doubts can keep us open and engaged with Jesus. It is my hope that in facing our doubts, remaining in the confusion, we will eventually come to the end of ourselves and meet God face to face. Short-changing this process often leads us to shallow faith, misguided rule-keeping, and a thoroughly compromised theology that considers Jesus' message to be one for the ages but not for *my* age. He is God—just not *my* God *today*.

Perhaps it will help any of us open to acknowledging some uncertainty about Jesus to consider C. S. Lewis's depiction of Jesus in the *Chronicles of Narnia* books. There we find that the Jesus figure, Aslan the lion, is not a tame animal. In other words, we cannot domesticate Jesus into being who we want him to be. It will also help us to dig into texts from Matthew that tell the story of first-century confusion through the words of Jesus and Matthew themselves.

We will consider the response of the religious leaders generally, then the startling response of John the Baptist who proclaimed Jesus the one—the Messiah—so many had awaited but later questioned this proclamation. The question of Jesus' identity, which he faced throughout his life and ministry, is the question of this chapter: *Is Jesus the one who is God and is Lord of my present life?*

THE ONE WHO EATS WITH SINNERS—MATTHEW 9:9–13

These five verses tell a short story with long implications. Probably nothing could have prepared the establishment for what amounted to a religious reversal of fortunes. Here is Jesus, a new teacher moving among the people, teaching the religious leaders and demonstrating a radical departure from their orthodoxy. Jesus turned their way of righteousness upside down.

Let's explore the implications of these verses by bringing the situation into the twenty-first century to get a feel for just how radical Jesus' actions and instructions were. It might be that we need to examine our own version of pharisaic attitudes, for we also might find ourselves questioning Jesus' actions and words.

Imagine living in a country controlled from a distance by a despotic ruler claiming to be God almighty. Enemy soldiers are commissioned by this ruler with guns everywhere, and if you step out of line, you will be shot. Now add to this situation a group of your fellow citizens who have become traitors and are helping the enemy by collecting your money to pay taxes to this evil, occupying state. That's what tax collectors were like in Jesus' day.

But it gets worse. These tax collectors are taking advantage of the situation by overcharging you and keeping the difference for themselves. They are getting rich while you are getting poor. If you want to stay alive, there is nothing you can do about this situation. Secretly, you hate these tax collectors!

Now imagine that your national religion, the only religion you have known since birth, requires that you stay holy by following a long list of dos and don'ts. At least this is how your religion has been interpreted to you by your leaders. What has developed is a clear-cut way of deciding who is holy and who is not. You want to be holy, so you try your best to follow the rules. While you are behaving, many unholy people are breaking the rules: prostitutes, homeless people, diseased people, and of course, the evil tax collectors.

Some of your religion's most important rules center on food preparation, cleanliness, and with whom one eats. As a person striving to be holy, you would never think of eating with people who break the rules. According to the religious rules, if you did eat with them, you would be as unholy as they are.

Here is the actual story from Matthew:

> As Jesus was walking along, he saw a man called Matthew sitting at the tax booth; and he said to him, "Follow me." And he got up and followed him.
>
> And as he sat at dinner in the house, many tax collectors and sinners came and were sitting with him and his disciples. When the Pharisees saw this, they said to his disciples, "Why does your teacher eat with tax collectors and sinners?" But when he heard this, he said, "Those who are well have no need of a physician, but those who are sick. Go and learn what this means, 'I desire mercy, not sacrifice.' For I have come to call not the righteous but sinners."

At the time of this story, Jesus was traveling around Galilee teaching and healing people. He was also going around selecting a special group of twelve people to be his closest followers. Believe it or not, those twelve people were to be a model of God's kingdom come to earth since more than anything else, the kingdom was to be a way of being in relationship. So, walking along, Jesus came across Matthew, a tax collector. Jesus invited Matthew to follow him and join his inner circle of followers. Matthew immediately accepted.

If you remember the equivalent situation today, you should be doing a double take. As a tax collector, Matthew would be someone you secretly hate and one of the most unholy people you could imagine! Just when you thought maybe Jesus was not so bad, maybe you were even considering this kingdom idea of his, Jesus personally picks Matthew over you. And then it gets worse—much worse: Jesus attends a big meal with *many* tax collectors and other unholy sinners. According to your understanding of religion, now Jesus is unholy too! He has just committed a whole host of unholy acts by touching, associating with, and eating with *those* people.

Table fellowship and hospitality are essential elements of your holiness code. Jesus has broken the rules in just about as bad a way as he could. He has done it knowingly and purposefully. Now it is time for you to take your tax-collector hate and begin to point it at Jesus. In your eyes, he has become one of the worst of the sinners, a so-called rabbi leading people *away* from a life of holiness.

How different is our present world? We may not be living under the harsh rule of a despot, but our ideas about who is holy and who is not aren't terribly different than those of Jesus' day. We may not live in a caste society, but our society may be just as divided. In many ways, people are separated, often *because of* religion, not *in spite of* it. I can hear Jesus saying to us, "Repent, for the kingdom of heaven has come near."

So let's look deeper into this passage, keeping in mind the question of this chapter: Is Jesus the one? *Is Jesus the one who is both God and Lord of my present life?*

In Matthew 9:9–13, Jesus saw Matthew as an outcast hated by his peers. Jesus saw the hurt behind the tax collecting, behind the cheating and collaborating with the enemy. Jesus saw a broken heart and knew how desperately Matthew needed a different life experience. Others looked at Matthew and focused their own pain onto him, pinning him against the wall of their hatred, keeping him stuck in his own pain. But Jesus reached out to him and included him, and a little piece of Matthew's broken heart came back together. Jesus invited. Matthew stood up and followed him. Just like that. Grant R. Osborne explains this call to Matthew in this way: "At any rate, Jesus commands Matthew, 'Follow me,' a present imperative that calls for a lifetime of discipleship. Matthew's immediate obedience is just as startling."[1]

Matthew may seem to us the least likely to make the cut, to become an inner-circle disciple of Jesus. Back in Matthew's time, everyone—including Matthew—would have agreed. But to Jesus, Matthew was the perfect example of someone he wanted to reach and invite into his kingdom. In so doing, Jesus showed the world how the kingdom of God really works, how God's will and way turn the world's kingdom ideas inside out and upside down.

If the story were to end here, we would be shocked but still on our feet. We could carefully chuck the call of Matthew up to some illogical action of Jesus. We could easily miss the significance of Jesus calling a champion sinner into his inner circle. *But this does not concern just one sinner; it concerns all sinners.* Jesus was not about to turn the world of just one man upside down. He planned to turn the world upside down for *all of us.*

In the gospel-writer Matthew's version of this story there is an abrupt shift from when Jesus calls Matthew to the phrase "And as he sat at dinner in the house" (Matt 9:10). Luke's version of this story gives us a bit more information: "Then Levi [who is understood to be Matthew] gave a great banquet for [Jesus] in his house; and there was a large crowd of tax collectors and others sitting at the table with them" (Luke 5:29). While the calling of Matthew could have been a relatively private matter, suddenly we have a very public celebration. Now a "great banquet" is taking place, with a crowd of Matthew's peers partying with Jesus and his disciples.

Note carefully, Jesus didn't put on his old clothes and sneak out to go slumming by himself. He publicly and dramatically lived out the kingdom by showing how *he and his followers* would together go beyond the religious holiness code of their day. Jesus and his inner circle broke the rules and became "unholy" in order to include displaced and forgotten people. Together they formed new friendships, new relationships, across the vast cultural divide of their day. Concepts like holiness and righteousness meant one thing to the religious leaders of the first century and something completely different to Jesus.

This story is crucial for our understanding of Jesus and his teachings. Whatever Jesus has taught about righteousness so far in the book of Matthew, he now teaches by

1. Osborne, *Matthew*, 181.

example, showing his disciples how to live. For any Christians today thinking Jesus' life and teachings were about his own journey through life and not about ours, this banquet of sinners and disciples should cause us to turn around and rethink. Why would any of us present-day disciples think we should party differently than Jesus and his disciples back then? Just because we are uncomfortable with "sinners," that does not mean God is. Jesus was clear about how God's kingdom on earth realigns our relationships with the very people we are tempted to exclude.

The drama really heated up when the Pharisees got involved. As a rather public display of rule-breaking, this party got the attention of the rule-keepers. Remember, when Jesus and his disciples broke important rules that governed clean and unclean actions *and* status, they themselves became impure. They took on the status of sinners living unholy lives.

In verse 11 the Pharisees ask Jesus' disciples for an explanation. What they get is a response from Jesus himself. He takes the initiative and makes clear that as the leader, he is responsible to answer for these actions. Everything in this story shows Jesus as the instigator: He approached Matthew and invited him to join his disciples. He led the way to the banquet. He was the one responsible for multiple people becoming unclean. Now he takes on the challenge of the religious leaders.

In Jesus' response to the Pharisees, he quotes Hosea 6:6. Here is a perfect example of what he meant in Matthew 5:17 when he said, "Do not think that I have come to abolish the law and the prophets; I have come not to abolish but to fulfill." Jesus not only fulfills the law and the prophets in this story; he also becomes the teacher of the law and the prophets to the very people who thought of themselves as the authorities over these matters. Though the Pharisees called him "teacher" in verse 11, they said "*your* teacher"—they did not think of him as *their* teacher. They saw themselves as *his* teacher. The irony is not subtle. But Jesus turned to the Pharisees and indeed took on the role of their teacher as he said, "Go and learn. . . ."

The words from Hosea 6:6, "I desire mercy, not sacrifice," are Jesus' way of saying that God wants us to love as God loves instead of practicing unrighteous acts in which mercy is withheld. The Israelites intended their sacrifices to cover their sins of injustice, but God, through Hosea, and Jesus, here in Matthew, are saying to stop the injustice altogether. Sacrifices are meaningless in the face of ongoing injustice, for when there is no mercy, it means the people have turned away from God, as Hosea describes in his chapters 6 and 7.

It is interesting that the Hebrew word *hesed*, referred to as "mercy" in English versions of Matthew 9:13, and translated "steadfast love" in Hosea 6:6, is often used in the Old Testament to describe God's unconditional and everlasting love. God wants us to love as God loves! God loves sinners with an everlasting love! Imagine then the over-against-God position religious people take when they write rules against sinners instead of embracing them with love. The Pharisees in this story showed themselves more interested in purity than in any real practice of God's love. Without *hesed*, God's mercy and love, flowing through them to sinners, the Pharisees were actually outside the righteousness of God and God's present kingdom on earth.

Jesus said, "For I have come to call not the righteous but the sinners." Think about it. Jesus came to call sinners. The word *call* stands out, loud and clear. Call sinners to what? Well, to what did he call Matthew, and why would he be banqueting with all these other sinners? Jesus' call is clear and consistent throughout the gospels. His call is to discipleship, which means to follow him, to love like he loves, to seek the outcasts and sinners like he did. Luke adds the word *repentance* to Jesus' call (Luke 5:32). Jesus loves sinners, invites them to be his followers, asks them to turn their life around. He is not preaching at them; he is showing them love and acceptance. Jesus is not monitoring a church membership list; he is breaking past any barriers that the idea of "membership" puts up.

So, does God love self-righteous people? We could certainly make a case that self-righteous people, including ourselves at times, are some of the greatest sinners. But we've just seen that Jesus welcomes sinners. So, of course God loves self-righteous people—God loves everyone! It's just that self-righteousness and following Jesus do not mix. The very substance of following Jesus means repentance, turning our lives around, and submitting to his will and way—his kingdom and his righteousness. By definition, *his* righteousness is in no way our own *self*-righteousness.

A Brief Summary

Let's quickly summarize this story:

1. Jesus called a super-sinner into his inner circle of disciples.

2. Jesus accepted an invitation to table fellowship with sinners and became unclean in the process.

3. As the leader of his disciples in this unclean action, he took others down with him.

4. He showed the sinners of his day that the religious rules did not apply.

5. He readily confronted the religious leaders and their rules.

6. He turned the tables on those who would teach him, and instead, he taught them.

7. He applied the authority of scripture and fulfilled it.

8. He declared his mission and God's mission to sinners.

9. And he upended the current religious understanding of righteousness.

Just one or two of these actions would have gotten Jesus into trouble. Add up all nine, and we can see how it all got him killed.

A Few Additional Thoughts

The healings in Matthew 8 and 9, along with this brief story, demonstrate the Godly compassion of Jesus. In the face of tradition and purity codes, former interpretation of Hebrew Scripture texts, and a building opposition from religious authorities, Jesus lived what he taught in chapters 5–7. Matthew carefully shows us Jesus' teaching ministry in chapters 5–7 and follows it up by carefully showing us Jesus' loving ministry in chapters 8–9. In this loving ministry, Jesus touched and healed a leper, the slave of a Roman centurion, Peter's mother-in-law, a paralyzed man, a hemorrhaging woman, two blind men, and many more. He cast demons out of the people, he raised a dead girl to life, and he threw his arms out in welcome to tax collectors and sinners.

For any who would call this kind of ministry wrong, Jesus is apparently *not the one*. He is not God and not Lord of their present life. If, on the other hand, you and I are seeking a Lord and Savior whose ministry is all about compassion to everyone in need, everyone left out or left behind, then he looks very much like *the one*—our God and the Lord over our present life.

Here might be the scary part. The fulfillment Jesus brought in this story—the "mercy, not sacrifice"—shows the lie and the illusion in any kind of exclusionary religion that places some people in and other people out. Jesus shows us a compassionate God who relentlessly pursues sinners. God is the judge in this life and at the end of this life—never us. The judgment of God cannot be separated from the mercy of God. In fact, it is the mercy of God that serves judgment. *God desires mercy. Where it is absent, no other pretend faith and religious practice matters.*

This story takes up only five verses of the Bible. Yet the earthquake-like impact of it still creates aftershocks throughout our world. Any time you or I decide to respond to Jesus' invitation to join his circle of followers, living lives of mercy together, we become a part of the aftershock, and joy is awakened in the world once more. Those who would recognize God in Jesus through this story will join Jesus in confronting self-righteous religion and its leaders by living God's compassion in the face of adversity or persecution. *If Jesus is the one, then his compassion is our mandate.*

THE DOUBTS OF JOHN THE BAPTIST—MATTHEW 11:2–6

If *anyone* would have understood Jesus' teaching and healing ministry, surely it would have been John the Baptist. It was John who baptized Jesus and claimed Jesus was far greater than himself. It was John who first proclaimed, "Repent, for the kingdom of heaven has come near" (Matt 3:2). John was there when God's Spirit "descended like a dove" onto Jesus and said, "This is my Son, the Beloved, with whom I am well pleased" (Matt 3:17). John himself challenged social and religious norms. He called the Pharisees and the Sadducees a "brood of vipers" (Matt 3:7). It was John the Baptist who represented the Old Testament prophet Elijah, preparing the way for the Messiah (Matt 11:7–10).

Yet, even John had some doubts about Jesus:

> When John heard in prison what the Messiah was doing, he sent word by his disciples and said to him, "*Are you the one* who is to come, or are we to wait for another?" Jesus answered them, "Go and tell John what you hear and see: the blind receive their sight, the lame walk, the lepers are cleansed, the deaf hear, the dead are raised, and the poor have good news brought to them. And blessed is anyone who takes no offense at me" (Matt 11:2–6, italics mine).

In prison, awaiting death, facing so much of life's cruelty at the hands of establishment religion and government—who could blame John the Baptist for having doubts? He himself was not being "saved" by the coming of the hoped-for Messiah. Surely, we can relate. Think of all the things in this world causing you doubt. The cares and concerns of life too often cloud our thinking and disable our faith in Jesus. Who would want to follow and become a disciple of a questionable Messiah, then or now?

I think it fair to put ourselves in John's place and honestly ask, *Is Jesus is the one?* As I said earlier, let's not think of our doubts as a bad thing; rather, let's face our doubts outright and allow God to touch and heal us too. I invite you to keep in mind your own struggles to come to terms with Jesus, and to dig deeper with me into this passage.

Verse 2 clarifies where John's question came from. He had heard reports about what Jesus was doing. No doubt this "doing" included Jesus' teaching, but it also lends specific emphasis to Jesus living out his mission. He embodied what he taught, creating a wholistic experience of God's message of kingdom and righteousness. So in verse 4, Jesus responded by telling John's disciples to inform John of what they *heard* and *saw*. The balance in this instruction is critical for the pivotal nature of this story.

John's question in verse 3 is the question of this chapter. Is Jesus the Messiah, the anticipated savior of Israel, both God and Lord of my present life? The question implies that Jesus has yet to prove himself to John amid whatever expectations John had. This is the question of the ages ever since Jesus walked this earth. How you and I answer it demonstrates the fulcrum point of our lives. To authentically and realistically answer this question for ourselves, we must understand both Jesus' teaching and his action ministry. We must both *hear* him and *see* him.

Jesus' answer to John's disciples continues (verse 5) with even more clarity. In effect, he said to John that what his disciples were hearing and seeing was this: healings of all sorts, including dead people raised (chapters 8–9), and good news shared with the poor (chapters 5–7). Jesus emphasized the balance in both his healing ministry and his proclamation of the good news of God's kingdom will and way. The Greek in verse 5 has Jesus literally saying, "Poor men are evangelized." Jesus' evangelical sermon is Matthew 5–7, which we examined in previous chapters. We, too, are called to evangelize people in need today through both our words and our actions.

The hope of Israel was that the Messiah would usher in the salvation of God. In Jesus' answer to John, he was, in effect, saying, "In me you are hearing and seeing the salvation of God. In me you are hearing and seeing the good news [related to the words *gospel* and *evangelism*] of God's kingdom come and God's will being done on this earth." If we today miss this astounding proclamation, we will miss the salvation God offers. We will miss the passion and compassion of God for all—for enemies and for us alike—indeed, for everyone!

The final thing Jesus says in response to John's question is, in effect, a beatitude, a wonderful blessing of God. The Greek word for *blessing* in verse 6 is the same used in the eight beatitudes in Matthew 5. Jesus is saying, "Joyful is anyone who does not find my teachings and ministry offensive." A positive way to say this would be, "Blessed, or joyful, is anyone who hears me and sees me. In the hearing and seeing, their salvation is at hand. Blessed is anyone who hears and sees that I am *the one*."

It is interesting how Jesus made the last sentence in verse 6 both a blessing for those who hear and see, and a dire warning for those who do not. Ulrich Luz, author of a three-volume commentary on Matthew, understands verse 6 as follows (if you find this passage a bit dense, no worries—I'll walk you through it in the paragraphs that follow):

> Only in the concluding macarism [ascription of a blessing] of v. 6 is the person of Jesus mentioned explicitly. *Skandalizow* [Greek for "take offense"], a late Jewish and Christian word, means "to set a trap," "to erect an obstacle," then more generally "to give offense," "to lead to ruin," "to seduce to sin." *En* [Greek word for "at"] designates the person or thing through which the offense comes. In Matthew and (Mark), the word is used of the final abandoning of Jesus in the passion (26:31, 33) and in the end-time (24:10). Our text looks ahead to these texts and to 13:57; 15:12. The general formulation in the third person shows that more is involved than a warning to John's disciples. Instead, here at the conclusion is the . . . point of our text that is fundamental for the evangelist [that is, for Matthew]. He is concerned not that one should have the right knowledge about Jesus but that one not reject the experiences of salvation to which Jesus extends an invitation. These experiences of salvation make a claim; they require a decision for or against Jesus. It is for just this reason that the evangelist, after Jesus' healing ministry in Israel (chaps. 8–9), had Jesus give the disciples the task of confronting Israel with a decision (chap. 10).[2]

Luz helps us with verse 6 in three important ways. First, he helps us understand the importance of the word that translates into English as "take offense." Anyone who takes offense at Jesus is like those from Jesus' hometown who rejected him (Matt 13:57). They are like the Pharisees who rejected what Jesus had to say (Matt 15:12). They are like all who deserted Jesus in his time of suffering and death, and like Peter,

2. Luz, *Matthew*, 2:135.

who said he would never desert ("be offended at") Jesus (Matt 26:31, 33), yet denied him three times. And they are like the many who will fall away, "be offended," at the end of the age (Matt 24:10).

In this term, "take offense," we discover the heartache of those who would reject, disown, and abandon Jesus. All who do so miss the blessings of hearing and seeing him throughout Matthew 5–9. For to not hear—and understand—his message and to not see his message in action—and act on it—is to reject, disown, and abandon him and, thus, to miss the salvation he offers.

Second, Luz helps us understand Jesus' words in verse 6 as they call us to *receive* Jesus in his teachings and his healing ministries, *not* only to *believe* the right things about him. No matter how well-written a creed, it is nothing compared to experiencing, accepting, and receiving Jesus' love given through his words and actions.

The third thing Luz points out is that it is decision time. Folks in Jesus' day had, and we today have, a decision to make. According to the Gospel of Matthew and from Jesus, our only salvation comes from the Jesus of chapters 5–9. We can be blessed by this, or we can reject it. Jesus himself offers the blessing and the warning. It would seem the core of our life and faith hangs in the balance right here. Jesus says to you and me: "Hear me and see me." Now we must decide.

A Final Thought

The waiting is over! We need not yearn for another messiah. Jesus answered John the Baptist's question in a wonderful way! The truth of God's salvation is in the love taught and shown by Jesus! So many people, Christians and non-Christians alike, are waiting on something else, some type of salvation other than Jesus, the Messiah staring them in the face. They are waiting on heaven, waiting on some other form of deliverance, waiting on some god who has not already come to them in pure love, grace, and forgiveness. In this brief story from Matthew 11, Jesus tells us that he *is* the one.

WHOSE LAW RULES?—MATTHEW 12:1–14

It will probably always be difficult for people to manage their life of faith without external rules. (We have talked about this in various ways in earlier chapters.) But in Matthew 12:1–14, a dependence on external rules is directly challenged by Jesus. Since the prevailing question of this chapter asks if Jesus is the one who is Lord and God, it will be important to understand another angle to this question: Is Jesus' authority the one that supersedes sabbath, temple, and all Old Testament law? *Is Jesus the Lord over any supposed religious "rules" we live by today?* Or in practice, is our religious propriety somehow the "lord" over our faith life?

Once again, I am thinking about all the ways Christians find themselves divided. I live in a small town with at least a dozen churches, all with different persuasions of biblical interpretation and the application of their faith. Rather than being a cohesive witness to the love of God in Christ Jesus, these churches too often display a lack of agreement and a focus on other things more important than fellowship, love, acceptance, and grace toward one another. In a world where people are looking for love and acceptance, wherever division is displayed instead of unity, the church at large is often seen as judgmental and even dangerous. Who would consider joining the Christian ranks, no matter the flavor, if it means joining a divided and seemingly mean-spirited group? People who don't associate with a church are usually masters at sniffing out the smell of rule-keeping Christians. Rightly or wrongly, this is often why people keep their distance from churches.

If we can rediscover Jesus as the one who is Lord, God, and authority over our personal and corporate lives, what would that look like in the face of church divisions today? Let's start by reading Matthew 12:1–14, separated into two parts.

> At that time Jesus went through the grain fields on the sabbath; his disciples were hungry, and they began to pluck heads of grain and to eat. When the Pharisees saw it, they said to him, "Look, your disciples are doing what is not lawful to do on the sabbath." He said to them, "Have you not read what David did when he and his companions were hungry? He entered the house of God and ate the bread of the Presence, which it was not lawful for him or his companions to eat, but only for the priests. Or have you not read in the law that on the sabbath the priests in the temple break the sabbath and yet are guiltless? I tell you, something greater than the temple is here. But if you had known what this means, 'I desire mercy and not sacrifice,' you would not have condemned the guiltless. For the Son of Man is lord of the sabbath." (Matt 12:1–8)

This bit about walking through the grain fields seems odd to us. No one would do that today. But in first-century Palestine, walking paths often cut through grain fields. Jesus and his disciples were simply walking a typical path on a sabbath day. Feeling hungry, the disciples reached out and picked some heads of grain, removed the husks, and ate the grain—normal, acceptable behavior. The problem came in how strictly the Pharisees interpreted the Old Testament law prohibiting work on the Sabbath (Exod 20:8–11; Deut 5:12–15). This law simply said to not work on the Sabbath. Since the law itself was so general, Jewish rabbis developed oral traditions explaining the law in more detail. It has been suggested that the Pharisees had about thirty-nine specific rules to follow regarding the prohibition of work on the Sabbath. These would have included rules against harvesting grain.

Exodus 31:12–14 adds a note of severity to this story:

> The Lord said to Moses: You yourself are to speak to the Israelites: "You shall keep my sabbaths, for this is a sign between me and you throughout your generations, given in order that you may know that I, the Lord, sanctify you. You shall keep the sabbath, because it is holy for you; everyone who profanes it

shall be put to death; whoever does any work on it shall be cut off from among the people."

With this text in mind, combined with first-century Pharisaic law, Jesus and his disciples risked banishment or worse for their actions in the grain field. The confrontation in Matthew 12 then takes on a rather serious tone. Even during the time of harvest, the law prohibited harvesting work on the sabbath (Exod 34:21). Of course, in this story, Jesus returned scripture for scripture, giving two examples of exceptions to the law. In the process, he also challenged the Pharisees' command of scripture, as he twice said to them, "Have you not read . . . ?"

If the confrontation had ended in this seesaw exchange of legalities, we would not have much to learn from this story. We are all too familiar today with scriptural food fights. But if we claim Jesus as the one God, then the life-changing moment of this story comes when he says, "Something greater than the temple is here" (v. 6) and "For the Son of Man is lord of the sabbath" (v. 8). With these words, Jesus makes a religious quantum leap! In essence, he claims two things: (1) the kingdom come and being done on earth through him is greater than the temple, and (2) he, the Son of Man, is lord—has authority—over sabbath, temple, and religious law. Only God or a crazy person would have made those claims in first-century Palestine.

Let's think about the significance of what we have just examined in this story. Once again, Jesus did not abolish the law and prophets (Matt 5:17). Instead, he claimed the authority to interpret scripture differently than the Pharisees did. But even more importantly, he claimed *rulership* over scripture. In so doing, Jesus claimed authority over all cultic (worship) life and practice known to first-century Judaism. He said a great big "I am the one!"

Everything Jesus said and did leading up to this story and this proclamation (Matt 5–11) sets the tone and the rhythm, the being and the doing, the faith and the life, the will and the way of all who would be his followers then and now. Jesus' authority over all cultic and religious life is exemplified in everything he has said and done. What we have covered in the first five chapters of this book clearly displays the very heart and function of Jesus' reign within us and in our world today. If Jesus reigns over all cultic and religious life then and now—if he is the one, the Son of God, the Savior of the world—then reality itself is transformed. We may think the world we know is reality, with myriad authorities ruling the ways of people everywhere. But if Jesus is the one, we are wrong about these other authorities and their rule.

How might this apply to the different interpretations of scripture and the rules extracted from scripture today? How does Jesus' claim to authority over temple, sabbath, and scripture put our rule-keeping and divisions to rest? The Pharisees were pros at rule-keeping. Today many church leaders and laypeople find themselves also caught up in rule-keeping, which, in one way or another, leads to divisions among us. We may look around and see all the divisions in the church and think these are inevitable, but I believe Jesus would say no. Instead he would say, "Believe me. I am the ruler of all of history."

The "Son of Man" figure Jesus identifies with when he says "the Son of Man is lord of the sabbath" comes from the book of Daniel. In Daniel 7 this figure is given authority over all earthly rulers and powers. It is this total reign over life that Jesus claims for himself. Everything else in our life experience is illusion! It will all pass away.

In this story we see that any kind of human-crafted oral or written law is superseded by Jesus' reign. His teaching and his ministry rule eternally. Jesus asks us to lay down our rule-keeping mindset in which we become locked up over who is right and who is wrong. If Jesus were here in person today, he would likely break plenty of the rules to which we humans cling. He would not care about who is right and who is wrong in all our religious disagreements. He would put an end to this mess and call us into the loving relationships for which we were created. He would tell us that all our biblical food fights only serve to take our focus off him and the will and way of his kingdom.

How Jesus Rules

In Matthew 12:5–8, Jesus claims to take over the rule of all life while overthrowing any and all challengers. But why would we *want* him to be the one? Why would we trust him with authority over our lives? This might sound like just another form of tyranny, another someone who wants to control me. Is it any wonder so many people, on seeing the ways of Christianity, want nothing to do with it? What people see in Christianity is too often a reflection of tyranny, control, and ruling over people, which many Christians seem to believe is the way of God.

Jesus, however, would have none of our tyranny and control, or of rules that separate us. Our rules and divisions are the things of earth that will pass away. The ways in which we try to control one another and our world are perhaps life's biggest illusion, for any attempt at control will, sooner or later, build a wall of isolation and pain around us. I think of Matthew 12:1–8 as the first half of this story. To overcome the illusions of our own control or our fear of being controlled, we need to keep reading. The second half of the story begins with Jesus very intentionally acting out the way of his rule, God's reign, the will and the way of God.

Jesus Acts on His Claims

As we noted above, Jesus made two astonishing claims in the first half of this story: First, he said that "something greater than the temple is here" (v. 6). Nothing (no religious rule) is to take our focus off the living out of God's kingdom and righteousness. Second, Jesus stated, "For the Son of Man is lord of the sabbath" (v. 8). We have already noted the reference to Daniel 7. It is important to hear this second statement both as a stand-alone assertion of Jesus' ultimate authority, and as a segue into the action he takes next. Here is the second half of the story:

> [Jesus] left that place and entered their synagogue; a man was there with a withered hand, and they asked him, "Is it lawful to cure on the sabbath?" so that they might accuse him. He said to them, "Suppose one of you has only one sheep and it falls into a pit on the sabbath; will you not lay hold of it and lift it out? How much more valuable is a human being than a sheep! So it is lawful to do good on the sabbath." Then he said to the man, "Stretch out your hand." He stretched it out, and it was restored, as sound as the other. But the Pharisees went out and conspired against him, how to destroy him. (Matt 12:9–14)

Leaving the field, Jesus went to "their" synagogue. In the spirit of the authority of which he had just spoken, Jesus entered the religious "territory" of the Pharisees who had just confronted him. This part of the story is not about the disciples of Jesus; rather, it is about action taken by Jesus himself, which builds directly on his claim of authority over the sabbath. If we thought the confrontation back in the field between Jesus and the Pharisees was startling, it now climaxes well beyond any conflict we have yet seen. In the same way Jesus has been emphasizing the importance of doing the things he teaches, he again follows his teaching with his own action. He literally confronts the powers that would withhold mercy for the sake of rules, disobeying them and their rules in a public and radical fashion.

Let's talk about some of the practical application of Jesus' actions. In the kingdom of God, as God's reign is enacted, people's needs are met. It is that simple. Wherever we can, we who would live in the will and way of God are to care for the needs of others through our actions. Nothing can supplant the importance of this caretaking; it is our calling as followers of Jesus. He has set the example by teaching what is greater than the temple and its rituals and rights; he has set the example by demonstrating how mercy is a higher priority than even the holiness of sabbath.

As Christians live God's kingdom today, we are called to apply Jesus' teaching and actions to all our religious ceremonies, buildings, programs, worship services, and any form of spiritual duty. Mercy is to be the very nature of all our relationships. Of all things within the church of Jesus Christ, showing mercy must guide us beyond our would-be religious food fights.

A few years back I experienced a heartbreaking situation in a congregation I loved. A young married couple from the congregation was heading toward divorce. It was a complicated situation involving mental illness, financial viability, and years of attempts to resolve these and other issues. Both the man and the woman were deeply hurt and struggling to figure out, as Christians, how to cope with divorce. During this crisis, church leaders met with the couple and threatened to take away their church membership because they were getting a divorce. Apparently, the church rule was that members could not divorce and remain as full participants in the life of the church.

The message given to this hurting couple was that they must adhere to certain rules of purity to be a part of us. The message also was given that purity of the church was more important than loving care for the wounded, and this message was communicated not only to this couple but to their extended families, other members of the church, and the wider community. Part of what was so tragic was the belief on the part of church leaders that threat of punishment, rather than love, was the way to treat the brokenness of divorce. They thought adherence to a rule, rather than compassion, was the teaching tool to use. They thought they could control this couple and others in the church by holding them to a certain standard of behavior instead of embracing them, crying with them, helping them carry the pain, and risking all for the grace and mercy of God.

This is just one example of a myriad of ways the church of Jesus Christ has put sabbath law—which is to say, any religious rule—above Christ's command to love. In so doing, the church has also put its "laws" above Jesus himself and his claim to lordship over the sabbath. Like the Pharisees, many in the church today mistakenly believe it is their job to control what people believe and do. Too often it is believed that if we can control people, we can prove the church worthy. We think it is our job to keep the church pure. Therefore, some beliefs are in and some are out, some actions are in and some are out, some people are in and some are out. In our attempts to form a holy church centered on our (supposed) right beliefs and actions, we can partially succeed at keeping people corralled in, but the tragedy is that we have kept the rest of the world corralled out.

Stepping back a few verses, in verse 7, and for the second time in Matthew 11–12, Jesus quotes Hosea 6:6: "I desire mercy and not sacrifice." He could just as well be telling us today, "I desire mercy and not religious rule-keeping." There can be no doubt about what Jesus will do upon encountering a man who needs his healing touch. And after the first half of our story, there is no doubt he will show mercy regardless of sabbath rules. In fact, based on Jesus' teaching and example, we could make the case that the sabbath is the *perfect* time to heal. We could make the case that whenever religious rules ignore the needs of people, that is *exactly* the time for mercy to overrule the rules.

Rules not only keep people out of the church; rules divide the church itself. Over the years, the church has divided itself over what clothes we wear, women in leadership, worship styles, worship songs, institutional hierarchy, authority of leadership, speaking in tongues, other gifts of the Spirit, forms of baptism, who takes communion, the meaning of communion, what day of the week we worship, whether or not gay and lesbian persons are welcome, beliefs about the end times, our political views, biblical interpretation, and so many more. And what does any of this have to do with following Jesus?

While Jesus claims to be the one who is Lord over all religious rules, we ignore him and divide ourselves over things that miss the entire point of why he came, what he taught, how he lived, and his calling on our lives. Every division that arises between people unveils the lie that we are obedient to Jesus as Lord. Anytime an argument cannot be settled in love, someone has claimed the righteousness of the Pharisees and the rule-keepers of a given generation. Whenever something keeps us divided, maintaining the painful distance of judgment, we have forgotten our true homeland, which is God's kingdom.

I know there will be kickback and rebuttal to what I am saying here. Many will want to list all the proper reasons why rules must be followed. Many more will want to withdraw and defend their spiritual turf. My challenge in return is this: Take the lessons we have learned from Jesus himself. Test his words, not mine. Ask yourself: What law did Jesus give us that is the law above all others? Are you living that law first, or are you living your own laws?

Back to Our Story

The ending of this story is stark in its revelation of ugly truth and divine truth, juxtaposed. The contrast could not be greater. Jesus has lovingly restored a man to complete health; meanwhile, the religious leaders begin plotting to destroy the God of the universe. We must come to terms with this dichotomy of God's way versus our way. In the story we are studying, the way of rules and judgment led to death; in fact, rules and judgment led to the torture and killing of God. What could possibly be worse?

During my years in church leadership, I watched hundreds of times as people grew divided. Some stayed in the same congregation, and some left one church for another or formed a new church altogether. Some left a denomination and joined or started another. The cycle of division can seem endless, with no apparent remedy for hurt and pain. What is needed is a transformation of our understanding of church and God. We have a great need for confession and repentance across the church of Jesus Christ. It is past time to take every disagreement and turn it into an opportunity to love instead of to judge. If we cannot do this, we are no different from those in Jesus' day who plotted to kill him instead of looking into their own controlling hearts.

In the end, what we see in this story of Jesus healing on the sabbath is God at work. Do we have the will and courage to see here that Jesus is showing us God's will and way as he heals both the man with the withered hand and the hearts of all who witness this simple act of healing? When we realize what was and still is at stake, we discover that it actually wasn't a *simple* act Jesus performed. His very life was at stake, and he did not falter or hesitate.

The divisions in the Christian church demonstrate that many of us have misunderstood God. To feel justified in our rule-keeping and judgments of others, we opt to believe in a god different than the God Jesus showed us. From beginning to end, the gospels show us Jesus, who is the one—the God of the universe. If we are open to it, we can see in Jesus the truth about a loving God who teaches us love, heals in love, casts out demons in love, challenges religious rules in love, and offers God's own body and blood in love. The cross is where we see the God of love most profoundly, but God's love as authority over all things is also visible in our story here in Matthew 12.

MOUNTAINTOPS AND VALLEYS

Let's shift our focus a bit. There are many mountaintop and mountain-related episodes, in the Gospel of Matthew, all of which involve Jesus in significant ways:

1. ". . . the devil took him to a very high mountain . . ." (4:8)

2. "When Jesus saw the crowds, he went up the mountain . . ." (5:1)

3. "When Jesus had come down from the mountain, great crowds followed him . . ." (8:1)

4. ". . . he went up the mountain by himself to pray." (14:23)

5. ". . . and he went up the mountain, where he sat down." (15:29)

6. ". . . Jesus took with him Peter and James and his brother John and led them up a high mountain . . ." (17:1)

7. "As they came down the mountain . . ." (17:9)

8. "When they had come near Jerusalem and had reached Bethphage, at the Mount of Olives . . ." (21:1)

9. "When he was sitting on the Mount of Olives . . ." (24:3)

10. "When they had sung the hymn, they went out to the Mount of Olives." (26:30)

11. "Now the eleven disciples went to Galilee, to the mountain to which Jesus had directed them." (28:16)

In this series of mountaintop episodes, Jesus is revealed. We see him tested by the devil, teaching the disciples and crowds, drawing the crowds, taking time apart to pray, healing many and feeding thousands, being transfigured, coming down from the mountain on his way to the cross, riding a donkey down from another mountain into Jerusalem, again teaching the disciples, praying before his crucifixion, and, finally, sending his disciples out to disciple others. Pardon the pun, but these experiences are highlights of Jesus' ministry and identity. It is as if Matthew and Jesus are saying, *Pay special attention to what takes place on mountains.* If we only had these mountaintop episodes by which to know Jesus, we would know enough to proclaim him the one who is the Son of God and the Lord of all.

Of the eleven mountain experiences listed above, we will look deeper into the up and down of chapter 17:1–13.

Six days later, Jesus took with him Peter and James and his brother John and led them up a high mountain, by themselves. And he was transfigured before them, and his face shone like the sun, and his clothes became dazzling white. Suddenly there appeared to them Moses and Elijah, talking with him. Then Peter said to Jesus, "Lord, it is good for us to be here; if you wish, I will make three dwellings here, one for you, one for Moses, and one for Elijah." While he was still speaking, suddenly a bright cloud overshadowed them, and from the cloud a voice said, "This is my Son, the Beloved; with him I am well pleased; listen to him!" When the disciples heard this, they fell to the ground and were overcome by fear. But Jesus came and touched them, saying "Get up and do not be afraid." And when they looked up, they saw no one except Jesus himself alone.

As they were coming down the mountain, Jesus ordered them, "Tell no one about the vision until after the Son of Man has been raised from the dead." And the disciples asked him, "Why, then, do the scribes say that Elijah must come first?" He replied, "Elijah is indeed coming and will restore all things; but I tell you that Elijah has already come, and they did not recognize him, but they did to him whatever they pleased. So also the Son of Man is about to suffer at their hands." Then the disciples understood that he was speaking to them about John the Baptist.

While many fascinating details make up this story, I include it in this chapter for two reasons: (1) the unmistakable emphasis on Jesus' glory as the Son of God, and (2) the way in which Jesus' divinity is wedded to his suffering. We simply cannot know the identity and authority of Jesus without knowing both his transfiguration *and* his suffering, for Jesus is both. W. D. Davies and Dale C. Allison place Jesus' glory and suffering side by side:

In the one [episode], a private epiphany, an exalted Jesus, with garments glistening, stands on a high mountain and is flanked by two religious giants from the past. All is light. In the other, a public spectacle, a humiliated Jesus, whose clothes have been torn from him and divided, is lifted upon a cross and flanked by two common, convicted criminals. All is darkness.[3]

One God, One Glory

We cannot fully know God without embracing both the mountaintop and the valley, the glory and the suffering. I do not mean these as different events or personality traits, or even two sides of the same coin. I mean that God's glory *is* God's suffering, and God's suffering *is* God's glory. Too often, and maybe even most of the time, Christians mistakenly view the glory and the suffering as two separate aspects of God. It is almost as though God had a split personality, a radiant side and a shadow side. Like

---

3. Quoted in Osborne, *Matthew*, 651–52.

we can choose which one we like best. Or we can worship the glory part and think of the suffering as a one-and-done event. Like we can share in the glory and benefit from the suffering, while still not realizing that the suffering Jesus *is* the real God.

Even for many Christians who believe in Jesus' death and resurrection, the cross is still too scandalous to accept as an indelible attribute of God. *Divine, suffering love is seen as a "once upon a time" thing, not as the way to know and follow God today.*

We will examine the topic of the cross at a much deeper level in chapter 11 of this book. For now, it is enough to say that Jesus is the *one* glorified and tortured God, and there is no other. In his transfiguration and his descent from the mountain, we see both the glory and the suffering. In this combination we witness something so amazing, so unthinkable, as to be nothing less than the God who is capable of transforming us and our world. No lesser god can do this. To the extent that you and I can acknowledge Jesus as the one God carrying his cross throughout the history of this world, we have the hope of our own transformation not later, but now.

THE QUESTION FOR US TO ANSWER—MATTHEW 16:13-17

Previous to this text, the gospel narrative has been leading up to the question Jesus asks in these verses: "But who do you say that I am?" In earlier passages, various voices and narratives have answered that question: an angel, wise men, John the Baptist, the voice from heaven at Jesus' baptism, Jesus himself, lepers, a centurion, blind men, and even a dead girl raised. All these announcements, events, and teachings have pointed to the power and authority of Jesus. Taken together, these passages point the reader directly toward the conclusion that Jesus is the one expected Messiah and Son of God. But all of this pointing toward his identity is not enough. Jesus wants to hear directly from his disciples who *they* believe he is.

> Now when Jesus came into the district of Caesarea Philippi, he asked his disciples, "Who do people say that the Son of Man is?" And they said, "Some say John the Baptist, but others Elijah, and still others Jeremiah or one of the prophets." He said to them, "But who do you say that I am?" Simon Peter answered, "You are the Messiah, the Son of the living God." And Jesus answered him, "Blessed are you, Simon son of Jonah! For flesh and blood has not revealed this to you but my Father in heaven."

This dialogue presents us with the pivotal moment between the first half of the gospel story of Jesus and the second half. Many biblical scholars have observed the importance of this moment. Once more, the overriding question is of Jesus' identity: Is he the one? All that has gone before now hinges on this question. All that follows the asking of this question explores the answer Simon Peter gives.

This central moment in Matthew's gospel is more than literary and Christological. It is also symbolized politically and geographically. It is no accident that Jesus asks this question as they "came into the district of Caesarea Philippi." This is the northernmost region Jesus visits, and from here he will begin his journey south toward Jerusalem. It is a Gentile region with historical roots deep in pagan worship and with a shrine dedicated to the pagan god Pan. The city was rebuilt by Herod Philip, who renamed it in honor of Caesar Augustus and himself. Jesus chose such a place as this—where the ghosts of Roman emperors, sold out kings, and pagan gods represented all the would-be authorities of fallen human nature—to make a crucial point about his own identity.

The way in which Jesus questioned the disciples set the stage for the oppositional views on his identity. The "people" were saying one thing and Peter, representing the disciples, said a very different thing. How anyone answers the question of Jesus' identity places them either with the general population or with the followers of Jesus. By this point in the gospel story, the followers of Jesus knew he was more than a prophet. In Mark's gospel, Peter answers Jesus' question by saying, "You are the Messiah" (Mark 8:29). Luke's gospel has Peter's response as "The Messiah of God," or "God's anointed one" (Luke 9:20). Matthew is even more explicit, having Peter say, "You are the Messiah, the Son of the living God."

What we have in the overall gospel story is now a clear delineation between serious followers of Jesus and the crowds of people who came and went. Though we are only at the midpoint of the story, followers of Jesus already know he is the one, the Anointed One, the expected Messiah, the Son of the living God. This may sound trite. We might say, "Well, of course they knew this!" But we have known it all along, based on the cross and resurrection. The disciples hadn't witnessed that part of the story yet. Jesus' disciples based their answer on knowing his teaching and ministry *so far*. They recognized Jesus as the Son of God when he taught them the will and the way of God. They recognized God in Jesus as he revealed to them their true identity in the beatitudes, in loving enemies, in seeking first God's kingdom and righteousness, in his instruction to not judge, in his command to do what he says, in his loving healings, and his compassionate casting out of demons.

The disciples were learning to have ears to hear Jesus and eyes to see him. All their ability to hear and see him as Son of God came from hearing and seeing the Jesus Matthew has recorded for us up until this moment. This is the Jesus many in the Christian church seem to have forgotten. How can we forget or overlook that which once was the very cause of faith for the first disciples? It is like knowing the ending of the story has enabled too many "believers" to forget the transformational ministry of Jesus that *led* to the cross and resurrection. It is as if the ghosts of emperors, sold-out kings, and pagan gods have, for some, erased the things God commanded. It is as if faith became a belief in a magical formula, a God-and-devil, one-time transaction at the cross, instead of a way of living as the image of God in the world today.

The Son of Man in the Emperor's Realm

Caesarea Philippi was the closest Jesus would ever get to Rome. Though he lived constantly under the oppression of Roman rule, and he died at the hands of Roman soldiers, Jesus contained his wandering ministry to Palestine. Caesarea Philippi was approximately 120 miles from Jerusalem. Jesus could not have gone much further north without entering the Roman province of Syria. Though Jesus was technically still in Palestine, he was certainly in a district heavily influenced by and named after Caesar. It is here that, once again, he calls himself the Son of Man. It is here that Peter, the mouthpiece for the other disciples, calls Jesus the Son of the living God.

You might remember our brief discussion of the politics of Jesus in chapter 1, where we talked about the opening line of the Gospel of Mark, which simply reads, "The beginning of the good news of Jesus Christ, the Son of God." As stated then, the Greek term, *euangelion*, meaning "good news," was used in first-century Palestine to describe conquests made by the Roman Empire. Matthew uses the term *euangelion* to proclaim the good news of the kingdom of the heavens, not of the Roman kingdom. Add Mark's and Matthew's uses of *euangelion* in the confession that Jesus is "the Son of God" (Mark) and "the Son of the living God" (in our present text in Matthew), and we can see that, indeed, something radical is being confessed. Something altogether opposed to any other form of earthly authority is being declared, and it is happening in the very shadow of pagan gods and rulers.

Let's not forget what we have said previously about the title Son of Man, and its claim to everlasting dominion over all peoples and nations (Dan 7:14). So, in Jesus' use of the title Son of Man, and Peter's use of the title Son of the living God, we have a double assault on the authority of human rulers. Why is this? Why is this so important for us in the twenty-first century? And what does believing Jesus have to do with emperors then and now?

In this passage we have two kingdoms represented: the kingdom of Caesar and the kingdom of Jesus. Caesar's kingdom is held together with violence. Jesus' kingdom is held together with love. Caesar taught conquering and control of enemies, punishment of enemies, killing of enemies, even torture of enemies. Jesus taught love of enemies and praying for enemies. Caesar taught obedience to Caesar and Caesar's way of control and violence. Jesus taught obedience to God and God's way of love. These two kingdoms could not be more different or more opposed to each other. Jesus never overtly challenged Caesar's kingdom, but he completely subverted it in the most effective way possible—with love. He taught and lived God's love regardless of the short-term outcome, knowing that love would win out in the end.

Consider the juxtaposition of these two kingdoms and ask yourself which one the church of Jesus Christ has aligned itself with for the past 1,700 years or so (since Emperor Constantine led the way to making Christianity the state religion of Rome). The honest answer is *both*. The world has suffered greatly over the past 1,700 years because, "both" is the worst answer imaginable. It would have been better for the church to deny Christ consistently than to say yes to Jesus in theory and no in practice. At least then, the non-Christian world would not have been exposed to a conquering, vengeful, racist, dominating, torturing Jesus. The history of Christianity over the past 1,700 years is replete with violence carried out in the name of Jesus. And Christians continue, even today, to espouse the right to dominate, fight, kill, and even torture in the name of Jesus. Christians still spend billions of dollars on war machines. In the name of defense and control of the world, we train our young men and women to fight and to kill. We do these things and many other hateful acts and bless them in the name of Jesus.

There exists a terrible irony in Christian history. The same Roman Empire that tortured and murdered Jesus, 300–400 years later adopted him in such a compromised way as to tame him for its use. With centuries-old blinders on, Christians today continue to tame Jesus, leaving him domesticated and in service to a different but similar Caesar. We may still pay lip service to monotheism, but we align ourselves with multiple gods. The biblical word for this is *idolatry*, and it is an ugly word. It is an even uglier way to live. If we call ourselves Christian while ignoring or remaining conveniently ignorant of Jesus' teaching, in effect, we say he is not the one Son of God. While we have examples of the early disciples claiming Jesus' name above all others, our example too often leaves a legacy of outright disobedience to much of what he taught and lived.

NEW TESTAMENT WITNESS

The book of Acts is all about witness. This word, *witness*, is the same Greek word that translates as "martyr." While following Jesus in the book of Acts, various disciples gave witness through their words, their lives, and even their deaths. Frequently and consistently, discipleship in Acts is chronicled as witnessing about Jesus to religious and Roman rulers. Here are just a few examples.

Speaking to the rulers, elders, and scribes, and to Caiaphas the high priest and his family, Peter and John say:

> Let it be known to all of you, and to all the people of Israel, that this man is standing before you in good health by the name of Jesus Christ of Nazareth, whom you crucified, whom God raised from the dead. This Jesus is "the stone that was rejected by you, the builders; it has become the cornerstone." There is salvation in no one else, for there is no other name under heaven given among mortals by which we must be saved." (Acts 4:10–12)

For these early disciples, Jesus was not just *the one*; he was *the only one*. For them, no other authority under heaven could tell them what to do and how to live. They could not have spoken more clearly. Think about what Peter and John meant when they said salvation comes only from Jesus' name—that is, by his authority. They were giving witness to the salvation they had experienced and were experiencing.

The council of rulers, elders, and scribes deliberated together and then called Peter and John before them again.

> [They] ordered them not to speak or teach at all in the name of Jesus. But Peter and John answered them, "Whether it is right in God's sight to listen to you rather than to God, you must judge; for we cannot keep from speaking about what we have seen and heard." (Acts 4:18–20)

How else could the early disciples claim their salvation and the salvation of the world? Their salvation was based solely on what they had "seen and heard." We are back again to the salvation Jesus brought and continues to bring through his teaching and healing ministry—crucial parts of his life that cannot be separated from his death and resurrection.

Once more the disciples are brought before the council of rulers and elders:

> The high priest questioned them, saying, "We gave you strict orders not to teach in this name, yet here you have filled Jerusalem with your teaching and you are determined to bring this man's blood on us." But Peter and the apostles answered, "We must obey God rather than any human authority." (Acts 5:27–29)

The book of Acts is the continuation of the gospel story of Jesus Christ. Throughout Acts, followers of Jesus are killed, tortured, and imprisoned by both religious and Roman authorities. After a long, long journey of imprisonment, persecution, and torture, Paul is taken to Rome and there placed under house arrest. It is in Rome that Paul achieves his goal of giving witness about Jesus to the ultimate earthly authority. It is also there that he is put to death.

If Christians today hope to discover the power and excitement of Jesus, we need to understand that Jesus did not teach some form of Roman rule in a milder, kinder tone. Rather, he taught the *opposite*. Christian leaders especially need to recognize Jesus as the only one in whom they hear and see authority, just as Peter and John did. Then Christian leaders across the board will stand up to earthly authorities and say no to violence in any form. In this twenty-first century, the time has come for Christian leaders to recognize the two separate kingdoms and choose God's kingdom of love every time.

WHAT IS AT STAKE?

Since Jesus was first co-opted by the powers of Roman rule, the Christian church has too often been guilty of preaching, condoning, and enacting genocide, racism, sexism, persecution, and murder of millions of Jews and Muslims; enslaving whole peoples, conquering native tribes, and stealing native lands; building up huge arsenals of weapons to kill and destroy human life, and fighting wars that have indeed killed and tortured millions. And on and on it goes.

What is at stake is simply more of the same. Oh, we would like to think of ourselves as beyond the dirty sins of the past. We would like to believe we have a future built on Jesus' love, forgiveness, and grace. But as long as we remain wedded to the powers of this world, we are lying to ourselves. As long as we still allow "Rome"—that is, worldly rule—to co-opt Jesus, we will continue to fund the military, serve in the military, and support the military. We will continue to live the lie of white, male, Christian dominance. We will continue to live subtle forms of racism and sexism that are just as harmful as the overt forms. We will continue to vote for and stand behind policies that retain wealth for the wealthy and keep the poor in poverty. We will allow our government to go unchallenged as it closes our borders and rejects people of other religions and lands. We will continue to put our trust in country instead of God, though we lie with every dollar we spend. "In God we trust" is a sad and truthless joke.

All the while, Jesus' question hangs there waiting for us to have the nerve to honestly answer him. Will we tell him that he is a subcontractor for earthly rulers, a mere prophet fantasizing reality? Or will we tell him from the depth of our hearts and lives that he is the Messiah, the Son of the living God? If the latter is our verbal answer, and if we are serious, then living his loving teachings and ministries will become the ongoing answer we live out with our life.

WHAT IT MEANS TO BE SON OF THE LIVING GOD—
THE CROSS DEFINES THE JOURNEY

We know that at this stage of the gospel story, Peter and the other disciples did not yet understand the full meaning of *Messiah* and *Son of God*. How could they have known the serious implications of all that Jesus had taught and done? They did know enough to answer John the Baptist's question, "Are you the one, or are we to wait for another?" They did know enough to counter the prevailing society's label of "prophet" for Jesus. Prophets came and went; they were important, but they were not God.

It must have been a heavy burden for Jesus to tell and retell the meaning and purpose of *Messiah* and *Son of God*—that suffering love was at the core of the journey of life, even in and through death. We pick up our story in Matthew 16 once again: "From that time on, Jesus began to show his disciples that he must go to Jerusalem and undergo great suffering at the hands of the elders and chief priests and scribes, and be killed, and on the third day be raised" (v. 21).

In this brief saying, Jesus confirms that we are now in the second half of the gospel story, when Jesus will take his disciples with him to Jerusalem and to all that awaits him there. Of course, Peter's immediate response is to take Jesus aside and rebuke him: "God forbid it, Lord! This must never happen to you" (v. 22). Imagine—having just proclaimed Jesus the Son of the living God, Peter now tries to tell *God* what God must not allow!

My heart goes out to Peter and to all disciples then and now who rebuke Jesus in this way. The path of ultimate and complete suffering love is so alien to everything we know in this life. We fight against this journey of love with our heart and soul. We simply do not understand! We present-day Christians who know the end of the story seem to relegate it to one-and-done; God's work, not ours; a love meant for a future time in heaven when all is light and happiness. When we, like Peter, catch a glimpse of the ultimate meaning of Jesus' teachings and the example of his life, we balk, blanch, and back away. After all, we are human, with all the anger, fear, and frustration of our condition. How can we ever get beyond our fear? Where would we possibly go with all our anger and pain?

Here truly is the critical moment when the question of Jesus' identity and our identity must merge:

> Then Jesus told his disciples, "If any want to become my followers, let them deny themselves and take up their cross and follow me. For those who want to save their life will lose it, and those who lose their life for my sake will find it. For what will it profit them if they gain the whole world but forfeit their life? Or what will they give in return for their life?"

Apparently, it was standard procedure under Roman rule for the accused to carry their own cross to the place of their crucifixion. This helps to define Jesus' meaning as he told his disciples to "take up their cross and follow" him. But Christians too often generalize the meaning of this saying, claiming it refers to some form of self-sacrifice that is, in fact, far from Jesus' original meaning. In so doing, we have unknowingly separated ourselves from both the meaning of his statement and from his transformational life. It is time to come back to his original meaning and then ask ourselves what this means for how we live transformational lives today. Remember, all the exploration of this chapter revolves around whether we believe and commit to Jesus being the one—the Son of the Living God.

For Jesus, the meaning of "take up their cross and follow me" had to be aligned with his journey to Jerusalem, his carrying of his own cross, and his suffering unto the point of death. Giving up life in order to find it had very specific meaning for him! Not only was his life's mission about giving up his life to find it; his mission was to teach and exemplify this for his followers. In this context, Jesus tells his disciples they, too, must live the life he is living, take the journey he is taking, and confront the powers just as he has done. Any other journey would not have the transformative power of everlasting love.

Though it was not until after Jesus' resurrection and the anointing of the Holy Spirit, the earliest disciples of Jesus came to understand the meaning of taking up their cross and losing their life so they might find it. They lived and died exactly according to Jesus' instruction in Matthew 16:24–26. They became witnesses—martyrs—to the world of their day. In the footsteps of Jesus, they are witnesses—martyrs—to us today as well.

WHERE DOES THIS LEAVE US?

If we say Jesus is the one, and if we are ready to stake our lives on it, what does it mean? How do we access his love that is so radical as to transform us and the world? Two answers stand out from the experiences of the first disciples:

(1) The first disciples saw and experienced firsthand all that we have been saying in this chapter. They saw and experienced the climax of Jesus' life and ministry in his suffering death and his resurrection. The first disciples went from utter despair at Jesus' death to utter ecstasy at his resurrected life. Before their very eyes, the greatest teaching moment of all time happened; indeed, the greatest demonstration of suffering love was confirmed in the most horrific way. But then, in his resurrection, everything Jesus had taught them and had lived out before them was vindicated—shown to be God's absolute truth regarding Jesus' life and the life he intended for them.

Like the early disciples, we live in disbelief when Jesus still claims that suffering love is the eternally transformative power of God in this world. We today, in the most normal human way, cannot imagine relying solely on God's love for us and the world. Because of our disbelief, we dilute God's love with the powers and securities of this world. Anything other than a melding of God's love with violent actions and systems seems to us an impossible way to live. We stand before the cross of Jesus, the way of Jesus, the loving journey of Jesus, the mission of Jesus, in disbelief.

If we are to live in the deep understanding that Jesus is the one, we, too, must come to the very end of hoping in the powers of this world and experience utter despair at the death of what we thought was God's will and way. We must see our misunderstanding—our idolatry, even—as Jesus takes it upon himself, along with all other sins, to die on the cross. We must let this sin die in us. We must reach the bottom of our addictions to the world's power just as any drug addict must hit bottom before anything changes in their approach to life.

The way of the cross of Jesus is the only true way to the release of whatever we have grasped for security and salvation. Jesus suffered a true and awful death, as did many of the first disciples. It will also be an awful death for us, in that we must be jarred loose from our hold on the limited and compromised form of life this world offers in order to be given a hold on God's eternal life of love. This is God's method and purpose. It is God's work in us. It is what God longs for and intends for us. It is the very core of all that Jesus taught and lived. It is why Jesus is the one.

(2) The second transformative experience of the first disciples came at Pentecost; (Acts 2). They were anointed with the power of the Holy Spirit of God in Christ Jesus. Jesus had promised he would send his Spirit, the Holy Spirit, and he fulfilled this

promise. But this could not have happened without their own spiritual and emotional death and resurrection experiences happening first. Without going through death and into new life, their spirits could not have received what God wanted to give them. At Pentecost, God gave them the power of love in an awesome way. The gospel of Jesus Christ, ongoing throughout the book of Acts—and up to today—flows from this Holy Spirit power of love.

Too many Christians today have mistaken this Holy Spirit power of love. We have made many claims in Jesus' name. We have often made use and misuse of the gifts of the Spirit. We have proclaimed Jesus in so many ways short of the Spirit's ultimate power of love. Whatever we have said or done or experienced of the Holy Spirit's power is worthless unless it is in service to the only real Holy Spirit power, which takes the form of suffering love, life-giving and releasing love, the love shared with us in Jesus' teachings and his cross. Without Jesus' transformational, unconditional love flowing throughout our lives, whatever else we accomplish is nothing. Such is the power of the Holy Spirit at work in us—it is God's love incarnate—that is, embodied—flowing to us and through us. It is our only salvation, both present and future. It is the only truth for us to believe—believing Jesus for the present as his life of love empowers our heart, mind, and soul.

If you think I have overstated the case for Holy Spirit love, I refer you to one of the best-known chapters in the New Testament: 1 Corinthians 13. There, Paul says what I have just said, but better and with more force. Love is the supreme gift of the Holy Spirit descended upon the first disciples. Love is and can be the supreme empowering of God in us too.

A WORD OF BLESSING

Answering the question of this chapter is serious business. I have attempted to say just how serious it is to claim that *Jesus is the one*. I have attempted, in as honest a way as I am able, to challenge anything less than a life commitment to this claim. What I have said here is not popular, not "orthodox Christianity," and not widely accepted. I have risked losing the approval of others, my credibility, and anything remaining of my own reliance on the safety offered by things of this world.

Yet, the joy I feel is real. It is as if I have entered a new room in God's house. I do not feel shame or fear or self-righteousness. I feel a sense of completeness of heart, mind, and soul. Whatever the inadequacies in my writing, God is writing new and blessed words, experiences of *Logos*—Jesus the Living Word—within me.

I want you the reader to know and experience this joy too. It is my hope that in believing Jesus, you will go through death to life, experience the horror and the ecstasy. I want you to know that in letting go of your need for this world's security blankets, when you lose the only life you have known, when you come to realize that Jesus is your only savior and his way of love is the only way he saves you, then you will be given so much more than you can ever ask for or imagine. I close this chapter with the words of Paul to the church at Ephesus:

> Now to him who by the power at work within us is able to accomplish abundantly far more than we can ask or imagine, to him be glory in the church and in Christ Jesus to all generations, forever and ever. Amen. (Eph 3:20–21)

7

KINGDOM PARABLES OF ABUNDANCE

FIRST, A STORY

I was a pastor in my middle years, finding my way through the challenges of life around me. His name was Mike, and he was dying of cancer. His belief was in music, especially Elvis. We played "You Ain't Nothin' but a Hound Dog" at his funeral, and for me it was a God moment.

But before that, as I ministered to Mike, I had to yell because he was 90 percent deaf. No normal conversation was possible. I yelled, and he spoke softly in return. I felt unequally yoked, like my yelling was an affront to his gentle nature. He did not seem to mind. I remember my first visit to Mike at his wife's request. He was already confined to bed. Making my way up the stairs to his bedroom, I wondered what I was getting myself into. I could not imagine how I might reach out to a deaf man who was dying and who did not believe in God or the church. His wife insisted Mike would welcome me.

When I entered his room that first time, I immediately realized there was no place to sit except with him on his bed. I could not imagine intruding on his personal space, the only place left to him in this world. I stood awkwardly, but soon Mike made it clear I was invited to sit. It was the first test to see if I was willing to become vulnerable too, with him in his last domain.

Our first conversation was aided by his wife, but as the weeks went by, Mike and I mostly visited alone. We got to know each other slowly. I became determined not to allow the awkwardness of yelling deter me from loving him. Part of my loving Mike came through my choice to regularly spend time with him. The other part simply came as a result of his wonderful, gentle spirit.

Slowly, as our friendship grew, I became relaxed about my and others' expectations that I somehow bring Mike to faith. As I learned more about his background and his past experience with religious people, I began to understand why he could not embrace faith in God. His painful experiences were a story all too familiar to me, of emotional abuse at the hands of so-called Christians touting a judgmental god and enacting that god's hateful attitude toward people—in this case, toward Mike and his family.

In my time with Mike, I learned two interrelated things. As the time went along, they became all that mattered to me and, I believe, to Mike. One of these things changed me, and the other, I believe, changed Mike. The thing that changed me was what was happening on my end of the friendship. I was learning that I could experience love and acceptance from someone very different from me—someone so outside the faith, so wounded by that which I cherished. Mike's love and acceptance of me was more profound than anything I thought possible as I first journeyed up those stairs to his bedroom. It was as if all my silly defenses were stripped from me. I had to learn to let them go, and Mike helped me do just that.

The second thing—the one I believe changed Mike—was his experience of my love and acceptance of him. Somewhere during our developing friendship, I lost my need to evangelize him in any "orthodox" way. As our cherished moments together accumulated, our love and acceptance for each other proved a safe space for clergy and pagan to become one, without anything but love and acceptance. I believe he came to fully trust in this love and acceptance that we held for each other. Though we had been worlds apart, we now were united in love. I am convinced this was God's love. Whether or not Mike knew it as God's love, I don't know. Regardless of whether it is recognized as such, God's love changes anyone whose heart is opened to it.

Eventually, hospice had to move Mike downstairs. The dining room became his final bedroom. My last visit to Mike was the day before he died. The cancer had overcome nearly all his body's defenses. But while his organs were shutting down, his mind remained clear. He could only talk in a whisper, and I still had to yell for him to hear me. So at the end of this last visit, I yelled at Mike, asking if he would like me to pray for him. I truly did not know how he would respond. Struggling to speak, he whispered a clear yes. By that time, I knew we could not have any real exchange of a shared prayer, so I attempted to pray for both of us. I trusted my love for Mike enough at that moment to pray from his perspective as well as mine. And no, I did not pray the "sinner's prayer" for Mike.

Twelve years have passed since my last visit with Mike, and I do not remember the words I prayed. I do remember holding Mike's hand and yell-praying for God's love to welcome him home and for Mike to welcome the love we had shared as God's love for him. I remember putting all I had into that prayer, attempting to assure Mike he was safely in God's love as he passed from the present life into his future one. I desperately hoped he could relax in the grace of God without any pain of bitterness about how Christianity and the world had treated him.

When I finished praying and a few more moments had passed, I yelled to Mike, asking if he had been able to hear me. I was crushed when he whispered back that he had not heard my prayer. Then he whispered, "But I felt it." I will never forget the joy I felt at hearing those four words.

I'll let you draw your own conclusions from this story. As for me, there is really only one conclusion. Having been given the gift of time with Mike, I am all the more convinced of the limitless bounty of God's love. God's love won the day regardless of anything I did or said or contributed. God's love won the day, no matter what defenses Mike had erected concerning his self-image and his worthiness of God's love. God's love and our exercise of God's love win the day every time. Regardless of the pain in this world, the misuse of God's name, the violent ways people devour one another, and the un-Christlike depiction of Jesus by too many Christians worldwide, God's love still wins at every moment of its intrusion into our world. Those who would be followers of Jesus have untold opportunities to channel God's love into every situation.

PARABLES OF ABUNDANCE

We will focus this study primarily on the first of Jesus' parables. In addition, we will engage the message of four other parables from Matthew 13. All the parables reviewed in this chapter can be described as "parables of abundance."

But first, I'd like to clear the air about what these parables are about. The parables in Matthew 13 are commonly understood as being about the kingdom of God on earth. We will explore this important aspect. But specifically, *the parables of Jesus are about what he taught and demonstrated throughout his life of ministry*. These imaginative stories built upon and extended the teachings of Jesus that we have been studying.

Over the generations, the church has enjoyed the parables of Jesus and explored them time and again. For example, most Christians have heard the parable of the sower and the seed (Matt 13:3–9) countless times. In Sunday school classes and Vacation Bible Schools, sermon illustrations, flannel-graph object lessons, and skits dramatized for effect, we have been immersed in the story of the sower and the seed. We know the meaning of the good soil and the bad soil—or do we? I contend that many Christians have not yet discovered what Jesus was really talking about in this parable.

I understand that my previous statement is controversial, and as such, it needs further examination; hence, this chapter. The reason I suggest many Christians have not understood this parable is because too many have separated it from Jesus' earlier teachings, especially the Sermon on the Mount (Matt 5–7). Without a deep understanding of Jesus' earlier teachings and a personal commitment to follow those teachings in this life, any interpretation of the parables quickly becomes "Jesus-lite." Jesus-lite is not a milder, but still helpful, form of Jesus; it is a dangerous, erroneous substitution for the real Jesus. Jesus-lite leads to a different religious experience than what Jesus taught and lived. Jesus-lite leads Christians today to espouse a faith in things alien to Jesus. The danger is that too much of Christianity becomes a different religious experience altogether, not one built on the solid foundation of Jesus himself.

In chapter 6, we emphasized the importance of hearing and seeing Jesus—hearing what he taught and seeing how he lived what he taught. The twin themes of hearing and seeing become ever more important as the story of Jesus unfolds. We have ample support for this in the parables of Matthew 13, as Jesus emphasizes again and again the importance of hearing and seeing. In fact, we could well interpret these parables as stories intended specifically to enshrine Jesus' teachings in our hearts and minds.

The Parable of the Soils

Jesus' first parable is primarily about the soils, though often it is often called "the parable of the sower" or "of the sower and the seed." Along with its explanation, it takes up the first twenty-three verses of Matthew 13. Because of its length and Jesus' careful explanation, this parable dominates the parables in this chapter. This one opens Jesus' use of parabolic teachings that will continue then, off and on, until Matthew 26. In a real sense, we could think of parables as Jesus' go-to teaching style through the remainder of Matthew, his primary method for following up his foundational teachings recorded in chapters 5–7.

Jesus' parables bridge the distance between expository teaching and real life. In Matthew 5–7, Jesus carefully taught the ways of surrender and love that lead to living God's kingdom here on earth. Now in the parables, he both invites and challenges his first hearers—and Matthew's readers, including us—to the same truths using word pictures and imaginative thinking based on images from everyday life.

Donald Senior explains parables in this way:

> Parables are extended metaphors or comparisons designed to draw the hearer into a new awareness of reality as revealed by Jesus, yet their artful nature adds a special twist of paradox and unexpected challenge. . . . The parables help amplify the profound Christology that suffuses Matthew's narrative, namely that, in Jesus, the reign of God has come. At the same time, the ability to penetrate the meaning of the parables and to "understand" them, or conversely, the refusal or inability to understand the parables, separates the disciples from Jesus' chronic opponents.[1]

Grant R. Osborne says it like this:

> For those who reject the presence of God in Jesus (as do the leaders of the Jews [in Matthew]), the parable becomes a sign of sovereign judgment, further hardening their hearts. For those who are open (e.g., the crowds), the parable

---

1. Senior, *Matthew*, 146–47.

encounters and draws them to decision. For those who believe (i.e., the disciples), the parable teaches them further kingdom truths.[2]

Osborne earlier states of Jesus' parables:

> These are parables centering on "the kingdom of heaven" (in virtually every parable), and they develop the implications of its arrival—about kingdom conflict, judgment, and decision, reflecting the implications of the preceding material, especially the controversy over Jesus.[3]

I will assume for the remainder of this chapter that the conflict, judgment, and decision called out by these parables will, for the duration of my life and yours, battle for our hearts—the softening or the hardening of our hearts. Or to use the quote Jesus uses from Isaiah, "For this people's heart has grown dull"; therefore they cannot hear and see" (Matt 13:15). Given the earlier teachings of Jesus, this comes as no surprise. For Christians, if there is no battle going on inside of us, it likely means we have succumbed to a world-friendly, comfortable version of Jesus-lite. Jesus speaks to us in parables; if we fail to hear and see, we will not understand with our hearts and be healed.

The Parable about Hearing and Seeing

With considerable accuracy, we could also call this a "parable about hearing and seeing." Approximately two dozen times in these twenty-three verses—more than once per verse!—Jesus mentions hearing/listening or looking/seeing. While the story told in this parable focuses on the sower, the seed, and the soil, Jesus' emphasis is also on understanding in our hearts by hearing with our ears and seeing with our eyes. The parable itself starts out with Jesus saying, "Listen!" (v. 3) and concludes with Jesus explaining the various types of soil in terms of whether someone truly "hears" the word of God such that it bears fruit in their life.

Without truly hearing and seeing, there is no understanding and no healing of our hearts. If we fail to get this message, we won't fully grasp this parable and those that follow. Yet, even if we comprehend Jesus' emphasis on hearing and seeing, a fundamental question remains: *What* are we to hear and see?

Let's consider the importance of context. If a third person had walked into Mike's dining room about the time I was yelling my final prayer with him, I might have been accused of abusive behavior. In order to make sense of what was going on, that third person would have needed to be a part of Mike's and my many visits leading up to that prayer.

Similarly, it is essential to pay careful attention to the specific situation in Matthew's narrative to understand its meaning at the time it took place. And it is equally

2. Osborne, *Matthew*, 504.
3. Osborne, *Matthew*, 497.

important to know as much as we can about what has led up to this text. Context is both specific—about the immediate setting—and extended—taking into account what has gone before. So, again, based on this parable, what are we to be hearing and seeing? The most obvious answer is that Jesus clearly longs for his disciples to carefully listen to his present words—to hear, see, and understand what he is saying in the moment. This is the first level of context—the specific situation, the current setting. There are plenty of good commentaries written on the book of Matthew that include insights into this first level of context. This is where most preachers and teachers spend their time studying and expounding, and with good reason. It is important to know what Jesus is talking about: Who is the sower? What is the seed? Who is represented by the different soils? As answers to these questions are clarified, the trouble comes when people assume they have understood everything Jesus was communicating.

With only the immediate context understood, the parable of the soils can be interpreted to confirm whatever theology, politics, or lifestyle the interpreter believes is right. While the interpreter correctly draws upon the immediate context of the parable, they are incorrect to draw upon their *own* extended context—rather than the extended context of *Jesus'* teaching and ministry—as they attempt to use Jesus to justify their personal brand of Christianity.

As I write, today is the fiftieth anniversary of the assassination of Dr. Martin Luther King Jr. We all know at least some of what he stood for, worked for, and died for. Slavery and its ugly aftermath are realities of the United States, past and present. Over the generations, white privilege has been preached and defended by many Christians. This can even be done using the parable of the sower. To illustrate, let's say the sower is God, the seed is the word of God, and the soils represent people who either do or don't hear, understand, and live out the word of God. Anyone with a preconceived bias toward white privilege can claim that the word of God supports white privilege and slavery. All they need to do is draw upon their own bias and a selection of biblical texts to draw the conclusion that the good soil that produces a bountiful harvest represents the white slaveholders who uphold society's values and contribute to (what the powerful consider) the common good. Slaveholders then become paragons of biblical virtue and followers of Jesus.

Any form of patriarchy can follow the same trajectory based on immediate context, added personal bias, misuse of scripture, and wrong conclusions. The outcome is tragic. Justification of violence, ethnic cleansing, economic oppression, us-vs.-them thinking, or any other personal bias can follow this same trajectory.

In other words, if we only take the present-moment context of Jesus' words of Matthew 13:1–23, we easily arrive at whatever meaning we want. When this happens—and it happens often—we lose any hope of discovering what Jesus intended to say, show, and transform. We lose the real Jesus and discover only our own shadow side. Above all, we miss out on the salvation Jesus brings. Jesus' message of salvation throughout the gospels is the most hopeful and joyful message humankind will ever hear! The parables in this chapter reveal this message in powerful ways, which is why I call them "parables of abundance."

A PARABLE BROUGHT TO LIFE

In this section we will bring together the immediate context and the extended context of the sower, the seed, and the soil. My hope is that we will discover the power, grace, and salvation of Jesus' mission and message. The future of the world depends on this salvation. We will follow Matthew's pattern of exploring the parable in three parts.

Part 1—The Parable as Told to the Crowd—Matthew 13:1–9

The first nine verses of Matthew 13 provide the immediate context and the basic story of this parable, which follows on the heels of the section we studied previously (Matt 12) about the escalating opposition to Jesus on the part of religious leaders. Now he also faces crowds of people gathered for healing. And he is leading a band of disciples who follow him but do not understand anywhere close to all that is taking place.

At the end of chapter 12 we find a short story where Jesus declares that his family is composed of anyone who does the will of his Father. In so saying, Jesus has redefined family in a culture where family ties were sacrosanct. We witness here Jesus' call to unbending allegiance to the will and the kingdom of God, as opposed to any other allegiance. Flowing from this conflict and Jesus' challenge for people to do "the will of [his] Father in heaven" (Matt 12:50), he chose to teach the crowds the parable of the soils.

> That same day Jesus went out of the house and sat beside the sea. Such great crowds gathered around him that he got into a boat and sat there, while the whole crowd stood on the beach. And he told them many things in parables, saying: "Listen! A sower went out to sow. And as he sowed, some seeds fell on the path, and the birds came and ate them up. Other seeds fell on rocky ground, where they did not have much soil, and they sprang up quickly, since they had no depth of soil. But when the sun rose, they were scorched; and since they had no root, they withered away. Other seeds fell among thorns, and the thorns grew up and choked them. Other seeds fell on good soil and brought forth grain, some a hundredfold, some sixty, some thirty. Let anyone with ears listen!" (Matt 13:1–9)

The first word out of Jesus' mouth is "Listen." Some translations use the English "Look" or "Behold." The meaning is the same: Pay careful attention; this is important! The same Greek word is used by Matthew in various places, including 1:20, where the angel of the Lord visits Joseph and speaks to him. The Greek actually means "to arouse the attention of hearers and readers."[4] There is apparently no exact English equivalent.

4. Bauer, Arndt, and Gingrich, *Lexicon*, 371.

Regardless of the specific translation, Jesus has taken the occasion to purposely stage an important teaching for a large crowd. While he has previously used short parabolic sayings and comparisons, like about new wine and old or new wineskins (Matt 9:17), Jesus' teaching at length in parables starts in 13:3. Matthew specifically notes this shift: "And he told them many things in parables." Together with the opening line of chapter 13, "That same day . . .," the wording links this occasion directly to the preceding verses, and we begin to see how the immediate context is that of heightening struggle between the "old wineskins" (traditional religion) and the "new wine" (Jesus' teaching).

Let's remember the purpose of parables. Jesus used them to tease the minds of his hearers into facing the truth about what was happening before their very eyes and ears. What we have in Matthew 13 is a litany of parables in which Jesus spoke the truth about both the rejection and the reception of his message and mission. He chose to confront all comers with word pictures intended to jolt, tease, and dislodge "old wineskin" thinking. Without his previous teaching and living of his message and mission, the parables would have no meaning specifically tied to him—they would have no extended context. If we do not understand the reason for the conflict, or do not understand this parable as Jesus' direct challenge to the conflict, we will almost certainly miss both its significance and true meaning.

What might Jesus' first hearers of this parable have possibly thought it meant? Even his own disciples didn't understand. This is important, for we who have so many layers of "understanding" regarding this parable probably can't imagine how perplexing it may have originally seemed. We wonder why the disciples were so dense. What we forget or don't take seriously enough is, again, the nature and purpose of Jesus' parables. They were intended to seriously shake things up. They were intended to shatter old thinking and transform people's hearts—certainly never an easy task or a simple process! We will come back to the specifics of this parable when we get to Jesus' interpretation of it. For now, let's pay attention to his concluding words in verse 9: "Let anyone with ears listen!" I don't imagine there were folks in the crowd who did not actually have ears, so this was Jesus' way of calling *everyone* to listen! He was also calling for everyone to understand and to respond. Osborne writes:

> Jesus calls for both a willingness to listen (present tense for an ongoing response) and a motivation to respond properly to the message. . . . Jesus is demanding a serious examination of [the parable's] meaning on the part of his hearers. Many have called this a prophetic warning to the hearers/readers to open their minds and hearts to the spiritual truths being conveyed.[5]

Jesus' emphasis on hearing, understanding, and responding will only intensify over the next fourteen verses. Two things to reiterate as we lean into the coming sections: (1) The conflict that is the present and extended context of this parable is

---

5. Osborne, *Matthew*, 508.

highlighted over and over by Jesus' repeated emphasis on the importance of hearing, understanding, and responding. (2) The spiritual truths underlying the conflict can only be those previously taught and lived by Jesus himself! So we begin to see how present and extended context fit together.

One final note for this section: Jesus' message and mission were intended to challenge, dislodge, and transform the whole world. That is what happened, and part of what this parable so aptly shows is how messy the transformation process is. Such an epic transformation would not be authentic if it didn't create a dividing line between those whose hearts are melted and those whose hearts are hardened. Much more on this below.

Part 2—Why Speak in Parables?

The disciples do us a great favor in asking this question. Not only was it a real and important question for them, but it helps again to emphasize for us the importance of the shift Jesus makes in his teaching style. Even Jesus' closest followers are surprised by this change. Their posing this question provided Jesus the platform for his explanation, which cuts to the very heart of things.

> Then the disciples came and asked him, "Why do you speak to them in parables?" He answered, "To you it has been given to know the secrets of the kingdom of heaven, but to them it has not been given. For to those who have, more will be given, and they will have an abundance; but from those who have nothing, even what they have will be taken away. The reason I speak to them in parables is that 'seeing they do not perceive, and hearing they do not listen, nor do they understand.' With them indeed is fulfilled the prophecy of Isaiah that says:
>
> "'You will indeed listen, but never understand, and you will indeed look, but never perceive. For this people's heart has grown dull, and their ears are hard of hearing, and they have shut their eyes; so that they might not look with their eyes, and listen with their ears, and understand with their heart and turn—and I would heal them.'
>
> "But blessed are your eyes, for they see, and your ears, for they hear. Truly I tell you, many prophets and righteous people longed to see what you see, but did not see it, and to hear what you hear, but did not hear it." (Matt 13:10–17)

A key phrase at the beginning of Jesus' answer to the disciples' question is "the secrets [mysteries] of the kingdom of heaven." Some have interpreted this as Jesus' way of saying that for some reason God has chosen to give some people this secret understanding, but not others. This then becomes a platform for anyone to claim that they are part of the elect while others aren't. In order to understand God as the "elector" of some and not others, and to make a case for this from the present passage, we would have to ignore all that Jesus has previously taught about the kingdom and his own extremely inclusive example of living the kingdom. We simply cannot ignore these unless we once again limit ourselves to the immediate context.

So what is Jesus saying in the immediate and the extended context of this passage? Most important are the qualifying words "of the kingdom of heaven." The mysteries given and not given are the mysteries of the kingdom of heaven. If we take the words *given* and *not given* literally, as indicating some form of pre-election by God, we suddenly lose the significance of the teachings and examples lived out by Jesus in chapters 5–12. Jesus' many kingdom-of-heaven teachings and examples of how to live were intended to challenge and invite *everyone*.

All of Jesus' parables, including this one, are descriptions of or invitations to the kingdom, the living reign of God on earth, now. Everything I have said so far about the kingdom is the ground upon which the parables are founded. We will take up the importance of kingdom again in the next section, but for now, we must simply say that God's will and way in this world are all-inclusive. God does not want a partial transformation, as we saw in Matthew 6. We cannot serve two masters. Also, in Matthew 6, we heard Jesus commanding *all* people to seek first the kingdom and God's righteousness.

The question of whether people are in or out of God's kingdom and righteousness is not God's doing; it is ours. Jesus makes this clear as he explains, "The reason I speak to them in parables is that 'seeing *they* do not perceive, and hearing *they* do not listen, nor do *they* understand'" (Matt 13:13, emphasis mine). Then he quotes Isaiah 6:9–10. Without knowing the context from Isaiah, we might again think that God is the instigator of the people's deficiencies. But if we read through Isaiah 5 and 6, we discover the true cause of their being deaf and blind.

Chapter 5 describes people of Jerusalem and Judah as a vineyard planted by the Lord, but this vineyard has gone wild. The Lord planted, expecting justice and righteousness, but instead saw bloodshed and heard the cry of the oppressed. This chapter continues to chronicle the sins of injustice and the inevitable judgment to follow.

Isaiah 6 begins by telling the beautiful story of Isaiah's commissioning. The quote Jesus uses in Matthew 13:14–15 is this commission given to Isaiah. This is a judgment on the people, for they have turned from God. They have sought wealth and ignored God and the justice and righteousness of God. While God has provided, cared for, and remained faithful to the people, they have not remained faithful to God. In the end, there is the justice of God's judgment. Yet even in quoting Isaiah, Jesus subtly changes the words, directing the guilt entirely on the people: "For this people's heart has grown dull, and their ears are hard of hearing, and they have shut their eyes; so that they might not look with their eyes, and listen with their ears, and understand with their heart and turn—and I would heal them" (Matt 13:15). Jesus opens the door to God's healing. If only they would open their eyes and ears and hearts!

Compared to the starkness of judgment Isaiah is commissioned to declare, Jesus' words remind us of his weeping over Jerusalem in Luke 19:41–42. While Jesus longs to heal all people and weeps over the violence and injustice of Jerusalem, the sad reality is that without repentance, destruction comes both in Isaiah 5 and in Luke 19:43–44. It is as if we are being told that destruction will always result for those who cause injustice and violence.

Thankfully, Jesus does not end his explanation with Isaiah 6:9–10. Rather, he declares a rich blessing on the eyes and ears of his disciples. What an amazing privilege they have been given! Why? Because they have seen and are seeing Jesus in action. They have heard and are hearing his teachings. Though often befuddled, they are beginning to understand in their hearts, and they are beginning to be healed!

Is this what we today see and hear? Is this blessing that Jesus declares true for us as well? Are our hearts and minds softened or hardened when we hear and see Jesus in action? We have the gospel accounts of Jesus that include his words and actions. In the verses ahead, as Jesus explains this parable, consider which type of soil you are.

Part 3—The Meaning of the Parable of the Soils

Jesus explained this parable, emphasizing the different soils. The sower (God/Jesus) is important, as is the seed (the kingdom message). But the purpose of the story is to reveal the truth about the reception that Jesus is receiving. In other words, this parable is about everyone who hears Jesus' teaching on the kingdom and sees Jesus' living example of the kingdom. It is about how each person responds—do they really hear, do they really see, and do they really bear the fruit of the kingdom of heaven?

Here is Jesus' explanation of the parable:

> Hear then the parable of the sower. When anyone hears *the word of the kingdom* and does not understand it, the evil one comes and snatches away what is sown in the heart; this is what was sown on the path. As for what was sown on rocky ground, this is the one who hears *the word* and immediately receives it with joy; yet such a person has no root, but endures only for a while, and when trouble or persecution arises on account of *the word*, that person immediately falls away. As for what was sown among thorns, this is the one who hears *the word*, but the cares of the world and the lure of wealth choke *the word*, and it yields nothing. But as for what was sown on good soil, this is the one who hears *the word* and understands it, who indeed bears fruit and yields, in one case a hundredfold, in another sixty, and in another thirty. (Matt 13:18–23)

I have added the italics above to be sure we do not misunderstand what is at stake here. *While the purpose of the parable is to reveal the truth of human response, it is the joy of the kingdom as Jesus has taught and lived it that will either become a bountiful harvest or seed sown in a wasted effort.* Once again it behooves us to remember the supreme importance of God's present reign on earth. Like the prayer Jesus taught us to pray, everything he has taught and everything he has lived reveals God's present kingdom. As such, every teaching of his and every healing act of his is a key for us to use to open the door of our understanding, to recognize what it is like for God to rule in us and our world right now.

The Soil on the Path

To not understand the present kingdom of God, in Jesus' words, is to allow "the evil one [to come] and [snatch] away what is sown in the heart" (v. 19). The seed is sown, but rejected. With everything that has gone before in the message and ministry of Jesus, to not understand the kingdom is to ignore Jesus, dismiss him, or refuse to believe him. Too many Christians find Jesus' teachings and example too difficult. They are looking for an easy out from life's demons and burdens, and for heaven when they die. *Sure,* they think, *there are rules to follow, like going to church on Sunday, serving on a committee, and behaving like a good person.* Although none of this is what Jesus taught and lived, this "lite" version of Jesus is all many people want. It is sobering to think that Jesus describes this as the evil one snatching the kingdom of God from our hearts!

All people are responsible for how receptive or unreceptive they are to Jesus' teaching and his invitation to follow him. We all have choices to make about the extent to which we believe what he has taught as the authority over our lives. Each and every person must decide if Jesus is Lord and teacher of their life here and now, and whether they will be a part of God's kingdom come to earth by obeying Jesus.

The soil that falls on the path can be illustrated by the person who has heard Jesus' teachings on the kingdom and has not accepted or lived them. We might think of all the reasons Christians and non-Christians reject the teachings of Jesus, but Jesus simply attributes these reasons to the evil one. We can make excuses about why we do not follow Jesus' teachings on the kingdom; still, what remains in our heart is pain, violence, fear, resentment, and unforgiveness. As much as so many like to say they believe in Jesus, to believe him fully and follow him fully eludes them because of these painful things. Jesus says this is of the evil one. Evil is alive and well and rampant on the earth. It is ready to snatch the hope of the kingdom of God on earth away from us if our hearts are not willing to fully understand and accept Jesus' teachings.

Sadly, for many in the Christian church—at least in the United States—it seems that not understanding Jesus is an intentional act. Anyone calling themselves Christian has access to Jesus' teachings in the gospels. Many willfully or selectively ignore these teachings. Some relegate the responsibility for understanding Jesus to someone else with whom they easily agree. Many simply listen passively and happily to sermons and teachings that do not represent sound understanding of Jesus, such as when this parable is explained in ways that confirm and uplift an American way of life.

Rocky Soil

Jesus dealt with a lot of crowds. Many people followed him and then left when things got rough. Even his most trusted followers deserted him at the most painful time of his life—during his suffering and at his death. Jesus says, "But when trouble or persecution arises on account of the word, that person immediately falls away" (Matt 13:21).

There is no sense mincing words here: like all the people of Jesus' day, we, too, are afraid of suffering, persecution, and violent death. These are primary motivators for most people who put their trust in world leaders, politicians, national legislators, military leaders, and lobbyists who tell us we need—and they will ensure—our protection in various realms of life. Yet Jesus tells us this fear restricts the depth to which our roots are able to grow in his will and way. Those who put their fears first, before the teachings and example of Jesus, are the ones in the parable who immediately fall away.

Now, you may be saying, *Wait a minute. We are not "fallen away" just because we believe in a strong military, or just because we believe in the right to defend ourselves.* Yet, think about it. What is the difference between (1) falling away from Jesus and the word of his kingdom because you feel threatened by trouble and persecution (such as Jesus' disciples when he was crucified) and (2) falling away by depending on the world's violent powers to keep you from trouble and persecution (like most people today)? Both versions of falling away involve the same rejection of Jesus' teaching and the same fruit of violence. Both versions are fear based. Both versions support and yield allegiance to a false-god kingdom instead of to living Jesus' kingdom of uncompromising love. *Both versions leave Jesus to suffer and die alone.*

It is interesting that Jesus says the seed that falls on rocky ground *receives* the word of the kingdom with joy. At first blush, our surrender to Jesus—to God's love and forgiveness, the Holy Spirit's infusion of excitement, and the clear realization of something new and radical—produces a wonderful high, like a joy never known before. There are countless stories of people whose life was on course for a train wreck, and suddenly they discovered God's love and forgiveness. We call these salvation stories. In those initial days of discovery, things seem so clear. We recognize the differences between the two kingdoms clearly, and this is a joyful part of the discovery.

Why, for so many people, does the joy not last? Because in their minds and hearts, the line between Jesus' kingdom way and the world's kingdom ways becomes blurred. Life gets rough, trouble comes, persecution and death threaten, and most people knuckle under. Most people decide to syncretize the world's offer of present protection and Jesus' offer of eternal life. The result is a kind of bottom line—when there is threat and fear, we accept and live in the kingdom of violence. In his explanation of the seed that falls on rocky ground, Jesus says that this immediately separates us from him and the joy he brings.

How many of us Christians can even remember the joy of God's love and acceptance overwhelming us? I am talking about the sense of oneness with the creator of all life! I am talking about a total realization that now we are fully in God's care with, literally, "not a care in the world." I am talking about what almost everyone would say is unrealistic, naïve, and fleeting in this present life. And I am sure these same accusations were repeatedly hurled at Jesus. He held firm and went to the cross despite what all the practical-minded people thought about it. He did not become our savior by bowing to the powers that promise to protect us from the world's cares.

Jesus tells a profound truth about the extreme danger of falling away. He says we will lose the joy of receiving the word, and too many of us have. But sadly, this parable has often been launched from pulpits entirely missing the truth about the initial joy and the falling away we experience as we flounder through life in our kingdoms of violence.

Thorny Soil

> As for what was sown among thorns, this is the one who hears the word, but the cares of the world and the lure of wealth choke the word, and it yields nothing. (Matt 13:22)

I'm sixty-five years old. My family has quite a history of Alzheimer's disease. I could share a litany of health problems I presently experience or fear. Add to this the extreme costs of health care, and I am left—as are so many in this world—to struggle with how to handle my finances and my "cares of the world."

Jesus knew how to name reality. Who among us does not face worldly cares? Jesus did not deny the existence of the thorns. What he warned against was allowing the thorns to choke us and therefore choke our ability to live God's kingdom word now.

So I ask myself, Are the cares of this life choking off my commitment to live the beatitudes as fully as I can? Does my love for God and neighbor, rather than my "cares of the world," clearly form the basis of my daily decisions? Has anything in my life compromised my vow to follow Jesus and practice nonviolence? Is my love of enemies and my praying for enemies diminished in any way by how I handle my finances? Am I protecting my way of life over against freely living the joys of the kingdom?

There is no simple one-time answer for these questions. They engage my conscience on an ongoing basis, not in a despairing way, but in a lively, challenging way. These questions force me to face my human weakness, my fears, and my failings. When I do that, I discover a freedom that makes room for the joy of trusting in God.

This thorny ground, the third type of soil, is a constant threat to the kingdom harvest. Everywhere we look today, we see the lure of wealth and the cares of this world. If anything, I imagine this type of soil is more destructive now than it was for Jesus' first-century hearers, mainly because here in the developed world, we have so much to protect and care about. The thorns we face in the United States are monsters with roots spreading constantly throughout the ground from which we are trying to produce a harvest for God's kingdom.

It seems the biggest, nastiest thorns are the ones that choke off any real sense of dependence on God, any need for surrender to the giver of all life, any serious interest in hearing the instructions of Jesus about love. The more wealth we have, the further science takes us, the more complete the worldwide web, the more wondrous the intricacies of technology, the more we believe in progress (and in ourselves), the more luxurious and easy the living, the more culturally advanced, the more powerful our militaries, . . . the bigger and nastier the thorns that would choke us.

We who dwell in the developed world have grown up amid the thorns Jesus warns against, so much so that often we no longer even recognize them as thorns. We say that these things are good, that they help make the world a better place. What we don't realize is that good can mask evil really well. Without a solid foundation of Jesus' teachings, hearts overflowing with love, and truly humble spirits, we inevitably become full of *ourselves*. When we are satiated with ourselves, good things become addictions and quickly become bad things. Dependence on anything not truly life-giving becomes addiction. Full of ourselves, we find myriads of ways to compromise the truth of love, the conviction of love, and the healing of love. Wealth and violence are intertwined in our world. When we compromise with wealth and power, violence, veiled as it may be with good, chokes us. These thorns choke us, and Jesus says we yield no harvest.

Let's step out from the soil descriptions for a moment. An important question to ask at this point is, Why focus so much attention on the negative response to Jesus? Why use this parable to challenge people to take Jesus and his teaching and ministry seriously?

To answer these questions, we need to ask a similar question: Why does Jesus tell this parable and explain it, including the first three types of soil, so carefully? We find our answer in the extended context of conflict—not just any conflict, but the conflict that eventually cost Jesus his life. To approach a deep level of understanding of this parable, even getting close to how serious this was for Jesus and his followers in the first century, we need to consider that the message is of life-and-death importance. Jesus is naming and calling out the harsh truth of rejection. He is making clear what was at stake for those who will, or will not, hear and see. And it was not just *his* life at stake. It was and is the lives of all his followers, the lives of countless victims of war and cruelty, abuse and neglect, bullying and privilege, bitterness and hopelessness, anger and resentment, murder and persecution, racism and sexism, injustice and inequality, dominance and manipulation. The list of evil in the world goes on and on, all around us!

In this parable, Jesus is holding up a mirror for all to look into and see themselves either rejecting or accepting him—not as their nebulous feel-good savior, but as the Lord over their everyday lives.

Think of the mirror Jesus holds up in front of us as functioning like a divine truth serum. This may seem like a strange mix of metaphors, but the function of the mirror is to force us to see what is true about our hearts. What rules us, what shapes our thinking and feeling, what clouds our judgment, what is the truth about that which lies at the base of our soul? For example, what is so hard about understanding Jesus when he tells us to love our enemies so that we might become children of God (Matt 5:44–45)? Nothing, except that which lies at the base of our souls. Look in the mirror, Jesus says!

It is a big mirror. If, like Jesus, we hold it up and see the true reflection of what is going on in the world today, to put it simply, we mostly see kingdoms of fear and violence. Hopefully, we catch at least a glimpse of the kingdom of God. But in Jesus' mirror those two kingdoms are wholly separate. God is love, and in this love there is no fear. In God's kingdom and God's righteousness there is only love in its many forms. Anything that is not a form of love or that does not flow out of this love is not from or a part of God.

To face the truth about the world around us, and the truth in our hearts, is the first fundamental step toward understanding this parable of the soils. This seems logical and obvious, like the acknowledgment that "the truth will make you free" (John 8:32). Yet I think we find this truth almost impossible to face because to do so would force us to decide once and for all in which kingdom we will live. As long as we can avoid looking in the mirror, we can pretend we live in God's kingdom. As long as we can imagine the parable of the soils as anything *but* a life-and-death matter amid this present world, we can pretend to be good soil. We can pretend to bear the fruit of God's kingdom even though the mirror shows how we compromise with fear and violence every day.

There are many great stories about the epic battle between good and evil. The *Lord of the Rings* trilogy by J. R. R. Tolkien is a good example. Stories like this show there is definitely a spark of recognition in our human hearts when it comes to Jesus and God's kingdom opposing the pain and suffering dealt by some representation of evil. The idea of two kingdoms—God's good kingdom and some contender's evil kingdom—is not unlike the typical epic. Jesus is clear as he teaches this parable that we all must choose which side we are on. Yet with Jesus, there is a fundamental difference, a mind-blowing difference in the kind of battle being waged. We will always love the idea of good triumphing over evil, but we will never know how this actually happens without the teachings and life example of Jesus. *Without Jesus, good in this world wins by using the same tactics as evil.* Good wins by evil means, and while we can hold on to our romantic notions that this evil-doing-good triumphs, the truth is that evil means produce evil results. Violence in any form, no matter how well intended, hurts, injures, kills, maims, intimidates, destroys, dominates, subjugates, diminishes, and enables the continuation of the kingdom of the evil one.

It is important in studying this parable that we pay careful attention to what divides good from evil. Why has the world around Jesus pitted itself against him? What has Jesus' world rejected by rejecting him? The answer is that Jesus has named good and evil without compromising tactics and without some halfway or pretend form of love. He has, with the authority of God, named love, and then named anything else as pretense. This is what he means when he says "the word of the kingdom" (v. 19). He's talking about his words spoken and his example lived out in the previous chapters of Matthew. In every one of the soil descriptions in verses 19–23, Jesus says the soil is the one who "hears the word." But what we do with that word is what divides good from evil. Three soil types fail. Only one soil type hears *and understands*. The odds are stacked against us. If we postmodern people living in the twenty-first century do not "hear the word," understand it, and bear fruit by it, our lives represent one of the first three types of soil.

What of the Fourth Soil?

Finally, some good news! Actually, some *really* good news. In the midst of life-threatening conflict, Jesus describes a fourth type of soil, and the entire parable changes hues before our eyes. Suddenly we catch a glimpse of what motivates Jesus, and of what motivated God to send Jesus in the first place. The gospel of Jesus Christ is, at its core, wonderful news—news that can heal and make whole persons and peoples and nations and our entire world. While conflict is so terribly real in our lives and must be dealt with directly and honestly, the power of God, the power of love, and the power of the kingdom inaugurated by Jesus is one hundred and sixty and thirty times more fruitful. The wonderful news of the harvest is the only part of this parable strong enough to convince me to face enemies with love. It is my life's compass setting—this divine infusion of unconquerable power, this joy unbounded!

The bountiful harvest is why I have named this "a parable of abundance." It is my way of saying no to the powers of evil and yes to the power of God's love. This is why I began this chapter with the story about Mike. I am convinced that this abundance of God's love is continually available, ready and eager to surprise us, waiting with anticipation in the corners and crevices of our world where we traditional Christians too seldom look. God's love is constantly seeping in and emerging, sometimes even storming the gates of our limited perception. Just as we often miss the dangers of the thorns growing all around us, we often seem to live unconscious of God's love blooming all around us in the Mikes and Marys of the world. Wherever there is real love, it is *God's* love.

But we are getting ahead of ourselves. Let's give the last explanation of soil its due.

> But as for what was sown on good soil, this is the one who hears the word and understands it, who indeed bears fruit and yields, in one case a hundredfold, in another sixty, and in another thirty. (Matt 13:23)

This last description of soil and the first one bookend the parable through use of the word *understand* in both places. Comprehension of the word of God's kingdom makes all the difference in one's heart and mind. Whereas with the first soil, there was no understanding in the heart, the key element with the fertile soil is understanding the word of the kingdom, which then leads to the action of bearing the fruit of the kingdom. It's important to recognize that the understanding Jesus is talking about in this parable is not only, or specifically, mental comprehension. Jesus is talking about a heart-level knowing that is interwoven with doing.

We must emphasize again *what* Jesus wants us to comprehend. Was it the rules of first-century religion? Was it the ways the world treats enemies? Was it some form of retaliation or graceless living? Was it something other than unconditional love? Was it simply a thankful heart that feels forgiven because of the cross? Was it the hope that heaven awaits because I say I am a "believer" and go to church? Was it comfort food for those who would solve first-century—or twenty-first-century—problems with violence and coercion?

I trust the questions above make clear how mistaken we are if we think Jesus was speaking about anything but his teachings, his life, and his example. The suggested answers above are so out of place with the life and ministry of Jesus, while the beatitudes he taught in Matthew 5 are the perfect example of what he meant by "the word of the kingdom." Everything Jesus taught and lived leading up to this parable he sums up in the phrase "the word of the kingdom." The core of how he has taught us to pray is all about God's will and way coming to reign on earth through Jesus and being lived out by his followers. The only pathway to follow, the only script we have, the only true alternative to the other kingdoms of the world, is Jesus' word. The Gospel of John goes so far as to say that Jesus *is* the "Word"—the very Word of God (John 1:1). What could be more important than understanding the word of God to such an extent that we can't help but live in the footsteps of the *Word* of God by following the example of Jesus?

But how do we become like the fourth type of soil—receptive to the seed being planted within us, capable of understanding, in a heart-knowing way, the word of God? Look again at the Isaiah 6 text Jesus quotes in Matthew 13:15. Notice the emphasis on the heart: "For this people's heart has grown dull . . . so that they might not . . . understand with their heart and turn. . . ." What could possibly remedy the dullness of our hearts? The healing of hearts is God's job and *only* God's job. It is *our* job to turn back: ". . . turn—and I would heal them" (Matt 13:15); note that "I" here is God. We turn our hearts over to God's heart, because our deep need for healing can only be met by the source and author of love itself. Any action, thought, intent, will, or way of our own will not be fully and truly loving. Our hearts can only be transformed into love by the God who *is* love. Whenever we try to love on our own, from our own heart's depth, our own wounded experience of life will limit us and compromise God's love in us. Remember Jesus' first word from Matthew 4:17, "Repent." *Repent* means "to turn." We must turn from any *semblance* of God's love that the world teaches, to the source of love itself. In this last type of soil, the evil one, trouble and persecution, and the wealth and cares of this world cannot counter the understanding of the word because it has taken root so deep in the heart of the one who has heard it.

Love can simply be a great *idea*, virtuous as a *concept*, yet meaningless within its mental prison. The love of God, on the other hand, is best shown in Jesus' message *and* ministry, culminating at the cross. This is self-sacrificial, giving love; it is active, doing love; it is knowing and doing linked, just as Jesus' instruction was followed by his action. It is this deeply rooted, fruit-bearing love-in-action that has the power to repel and resist the evil one, to overcome the lure of wealth, to stand strong in the face of persecution. It is this fruit-bearing "Word made flesh" (John 1:14) working in us that creates the harvest of abundance!

Finally, in this last example of soil, we have the image of harvest. What is the harvest? Well, it is not "saving souls" for heaven. Rather, the fruit of the word of the kingdom is love incarnate in us, producing hearts and minds—people—that are changed because of God's love working in and through us! This is a very specific kind of fruit!

The fruitful harvest is not about saying the "sinner's prayer" as if it were a magic formula. To bear the fruit of the kingdom we must repent of any other kingdom. We must live in the kingdom of Jesus. Our hearts must soften so we will spend the remainder of our lives leading people to Jesus along with us, and to a repentant, new life bearing the fruit of his words.

The Abundant Harvest

If we come even close to comprehending God's love for us and the world—a love that truly conquers all evil, hatred, violence—it leads us to hear differently, see differently, and understand differently. There is a healing so deep in our hearts as to transform our reality. Life is never the same again. Love becomes our way of life, of hearing and seeing all our surroundings and all people around us. We recognize God's love in the oddest of places. We develop a sixth sense for knowing when God's love is absent or when "love" is not genuine, perhaps purported but not performed. Any hurtful thought or action becomes an affront to our sense of the well-being intended for the world. Our life journey is defined by loving everyone and forgiving everything.

Love has a script to follow. God wrote the script in the person and presentation of Jesus. We have enough, know enough of Jesus to change the world we live in. We find our love script written in Matthew, Mark, Luke, and John's accounts about Jesus. The love Jesus taught and lived produces bountiful harvests. This is how Jesus sums up this parable. If we understand and take this love to heart, Jesus says we, too, will produce the abundance described here.

To imagine the harvest Jesus speaks of, think about how you would live your life if you were unrestricted by worry, fear of rejection or harm, or distractions of any kind. Think of your life unencumbered by anything that might restrict the flow of God's love to you and through you. You are probably thinking that this is impossible, but it is exactly what Jesus has been teaching us. This is the sum of the will and way of God, God's kingdom come on earth, in and through you.

Stop thinking about your life as one lump sum. Stop disbelieving Jesus. Stop believing in violence and pain and death as things with any genuine power. Jesus knew what he was talking about, and he knows your heart and mind better than you do. God created your heart and mind for love, and God knows how to heal your heart and mind from the world's hurts. God knows how to replenish the love in you. Fear of any kind is never, ever a match for God's love, which creates and sustains the very world in which we live. We think fear is too strong for us and for God. We need to confess that we have believed a total lie! God can and does heal any hurt, any pain, any struggle we could possibly face in this world! Jesus has cut through the lies of this world once and for all. He has shown us what we were created to be—images of God's love bearing the bountiful harvest of this love. Nothing can stop us once we understand and bear this fruit. Nothing.

The way in which Jesus ends this parable should prompt us to stand up and shout for joy! He has given us a guarantee. His mission and message taken to heart will produce amazingly. Why are Christians not celebrating and reveling in the extreme transformational power of God's love shown and taught by Jesus? At least part of the answer to this question is that we have mis-defined Jesus' mission and message. We have limited it to things like church membership rolls, attendance numbers at worship, the number of people "saved," how many tracts have been handed out, how many Bible verses have been memorized, how many committee meetings we've attended, right doctrines, rules observed, prayer meetings called, and on and on.

None of the above are really bad things. They are just beside the point, and they mostly distract us from the real point. They are not what produces the bountiful harvest, and they are not the fruit. Too often they serve as discouragements and cause good people to burn out on church and the trappings of religion.

The actual word of the kingdom and the fruit of its harvest are so much simpler and more profound than the things I named above. This is all good news to the extreme! Over all the years the church has existed, we have somehow done the human thing, thinking the mission and message is up to us to figure out, plan, and accomplish. We think the mission and message is something we can wrap our minds around, contain in a sermon or a meeting, and then proclaim to people less connected to God than we are. We have institutionalized, tamed, and systematized something totally illusive to any of these. We have tried to define God's love, and in so doing, we have dumbed it down to look like our practical actions in the world. We have tried to master God's love with the tactics of earthly kingdoms. We have forgotten that Jesus claimed lordship over all things through love. Indeed, we are not the lords of the universe we thought we were. But that's *good* news!

THE SIMPLE AND PROFOUND HARVEST

Several years back, I was pastoring in a rather large congregation. I had been there about six months and had not yet learned to know all the congregants. One night I was eating alone in a local restaurant. I was surprised when my waitress knew my name and referred to me as her pastor. I was vaguely able to place her face among the sea of Sunday morning worshipers I was slowly coming to recognize. But what truly surprised me was that when I picked up the bill at the end of my meal, I found it was marked paid. She had bought my meal on her waitressing salary. She had recognized me, honored me, and given me a totally unexpected gift—one I considered undeserved.

About five years have passed since she paid for my supper. I now live hundreds of miles from that restaurant. You'd think it was not that big a deal. Yet, I cannot forget this kindness. Every so often, something reminds me of her gift. In the life of a pastor, many people show you kindness, but the one I remember most vividly is the meal paid for by the woman waiting my table that night.

That gift came from a loving heart, and that simple act of love affected me more profoundly than I could have imagined at the time. It has stayed with me, gone before me, and challenged my heart. I am at least a slightly better and more loving person because of her simple act of love.

Simple acts of love are profound acts of love. They are the fruit of the word of the kingdom. They produce the plentiful harvest Jesus proclaims. Hearts overflowing with God's love produce the abundant harvest of love God seeks. God sent Jesus to fill our hearts with this love. Jesus' message and mission *are* this love. Humans cannot create it or contain it in our religious "boxes" no matter how hard we try. God's simple and profound love is the real thing. There can be no pretense or substitute, no human legislation of it, and no human limitation of it.

After living and working for many years within the structures of the church, I am not opposed to these structures. I am not saying we should abandon all institutional forms of religion. Not all "old wineskins" (Matt 9:17) are bad. But if we try to put God's boundless love into structures that can no longer contain it, the structures—one way or another—will burst. Then we must allow love to win, our old wineskins to pass away, and new wineskins to be utilized.

Jesus taught us to love in simple and profound ways. He cut through all the trappings of religion in his day, trappings that could not contain God's amazing love. Jesus paved the way for God to re-enter the human heart and transform it into a fountain of God's amazing love. God's love, in its simplicity and its profundity, radically changes life around us. Imagine your life without any enemies, no one to blame or scapegoat, no neighbor to dislike or international regime to despise, no emotional energy needed to hold hurts that lead to bitterness, no need to arm yourself physically or emotionally, no one to fear, no relationships lost because of past pain, no need to take sides against anyone ever again.

Now imagine God's love bursting from your heart and into the world around you. Unfettered by the limitations listed above, this love of God now reigns in and through you. You smile more, laugh more, relax more, and you spread this change like sunlight to the people in your life. Your life becomes a constant flow of love as you seek out people in need, such as the unrecognized, spiritually depressed people in your family, church, and work place. You enter a room and the love of God enters with you. You are a salve to the brokenhearted. You are a worker for justice. You retain the overwhelming power of God's love to hold at bay any desire or thought of violence. You now can enter any conflict situation with an inner peace and calm that helps others ratchet down the rhetoric and impulse of their own violence. You have eyes to see and ears to hear whenever the world proposes actions foreign to God's love. In all the politics, policies, and public displays of human will, you now only see and hear through the eyes and ears of Jesus, his teachings and his understandings. His clarion call to God's loving will and way in this world is alive in you.

Once again, you may be saying that this all sounds nice, but it is not possible. If this is your response, it comes directly from the lies this world has taught you. This is the evil one snatching God's love from you. I have seen and experienced the joy of the above blessings in my life and the lives of Jesus' followers. These are the bountiful harvest. These are the unstoppable bearing of fruit by everyone who hears and understands Jesus' word of the kingdom. These things are the very reason Jesus came to earth, taught us, and lived among us. These are the reason he allowed himself to be tortured and murdered. Jesus simply and profoundly taught and showed us these very blessings! Then he said, "Follow me."

This is what God's amazing love does: it transforms our hurt and pain into the joyful expression of justice, mercy, grace, forgiveness, reconciliation, and peace. This amazing love spreads with a rush as it touches hurting hearts, the people with whom you and I relate every day. *Yet another powerful point of this parable is that the harvest is real!* Yes, the conflict is real, but the harvest is so much *more* real!

Rather than setting the goal of getting the Mikes and Marys in your world to attend church or say a traditional "sinner's prayer," how about simply and profoundly loving them in the blessed name of Jesus? Think about the abundant harvest this love would provide, guaranteed.

LOVE'S ABUNDANCE FLOWS ON

While the parable of the soils is the one that gets the most attention by Matthew in chapter 13, we should note that Jesus tells other parables here as well. In fact, in verse 34 Matthew writes, "Jesus told the crowds all these things in parables; without a parable he told them nothing." From this verse we get a pretty good idea of how important parables were to Jesus as a way to teach, and perhaps we can appreciate the significance of the parable of the soils all the more. This first parable sets the stage for those that follow. They, in turn, enrich and expand the meaning of the first.

In Matthew 13, it seems Jesus was not content to teach only one parable of abundance. Instead, *four more times* he promises the unstoppable harvest of God's love! The key phrase in each of these parables is, again, "the kingdom of heaven," and each of these parables teases out and reveals the truth about the kingdom of God on this earth, here and now. In the additional parables of abundance, he is declaring that God's kingdom of love is the only true kingdom. God's kingdom of love is like:

1. a mustard seed—the smallest of all seeds, but it grows to be great in size (vv. 31–32)

2. yeast that leavens an entire loaf of bread (v. 33)

3. treasure hidden in a field—it brings great joy and is worth the price of everything we have (v. 44)

4. a pearl of great value—again, worth selling everything we have in order to obtain it (v. 45)

Jesus is saying in various ways that the harvest of God's will and way of love is unstoppable, and the value of the will and way of God's amazing love is beyond compare to anything else we might possess.

Why this need to keep hammering on the abundance, the growth, the value, and the surety of the kingdom of heaven? We obviously need convincing. To really believe Jesus, we need all the help he can give us. This is why he takes a variety of opportunities to illustrate God's loving will and way, hoping to finally get us to understand with our hearts. In a world of hurt, pain, and violence, we have learned to accept and live with adaptations based on the same hurt, pain, and violence. We know no other options, and we accept no other options. Anyone suggesting that love is the only way out of our human dilemma is branded a simpleton. This is why almost everyone turns aside from Jesus when he teaches love of enemies. We do not actually believe God's love is the answer, so we do not believe the salvation Jesus offers.

In all this kingdom-parable talk, it is time for the weary peace-and-justice workers, the discouraged mourners of embittered rivalries, the heartsick souls hoping beyond hope for relief from retaliation, and the politically exasperated seeking a way out of partisan politics to consume the quenching waters of joy and renewed determination. *The present rule of God's love is the surest thing in which you will ever participate.* It is God's amazing love available to us and through us that offers the same good news of salvation Jesus offered the world of the first century.

OUR PERSONAL EXPERIENCE OF GOD'S HARVEST OF LOVE

The parables of Jesus challenge us with critical lessons illustrating the power and guarantee of God's loving will and way in our earthly life. While we live this life, we will never become perfect conduits of God's love; nevertheless, God's kingdom come transforms us and life around us every time we allow it. The change happens something like this:

Believing God's Love Can Heal You

When we come to the end of our own efforts to satisfy life's longings, we come to the place where all the wounds we have ever endured can be submitted for transformation. This is truly a turning point necessary in each of our lives. This is a place of self-emptiness, a dark and dangerous place to walk spiritually, a place of desperation and deep longing, a place of unknowing, a place that calls for great inner courage. It is a place where we carry our pain openly in outstretched arms, carefully lay it down before God, and back away.

Allowing God's Love to Heal You

We stand in God's presence while the pain lies at a distance. We feel totally vulnerable and alone because we are used to using our pain as a crutch as we limp through this hostile world. We have relied on it as justification for our actions and beliefs, for living in anger and hatred, for relying on violence instead of trusting God's love. Without this crutch, we stand trembling in fear of falling into an endless abyss. But finally we are willing to admit that enough is enough. We have concluded that carrying pain is the lie of all lies, the accumulation of the world's addictions forcing their will on our heart.

It's tempting to return to our pain and pick it up again. But here we must keep believing Jesus, knowing it is he who has invited us to this place. He is the one who cleared the way for us to find our repentant moment, the turning point in God's timing for our life.

We feel something stir in us like a slight shudder of the earth. Now, before we have any sense of it, we are falling, but not into an abyss. It is a warm ocean, outstretched arms of eternal embrace. In this enveloping and swelling tide, we realize, like Job experiencing God's presence, "I had heard of you from a distance, but now I see you face to face" (Job 42:5, my paraphrase). We are welcomed home by God's pure love, and it is overwhelming.

Hearing and Seeing God's Love Everywhere

We live in a different place now. Like rising to the top of a mountain, we see and hear and understand from a fully transformed perspective. We see through the lens of God's love, and nothing in our experience of this world is the same as it was before. Our understanding is aligned with God's heart—that same heart that created and sustains all life, the heart that loved the world into place and keeps loving it in its place. Yes, the world still turns on its addiction to violence; cruelties continue; life in the trenches goes on. But our hearts no longer accept this reality as ultimate truth. Our hearts refuse to return to the pile of pain. Our hearts thrive on God's loving embrace of it all, even the worst of the worst. Everything now is understood from within this embrace of God's love.

Living Thankfully

In the deepest recesses of our hearts, we now know for certain that God's amazing love is eternal, and it lives in us as we live in this world. Sure, doubts and failings will come and go within our lives, but these cannot change the certainty of love on which our lives are now founded. There is now a permanent smile in our hearts. It is often evident in our walk and in our talk. We simply cannot hide a thankful heart. To fully know God's amazing love is to have full assurance that regardless of what tragedies or disasters befall, we are safe in God's love. I know this is not logical, but it is the truth, because God's love is the truth. Out of assurance flows gratitude, and it is unstoppable. Any heart filled with God's love is a heart rejoicing in the experience of life because now that heart knows life as surrounded by God's love—divine arms stretched open and a caress like a warm ocean.

Spreading God's Love

By now, we are out of control (in a good way)! Loving life is the demeanor with which we greet the day and how we watch the sun set. Religion is not important. Loving and sharing God's love is the whole point of life. The only rule is love, and it now flows from our hearts as if from the very DNA that makes us who we are. It does not come from a script handed to us. We live and share the abundance of love Jesus has described in the parables of abundance. We no longer have a "strategy" for sharing our faith because life itself is opportunity enough. There is not one moment of one day for the rest of our lives when we need to wonder about how and when to share God's love, because the answer is forever *yes!* Imagine never needing to convince someone about faith or God. Now, simply—and profoundly—loving them is the sum of faith and God. We are spreading the heart of God to everyone all the time.

Watching God's Love Grow

Here is perhaps the pinnacle of faith in God: trusting that God's love is enough to recreate the world and all relationships in it. Violence is not necessary. This is what Jesus has promised in the parables of abundance. The harvest is sure. The mustard seed will grow huge. The leaven will spread throughout. The joy of God's loving kingdom is worth all the gold in all the world, all other things we might ever hope for, and all the pearls of lesser price. It is this simple: if God is God, then God's love will grow. Whenever and wherever we plant God's love, the harvest swells around us and spreads out from us. There is no greater blessing than watching God's love grow.

8

IS THERE A LIMIT TO FORGIVENESS?

We begin this chapter in approximately the middle of Matthew 18. I suppose this is as good a place to start as any, since forgiveness is a vast ocean to sail. Many people make the mistake of thinking they understand forgiveness, yet forgiveness is not so much something to understand as something to live. Too often our conclusions about forgiveness have restrained the living of it. Some of our conclusions have, in fact, walled us off from forgiveness completely. When we leave God's forgiveness out of our living, we wander life's ocean directionless. Whatever wind comes upon us will blow us on an ill-fated path of unresolved pain.

Part of why forgiveness is hard to live and easy to wall ourselves off from is because it is so utterly personal. In nearly every instance where forgiveness is sought or evaded, the trail of emotional bread crumbs leads back to us. We will explore the deeply personal nature of forgiveness and seek the courage to be vulnerable enough to embrace God's forgiveness in new and more meaningful ways. Hopefully, then, we will discover the healing power not only of being *forgiven* but of being *forgiving*.

THE HUMAN QUESTION

Peter asked Jesus, "Lord, if another member of the church sins against me, how often should I forgive? As many as seven times?" (Matt 18:21)

This is an important question because of both what is said and what is not said. First, let's look at what is said. Peter's question is stated conditionally. The word *if* is peculiar when we are honest about human relationships. Has there ever really been any question about just how inevitable sin is? Would it not be more accurate to ask, "*When* a brother or sister sins against me . . . "? Though Peter may not have intended it, the conditional use of *if* seems a subtle form of denial, which is in keeping with the long human legacy of denial in dealing with conflicts and the need for forgiveness.

We begin here by acknowledging that people—even in our most cherished relationships—do hurt us, use us, misunderstand us, say wrong things about us, and misjudge us. This is a problem, Lord! What are we to do about it? Was this perhaps what Peter was trying to say?

Peter's question leaves open a potential limit to forgiveness. Surely this is our question too. There *has* to be a limit, right? We often call this limit to forgiveness "justice." Somebody sins, somebody pays. Right? Peter's question about forgiveness could easily be based on what he knows of Old Testament law. We well know the saying "an eye for an eye" (Exo 21:23; Lev 24:19–20). In Old Testament law there were many such severe repercussions for sins. Where does forgiveness fit in with the laws of justice?

While Old Testament law served the purpose of limiting retaliation, it did not address transactions of the human heart. When my neighbor's ox gores my child, does killing the ox or retaliating more directly against my neighbor heal my heart? When a rapist or murderer is put away for life, does this bring true healing to the heart of the victim or the victim's family? Where does forgiveness fit in?

Why is Peter even thinking about this? Why ask about forgiveness at all? Isn't meting out justice enough? Well, think about who Peter has been hanging out with. Think about what Peter has been learning from the instructions and actions of Jesus.

Why is Peter asking this question of Jesus? Why not simply review scripture? Why not ask around next time he's at synagogue? A likely answer comes from his direct experience of Jesus' teaching and healing ministry. Also, remember how Peter confessed in Matthew 16:16 that Jesus was "the Messiah, the Son of the living God." By now (two chapters later), Peter recognizes Jesus as so much more than any other religious authority. It would seem natural for Peter to bring a question that troubled him to "the Son of the living God."

The most specific answer to why Peter asked Jesus this question likely comes from the immediate context in Matthew 18. Jesus has just finished describing a process of reconciliation between members of the church. In a sense, Jesus himself initiated the conversation on forgiveness. Not surprising: forgiveness was very important to Jesus.

Now let's consider what is *not* said in Peter's question. Peter did not ask how many times his brother or sister should forgive *him*. Nor did he ask how many times he should *ask* for forgiveness. Far too often when there are issues or conflicts between people, the "offended" party convinces themselves they have done nothing wrong. Or they downplay their role in the conflict while focusing on the "sins" of the other. I would argue that Peter's question and Jesus' answer are at least as concerned with Peter's *own* sin—and, by extension, ours—as with the sin of others. As I said earlier, the emotional bread crumbs in our struggle to forgive lead back to our own heart. *Forgiveness, in perhaps its most raw and revealed nature, is a process concerning our healed or unhealed heart.*

TRACING FORGIVENESS THROUGH THE TEACHING AND MINISTRY OF JESUS

What, specifically, has led up to Peter's question? Let's do a quick run-through of what Jesus has taught and done concerning forgiveness so far in Matthew. It turns out to be quite a lot!

1. The initial preaching of good news and healing of "every disease and every sickness among the people" (4:23). Given the first-century belief that disease was the result of sin, to heal people prompted questions about God's forgiveness.

2. "Blessed are the merciful, for they will receive mercy" (5:7). Think about the ways mercy relates to grace and forgiveness.

3. "Blessed are those who are persecuted for righteousness' sake, for theirs is the kingdom of heaven" (5:10). Jesus was speaking of situations where, clearly, people would be sinning against his followers. What is his instruction lacking? Where is retaliation? Where is justice? Perhaps justice comes in the form of all the blessings of living in the kingdom, and not in some form of vindication.

4. In summing up all the beatitudes, Jesus declares that these good works of living the beatitudes "give glory to your Father in heaven" (5:16). Many, if not most, of Jesus' listeners would have had plenty of reason to be angry, jealous, resentful, vindictive, and longing for justice. Jesus makes no mention of these things; rather, he speaks blessings on those who would bless others.

5. In 5:21–26 Jesus puts an end to any thought of staying angry, acting in anger, accusing in anger. He places reconciliation between brothers and sisters first, even before seeking reconciliation with God. He severely warns us against the dangers of not reconciling. How could reconciliation possibly happen without forgiveness?

6. In 5:38–42 Jesus gets more specific regarding what to do when faced with an evildoer. Perhaps Jesus should have answered Peter's question about forgiveness in chapter 18 by repeating this instruction from chapter 5. Here he spells out his fulfillment-of-the-law equivalent of retaliation. He transforms the situation of being "[sinned] against" (to use Peter's words, 18:21) into an opportunity to love and serve the one who has sinned.

7. As we have discussed earlier, 5:43–48 sums up Jesus' fulfillment of the law and the prophets. There is no way to love and pray for enemies without forgiving them. Add to this astounding reversal of human nature Jesus' declaration that this is God's way and should be ours because of divine and complete love.

8. The Lord's Prayer (Matt. 6:9–13) and Jesus' additional instruction in verses 14–15, presents his most pointed teaching on forgiveness yet. Our spiritual

well-being itself depends on our willingness to forgive. Without forgiving others, we cannot experience God's forgiveness.

9. In chapter 7:1–5, Jesus strictly warns against judging others. Here we get his take on that emotional and spiritual bread-crumb trail mentioned earlier. He makes clear how accusing someone else often (maybe always) reflects back on us. Jesus defines as hypocrites those who will not deal with what is in their own heart.

10. The "golden rule" is well known (Matt 7:12). Who among us does not desire forgiveness from others? "Doing" to others surely involves granting forgiveness.

11. At the end of chapter 7, Jesus emphasizes and re-emphasizes the importance of doing the will of his Father and acting on the words he has taught. Without taking his teachings to heart, our lives are destroyed, like the house built on the sand (7:27). As we have seen in the passages listed above, Jesus clearly taught the importance of forgiveness. To not obey his teachings on forgiveness would amount to our own destruction.

12. Chapter 9 begins with the story of Jesus healing a paralyzed man (9:2–8), declaring outright the forgiveness of his sins. This pronouncement illustrates the linkage between forgiveness and healing. We would be remiss to not view all Jesus' healings as stories of God's grace, mercy, and forgiveness.

13. Previously we looked closely at the story of the calling of Matthew and the party at his house (9:9–13). Consider what Jesus offered Matthew and all those attending the party. He reached out to them in their state of sin and showed God's welcoming love. Jesus offered them forgiveness.

14. Consider Jesus' saying concerning new wine and old wineskins (9:16–17). How might forgiveness fit into this? If part of the old wineskins is the Old Testament laws of retaliation, it makes perfect sense that Jesus' teachings and examples of love, mercy, and forgiveness are new wine bursting the old skins.

15. The final verses of chapter 9 again chronicle Jesus' proclamation of the "good news of the kingdom" and his "curing every disease and every illness" (v. 35). Then it says, "When he saw the crowds, he had compassion for them, because they were harassed and helpless, like sheep without a shepherd" (v. 36). The compassionate message and ministry of Jesus are the good news of God's kingdom come into this world! Pretty much all of Jesus' ministry was taken to the people. This is directly opposite to the religious expectation that forgiveness was a transaction that could only take place at the altar in the temple in Jerusalem.

16. In chapter 10, Jesus sent his disciples out on a mission patterned after his own. Again, the kingdom of God was brought directly to the people with good news and healings of all kinds. This is a freely given gift of the kingdom where God's

mercy and invitation to relationship reign. "You received without payment; give without payment" (v. 8). Think of the threat Jesus' message and ministry were to the sacrificial system of his day. The sacrificial system, with its expected "payments," found itself under full attack by Jesus. Why would anyone want to return to the old system for obtaining forgiveness once they discovered the realities of God's kingdom come in Jesus?

17. There is much in chapter 11 we don't have space to go into. That said, considering all we have listed above, read verses 28–30. What a wonderful invitation Jesus made to all people. After years of trying to placate a God who seemed distant, think of what it would be like to suddenly find that God is not distant at all, but right there, offering you a gentle and humble heart and providing rest for your soul. How could God's welcome not include the free offer of forgiveness?

18. Amid the healings Jesus performs in chapter 12, Matthew quotes from Isaiah 42. This, in part, explains why Jesus wanted his healing ministry kept quiet. But the passage from Isaiah twice refers to God's servant's justice—". . . he will proclaim justice to the Gentiles"; ". . . until he brings justice to victory" (vv. 18 and 20)—and Matthew here indicates that this servant is Jesus. Think about God's justice as the offer of forgiveness and rest for our souls. This is the nature of God revealed to us by Jesus.

19. Read the parable of the lost sheep as Jesus briefly told it in 18:12–13. Of the one hundred sheep, the one that has "gone astray" gets the shepherd's (God's) sole attention. This is just the latest example of God's unrelenting pursuit of "sinners." God's desire to offer love and forgiveness is surely the motivation for the seeking.

When all these examples are added together, we see the overwhelming grace and mercy of God taught and lived by Jesus, and Jesus clearly saying that we must live this way as well. Peter has been hearing and experiencing this overwhelming mercy and grace throughout his time with Jesus. Slowly, Peter's personal hold on retributive justice has eroded and forced the human question "Is there a limit to forgiveness?"

RECONCILIATION WITHIN THE FAITH COMMUNITY—MATTHEW 18:15–20

In the early verses of Matthew 18, Jesus placed great emphasis on the careful treatment of children to illustrate how his disciples were to care for others in general. Further along, he declared God's intent that not one sheep be lost. Seeking the lost, along with humble and loving care given to the "least" in God's kingdom, is the way of Jesus.

These earlier instructions of Jesus set the stage for what he says here about a process for reconciliation:

> "If another member of the church sins against you, go and point out the fault when the two of you are alone. If the member listens to you, you have regained that one. But if you are not listened to, take one or two others along with you, so that every word may be confirmed by the evidence of two or three witnesses. If the member refuses to listen to them, tell it to the church; and if the offender refuses to listen even to the church, let such a one be to you as a Gentile and a tax collector." (Matt 18:15–17)

The object of this passage is reconciliation. Reconciliation is not the same thing as forgiveness, but they are closely related. According to this passage, in a situation of sinning against a brother or sister, reconciliation is always the goal but is not always attainable. Forgiveness, on the other hand, is always the goal *and* is always attainable.

One reason to look at this passage specifically in relation to forgiveness is to challenge interpretations of these verses that call for some form of disciplinary action, like excommunication (formal or informal). To counter such interpretations, the full trajectory of Jesus' message and ministry of forgiveness must be brought to bear; thus, the carefully listed examples above. Without Jesus' overall message of forgiveness, these present verses can easily be misinterpreted and used against an offending party.

Let's be clear about the intent of the reconciliation process outlined by Jesus. It is all about *seeking the one lost sheep*. It is all about God's desire that "not . . . one of these little ones should be lost" (Matt 18:14). In verse 15, Jesus now places the heart of our shepherding God into the situation of conflict among brothers and sisters in the faith community. Whatever the issue, hurt, or trespass, as members of the faith community we are obligated to do everything possible to reconcile with an offending party. The responsibility to begin and continue restoring relationship is ours. We are, clearly, not to *wait* for the other to come to us. Nor are we to, in any way, force the other to comply. They are free agents; our responsibility lies with *us*, not them. We who are to love enemies, turn the other cheek, and forgive as God forgives us—*we* are the ones whose job is reconciliation. To quote Paul, "All this is from God, who reconciled us to himself through Christ, and has given us the ministry of reconciliation" (2 Cor 5:18). Furthermore, Paul goes on to say that this reconciliation of God is for the whole world. He then adds that we are to be ambassadors for Christ in this reconciliation ministry. Nowhere in this ministry of reconciliation is a limit placed on God's mission or ours. Reconciliation of the whole world is God's goal in Christ and is to be our goal as ambassadors of Christ.

There is a certain history in the Christian church of using Matthew 18:15–17 to formally or informally enforce discipline, ban, or even excommunication against offending parties. Today, many formal and informal means persist of banning people who either offend us or believe differently than we do. For the most part, this banning produces separation and the opposite of reconciliation. Even in cases where a ban is placed with the sincere intention of reconciliation, this often fails. The various formal or informal forms of excluding others are typically veiled attempts to control them.

Even when these forms of exclusion seem to succeed, the results can be people united with a faith community not out of love, but as a result of fear and control.

So if these verses do not support exclusion of someone from the faith community, what might Jesus mean when he says, "If the member refuses to listen to them, tell it to the church; and if the offender refuses to listen even to the church, let such a one be to you as a Gentile and a tax collector" (Matt 18:17)?

Treating People as Jesus Treated Them

This would be a good time to consider whether we truly want to hear and see Jesus. Is his way of unconditional love and grace growing in the depths of our hearts? Are we committed to and actively engaged in loving enemies? Have we let go of our hurts, our anger, and our deep-seated disappointments regarding people in our relationship circles? Have we humbled ourselves spiritually to the extent that the Holy Spirit guides our thoughts and actions in any tension-filled exchange with a sister or brother? Can we allow God's Holy Spirit to freely work in the heart of the other? Can we trust God that much?

It will help our understanding of Jesus to recall some of his actions in the chapters preceding our present text. In chapter 8, Jesus healed the Roman centurion's servant, saying of the centurion, "Truly I tell you, in no one in Israel have I found such faith" (Matt 8:10). Jesus chose Matthew, a tax collector, as one of his twelve disciples (Matt 9:9). He then partied at Matthew's house with many other tax collectors and sinners. Jesus' ministry focused significantly on reaching out to crowds, outcasts, and sinners.

The problem with any form of ban or exclusion of "sinners," or our withdrawal from them, is that anything less than love, healing, and outreach toward them ignores the mission and ministry of Jesus. Simply put, how could Jesus be telling us here to treat Gentiles and tax collectors any differently than *he* did? If we are not steeped in Jesus' will and way, we cannot understand his intent in this instruction. Jesus never banned or excluded *anyone*. Let's not misuse a teaching of his to treat people in ways Jesus would never have done.

I know some people will want to contest the above conclusion, saying this leaves the church vulnerable to sin and to terrible doctrine. I understand this fear. Yet, as 1 John 4:18 says, "There is no fear in love, but perfect love casts out fear; for fear has to do with punishment, and whoever fears has not reached perfection in love." The point is that fear and punishment are the wrong answers to conflict among sisters and brothers in the church. The right answer comes in the form of love—not easy love, not simplistic love, and not warm-fuzzy love.

Continuing in the Context of Reconciliation

> [Jesus continued,] "Truly I tell you, whatever you bind on earth will be bound in heaven, and whatever you loose on earth will be loosed in heaven. Again, truly I tell you, if two of you agree on earth about anything you ask, it will be done for you by my Father in heaven. For where two or three are gathered in my name, I am there among them." (Matt 18:18–20)

Too often the verses above, which follow the text about reconciliation in the faith community, have been taken out of context. The terms *binding* and *loosing* have been used for any number of decisions and actions Christians wish to take. At times, this binding-and-loosing process seems to be viewed as license to put God's stamp on anything *we* wish to authorize, even when it creates more division and hurt. We tell ourselves that if a few faithful agree on anything, we have the right to act with the authority of our Father in heaven. We regularly affirm ourselves as we gather with two or more in prayer, believing we are gathered in Jesus' name. We mistakenly think this gives us the right to pray for anything we want.

I'm not saying the above conclusions are *always* wrong; I'm saying they are wrong when understood out of context.

Jesus' repeated use of the phrase "truly I tell you" signals both the importance of this instruction and its connection to verses 15–17. In the broadest sense, the context of verses 18–20 is God's ministry of reconciliation for all the world. In the specific sense, the context is the reconciliation process between sisters and brothers in the faith community.

In addition, the meaning of this passage is bathed in the authority (name) and presence of Jesus (v. 20). It is imperative that we understand these last three verses of Jesus' instruction in full light of his ministry and mission. For if we are to be about deciding heavenly things, they must align completely with him. We will address forgiveness more fully in the next section. For now, simply know that without forgiveness reigning in our hearts, what we do and decide will not align with heaven. Without forgiveness reigning in our hearts, our connection with heaven is broken (Matt 6:14–15). In an atmosphere without full forgiveness, binding and loosing becomes no less than a further type of sin (separation from God and others).

Let's remember that Matthew 18:15–20 is about reconciling with our sisters and brothers. Jesus was not handing out blanket statements about how Christians are to make decisions. He was explaining a process for bringing hurting souls back together with God and one another. No matter the context or the amount of hurt and pain between people, Jesus would have us be out there seeking the one lost sheep. How we treat "strays," how we pray for them, how we bind and loose them will ultimately show whether God's unconditional love for strays resides in our hearts—or not. *It is always a terrible mistake to invoke heaven and the name of Jesus through our actions and prayers while ignoring the full message of reconciliation and forgiveness throughout*

Jesus' life and ministry. We simply must consider how our thoughts and actions can best model everything Jesus taught and lived. It is easy to live Jesus' love when things go well in the faith community. But it becomes *imperative* to live Jesus' love when tensions arise, for this is the true test of God's love within our hearts.

Replacing Any Ban with God's Love

If for even one moment we think Jesus was just a warm-fuzzy guy, we have not carefully read the gospels. It is important to know that God's love is *real* love. God's love, as taught and shown by Jesus, is the ultimate challenge to division and separation. This real love of God flows powerfully even in the face of the worst evil possible. God's love is never punitive, vengeful, or weak. God's love is always love in action. It is, in fact, at its best when challenged by any sort of separation from God and others. Therefore, formal or informal shunning, banning, or separation of people is foreign to all Jesus taught and lived.

Consider the shepherd who discovered that one sheep out of the one hundred in his care was outside the fold and lost (Matt 18:12–13). If this shepherd had practiced some form of shunning, he would have left the one stray sheep to fend for itself until, hopefully, it wandered home on its own. In fact, the shepherd would have instructed the other sheep to also ignore the lost sheep. The point would then have been to teach the lost sheep a lesson, right? That lesson today is: "We will forgive you if you come home. We will love you if you return to the fold. Our love is conditional on your change of heart and mind." This is the opposite of what Jesus taught in the parable of the lost sheep. It is also the opposite of the gospel message in general: "When we were dead through our trespasses, [God] made us alive together with Christ" (Eph 2:5).

All this thought of separation or shunning would not be so important to this chapter on forgiveness if it wasn't so pervasive in human relationships. Who can honestly say they have not "banned" someone from their life, ignored someone, left someone on their own to "see the light" and repent, or decided to whitewash the conflict separating them from others? We might call this form of banning "sweeping it under the rug." When we do this, we risk blocking forgiveness from our hearts and reconciliation from our relationship.

So, what does it mean to apply God's love in a situation where a sister or brother has strayed? What does it mean to bind and loose a member of the faith community? How are we to pray in Jesus' name for the wandering soul out on their own somewhere?

Years ago, my wife and I were sharing a three-quarter-time pastorate in a church of around fifty people. About six months into our time with this congregation, we discovered that the congregational chairperson had become deeply involved with sexually inappropriate behavior involving teenage girls. In addition to the damage to his victims, his behavior destroyed his marriage and left our small congregation in great pain and disbelief. Since there were several teenage girls in the congregation, this problem brought with it much fear for their well-being anytime we gathered.

As a group, we did a lot of praying and soul-searching. We brought in a professional sexual-abuse counselor to help us work through our pain and take appropriate steps as we attempted to disciple our brother who had strayed. Following a careful congregational healing process, we embarked on a journey of reconciliation with our brother that went like this:

1. We asked our brother to temporarily refrain from meeting with us. This was to provide temporary safety for the girls and families in our group.

2. We continued to relate to this brother, care for him, and show our love for him.

3. After long and careful processing, we decided we would again welcome him and embrace him as a member of our community.

4. Once we came to a place of healing ourselves, we formed a plan to include our brother fully in our faith community while also providing both healing for him and safety for us. This plan included counseling for the brother. It also included an accountability group of three men from our congregation. This group was to walk with the brother through his healing process. This group would also ensure that the brother was never left alone in a situation where any in our congregation would be vulnerable to a sexual encounter with him.

5. As the male pastor on staff, I was tasked with spending time with the brother, helping him to understand both the continued love of the congregation and the seriousness of the road to recovery.

I would like to say that after years of counseling and careful accountability, our brother was fully restored to our faith community. Instead, he chose not to remain with us. This was a great loss to us as a congregation and, I believe, a great loss to him. The good news, and the reason I tell this story, is that as a congregation, we discovered a way to work through our pain, reach out sincerely to the offender, take the sin seriously, fully forgive him, and do our best to reconcile with him. It would have been so much easier to impose a full and permanent ban on our brother while ignoring the depth of our pain and the necessary process for healing. All the while, we would have missed the deep lesson of forgiveness required for our spiritual and emotional well-being. We would also have missed the chance to show God's true nature of love to our brother.

A traditional understanding of the concept of binding and loosing is that of withholding (retaining) forgiveness and offering forgiveness (John 20:23). But another interpretation, more consistent with Jesus' life and teachings, would be to hold up the standard of love in *both* the binding and the loosing. The binding in the example I shared was to stand firm against sexual abuse of young girls (evil in any form) while holding the abuser accountable. The loosing was to release the love of God in a fully forgiving process with potential to heal both us and the offender. In this way, the binding and loosing process is not focused on exclusion or inclusion; rather, binding and loosing represent a holistic process of redemption, maintaining Jesus' clear emphasis on seeking the lost with God's unconditional love. I contend that in Jesus' teaching and in the example of his life, we have a clear illustration of binding and loosing that always seeks to restore people in loving relationship with God and with one another.

Simply put, binding, or retaining, is the process of clearly identifying the boundaries of what is and is not God's love. Loosing is the process that provides a path forward to love and restoration of relationship. It is crucial to notice Jesus' words in verse 18: he said "whatever," not "whoever." Jesus was not specifically speaking about *people*. This has been missed for too many generations of the church. What an amazing statement of Jesus we now discover—God's ever-redemptive love is to be displayed in the binding and loosing *on earth as in heaven*. The redemptive love and the will of God are to be enacted the same way on earth as they are in heaven. In the church of Jesus Christ, the distance between heaven and earth narrows as we reach out to the offending sister or brother in consistently redemptive ways.

In verse 18, Jesus is not saying we have the choice to forgive or not forgive the sinner; this would contradict his instruction to Peter just a few verses later. If we put these present verses in the context of seeking the lost, loving enemies, calling tax collectors to be disciples, and Jesus' constant outreach to all, we would more easily see the consistency of dealing authoritatively with sin and redemptively with the sinner. Now, in the name of Jesus, his teaching and his ministry, two or three of us can gather in prayer intending to bind ourselves to the hearts of all offenders regardless of the offense.

AN EVER-EXPANDING FORGIVENESS—MATTHEW 18:21–22

> Then Peter came and said to him, "Lord, if another member of the church sins against me, how often should I forgive? As many as seven times?" Jesus said to him, "Not seven times, but, I tell you, seventy-seven times." (Matt 18:21–22)

In the beginning pages of this chapter, I was a little too hard on Peter. In Matthew 18:21, Peter asks a good question. With the Hebrew understanding of 7 as the perfect number, Peter is probably not asking Jesus if he can stop forgiving after seven times. I appreciate the clarity Ulrich Luz brings to this verse as he states, "That Peter suggests forgiving seven times does not mean, therefore, that he wants to grant his brother only a limited forgiveness. Instead, the sense of Peter's question is: 'Is perfect forgiveness expected of me?'"[1]

In fairness to Peter, it seems he has already come a long way toward understanding Jesus' teaching on forgiveness, non-retaliation, and radical love. Perhaps his

---

1. Luz, *Matthew*, 2:465.

question is a way of asking if he has really been hearing and understanding Jesus correctly. (You may find it helpful to review the nineteen examples from Jesus' teaching and ministry listed earlier in this chapter.) Peter has heard and seen Jesus teach and live these things. He has acknowledged Jesus as the Messiah and the Son of the living God. Surely he was putting all this together in his mind, along with Jesus' most recent teaching on reconciliation (Matt 18:15–20). I can only imagine that Peter remains amazed by what he hears and sees Jesus do! Here, then, he is basically asking, "Jesus, are you honestly saying I need to forgive completely, all the time, in every situation?"

If we think about it, Peter's question should startle us. Can we imagine forgiving completely, all the time, in every situation? This question should frighten us. What if God's answer is *yes*? Where would that leave us? How could we continue to hold on to hurt, frustration, or resentment? That separate room in our heart where we hide these things would suddenly need to be cleaned out. A lot would have to change about how we negotiate relationships with others.

Jesus could have answered Peter with a simple yes. Instead, he chose to erase any remaining doubt in Peter's mind about the full extent of forgiveness required. Jesus did not just say yes; he said a resounding *YES*! Again from Luz: "The most perfect, boundlessly infinite, countlessly repeated forgiveness is demanded of Peter."[2] I wonder if Peter fell over from shock when he heard this! Maybe we should join him on the ground.

A Practical Application of Forgiveness

During the years I was a pastor, I did a lot of marriage and pre-marriage counseling. One of the most helpful tools I used with almost every couple was a simple circle. On a whiteboard or easel, I would draw a large circle. Then I would ask the couple to tell me about a repeated conflict in their relationship, something that never seemed to get fully resolved, something that would either regularly or periodically repeat itself and leave them once more at odds with each other. I never met a couple who could not immediately think of one or more of these unresolved conflicts.

Once we had established an ongoing conflict they were experiencing, I asked them to describe the sequence of the conflict, how it started, who did or said what, how it escalated, and how it ended. Again, every couple was able to easily identify the stages of the conflict, and even though they were describing a conflict *between* them, they were always able to *agree* on the stages. They knew the conflict well.

As they described the stages of conflict, I would write these into the circle in the order the couple gave. I put arrows showing the direction of the sequence from the top of the circle, clockwise all the way around to the end of the conflict, back up at the top of the circle just to the left of the beginning point. Once this was done and the couple could look at it, they confirmed my accuracy every time.

2. Luz, *Matthew*, 2:465.

Of course, the so-called end of the conflict was never really the end. It was just where they ended up leaving it each time, unresolved. The whole point of this exercise was for them to be able to visualize the repeated cycle of conflict, and for me to be able to tell them they could choose to speak or act differently at any point in the cycle. At any point, they could break the cycle and end it. They were not constrained to endlessly re-cycling their conflict.

I use this illustration of the conflict cycle to suggest that we all live within relationships where we experience conflict. Even if we avoid or ignore the conflict, the potential is there for it to emotionally and spiritually harm us and others. Hurts left unresolved always come back around. Not only do they harm our relationship with the party with whom we are in conflict; they also harm our ability to function as a fully healed person within our other relationships. I know of no one who lives completely free of ongoing conflicts with others. Thus, we all need practical ways to break the cycles of conflict that ensnare us.

One practical way to break a conflict cycle is forgiveness. This does not mean there will always be reconciliation between parties. What it does mean is that the forgiving one will speak and act differently during one or more of the circular stages of the conflict. When this happens, the conflict cycle is disrupted and the door to reconciliation is opened.

The Resounding Yes That Ends All Conflict Cycles

In Matthew 18:22, Jesus leaves no doubt about God's will and way in this world. Let's not forget what we have been learning about the kingdom of the heavens and how all that Jesus taught and lived illustrated this kingdom come to earth. Now, as Jesus answers Peter, he makes clear that God's will and way, God's kingdom come, is total and complete forgiveness in every situation and relationship in which we will ever find ourselves. Jesus is a master at not giving us wiggle room to slip out of our kingdom-of-God commitments!

If we look back at verse 17, we see that it is important that we apply this total, uncompromising forgiveness especially to folks who offend us and then choose to remain apart from us. How better to keep the door of reconciliation open to them than to relate to them from a stance of full forgiveness. There is no better leverage toward reconciliation than loving forgiveness shown in all the ways we speak and act toward an offender! If we can live out this loving forgiveness with offenders, it will alter the hard-wiring of our own brains and hearts. We will be able to recognize the offense not as against *us*, but as against God's way of love. We will be able to live within the redemption of God's love while extending God's love open-handedly to the offender. Jesus is telling us to never withdraw that extended hand. We will not always do this perfectly, but Jesus expects us to always do it. In so doing, we permanently step outside of whatever conflict cycles we have entered.

The Expanding of Forgiveness within Us

Perhaps a deeper way to hear Peter's question in 18:21 and Jesus' answer in 18:22 is to think of the ways we take offense. There seem to be unlimited occasions to take offense—from someone cutting us off in traffic, to when we feel unheard or ignored, to hearing an unkind word directed our way, and a whole host of more egregious sins against us. In addition, we daily experience the frustrations of life in general, and we struggle to not take these personally. Sometimes it feels like life itself is conspiring against us.

The way Peter asks the question—"If my sister or brother sins against me . . ."—we assume the sin and the automatic nature of taking offense. This happens so often that we believe that taking offense at a sin against us is a given. But it is not. If we plan to follow Jesus' instruction on total forgiveness, we will need to deal directly with our own problem of feeling offended. To learn to approach life from a stance of full forgiveness means to learn ways to lay down our defenses against offense. We will need to discover new ways to be spiritually and emotionally whole even in the face of insult and injury. Remember the blessing Jesus pronounced on us with the eighth beatitude:

> Blessed are those who are persecuted for righteousness' sake, for theirs is the kingdom of heaven. Blessed are you when people revile you and persecute you and utter all kinds of evil against you falsely on my account. Rejoice and be glad, for your reward is great in heaven, for in the same way they persecuted the prophets who were before you." (Matt 5:10–12)

God has a blessing waiting for those who withstand attack, insult, and persecution.

This idea of approaching life from a position of no defense is huge. Completely letting our guard down in this way seems to leave us vulnerable to attack. Think of all the people who might take advantage of us, hurt us, even kill us! Some reading this chapter might now say that this is impossible and not what Jesus had in mind. But perhaps we should listen more carefully to what Jesus instructed.

What would life be like if we actually laid down our defenses and no longer took offense? No doubt, we would be more vulnerable, and for at least a while we would probably not like that feeling. It would greatly change how we approached life. We might withdraw from any chance of conflict, but of course that would simply be a new form of defense. We might try to ignore the offense, but again, that would be an alternate form of defense. We might simply attempt to charge through life thick-skinned and tough enough to absorb any offensive words or actions. And yes, this too would be our defense.

But what might our life be like without *any* defense against offense? For starters, we would need to become more aware of our own reactions to situations of offense. We would need to choose to replace our reactionary ways of relating to people with positive action. To do so, we would need careful thought, and time to experience and experiment with what kind of positive responses we can nurture within ourselves. We would definitely need a power beyond ourselves. It would take a deep dependence on God. And it would be a lifelong endeavor to explore how to let God's love move through us unconditionally.

We will never do this perfectly, but consider how a positive response based on God's love directed through us into an offensive situation would change the dynamics and outcome of that situation. Instead of pouring conflict accelerant on the situation, we would infuse God's love. Imagine how that would alter anxiety-ridden, stress-filled moments of hostility between people!

The next time someone launches an angry attack at you, your first reaction will likely be the old fight-or-flight mechanism that is hard-wired into your brain. But how will either fight or flight help you, the situation, or the other person? You may feel more protected as you fight or flee, but all you have done is contribute to the conflict. In the end, by fighting back or fleeing the scene, you have merely added to the angst you all feel. You have solidified your defensive wall, which now separates you long-term not just from the one with whom you are conflicted but, at least to some extent, with other people, and certainly with God. The cycle of conflict will go on and on, restricting you spiritually and emotionally.

Now consider what might happen if you respond to an angry person with a heart flowing with God's love. I don't mean just a warm-fuzzy expectation that everything will be okay. Think about a serious situation when someone is angrily attacking you. Think of how devoid of God's love that person is at the moment, how lost and out of control, how deeply frightened and desperately frustrated. If God's love is flowing in and through you, the first thing that changes in a conflict situation will be your thoughts and desires. Instead of being focused on yourself—fight or flight—you will be focused on the hurts and needs of your brother or sister.

I understand how crazy and impossible this sounds. Allowing God's love to flow through us during conflict is opposed to everything our world teaches, and the church of Jesus Christ has too often adjusted its understanding of Jesus to accommodate it. Christians who claim Jesus as Lord and Savior generally act and react in conflict situations just like anyone else, responding in fight or flight. We vigorously defend our Christian right to defend ourselves.

But I am proposing that we choose to believe Jesus instead of society. Then a wonderful world of love and freedom will open to us, a world that formerly we could not begin to imagine. Jesus told Peter to forgive totally, every infraction and every time, no matter how many. If we are to take Jesus' words to heart for our everyday lives, forgiveness—not fight-or-flight—must be our automatic response to everyone, in every situation, for all of our life's experience. We might even learn daily to forgive life itself and no longer carry a chip on our shoulder. This will become a profound journey into self-discovery and God-discovery.

In essence, we can choose to open ourselves at a deep level of heart, soul, and mind, where God's love heals us, frees us, and empowers us. This will demand our willingness to be fully vulnerable to God's love. If we are to be freed from the power of hurt and attack, it is here in the presence of God's intensely personal love for us. Here is the only place we will ever discover a lifetime of forgiveness, the shocking realization that the Creator of the universe holds nothing against us, and the totally humbling experience of knowing the completely unearned, yet all-encompassing love of God.

This is where oneness with God is found, and this oneness is everlasting love. At the center of this oneness is the very love Jesus experiences with God and prays will be ours as well: ". . . so that the world may know that you have sent me and have loved them even as you have loved me," Jesus prays to his Father, ". . . so that the love with which you have loved me may be in them, and I in them" (John 17:23, 26).

When we experience oneness in God's love, it frees us in two life-changing ways. First—and this really does need to come first—is the freedom we experience from self-incrimination. When God's love frees us from our personal storehouse of shame, all the world looks like a different place because we are released from the primary blockage holding our hearts back from receiving and giving God's love. We have no more need for self-protection or self-preservation. We are safe in God's loving embrace, a resting place from which to respond to life's joys and challenges.

The second way oneness in God's love frees us is from our need for justice, in the sense of fairness, recompense, apology, or "getting" anything from the offending party. No longer is our safety, well-being, or justification dependent on someone other than God. We have been healed of any ego needs requiring the approval of others. All aspects of any offending situation have already been resolved at the deepest levels of our conscience and subconscious minds.

Now the offending situation, no matter what it is or who is involved, is simply not about us at all! Because we are *freed from* our need for something from the offender, we are *free to* offer God's love and grace to them. Our needs and desires have been replaced by the ever-hopeful sharing of God's love. So, now, in a personal way, we understand how, in situations of offense, conflict, tension, and anxiety, God's love shines brightest, does its best work, and is most demanded.

Hurts Are Opportunities for God's Love to Flow

Conflict situations present the perfect opportunity for God's love to flow to all parties. In fact, the greater the conflict, the greater the opportunity for God's love to alter life on earth. There is no more powerful example of this truth than the cross of Jesus, his suffering death, and his resurrection. In a very real sense, we, too, can lay down our lives in any conflict situation so that God's love will work its healing and transforming power in the world around us.

The will of God was at work as Jesus laid his life on the line. Indeed, in the Garden of Gethsemane Jesus prayed that ultimately God's will would be done. As God's will was done through Jesus loving his attackers even as they killed him, God's will is also done as we lay our lives on the line when faced with attack. In this way, we join Jesus in his powerful reconciliation work. Like Jesus' life, our lives can become pivot points in turning the world's attention away from conflict and toward the radical love of God. Likewise, when we fail to face conflict with God's love, we miss the opportunity to do God's will and heal a part of the world.

It might be worth thinking about how little persecution most Christians face in North America. We generally think our lives are free of persecution because we live in a democracy where we have freedom of religion. This is partially true, but there is another huge reason we do not suffer persecution. It is because we have not yet discovered full forgiveness for ourselves and others. Consider conflict situations where you have shied away from the tension and, thus, the opportunity to share God's redeeming love. Consider the ways our society ignores Jesus' radical teaching on forgiveness while we remain silent, either not knowing better or not willing to confront the hurtful ways of the world with the way of God's healing love. Think about the impact our lives would have if we faced this hurting world with the radical love of Jesus every time there was conflict on any level. Yes, we would risk much, but we would gain much more. We would experience hurt, definite resistance, and angry challenges. But we would also experience God's flowing love at such a deep level that whatever persecution we might undergo would only strengthen God's love in and through us.

Ways to Allow God's Love to Strengthen Us

Let's ask again what brings the forgiveness question to Peter's mind. We suggested earlier that he had been listening to Jesus and observing Jesus' ministry. For us to also get to the point of asking Jesus if total forgiveness is required of us, we need to spend significant time with him. During the past sixteen months I have been a member of a small church group that meets every Wednesday night to spend an hour or so studying Jesus' teachings and ministry in the book of Matthew. After these many months we are now only through Matthew 9. It would appear we have a few more years of study before we finish the book!

As a pastor for many years, I studied and taught the gospels often. Even so, I have learned more, I have been challenged more, and my life has been changed more in these past sixteen months than ever before because of Jesus. I have learned at a much deeper level how the teachings and ministry of Jesus are intended to reform my inner and outer life in him. For example, until our group started this study, I thought I pretty much understood the beatitudes. What I have learned is the difference between understanding the beatitudes in my head and living the beatitudes as God's image on earth. One is great food for thought and reflection. The other is real life with God in total control, a discovery of all I was created to be and become.

If you long for God's love to overtake you and infuse you with forgiveness, I suggest that you take time to allow all of Jesus' teachings into your soul. Take time to allow all the different examples of Jesus' ministry to form you from the inside out. Dedicate yourself to walking with Jesus throughout his life and ministry with the intent and the hope that his life will become your own. Search for, and seek in him, the true life God has planned for you here on earth. This is not so much about your career choice, the school you should attend, where you should live, or who you marry. This true life that God has planned for you is yours to discover in following Jesus, his teachings, and his way of ministry. Jesus' life example is your template for living God's will and way.

As part of your time spent with Jesus, the Lord's Prayer is a wonderful resource, especially in this area of forgiveness. The simple phrase "forgive us our debts as we forgive our debtors" is often recited without any real prayerful thought. May we take this simple statement as a mantra, allowing it to sink into our hearts. Along with Jesus' additional emphasis on forgiveness in Matthew 6:14–15, in repeatedly praying this prayer for forgiveness, we sink deeper and deeper into the realization that forgiveness is *God's* work in and through us. Forgiveness is a whole way of knowing and being in relationship. Forgiveness is the process whereby all relationships can be restored. If any relationship remains broken, to some extent all relationships remain broken. Total forgiveness is God's will and way in this world. As this piece of the Lord's Prayer becomes a significant part of your daily life and your dependence on God, your realization of God's important reconciliation work in you will fuse you more and more to the life and work of Jesus. His authority and power will become increasingly available to you.

While chapter 11 of this book is dedicated to the meaning of the cross and salvation, let's not miss here the importance of Jesus' words from the cross—words of forgiveness for his tormentors: "Then Jesus said, 'Father, forgive them; for they do not know what they are doing'" (Luke 23:34). These words are echoed by Stephen in Acts 7:60, and by many other Christian martyrs through the centuries. It will strengthen us as we learn to live out forgiveness to reflect on how Jesus and others, in the face of suffering and death, have been able to offer forgiveness to the very ones torturing and murdering them. The same forgiving love that Jesus expressed from the cross is fully available to us. It is the reality we live when we boldly respond in love to an offense done to us.

I know it is easy to take this last thought too lightly. We sometimes assume Jesus' statement of forgiveness is just a minor part in the whole crucifixion story. We say to ourselves that this power to forgive in horrific situations is given to Jesus and other martyrs under special circumstances. Somehow these circumstances seem to have little to do with *our* everyday life and the offenses we face. But in placing such light emphasis on Jesus' forgiveness from the cross, we miss one of the most empowering blessings God has for us. There is a sad irony in how seriously we take Jesus' forgiveness of *our* sins at the cross, yet not his example of forgiving *others*. But Jesus' example at the cross demonstrates that no situation on earth is beyond forgiveness, and no people on earth are beyond forgiveness. With confidence we can enter any place, any relationship, any situation knowing that God goes before us, showing us how to forgive and providing us the wherewithal to follow Jesus' lead in doing so. Forgiveness does not become any more radical than this.

One more thought about how God's love strengthens us for the task of forgiveness: There is a reverse flow about forgiveness. Whenever we open our hearts and let God's loving forgiveness flow unimpeded to others, we experience both the release of pain and the renewal of God's joyful and loving freedom. The pain we were carrying is replaced with God's healing love every time. The more times and the more situations in which we undergo this inner transformation, the more we are encouraged, strengthened, and blessed. While the conflict cycle breeds more and repeated conflict, the forgiveness cycle breeds more and repeated healings. Each time we forgive, God pulls us farther along in the direction of ongoing forgiveness. Rather than ignoring or sweeping small conflicts "under the rug," we will find it helpful to take these opportunities to fully forgive, because that, in turn, will strengthen us to forgive also in more painful situations.

Experiences of forgiving others are also powerful because of the joy of recovering what was lost in the broken relationship. In Genesis we read of Jacob reuniting with his brother Esau. The burden of their pain-filled relationship had plagued Jacob for years. Though he feared his brother Esau, in their time of reunion Esau "ran to meet [Jacob] and embraced him, and fell on his neck and kissed him, and they wept" (Gen 33:4). For both brothers these were tears of joy and relief. While not every relationship is reconciled by forgiveness, many are. Such a reunion of sisters and brothers is like a lightning bolt recharging our forgiveness energy supply. Literally years of burden can be lifted in seconds as our forgiveness finds forgiveness returned. Always remain hopeful about what God can reconcile in any relationship.

A KINGDOM-OF-HEAVEN PARABLE ABOUT FORGIVENESS

[Jesus said,] "For this reason the kingdom of heaven may be compared to a king who wished to settle accounts with his slaves. When he began the reckoning, one who owed him ten thousand talents was brought to him; and, as he could not pay, his lord ordered him to be sold, together with his wife and children and all his possessions, and payment to be made. So the slave fell on his knees before him, saying, 'Have patience with me, and I will pay you everything.' And out of pity for him, the lord of that slave released him and forgave him the debt. But that same slave, as he went out, came upon one of his fellow slaves who owed him a hundred denarii; and seizing him by the throat, he said, 'Pay what you owe.' Then his fellow slave fell down and pleaded with him, 'Have patience with me, and I will pay you.' But he refused; then he went and threw him into prison until he would pay the debt. When his fellow slaves saw what had happened, they were greatly distressed, and they went and reported to their lord all that had taken place. Then his lord summoned him and said to him, 'You wicked slave! I forgave you all that debt because you pleaded with me. Should you not have had mercy on your fellow slave, as I have had mercy on you?' And in anger his lord handed him over to be tortured until he would pay his entire debt. So my heavenly Father will also do to every one of you, if you do not forgive your brother or sister from your heart." (Matt 18:23–35)

One of the most important things we can say about this parable is also the simplest. It is an exclamation point placed at the end of Jesus' answer to Peter that constant, continual, and unending forgiveness is indeed required of us. This parable also serves as an expansion of Matthew 6:14–15, where Jesus clearly states how God's forgiveness and our forgiveness are a package deal. You don't get one without the other.

Remember that Jesus' parables are all kingdom parables. As such, this parable describes what life is to be like in God's kingdom while living God's will and way. This parable is a resounding amplification of the unconditional love and forgiveness required of Jesus' followers. The first servant's debt is huge, incalculable. This aptly describes our own human state in the presence of God's mercy offered to us. The second servant's debt is extremely small in comparison to the first servant's debt. The second servant's debt is minor but unforgiven, much like the offenses we so often find difficult to forgive.

This is Jesus' way of summing up the absolute necessity of forgiveness. In the will and way of God's kingdom on earth, there is no place for an unforgiving follower of Jesus. Our forgiveness of others is a requirement of living within God's kingdom. We are simply to forgive in the same way God has forgiven us. If we do not forgive others, God's forgiveness to us is cut off by our own rejection of forgiveness.

This parable is intended to shock us, rebuke us, and reveal the light or darkness in our hearts. Any of us followers of Jesus who thinks we can fudge on forgiveness in small things or big things ought to feel the full conviction of this message. Mercy and forgiveness are a given in God's will and way. Nothing could be more important within our relationship with God and others. Jesus leaves no room for any follower of his to withhold forgiveness, no matter the size of the debt. (I realize there are situations where forgiveness seems impossible. We will consider these before the end of this chapter.)

What Jesus is warning us about in this parable is how we block God's love and mercy for us when we hold on to hurts in our hearts, when we hold others at bay, and when we dwell on their offense. When we hold others at bay, we hold God at bay as well. We have effectively staunched the flow of grace and love to us and through us. The absolute law in God's kingdom is the law of love. Without forgiveness there can be no love. I know we want to find ways around this truth, to soften it, and to slide out from under it. But when we do this, we are committing spiritual suicide, for we are rejecting the life of love God freely offers us.

Some will want to make claims about God's judgment based on the conclusion of this parable. We will take up the theme of judgment in chapter 10. For now, I will simply say, keep the focus on the purpose of this parable—that is, to startle us into full understanding of the absolute law of love and forgiveness required of us as children of God.

FORGIVENESS AS A WAY OF LIFE IN GOD'S KINGDOM

Possibly the biggest mistake most people make is thinking that forgiveness only applies to certain obvious situations of offense. This allows us to forget forgiveness in the give-and-take of everyday life. I am discovering as I write this chapter how invasive offense is in so many aspects of my life. Consider the number of times per day we think an angry thought, get exasperated at someone at work, mentally call someone nuts, or resent something our spouse, our child, or our best friend said. In this earthly life, there is an inexhaustible supply of general irritations and interpersonal friction. These are ongoing and invasive every day.

The study where I write is upstairs in a separate room of our loft. Presently, my wife is preparing for a trip to Bolivia. This morning she has interrupted my writing three times with concerns over her travel preparations. I tend to be able to accept one interruption, but three borders on inexcusable. How funny to think that while I am writing this chapter on forgiveness, I am keeping score of my wife's "trespasses" against me!

You may think that example of score-keeping insignificant. It is only insignificant if I can forgive and let go while learning to appreciate the give-and-take of helping one another in a relationship. It becomes anything *but* insignificant as the score-keeping mounts through the day. How you and I respond to situations, big or small, truly does matter. Is it any wonder we have so much trouble forgiving a serious offense when we have not learned to forgive the little offenses bombarding us throughout each day? Any small amount of friction can build into great anxiety as unresolved tension mounts. Like it or not, unresolved tensions are a magnet for additional unresolved tensions.

This is not the place to go into detail about how we deal with our past. Suffice it to say how important it is to find ways to forgive the people in our past, and our own past words and actions. I have never known a person who did not carry at least some baggage from their past. The question is, Is it healed? Have we released hold on it? Can we embrace the past in love and forgiveness? Can we allow our past pain to fully surface and then let God replace it with wholeness?

Directly related to our past pain are our present frustration and impatience with the world. Let's face it, much goes wrong in this world. Any unloving act, insensitive comment, willful intrusion, or outright aggression, local or global, can add to the disturbance of our day. I find I am particularly vulnerable to this kind of disturbance. When I allow my frustration with the ways of this world to add to my marriage score-keeping and throw in one or two other disappointments, my day is shot. I soon have little resilience left for anything unanticipated. I then invariably contribute to the day's supply of disturbance for people around me. And likewise, if we are not careful, all these things can become the pattern of our lives, making it impossible for us to re-spond to insult or injury with grace, love, and forgiveness. It is just not in us because the burden of unforgiveness we carry in our heart occupies the space God would like to fill with love. It is as if our hearts are broken not for the moment but for weeks, months, and years to come.

Forgiveness or unforgiveness shapes our everyday lives whether we are aware of it or not. Therefore, forgiveness needs to become an important spiritual discipline we practice daily, and some days even moment by moment. Imagine your heart as a wheelbarrow that you push around throughout the day. Each day, your wheelbarrow gets filled with rocks. Some are your own contribution, but many come from the of-fenses of others, ongoing conflicts in your life, past hurts, crazy insensitive words and actions in society and the world. Some of the rocks are big and some are small, but they all add to the weight in your wheelbarrow, and every rock makes it more difficult to push your way through your day.

Why are we so willing to push the weight of numerous rocks around in our wheelbarrow every day? Many of us, maybe most of us, have come to believe that because rocks are inevitable, so is the burden of lugging them around. We are stuck in our inner conflict cycle of unresolved pain with others and the world. This inner conflict cycle has been going on for a long time, so we have adjusted how we approach life in order to accommodate it. We do not realize the extent to which our spiritual and emotional energy is used up lugging around life's rocks. I say "life's rocks" for a reason: these are not your rocks!

It's about time for us to come clean about whose rocks we are lugging around and where they belong. It is pretty easy to dump a wheelbarrow full of literal rocks. It is not so easy to dump the rocks weighing down our soul. We accommodate the weight of these rocks through resentment, anger, general displeasure, and self-pity, for start-ers. Because we are accustomed to the weight, most days we do not even realize these things are there, but they are. If asked, we might gladly lay down the *rocks*, but are we as ready to lay down the ways we *accommodate* them? While the rocks are not ours, the resentment, anger, displeasure, and self-pity are.

I live in northeastern Minnesota. As I look out the window of my study, I see literally hundreds of rocks scattered across the forest floor. Just as the ground around me holds many rocks, the world around us holds many hurts and pains. It would be wonderful if we could learn to recognize the hurts and pains in the world without picking them up and putting them in our heart's wheelbarrow. And *here* is the es-sence of the spiritual discipline of forgiveness—seeing the hurt and pain of the world, including specific offenses thrown our way, yet resisting the temptation to own and carry it.

It is important to learn when we have begun to accumulate the rocks of the world and how to put an end to our accommodation tactics. We need to allow time and spiritual space for God's love to fill our heart's wheelbarrow, leaving little or no room for hurts and pains to accumulate. Then, when we experience the pain and hurt of this world, instead of putting it into our heart's wheelbarrow, we can meet it with overflowing, loving forgiveness, which comes directly from God's heart.

Probably the most practical advice right now would be to suggest that we all start practicing the spiritual discipline of forgiveness moment by moment from the time we read these words and throughout this day. Do not gloss over the negative thoughts and feelings you experience, no matter how small and insignificant they seem. If it helps, visualize taking the "rock" of any negative thought or feeling out of your heart's wheelbarrow and giving it back to the earth, back to this life on earth. See the negative thought and the hurtful feeling not as yours to hold and carry, but as something hard and heavy but with no power to ever weigh you down again. And in the moment you first recognize the negative thought or feeling, remember your heart's real purpose, which is to carry the love of God in all its joyful wonder. In this way, you will realize that you have so much to *offer* the world, instead of *taking on* the pain of the world in a personal way.

When the Offense and the Pain Are Too Great

Perhaps the greatest teacher of unconditional love is the pain of unbearable offense. This may surprise you. Of course, for many, the pain of unbearable offense becomes a dump truck full of rocks weighing down their hearts long-term. It does not have to be this way. When God's loving forgiveness is channeled in and through us, even the most terrible offenses can become occasions for healing and hope.

It is too easy for us to gloss over the pain and suffering God went through at the cross. I don't mean we gloss over the suffering of Jesus so much as we gloss over the suffering of the whole world. As a defense against the unthinkable, we all choose not to think about horrible offenses happening to us. If we did think deeply about such things, it would likely debilitate us and cause us to withdraw from the world. So when the unthinkable happens, we are left in shock, disbelief, and despair. If and when we find ourselves overcome by tragic attack, abuse, or death, our typical defense of denial falls apart and we are left to the hopeless reactions of fight or flight. But what if we could be prepared to respond with God's love and forgiveness even in the worst of times?

A novel called *The Shack*, by William P. Young, was published in 2007 and caused quite a stir among some Christians. Others found it a wonderfully fresh approach to understanding tragedy, God, and healing. Despite being fiction, in my experience the book carries great truth. It is a story of how one man, Mack, came to deal with the abduction and murder of his young daughter, Missy. It is also about how Mack's experience of God changed him forever.

Chapter 11 of *The Shack* deals with letting go of judgment of the offender. While other books deal with letting go and allowing God to heal us, I found this chapter especially helpful because of its raw portrayal of emotions and how clearly it depicts our relationship with God. Mack's broken heart left him living in extreme pain and bitterness. Though Mack was unaware of the depth of his bitterness, what he did feel was a heavy and constant weight of sadness.

One day, Mack finds himself sent by Jesus into a dark chamber, where he is greeted by an emissary of God. In his conversation with the emissary, he discovers that the room is a judgment chamber. At first, he thinks he is the one to be judged; instead, he is told he will *be* the judge.

In addition to Missy, Mack has four other children. The emissary asks Mack which of his children he loves the most. This line of questioning helps Mack face his belief that God does not love all God's children equally well. How could God love all God's children well and yet allow what happened to Missy?

Mack is then given the judge's seat, where he is to judge God and the human race. Mack, of course, protests and claims no interest in this role of judge, yet the emissary easily reminds him of how practiced of a judge he has been in life. Under the pressure of being asked to judge God and humanity, Mack begins to think about how self-centered his many judgments of people have been.

Mack can't believe he is being asked to judge God! Yet that is what it all boils down to. Mack is ready to damn to hell the one who abducted and murdered Missy, and the ones who helped create the monster that murdered Missy, and evil people back through history. But where this all actually leads Mack is to his judgment of God. Ultimately, Mack is led to admit he is judging God for creating and not restraining evil in the world. Mack says, "Yes! God is to blame!"[3]

In real life, this kind of honesty is rare. Who among us has never blamed God? Who among us is willing to admit that we have? And that perhaps we still do?

The pivotal question comes when the emissary asks Mack which of his own five children he will damn to hell and which two he will send to eternity with God. Of course, Mack is now in total disbelief and despair, refusing to judge his children in this way. Through the excruciating dialogue, the emissary eventually leads Mack to his breaking point. Mack falls down weeping and pleading to be sent to hell instead of any of his children. At this moment in the story we begin to grasp just how much Mack's weeping and pleading remind us of God's heart and the willingness of Jesus to take our place at the cross.

Eventually, the emissary helps Mack begin to allow the thought of a fully loving God instead of a God who would damn anyone: A God who is responsible for all

3. Young, *The Shack*, 161.

the wonder of creation and all goodness. A God who is not responsible for the great offenses of the world. A God who loves all God's children with a perfect love. In this realization, Mack asks to be fully relieved of his role as judge of God and the human race.

My brief recounting of this story does not do justice to the heart-rending dialogue found in chapter 11 of the book. I recommend that all who struggle with judgment (unforgiveness) of any kind read and reread this story. In my experience with people, I have found few, including myself, who have gone deep enough into their own cycles of conflict, judgment, and unforgiveness to become as in touch with the true source of their sadness as is described of Mack.

We live in a glorious but broken world. If we are to realize the true love and goodness of God, we must first face the brokenness in the world and in ourselves. It is impossible to go through daily life without experiencing this brokenness. We all carry pain with us wherever we go. Most of us, maybe all of us, will sooner or later reach a breaking point where the offense is more than we can bear. And when we come to this point, we have come to the opportunity of a lifetime.

While we have known a lifetime of judging others and God, veiled though it might have been by our religious guise, now comes a reckoning. Will we fall down weeping in the presence of God who loves all God's children perfectly? Who perfectly loves the haters and the evildoers, including those who have offended us grievously? Will we acknowledge God's perfect love for us? Can we finally accept a God who fully loves, always forgives, never destroys, never acts in harmful judgment, never authors an evil thought or act, and is never in any way responsible for the terrible plight in which we find ourselves and our world?

What is now revealed is what is really at stake. It is our own hold on a lesser god, a god who would support our holding on to pain, retaliate with us, and respond as we would to injustice and offense. At some point in life, we all refuse to let go of this god. Even when we clearly see the true God on the cross, we find a way to accommodate the god in which we want to believe. Possibly the greatest sin of humankind is our creation of a caricature god in our own image. This is a god we can live with. This is a god we can believe in. This is also a god we can stay angry at and mistrustful of, a god who cannot save us at our times of greatest need because this god dead-ends in our own hearts.

Yet the real God offers us a relationship from outside ourselves. This is a relationship of pure and perfect love from One who is the essence of pure and perfect love. If we are to enter into relationship with the One who is pure and perfect love, it will need to be on this God's terms. Our former ideas about some other god will need to be transformed by an experience of Love Incarnate living in us. We cannot comprehend the existence and experience of this loving God without first being stripped of our hold on any other god. Tragedy, terrible offense, a face-to-face encounter with the deepest of evils—these reveal the hopelessness of our self-made god. When we truly come to the end of all our hope, we are vulnerable to the discovery of the One waiting for us with outstretched arms. Waiting to embrace us and to heal our deepest wounds. Waiting to shower us with pure and perfect love every time.

Laying Down All Our Weapons but the One God Gives Us

Self-protection is not a part of real, loving forgiveness, yet we all try hard to live love while holding on to our hurt like a shield. It cannot be done. Jesus said this in so many ways and offered life examples over and over. Why is God's forgiveness of us dependent on our forgiveness of others? When we cling to our hurt as a shield, when we hold out on love of enemies, when we judge others in any way, we block pure and perfect love. When we hold on to hurt, great or small, we say no to God's pure and perfect love, and to the healing we so desperately need from God.

This may sound callous toward those who suffer the most horrible of this world's offenses. What about survivors of abuse? What about survivors of torture? What about survivors of deep emotional wounds? What about all who are desperately stuck in their ongoing pain while struggling to get through each dark day of their lives?

It would be *truly* callous to tell those who suffer greatly that the only hope beyond despair is their own defenses, or a weak god to bolster their own defenses. Anything short of God's pure and perfect healing love *is* the callous answer. Anything short of helping suffering people find ways to become open to God's healing love *is* the callous answer. What works against us is a world full of callous answers that only intensify the cycle of conflict and pain. And too often, we have a church that, like the world around it, also settles for callous answers.

In the mid-1990s I lost my marriage, my family, my home, my job, and my career. I was dangerously suicidal for six months. During this time, I awoke Christmas morning to find a Christmas tree that had literally lost all its needles. It was laid bare and quickly became a symbol of my hopelessness.

In the following weeks and months, I continued to struggle desperately, trying to hold on to what little was left of my life. For some reason, I did not destroy or dispose of the Christmas tree. By Easter, I finally decided to do something about the tree. I stripped the branches, cut the tree into two pieces, and formed these into a rough cross. I then placed the cross in a private place where I could go whenever my despair overwhelmed me. During the next year and a half, the barren and hopeless tree became a place of great relief and healing for me. The rough cross, a symbol of Christ's own suffering, became a place for me to lay down my sorrow, my hopelessness, and my hold on blame of others and of myself.

I'm not describing a quick and easy course, but a slow and arduous journey. In a very real sense, I had to learn a new way of life from the inside out. I discovered that if there was any hope for my healing, I had to lay all my weapons down—all my hurt, all my pain, and all my blame. Forgiveness of everyone and everything—myself, others,

God, life—was required. Even though I knew what was necessary, the letting go and the healing process took me years.

Prolonged grief work, extreme emotional trauma, severe emotional and spiritual offense, my own shame and blame—God has brought me through all these horrors. I can say most assuredly that God's pure and perfect love heals all. This is no quick and easy fix of the deep brokenness inside us. To know and experience God's pure and perfect love requires us to first make room for it in our hearts—to do a kind of spring-cleaning beyond any we have ever known!

In my years of pastoral ministry, I have watched many people carry their pain, some more quietly than others. Any form of holding and carrying pain is emotional and spiritual drudgery. Whole communities of people become divided, discouraged, and withdrawn from one another as a result. So much that could be forgiven is not. So much suffering that could be avoided continues to be endured. We remain wounded and broken inside, all the time feeling trapped in sorrow.

God offers us one, and only one, weapon. All others are spiritually forbidden by Jesus himself. Anything that would prolong conflict, prolong our suffering and that of the other, is declared outside the bounds of God's kingdom come on this earth. The very will by which we hang on to our pain is opposite God's will for us. The time for our confession is now as we come before the cross of Jesus and release our hold on anything other than what God has given and ordained for us. The one weapon God offers us is the cleansing, renewing, healing power of love; yes, even pure and perfect love. To know this love is to know complete forgiveness. To know this love is to live complete forgiveness of all others.

There is nothing like being washed in God's love. No self-satisfied feeling of revenge or retaliation or withholding of forgiveness compares to experiencing total freedom from these things that bind our hearts to pain. If after reading this chapter, you still do not know this wash of love, the experience of a lifetime awaits you! The flowing, cleansing love of God is the life force you are missing. This love of God is free, it is offered to you moment by moment. It is as accessible as the air you breathe. It is for you to choose to enter into a deeper relationship with this God of love.

The Ever-Flowing Stream of Forgiveness

Forgiveness knows no boundaries. Jesus said it and lived it. Once we begin to forgive everything that formerly obstructed God's love from flowing into and out of us, we discover that there is no end to the joy and freedom of forgiveness. The application of forgiveness plays out in every aspect and at every level of life. We experience an ongoing infusion of God's love that carries us through each day. We now know why Jesus replied to Peter's question about forgiveness by telling him that complete and never-ending forgiveness is required. It is the pathway to living in God's kingdom will and way while we walk this earth. And it changes everything!

9

IS GOD'S LOVE REAL?

When the Pharisees heard that he had silenced the Sadducees, they gathered together, and one of them, a lawyer, asked him a question to test him. "Teacher, which commandment in the law is the greatest?" He said to him, "'You shall love the Lord your God with all your heart, and with all your soul, and with all your mind.' This is the greatest and first commandment. And a second is like it: 'You shall love your neighbor as yourself.' On these two commandments hang all the law and the prophets."

—MATT 22:34–40

You might think that after about two thousand years of church history, enough would have been written about God's love. The books and articles about God's love could surely fill a library, so why include a chapter on love in this book? Is it not enough to say enough has been said? Probably not.

The undeniable truth of the absence of love can be read in the present and past of the world and the Christian church. The stories of unloving behavior could also fill a library. Something has gone terribly wrong, and the proof is in the destruction of God's creation and the violence among God's human creatures.

We come back to a central challenge in this book: to believe *and* follow Jesus, not just to believe in him. To believe in Jesus for many Christians has equaled something like small children believing in Santa Claus. The idea of Santa Claus (or Jesus) is a warm-fuzzy hope for something special under the Christmas tree in the future. It is not about a core change of heart, mind, and daily life.

Not much could be more difficult for the human heart and mind to believe than God's total love shown in Jesus. The proof of our unbelief is on display as many followers of Jesus harbor offenses, create enemies, support billions spent on weapons of mass destruction, fight in the militaries of the world, allow fear to rule how we treat others, and generally leave a wake of pain and hurt in our path no different from that of the non-Christian world.

It might help if we could be honest enough to admit, "This love of God in Jesus is unbelievable!" Here is a starting point that may allow us to hit the pause button on living life from our own power and might. Perhaps we could start by realizing that God is bigger, more amazing, more loving, and more of everything than we could ever imagine. It would be wonderful if we could stop boxing God into what we think love and love's limits are.

The core human problem of sin (missing the mark) is not about our life's failings and inadequacies. The core human problem of sin is our inability or unwillingness to believe that God is pure love, God's love is forever real, and God's love is never-failing. If we truly believed this God of complete love as shown in Jesus, we would face the choice either to run headlong into God's loving arms or to walk away. But instead of believing the seemingly unbelievable, many hedge their bets, say it can't really be true, Jesus did not mean it for us, his teachings and example do not apply to us for all sorts of reasons. So, we run into the loving arms of a Santa Claus–like god who denies us any chance of discovering the real God of complete and unconditional love.

It would seem this human misbelief and disbelief would be very bad news. It *is* bad news if we continue to focus on ourselves, our inabilities, and our weaknesses and project them onto God. But that is not the message of this chapter. We will instead focus on the God of amazing love as shown in Jesus, who is himself the "image of God" (Col 1:15), the "reflection of God's glory and the exact imprint of God's very being" (Heb 1:3), the "Word [who] was God" (John 1:1), the "eternal life that was with the Father and was revealed to us" (1 John 1:2), and the "Messiah, the Son of the Living God" (Matt 16:16).

This chapter points to the best news you will ever hear, whether you have considered following Jesus or not. It does not matter where you have been, in the fold or out of it; God's perfect love is all for you, and you cannot possibly have grasped the full meaning of it—no one ever has.

This chapter is divided into two parts: The first part looks at what has gone wrong in terms of how people understand God. It is important to take an honest look at where we have been mistaken, misled, misinformed, and, of course, where we have made our own wrong choices. The second part is about how we might realign our thinking with God's love, and how we might speak and act with the true heart of God in Jesus Christ. *Part 1 is confession. Part 2 is celebration. They are both wonderful news.*

PART 1. CONFESSION: WHY WE STILL NEED TO WRITE AND READ ABOUT GOD'S LOVE

Why We Think We Need an Unloving God

Whether we admit it or not, there is darkness within all of us. I'm not talking about horrible evil. I'm talking about real-life issues of hurt, anger, and resentment. Pains that will not fully go away. Disappointments that cloud our day. Physical and mental injuries and limitations. Love lost. Rejection. Shadows of shame past and present. Even bitterness and severely wounded spirits. All these and more plague the human heart and have a narrowing effect on our ability to love, on our ability to recognize and accept God's love.

Everybody lives with some degree of pain. We all have a great need to manage this pain, and most of us seek to manage it well. Part of how we do so is to lower our expectations of ourselves and life. We try to balance a sort of realism about life with a solid sense of self-esteem. We have just so much capacity to deal with our own struggles, and in the end, we settle for less of life than we hope for. All this is normal and maybe even a natural, mostly healthy way of coping. We are unable to meet all of the world with love. We know this in the depth of our souls. *The enormous spiritual problem comes as we project our inadequacies onto God.*

We all, some of the time, feel we need a God who is less than perfectly loving, not always full of mercy and grace, and not constantly accepting of us and of everyone else. We use this less-than god to help us in our desperate search for wholeness. It is, of course, a fallacy of the human heart to think that God must in some way be like our own imperfections.

There are several reasons we find it difficult to accept a completely loving God. For one thing, we struggle to face our own painful inadequacies, yet we long for a sense of self-worth that, in the presence of a fully loving God, might (we think) not be possible. If we can project our limitations onto God, we can ease up on our own self-condemnation—we can surmise that we are whole as God is whole. We can find a certain solace in the ways of the world's violence and pain because this is the inescapable way of life. We can absolve ourselves of culpability with, and participation in, the violence and pain of the world. We can enjoy peace of mind even though we are not living peacefully. We believe we can love a god who is not perfectly loving because we can understand something elemental in God's supposed nature—that is, the need to avenge. It's only natural, we can then think. This is the way the world works. There's nothing we can do about it. God doesn't expect us to be perfect in love. After all, *God is vengeful, right?*

Another consideration is the fear we talked about in earlier chapters. Along with our struggle for self-worth comes our struggle to feel safe. To feel safe, we need a certain sense that we are in control. When we are afraid and feel out of control, our need for protection becomes overwhelming, and we naturally respond in less than loving ways, so we dare not imagine a God who would not act this same way. We cannot bear the fear and guilt of knowing God disapproves of our unloving responses to fear. We need a less-than-loving god if we are going to strive to be like God while living in the scary realities of the world.

Here then is our need for confession. The god of retaliation, divisions, self-defense, and war reflects our own self-image and self-protection. Rather than being made in the image of God, we have now made God into our image. There can be no clearer transgression of the first commandment (Exod 20:2–5). We have formed a deeply flawed, graven image of God in our minds and in our way of life.

It's Not Your Fault

In the 1997 movie *Good Will Hunting*,[1] Will's therapist finally confronts him with the crucial words to enable his self-acceptance. The therapist repeatedly says to Will, "It's not your fault." He comes closer and closer to Will until he is right in his face, saying, "Will, it's not your fault!" This may be my favorite line from any movie I have ever seen.

In the context of the movie and this chapter, the line "It's not your fault" means that, fundamentally, you and I are wounded and battered, and helpless to change that ourselves. Yet God loves and accepts us fully! Despite, and even because of, our shame and fear, God comes to us in the form of the living, loving, crucified, and resurrected Jesus to embrace us. But we have thought God's love in Christ Jesus impossible. The confession we most need to make is that we have disbelieved. We have prejudged ourselves and our world. We have not allowed God to be God and Lord of all.

This confession takes a whole lot of courage. It would represent a turning point in our lives. This would become the point when we allow God to love all that is in us and all that is in the world. This is where, perhaps for the first time in our lives, we allow God to be God in us. We would allow Jesus in his words and actions to truly be God's incarnate Word written with perfect love in our minds and hearts.

This confession, of course, is just the beginning. We will stumble and fall, bringing aspects of violence back into this world. But we will now know enough and trust God enough to always come back to God's love. The remainder of our lives will be a continuing confessional return to God. Now, even in the face of our shame and fear, we will find, more and more, the true peace and joy of God's love flowing through our lives. We will no longer think of Jesus' loving life and teachings as impossible because we will have discovered his life as the love of God flowing in us.

Further Need to Let Go of Shame and Control

I doubt anyone has ever been completely free of judging others. I struggle with it just about every day. Mostly, the judging goes on in my mind and—thankfully, less

1. Damon and Affleck, *Good Will Hunting*, 1997.

often—creeps into how I treat people. At least this is what I hope. The point is, (1) the tendency to judge others accompanies us through life, and (2) it is *always* about the log in our own eye (Matt 7:3). Our seemingly relentless need to judge others does not come from hearts filled with God's love, but from our own broken hearts; from our shame, pain, and fear; and from disbelieving God.

Paul tells us in Romans 12:19, "Beloved, never avenge yourselves, but leave room for the wrath of God; for it is written, 'Vengeance is mine, I will repay, says the Lord.'" This is a well-known quote from scripture, yet we are largely unwilling to let vengeance be God's job. Think of all that goes wrong in this world, and God does not appear to do God's job of vengeance. Think of all the horrible people in this world, and God does not repay them with vengeance. Since we do not believe God is doing God's job of vengeance, or at least not doing it right, we gladly volunteer for this duty. In the apparent absence of a judge over life, we appoint ourselves.

Once again, we have allowed our own struggles in life to paint a picture of the God we think we know. We have projected our own sense of justice and our version of retaliation onto God. The enactment of our judgment and vengeance occurs on every level of human relationships. It begins with an unkind word and ends in a world war. Most people think violence is inevitable in this world, but that depends on whether we remain the judges instead of choosing to leave the judging and vengeance up to God.

The most frightening aspect of our judging and vengeance is how readily we ascribe our version of judging and vengeance to God. Pretty much every nation does some form of jihad, or holy war. There are countless ways to rationalize the need for violent self-defense and aggressive, nationalistic retaliation, but none of them come from Jesus. He taught, lived, and died the exact opposite of all our rationalizations for violence. Still, far too many Christians refuse Jesus' version of judgment and vengeance while telling themselves they are doing God's will.

It is time for more confession. To the extent that we continue judging others, we are judging God and usurping God's role. Judging others, and ultimately judging God, is a symptom of the shame, pain, and fear in our hearts, and reveals the lack of God's love within us.

Whenever we succumb to the temptation to judge, there is a love-void in our heart. We need to learn to recognize the small daily occurrences of our judgmental attitude, to admit how our judgmental attitude reveals our dissatisfaction with God's world and God's way. We need to confront in ourselves the need to wrest from God control over life, and allow God to remove our shame, pain, and fear while refilling our heart with unconditional love. This letting go and allowing God to regain control in us will become a lifetime pattern of releasing our misery while embracing God's grace and love. This is why confession is wonderful news. Real confession frees us to live as God always intended us to live.

This chapter is focused on God's love. Chapter 11 takes up God's judgment. For now, it is enough to say that they are so closely linked that we could argue they are essentially the same.

Think of it this way: When we judge others, we take control of life on our terms. Any form of violence is an expression of control on our terms. We cannot access God's love this way, for God's love is not controlling of anything. God's love is inviting, welcoming, sharing, helping, renewing, forgiving, and, yes, sometimes confronting.

Few, if any, of us can imagine letting the world be completely within God's control. But what if we did allow God's love to fully have its way in us and all that we influence in this life? What if ten people in our church or community allowed this? What if 100 million followers of Jesus living all over the world allowed this? It either starts somewhere, or the world will never know God's complete love. For you and for me, it starts with confession.

Is There a Limit to God's Love?

I'm no mechanic, though years ago I drove a truck with a governor on it. I do not really understand how it worked. Mechanically, the truck could easily have gone 100 miles per hour. The governor's job was to limit the speed to about 60 miles per hour. Back then 60 miles per hour on the roads I was driving was just about the right speed. The governor was helpful, and it served a good purpose.

Let's say God's love is a 100-mile-per-hour love. On the rough roads of this life it would seem to us too dangerous to travel at love's full speed, so we act much like a governor limiting God's love to 60 miles per hour. Is there a limit to God's love? The answer is yes, and it is us. But is our limiting of God's love helpful? Does it serve a good purpose? Some would say yes; in fact, in some ways the church of Jesus Christ has said a resounding yes for centuries.

Maybe the question we should ask is this: Is the partial love of God the same as the full love of God? Or we could ask, does God's love seek only partial fulfillment? Or, who assigned us the task of governor? Or, when the church of Jesus Christ shows anything but complete love of God, is the resulting message one God hopes the world will hear? Should Jesus have been more sensible and limited his love to 60 miles per hour? Or try this: Who is best served when we love at 60 miles per hour instead of 100? Perhaps the most scathing question is to ask whether love at 60 miles an hour is God's love at all.

In the last chapter we looked at how forgiveness is to be unlimited. It is to be complete and constant and always. God's love, too, is complete, constant, and always.

Jesus did not give us instructions about how to be mechanical governors of love. In the Great Commission (Matt 28:18–20), Jesus told his followers to teach others *everything* he had commanded. On the rocky roads of this earthly life, acting as governors—limiters of love—serves only one purpose: ours. We are not yet ready to accept

God's 100-mile-per-hour love, for it would then ask us to also love at this speed in situations and with people where love seems too difficult.

The Counterweight to God's Love—The Damage Done

In not accepting an ultimately loving God as shown in Jesus, we join Adam and Eve hiding out in the Garden of Eden (Gen 3:8). Without an understanding of love as the anchor and the defining concept of the universe, we will always be left to live in doubt and fear. Just as the "original" sin was to doubt God, our "continual" sin is to doubt God. All our fear originates in this doubt. Left to our doubts and fears, we mask the identity of the only One who can heal us.

Mistrust of God kills creativity, destroys relationships, and diminishes hope. This mistrust is the result of damage done over centuries by Christians and non-Christians alike. Who will believe again? How might we ever stop the doubting? Have we ever trusted, and will we ever trust, the full love of God?

The results of original and continual sin have too often made liars out of those who profess to be Christian believers. Believers in what? If we have pushed God's ultimate love out of our lives, what are we left with? To say we are believers while not really believing makes *us* the untrustworthy ones. We have become deeply conflicted at such a level as to render ourselves ignorant of love's potential. Thus, we give witness to God's love with our lips and live the idolatry of vengeance with our lives. All the while, we remain unconscious of the living lie we have become. Our souls are crippled, but we have no knowledge of it.

This unconsciousness and crippling of many Christians is seen in their adherence to a certain understanding of Scripture that leaves Jesus' life and teachings on love largely out of the picture and, instead, normalizes violence, judgment of others, and vengeance. The greatest biblical teachings about God's love are lost to us, and we don't even know it! We are left vulnerable to our doubts and fears. Divisions define us and issues alienate us from one another, while the doubts and fears we hide within ourselves leak out all over the map of our relational lives.

Surely it is time for confession, to be fully honest about when and where we seek to limit God's love because we don't believe what Matthew portrays: that Christ Jesus reveals the fullness of God's love. It may be time to admit we doubt even the existence of a God whose love is free of human limitations. It may be time to face our inability to imagine that God is *complete* love, and to confess our failure to acknowledge that God loves *all* people completely.

More Damage Done—Division and the Inconsistencies of Human Love

It doesn't matter if we are on the left or right politically, the pro or con on any issue, the right or wrong of a belief system. Whenever humans become polarized, there is scapegoating, blame, and shame. Choosing sides works great in a pick-up game of basketball, but it is devastating to a loving community. Choosing sides happens when we lack a love deep and expansive enough to truly love the other, no matter our differences. That form of true love is impossible until we release ourselves into its source, which is God.

Let's look at the macro picture of division: In the United States, we seem to be experiencing an ever-increasing political divide. I know wonderful people of every political flavor, and everyone I know has some degree of trouble loving other people consistently. No matter your politics, the more you feel you are right, the more you will likely feel others are wrong. Those most strongly on either side are the ones who most often stop loving and start judging most harshly. Here is proof enough that right belief is not what love is or what creates a loving space. In no situation, issue, or circumstance will right belief ensure love's reign. Without God's ultimate love flowing among us, we will always operate out of a defensive/offensive mindset. We will wall ourselves off from anyone who holds a position opposite ours.

Human love, left on its own, will always be inconsistent, diminished by judgment, and veiled by the ego. In this atmosphere of inconsistent love, is it any wonder there is so little trust among us? All we have as a basis to gauge empathy is a shadow of love that comes with almost a guarantee of rejection. At the first sign or hint of disagreement, our defenses go up and any hope of experiencing real love disappears.

Jesus never told anyone to believe the right way or to take political sides. He did tell us how God loves, and he challenged us to love as God loves. Once again, in Matthew 5:43–48, Jesus told his followers to love and pray for their enemies, to love those who do not love them back, and to greet those who do not greet them. According to Jesus, this is how we qualify as children of God. This is how we become complete ("perfect") in love, as God is complete. This love of God is not a belief system, not dependent on any country's politics, and certainly not based on any human standard of judgment. But many Christians and non-Christians act the opposite of what Jesus instructed. Worse yet, we convince ourselves that doing the *opposite* of what Jesus taught is actually the way to love like God loves. In so doing, we live a lie, and those looking at the Christian church from the outside see the sham.

If we are to believe Jesus and commit to loving as God loves, we first must confess that *we* have decided when, where, and whom we want to love. We have often not loved the very people God has called us to love—those who, if we had loved them, would have come to know God's love and its power to transform their lives, and perhaps the tilt of this world's axis would have shifted away from violence.

There are at least two important reasons our inconsistent love is so serious. First, over many generations we have effectively inoculated millions of people from accepting Jesus as their Lord and Guide through life. Second, to those we have convinced to adopt our faith, we have provided a false god who does not love as the real God loves. In the process, we contribute to the destruction of our planet and of our relationships with others and with God.

There is only one way out of our inconsistent love and divisions—especially those concerning religion and politics. The way out is to discover something so amazing, so radical, and so powerful that our lives and the lives of all we influence will be fundamentally changed forever! That we would begin to know the real God of love, learn to love as the real God loves, and live renewed lives in God's love—these are the longings and hopes behind all our confessions.

A Final Question for Part 1

What is at stake if we believe and follow a God of complete love? We will each answer differently. This question is something of a warning before you continue reading— not of danger but of an opportunity you won't want to miss. It's like the sign along a mountain road that, just in time, says "Scenic View: Pull-Off Ahead." What's at stake if you hastily opt to pull your car over and step out? Your original travel plan might get a little disrupted if you stop to see what awaits your discovery. But trust me—you will never regret taking in the breath-taking view. It might even change your life.

God's real love is the breath-taking view, and it may shake the foundations of our understanding, our lifestyle, our politics, and our faith.

PART 2. CELEBRATION: GOD'S LOVE INCARNATE AND REAL

First, Remove Some Clutter

As we venture from confession to celebration, we still have some serious clutter to wipe away to gain a deeper understanding and experience of God's love. Love is a serious matter, and God's love comes with an ultra-serious label. Most people I know think of love as a positive influence, a warm-fuzzy feeling, a spiritual experience of light, renewal, hope, and joy all rolled into one. God's love is all these things, but so much more.

God's love is also the knife that cuts across the grain of our lives, and this love sears a chasm through human history and culture. Anyone who presumes that love is weak or helpless in the face of death and destruction has lost touch with the depths of God's love. Anyone who thinks love is silent in the face of evil, large or small, is sorely mistaken. Love has a voice, and it cries out in the face of injustice. Love has a voice, and it confronts apathy. Love has a voice, and it will not tolerate the destruction of human life or harm to our planet. An unkind word is rebuked by love. A heartless act is condemned by love. Anything not motivated by love is judged by love.

It is vital that we understand the enormous capacity of God's love when it comes to telling and living the truth. Think of God's love as the litmus test of our life's motivations, intentions, and actions. Are we fully living out of God's love if we behave lovingly toward some people and not others? Are we living God's love if we manage our mild disagreements with kindness and forgiveness but not our violent exchanges? Are we living in God's love if it affects some parts of our thinking and relationships but leaves the remainder to the whims of our doubts and fears? Are we fully living in God's love if we remain on the sidelines of the world's turmoil instead of stepping in to help the most vulnerable? The answer to all these questions is no, for God's love is complete and all-encompassing.

It is our desperate human need to swim in the deep end of love's pool, to be "all in," as God's love itself is. God's love completely unveils the truth of our lives—including our frailties and missteps and failure to love fully—and challenges us to grow in God to become the most loving we can be. Only God can give us this love—and God wants to give it as desperately as we need to receive it. God's love is more than we can ever imagine, more than we have yet experienced, and a driving life force challenging us to ever greater good.

Mystics talk of the true self and the false self. The false self focuses on *me, my* ego, *my* sense of self-worth, and *my* capacity to manage life from *my* perspective. The true self is all about discovering my identity in *God* and then living life out of *God's* self as *God* lives through me. There is a profound difference between these two ways of knowing and living. Our true self is found only in God's love and truth expressed through us. Nothing could be more life-transforming than knowing so deeply that God's love inhabits and enlivens us.

As our life is transformed, we become an extension of God's powerful presence in a world often wholly unprepared to accept it. We become a force of light, life, and truth in the face of evil or destruction. We bring God's love to bear on the world and its harmful complexities. Though we may find it hard to believe, as we live out God's love and truth, we serve as God's very real presence transforming the world around us.

There is nothing as powerful as God's love. This is not a romantic notion. It is who God is in all that God is and does. God's love formed the universe and sustains creation. Any lesser notions of love are fleeting glimpses of the real thing. Sadly, too many Christians settle for love as something only understood and accessed within the realms of human experience and culture. There is nothing supernatural about loving only those who love us or being at peace with those who do not bomb us.

By *supernatural* I don't mean "unnatural" or "other-worldly." Supernatural love is the kind of love God intends human beings to express consistently. In truth, it is the most *natural* love for life in God's kingdom here on earth. If God's love forms and sustains our universe, when we humans choose a different, lesser form of love, it is actually more accurate to call *human* love "unnatural."

If we could reverse our thinking and our way of life from viewing mere human love as the norm, we would become vulnerable to God's love in previously unimaginable ways. If we centered our lives on the experience and expression of God's super-normal/supernatural love, all our relationships would be transformed. God's love is *that real*! This also means our lives can become this real too, for we have been created to be of one heart and one mind with God.

Commandment as God's Call to Love

We are now ready to look again at Jesus' teachings from the book of Matthew. This time, our scripture is Matthew 22:34–40:

> When the Pharisees heard that [Jesus] had silenced the Sadducees, they gathered together, and one of them, a lawyer, asked him a question to test him. "Teacher, which commandment in the law is the greatest?" He said to him, "'You shall love the Lord your God with all your heart, and with all your soul, and with all your mind.' This is the greatest and first commandment. And a second is like it: 'You shall love your neighbor as yourself.' On these two commandments hang all the law and the prophets."

Here in the United States, the idea of a commandment is not popular. It seems no one likes to be told what to do or not do. Jesus' command to love grates against our sense of propriety. We wish he would have *invited*, *suggested*, or *enticed* us to love instead of *commanding*. Is life not about *us*, *our* choices, and *our* free will? If so, how we feel about life and what we believe about life will be the limit of our understanding of love, and our restricted ability to love will make for a limited existence.

What if God's love really was real?—constant, consistent, ultimate compassion, unconditional, yours for the receiving, never-ending, present? What if nothing from the mouth of God could be less than such ultimate love? There are hundreds of commandments in the Bible, but Jesus says they all come down to the commandment to love. What if you and I could reach a place in our lives where we heard this one commandment as the most loving thing God says to us? What if this is the most compassionate and life-giving thing God has ever said? *What if this is God's invitation to a life of oneness with God for all eternity, starting right now? Is God not simply saying to us, "Love as I love. Join me forever in this love!"?*

If we are to hear and understand God's command of love, embrace it, obey it, and live it, we will need to undergo a process of confession as described in Part 1 of this chapter. If we try to skip that step, we will remain locked in our own limited form of love, and in society's endless cycle of judgment and violence.

How could anyone be expected to love God with all their heart, soul, and mind? Isn't this impossible? Only if we refuse the transformative experience of God's ultimate and complete love showering upon us. But the only way to undergo this transformation is to let go of our control of life and submit our self to the loving care of God. As Jesus said in Matthew 16:25, "For those who want to save their life will lose it, and those who lose their life for my sake will find it."

For the purpose of gaining clarity, let's ask, "What would it be like to love God with all our heart, soul, and mind?" Here are some suggestions to consider:

1. We would give ourselves completely to God's will and way in this present life.

2. We would trust God and God's control over all the world.

3. We would find ourselves lost in the vastness of God's great mercy.

4. We would come to recognize all words and deeds either as an act of love or as a false front for a self-controlling life.

5. Our compassion for others would be automatic.

6. We would learn to love the unloving and to have compassion for the compassionless.

7. We would find ourselves open to receiving God's love in all its life-transforming power.

8. Regardless of circumstances, we would not feel the need to hide from God.

9. Though still certainly human and fallible, our constant goal in life would be to show compassion and mercy instead of any form of violence or judgment.

10. Looking through love's eyes, we would experience God's ever-flowing blessings in the world.

11. Our life's mantra would become "Love everyone. Forgive everything."

If you are thinking that the eleven statements above are idealistic or impossible, ask yourself, "What is holding me back from experiencing them? What other voices in my head are commanding my attention? What experiences am I relying on to guide my conclusions? What would it take to draw me nearer to God and help me believe Jesus and the gospel story Matthew is telling?"

Disbelieving Jesus Has a Long History

Jesus' command to love comes to us amid controversy. Matthew states, "When the Pharisees heard that he had silenced the Sadducees, they gathered together, and one of them, a lawyer, asked him a question to test him" (Matt 22:34–35). In Matthew's account, the controversy begins way back in chapter 9, while Jesus is eating with his disciples at the home of Matthew the tax collector. There, the Pharisees challenge Jesus' disciples, "Why does your teacher eat with tax collectors and sinners?" (Matt 9:11). The conflict escalates throughout the gospel, turning ominous in Matthew 12:14, where we read that the Pharisees "went out and conspired against him, how to destroy him." Of course, the climax of the resistance to Jesus comes with his torture and crucifixion in chapters 26 and 27.

We already know this story of conflict, torture, and murder. My point in highlighting it here is to draw attention to the centuries of systemic violence that continues to deny what Jesus taught and lived. I say "systemic violence" because of the insidious and consistent way so much of humanity has resisted Jesus throughout the generations since his first call for mercy instead of sacrifice. It started in the first century, and it continues into the twenty-first century.

It may sound radical and out of bounds to some Christians, but it is of utmost importance to recognize the extent to which we in the twenty-first century continue to counter Jesus with our violent, death-dealing, destructive ways. Every person who ever lived has to some extent been caught in this web of systemic violence. It is like the very air we breathe. Violence was the most typical human response to conflict in Jesus' day, and it still is now. Today, many religious leaders resist Jesus in no less destructive ways than those who killed him in the first century. The difference is in the subtle ways we and our leaders have learned to embrace the cross while rendering its essential message of nonviolent love impotent. Too many have taken God's radical message of love and twisted it into an agreement with the twenty-first-century version of systemic violence.

Considering our willing assent to systemic violence, it's not surprising that people disbelieve Jesus and how God's love can transform us. On the other hand, if Jesus' followers lived out the eleven ways listed above for obeying God's command to love, it would bring down the violent system. Few in Jesus' day were prepared to live this way, and few today are ready to do it either. For those who are ready, believing Jesus starts with recognizing and stepping out of our involvement in systemic violence. A part of our healing from systemic violence will be learning redemptive ways to confront it.

My plea throughout this book is for Christians and non-Christians alike to return to Jesus as our primary source for knowing and living God's love. The very fact that first-century religious leaders felt they had to kill Jesus to stop his message of love should tell us just how threatening he was to any form of violence. Jesus brought God's message of unconditional love to a broken human system. In doing so, he threatened the very existence of the system, along with all the justifications, rationalizations, and lifestyle choices that went with it. It should not surprise us that religious leaders are often the first to feel threatened, to defend the system, and to resist Jesus. The Christian church today continues to be led by some who, when threatened, choose to disbelieve Jesus and respond with violence instead of love.

Real Love Is Complete Love—"All the Law and Prophets"

Jesus' commandment to fully love God, others, and self did not come as an outside-of-the-box new teaching. Remember, at the time of this instruction on love, he was being tested on which commandment from what we now know as Old Testament law was the greatest. His answer reflected quite accurately both Deuteronomy 6:4–5 and Leviticus 18:18. Jesus did not challenge the religious legal system from outside it but from within it.

Jesus made an all-inclusive statement when he said in Matthew 22:40, "On these two commandments hang all the law and the prophets." Most people have taken the word *all* too lightly. How else could we possibly explain the continuing hurt of division, bitterness, anger, violence, and the distance from God's unconditional love that is experienced all around the world? The Christian church itself is rife with corruption, sexual abuse, divisions, judging, blaming, and the support of systemic violence. How is it possible for this to continue in light of Jesus' claim here? We may as well be honest and admit that for many of us, *all* does not mean "all."

It is long past time to return to this word, *all*, as it defines the scope of God's command to love. Here begins the most wonderful news of the universe! No matter your life situation—devotedly religious or atheist, Christian or of another faith, destitute or living in the realms of wealth and power—God's love is complete, and completely available to *you*. It is all encompassing! In Jesus' world of the first century, he defines love as the commandment of God, the way and will of God, as the very way to understand everything in Scripture. Love is the test of everything in religious teaching. Jesus took on the length and breadth of around two thousand years of Jewish history—indeed, the whole of human history. For us to take Jesus at his word would change the course and make-up of any religious system. All our traditions, statements of faith, belief systems, and hallowed history, as well as all our disagreements and divisions, just might fall away as we listen to Jesus and his message of love.

We might even argue how this message of love potentially supersedes any divisions between people of faith and those who don't identity with a faith. Consider the increased chances for dialogue if religious folks and nonreligious folks had much less on which to focus their disagreements. Take away centuries of church protocol, emphasis on believing the right doctrines, the where, when, and how of worship; then, just maybe we could all talk about and act on the best ways to love one another. If loving God completely, while fully loving others and self, is the key to unlocking all other spiritual truths, what really has divided us for so long is not the issues themselves, but the lack of love on our part.

All means "all." At least from a Christian perspective, if we accept Jesus as Lord of our lives, nothing in all of Scripture comes close to the importance of loving as he has commanded us to love. Take any strained or broken relationship in your life. Take any disagreement over worship style, doctrine, sexuality, male and/or female leadership, end times, expression of spiritual gifts, predestination, purpose, mission, or anything else. These all fall like a house of cards when unconditional love enters the room. While we still might disagree, our love for one another would overpower the emotional and spiritual distance between us.

The excuses made for not believing Jesus when he says that love trumps all else come in many categories. But the wonderful news is that the love of which Jesus speaks is the greater truth and the rebuttal to all our excuses. For example, plenty of us have been deeply hurt through church divisions and splits. While I have a pastor's heart of compassion for the hurting, the only pathway to healing is the one Jesus has commanded. To love all and always, we must submit to God alone, get beyond our personal pain, and find true healing. There is not space here to give spiritual direction for a process of healing, but please know that the path to healing is the path of receiving and then giving unconditional love.

If you are hesitant to embrace the all-in-all of God's love, at least give Jesus and his teachings another look. At least consider that if God is God, then God knows your deepest need, your greatest hesitation, and why it has hold of you. Take your hesitation directly to God. Lay your roadblock to unconditional love before God. Make it a matter of constant prayer. Believe Jesus and hope in his power to restore you to a place of unbelievable love.

God Is as God Commands

Throughout this book, we have been careful to take the story of Jesus as a whole. One chapter, one verse, one action, one teaching does not make up the story of Jesus. Not even the crucifixion and resurrection of Jesus can stand alone. The whole story must be told and heard if we are to understand and then with our own life enter this story. From within the whole narrative of Jesus, we are exploring how God is a God of unconditional love. In Matthew 22:34–40 Jesus commands us to love completely. What does this say about God's love?

If I were to ask one of my children to love others, but then I demonstrated my lack of love for others, what kind of a father would I be? The word *hypocrite* comes to mind. Somehow, I can't imagine any of us calling God a hypocrite. If God commands us to love completely, while not being the ultimate example of complete love, would this not be a prime example of hypocrisy? The wonderful news of the gospel of Jesus is that God is not a hypocrite. If we are ready to believe Jesus (and the other New Testament writers), we will joyfully discover just how amazing God's love is. It is complete, consistent, and offered to us moment by moment throughout our lives. To hear and understand this message of love in its completeness, it is critical to put on hold our inclinations to govern God's love by human standards.

In case you have lingering doubts about the complete love of God that Jesus taught and lived, spend time soaking up these examples from his life of ministry as told in the Gospel of Matthew:

1. He spent most of his ministry wandering the hills of Galilee, giving all his time and attention to the needs of his closest followers and of the crowds desperate for his message.

2. He did not take on a mantle of authority other than the power of his words and actions. He purposely chose to let his message fall on eyes and ears that could see and hear the truth and love of God.

3. Nothing in his manner or method coerced his listeners.

4. Through his teachings and example, he laid bare the absence of love and the hypocrisy of the religious system of his day.

5. He invited all people into a relationship of amazing love with God.

6. He took great pains to tear down religious walls and boundaries separating people from God.

7. He gave everything he had to dispelling the shadows hiding the truth and love revealed in Scripture. In his own words and actions, he fulfilled all prior religious teaching.

8. He supplanted human understandings of religious law with God's law of love, paving the way for human hearts to receive God's heart of love.

9. He taught and demonstrated for all to hear and see how to return to being images of God created in love and sustained by God's love.

10. He made love personal, inviting people into direct relationship with God.

11. He taught people to fully and completely love all others as an essential part of their loving relationship with God.

12. He openly challenged and defied any religious rule or authority that demonstrated anything less than God's complete love. He did this knowing that it would lead to his suffering and death.

13. He fed the hungry, healed the sick, raised the dead, cast out demons, returned sight to the blind—and did it all with the compassion of God.

14. In a demonstration of God's total love for all humanity, he allowed the authorities of his day to torture and kill him in the most brutal of ways.

15. Following his resurrection, he commissioned his disciples to teach as he did and to live as he did so that all the world would come to know the living, loving presence of God.

The sum of Jesus' words and actions (and the list could go on) demonstrates the character and nature of God. Out of God's loving heart and mind, Jesus commands us to love. Other New Testament writers, too, affirm that the very essence of God in Christ is love. Their writings call upon us to know God is love, to enter complete union with God and others in love, to demonstrate our love of God through love of others, and to lay down our lives in love for others as God has done for us in Jesus.

In light of all of this, how is it possible for Christians to deny a God of complete love and defend a god who justifies revenge and violence? Why are so many Christians and non-Christians at peace with a god of *incomplete* love?

Clinging to Life, Accepting Less Than God's Real Love

Those who believe that violence as a means of defense and that retaliation for offense are necessary, whether on a personal or a national level, have accepted less than a God of complete love. This is not a problem of biblical interpretation. We can think of all the arguments for biblical literalism and biblical infallibility, all the Old Testament stories showing a God of war, and the various theories of an unchanging and all-knowing God of the Bible. I have spent my life since my middle teens amid these conflicting messages—the justification of conflict touted by much of Christendom.

As the Christian church in general, we have lost our way beginning at least from the time of the Roman emperor Constantine (312 AD). To state this so plainly may sound naïve or judgmental, yet someone needs to call out the truth of real love and name when we are practicing incomplete love. No unkind word or violent deed will stand the scrutiny of God's love. If this is not the truth about God's love, we have thrown out the foundation and centerpiece of the New Testament and the gospel of Jesus Christ. God's complete and unconditional love is the irrefutable core of New Testament scripture. Thus, all understandings of God and all extrapolations to the day-to-day lives of God's people must be guided by complete and unconditional love.

Many will challenge the above statements by quoting Old Testament scripture. Many will refuse to accept Jesus at his word, rationalizing various ways his teachings do not apply to the complexities of the twenty-first-century world. Many will choose to take Jesus' cross as a ticket to theoretical forgiveness and a free pass to heaven. Many will pick and choose from Jesus' teachings to balance their human desires with God's commandment to love. Many will simply choose the name of Christ as their security blanket in case there really is a God of judgment. Fear of hell has often been a great motivator to sign on to a so-called Christian life.

All such attempts to contradict and circumvent the core New Testament teachings on God's complete and unconditional love fall short of the real problem. No amount of debate over scripture will help us out of our desperate human dilemma. In fact, the more we debate these matters, the more we keep the real problem hidden from our conscious minds. To get hooked into arguing scripture is to miss the reason we suffer through life and project this suffering onto others in violent ways. Meanwhile, all the divisions in the Christian church provide the evidence of the great extent to which we have lost our way. And the fact that so many people scorn the Christian church is further proof.

The primary reason we have held back from full acceptance of the love Jesus taught and lived, died for and rose for, is self-preservation. Self-preservation comes in many forms and disguises. Self-preservation plays a heavy role in all our relationships regardless of how intimate or shallow. Each human being is a complicated mix of motivations focused on both self and selflessness: Who am I, and who am I in relationship?

We are in an endless struggle for self-preservation until we realize that the only way beyond this fate is to stop struggling. The image that comes to mind is a person who has stepped into a pool of quicksand. Desperately, this person grasps at anything they can reach to keep them from sinking deeper. The more they struggle, the deeper they sink and the more desperate they become. This is how many people live their entire life—struggling and grasping for whatever they can grab to save themselves.

The greatest lie of all, the most insidious falsehood, the evil of all evil harbored in the human soul is the notion that the quicksand is to be feared and that the life we have made for ourselves is to be saved. Nothing could be further from the truth.

We cannot be drawn into the heart of God while holding on to life fashioned by our own hands. God will not break our hold on life. God will not cross our will. God will not force us into a quicksand of total mercy. God is not a pool of quicksand pulling us forcibly into immense love. God will not trick us or manipulate us or intimidate us into welcoming arms of compassion beyond knowing.

Jesus said it so simply, so plainly, two thousand years ago, and we still do not understand and believe him. We have failed to realize that he gave us the greatest truth of life, which is also the greatest love in life: we must lose our life if we want to find it. That is what he said. In every waking moment of our lives, most people choose not to hear, not to understand, and not to believe him. As long as we hold tight to the life we live, we will never know the boundless possibilities of unconditional love.

Our problem is not somewhere "out there" amid differing doctrines or competing scriptures. Our problem is a heart problem, and it is all about whose heart will beat in us. We cannot choose both God's heart and a heartless form of self-defense. Many Christian leaders, writers, and teachers have failed to find a way to release their hold on life. Because of this, they have led Christianity into divisions and holy wars. The devastation of this hold on life and its influence on countless generations has helped bring our world to the brink of annihilation.

Who will let go? Who will choose God's love over their hold on life?

From Terror to Life Transformed

If we were to gather the whole story of the Bible and wrap it up into one package, what would that story tell? Jesus said it would be all about love—God's love, and our call to practice this same love. Have we met this Jesus? Have we heard this call on our life? Can we hear it now? It doesn't matter if we have been religious or not, gone to church or not, fallen in line with Christian doctrine or not. What matters is our heart, what lies at the core of our life, and the choices that flow from our deepest knowing. When we become tired of struggling to find our own way and grasping for our personal life's meaning, it is time to reconsider that constant, quicksand-like tug. Might that tug be God's love calling to us from a depth we have not yet known?

The apostle Paul's ode to God's love 1 Corinthians 13 is one of the most beautiful and significant passages in the New Testament. Here Paul challenges us to not understate the power and significance of God's love. He essentially states that we have nothing without love, and that love is above and beyond the greatest of all virtues. Similarly, 1 John 4:8 says, "Whoever does not love does not know God, for God is love." In the Gospel of John, chapter 17, Jesus prays the most beautiful prayer in the Bible, calling repeatedly for his disciples to be one in love with him and God the Father. John 3:16, the best-known verse of the Bible, declares, "For God so loved the world that he gave his only Son, so that everyone who believes in him may not perish but may have eternal life."

These texts highlight and expand the message that God's love is real—the supreme reality. When Jesus commands us to love completely, he does so from God's heart full of total love for us. Apart from this love that Jesus commands, we humans can never *fully* know God.

God's real love transforms every life it engulfs. This transformation is what awaits us in the quicksand of God's embrace. When we put aside our fear of losing life, we will realize the true life that God has created and intended for us from the beginning. Love's transformation will turn our lives around in such undisputable, blessed fashion that we will no longer dismiss it as impossible; instead, we will celebrate it with joy.

Loving Completely—Becoming One with God

Returning to Matthew 22:37, this phrase that Jesus used—"with all your heart, and with all your soul, and with all your mind"—brings to an end any halfway attempt at love. God asks *everything* of us, not out of selfish desire but out of God's own selfless love. This is our invitation to oneness with God. Even more, Jesus is saying that this is the path of discipleship. This is "the way, and the truth, and the life" (John 14:6). You and I were created to live in union with God through love. This is God's call to us, expectation of us, and commandment for us.

In order to let go of ourselves and live fully in oneness with God, three understandings are key: (1) God is love, pure and simple. (2) Jesus defines God's love. (3) Life itself is redefined by love. We have touched on these before, but let's explore them in a bit more detail here.

God Is Love, Pure and Simple

What we believe about God may largely be a statement about us. How many people want a completely loving God? Many people are comfortable knowing God as partial in terms of love, judgmental toward sinners, and more than ready to mete out some horrible punishments. However, what you and I want God to be does not define God, and our wishes may be the furthest thing from the truth. God is love, pure and simple.

The angel's opening line to the shepherds in Luke 2:10 says it all: "Do not be afraid; for see—I am bringing you good news of great joy for all the people." This line is stated throughout the Old and New Testaments. People have been afraid of God throughout the generations, and we have defined God, at least partially, based on our fear. Fear has cut us off from God, instilling in us doubt and disbelief about God's completely loving nature.

"God so loved the world." These are Jesus' words, not mine. For generations, some Christians have masked the truth of these words by portraying God as vengeful and scary, to convict "sinners" of their need for God. But "perfect love casts out fear" (1 John 4:18).

Imagine waking up from a terrifying nightmare to find you are being held tight in the embrace of someone who loves you beyond measure. Now imagine that this someone is the Creator of the universe. The love that surrounds you is the creative power by which the universe came into existence. The fear of your receding nightmare is like the grit of life being cleansed from your soul by the power wash God's love delivers.

Throughout the book of Matthew, Jesus is saying, in a sense, "Wake up! The nightmare is over. You're safe." The terror is past. Don't relive it. Don't believe it. Love transforms the world, and love will transform your life. Everything Jesus said and did is the ultimate embrace of God's complete love waiting for us as we wake up. Over and over Jesus calls us to live lives that are fully awake to God's love. Hear and see with ears and eyes awake to the call of God's love on your life. Experience the healing of God's complete love. Experience the casting out of demonic dreams. Wake to your full inclusion in God's reign! Jesus proclaimed life's awakening to all. The love and joy of God's kingdom come are eternally alive in resurrection, have defeated death, and refuse any form of terror we might dream up.

How many people throughout the generations have longed to wake up from the death and destruction strewn across human existence? Countless people have longed to awaken to a new world, a new hope, a new life, only to rediscover cycles of violence in its myriad forms. We all need another angel to tell us the "good news of great joy," to tell us we need never again be afraid, to help us truly wake up.

To wake up to the truth of God's love for us and this world is to open our eyes and ears to the eternal message of Jesus instead of to the hurt and anger, fear and resentment we have projected onto God. To wake up is to somehow know beyond our knowing that God is God, not an idea from our own head or heart. It is to finally accept the limitless love, the power beyond power, the bottomless depths into which we are falling into God. In losing our life by giving in to the loving embrace of God, we will find oneness with love itself.

Now in our truly wakeful state of heart and mind, God will live the ways of love within us. There will be nothing left in us of the false concepts of a vengeful, angry god, but only the truth of the God of love. All the half-notions of God that simply mimicked our own resentments, prejudices, jealousies, and judgments will have passed away. Our former life of believing in violence will have vanished along with the last vestiges of our fear. We now recognize the idea that God would ever have us fight and kill our enemies, hold on to divisions, or spout angry words as just a part of fear's repertoire of lies.

Consider once more the "good news of great joy to all the people" that the angel proclaimed in Luke 2:10. Again, we highlight the word *all*. A God who is angry, judgmental, punishing, exclusive to baptized Christians, or the sponsor of eternal torture is not good news and never has been. But the God of complete and everlasting love, known to us in our fully awakened state of heart and mind, is in fact the ultimate good news to all. Imagine how such good news changes the message we live out among people who don't yet know God's love! Imagine the barriers we have formerly enforced between ourselves and "unbelievers" crumbling to the ground! In our awakening, what is being revealed to us and through us is this: that God is wholly trustworthy, totally safe, absolutely redeeming, forever available, 100 percent merciful, and never reflective of anything we have ever feared. Now *we* can be the angel God sends to humanity with the message "Do not be afraid."

For God is love, pure and simple.

Jesus Defines God's Love

Jesus defines God's love as perfect, complete (Matt 5:48). It is of great importance to understand just how fundamentally Jesus has changed our understanding of God. To help us grasp both the importance and the radical nature of Jesus' instruction about God's complete love, I refer to these words from Ulrich Luz in his commentary on Matthew:

> In the basic text of Lev[iticus] 19:18 ["you shall love your neighbor as yourself"], "neighbors" are only Israelites, the people for whom God has given his laws. . . . A difference first appears in the context of the Jesus tradition. Along with the entire Jesus tradition Matthew expands "the neighbor" . . . to include everybody.[2]

Matthew's account of Jesus' life and teaching leaves no doubt as to the all-inclusive, limitless love of God. Whereas Hebrew scriptures offer great insight into God's love and mercy, there remains the specific question of our relation to the enemy. It is finally in Jesus' life and teachings that the full meaning of love is revealed, both through his words and, most conclusively, in his actions as he endures torture and faces death. Luz is correct in his assessment that *neighbor* now includes everybody because love of enemy stretches love to the fullest perimeter possible.

The love to which Jesus calls us applies to all people, situations, and time. Jesus leaves us with no exceptions in his fulfillment of the rule of love. It is hard to imagine anyone successfully defending the use of violence in any form (any unloving word or action) by using Jesus as their teacher or example. The truth of Matthew's Jesus is rather the opposite. Anything other than the message of complete love is not Christ-like and, therefore, not Christian. Defense of any unloving word or act draws its source

2. Luz, *Matthew*, 3:83.

from outside of Jesus, and indeed, from outside of New Testament scripture. For all who claim to follow Jesus, it is time to reevaluate the use of violence in light of Jesus' transformation of the scope of love.

Nothing ever written can fully and accurately describe God's love in Christ Jesus. Even the words of the Bible are not enough. Instead, it simply needs to be experienced. Our reading of scriptures and our experience of God's indwelling are not the same thing. Matthew's way and Jesus' way of saying this comes in the form of the commandment to love God with everything we have, all that we are. God's love in Jesus can never be contained in ideas on paper or in our brains. While the experience of this love involves our brains, more importantly it captures our heart and soul. *All* means "all." Real love is *that* inclusive.

A wonderful illustration of an experience of Jesus' complete love comes in chapter 9 of the book of Acts. This is the story of Saul journeying to Damascus to ferret out followers of Jesus so they could be captured and killed. Saul was part and parcel of the systemic violence perpetrated by the collaborating religious and political forces of his day. But in loving and dramatic fashion, Jesus confronts Saul and leads him through a repentance—a turning from violence to following Jesus—that fully turns his life around. (He even gets a new name to symbolize the extent of the change.) Out of this encounter with Jesus flow the writings of Paul, the premier evangelist of the New Testament. And from Paul's writings we repeatedly glimpse the wonder and power of the transformation of a human being exposed to the complete love of God in Jesus. From the time of his encounter with Jesus, Paul devoted his life to living "in Christ." Paul had been shocked to discover himself engulfed by God's love.

Romans 12 is a powerful indication of how Paul took the message, ministry, death, and resurrection of Jesus as the foundation of his own life and teachings. If we read Romans 12 carefully, we hear the very message of Jesus being described. Paul claims the complete love of God in Christ Jesus, as taught and lived by Jesus. Only in and through Jesus can Paul now write about and live this love himself. As a result of Paul's union with God in Christ Jesus, we become recipients of Paul's invitation to the shocking transformation of real love.

It is Jesus who fundamentally changed history with the earth-shaking gospel of God's real and complete love. For Christians, as for Paul nearly two thousand years ago, there is no other voice, no other calling, no other witness so strong.

Life Itself Is Redefined by Love

Real love takes control of everything, in a wholly safe and wonderful way. We find that love's grip is the touch of healing, grace, mercy, and peace that we have long hoped for and dreamed of. There is nothing else like this hold that God now has on us because now we know, for the first time, the truth about ourselves—not who we have been, but who we are meant to be. Love is how we were created; love is the purpose for which we were created; love is the very DNA of God. Once this reality takes hold of us, nothing in this life is ever the same. God's complete love is now the only thing real to us. It redefines all else—self, others, situations, how we hear and see life—in light of the kingdom of God.

As human beings in this present life, we will not live out God's kingdom perfectly. This must never become our goal. Our goal is to keep our focus on Jesus. His example, his teachings, and, most of all, his dwelling in us will now set the course of our heart, mind, and soul. This is the only way we will remain truthful and practical as we live out our faith from day to day.

Anyone whose life is focused on Jesus' example and message will find their life redefined by God's love. As frail human beings, both our successes and failures at love will require God's merciful presence moment by moment. Within our redefined lives, the best thing we can do is confess God's love for us and for the world moment by moment. In both our confession and our celebration of God's love, we will find ourselves healed and transformed. The world around us will be transformed as well, and all of life will be redefined.

From Confession to Celebration of God's Love

Amid all the ways that religious people in first-century Palestine expressed their devotion, Jesus chose to be the prophetic voice calling people back to the God of love. Jesus was not a violent revolutionary out to overthrow Roman rule. He was not a collaborator. He was not a legalist. He certainly was not one to withdraw from the fray. He rejected these options, as should we, today. When we commit to focusing on Jesus, other forms of religious devotion fade into the background as failed attempts or lesser ways to know God and live as God's children.

Human attempts to pursue God have not changed much since Jesus' day. To the extent that we have believed and lived things *other than* God's will and way as modeled by Jesus, our lives, too, have become ruled by fear and violence. But as Jesus redefines our lives, the things we have depended on become known to us as falsehoods. Love's truth is now our only guide.

Violent Resistance: From Confession to Celebration of Love

Attempting to right the wrongs of the violent system we live under is in many ways based in righteous anger. Righteous anger is not a bad thing, but it becomes a bad thing when we allow our anger to dictate our response. Whenever anger dictates, we succumb to the very violence we claimed to be against. Whenever anger dictates, our focus is misplaced; we have taken our eyes and ears off Jesus and placed our attention on the wrong, which, then, is sure to overtake us. As the wrong overtakes us, we respond with more anger, we become impatient, we risk depression, and the fruits of the Spirit (Gal 5:22–23) are diminished in us.

Whether our anger is expressed overtly or covertly, it comes out in some form of violence. In effect, we become ambassadors of the violent system instead of emissaries of love's hope for the world. Our righteous anger is now wasted and used by the system we oppose. But righteous anger does not have to lead to love's defeat.

My personal experience with righteous anger is ongoing. Slowly, I am learning to recognize this anger both as an alert to love's truth-telling and as a prompt to confess my need to control things that are not mine to control. If righteous anger wakes us and helps us respond honestly in love, it has served a great purpose. If instead we remain angry, it will turn inwardly or outwardly violent. In confessing our own violent nature, we find the grace and wisdom to respond to violence in our world with God's love. We learn to think the truth in love, speak the truth in love, and live the truth in love.

When you feel righteous anger in the face of injustice or violence, thank God for that. Then allow God to shape your anger into a world-transforming love. Let God's love stir your heart to celebrate love, even and especially in the worst of times. Celebrate love with all the world, especially where the world needs it most. Take the most offensive person or situation you know and choose to love and forgive. In this celebration, violence in and around you will come to an end.

Withdrawal: From Confession to Celebration of Love

Withdrawal takes various forms. It can come from or turn into apathy. It can stem from fear. It can be our response to hopelessness. It can represent our attempt to live idealistically apart from the evils of the world. Whatever form withdrawal takes, it circumvents a life lived as Jesus taught and lived. Withdrawal takes us out of the game and renders God's love in us ineffective, just when the world needs it most. Withdrawal also claims in our absence from life a sure defeat of God's love in us. Where now is the purpose of God's love?

God's real love is real all the time. It does not surrender to evil. It does not hide. Rather, it stands firm in the face of either good or evil.

It is natural to seek protection when life gets rough, but which protection will we seek? Any form of self-protection signals our need for confession. Withdrawal in whatever form is our attempt to self-preserve. When we are in self-protection mode, our focus is not on Jesus, and God's love will not reach us through the walls we have raised. When we hide from the world, we hide from God's love, because the world is where God meets us, especially in the form of Jesus: "for God so loved the world that he gave his only Son."

All who hide or attempt to withdraw in part from the world have a wonderful discovery waiting: God's love is the best and only *real* hiding place. In God's love, hiding becomes filling and braces us to return boldly to the world. Instead of sharing our quiet withdrawal, God leads us into the battle of good versus evil with the only sword God ever wields, the sword of love. Along the way, we discover a much greater purpose than self. We discover love's protection beyond anything withdrawal could give. We begin to see and hear how life in Jesus becomes eternal. It is not a life we will risk losing ever again. We celebrate the gift of receiving and giving love, for in God's kingdom, this gift is forever.

Collaboration: From Confession to Celebration of God's Love

The Sadducees of Jesus' day were the ruling class of religious leaders, and they collaborated with the Roman occupation of Israel. Similarly, many Christians, and many Christian leaders, have been collaborating with the rulers of this world for centuries. Such collaboration, then and now, represents a sell-out to systemic control that operates through violent means.

As many have pointed out, Paul affirmed government as ordained by God and called Jesus' followers to obey government (Rom 13). This does not take God's love out of the equation, however. Paul did not tell us to collaborate with anything except the love of God (Rom 12). We must be willing to hear Paul in the context of the full book of Romans and of his life's journey, bearing witness to God's love before agents of the government all along the way, culminating at Rome. Paul was not a collaborator. He was a faithful witness. He became a martyr for the cause of Jesus' way. He stood up not in opposition to government, but in full compliance with God's love for this world. His witness was done in the name of Jesus and by living God's love. Paul wanted, more than anything, for all to hear and experience God's love in Jesus Christ. He took this message everywhere he went from the communities of Asia Minor to the halls of Roman power. Paul's life is an example of how God's real love can be brought to bear on government. Let's not forget who killed Jesus, who killed Paul, and why.

Collaboration with the world's system of violent power is defiance against God's love. To cease such collaboration does not mean we are bad citizens or that we resist the governments of today. Bless Paul for Romans 13. We are to treat our governments as good entities and rejoice in all the good they do. In the process, we are to obey the good and bear witness to God's love in the face of violence, in the same way Jesus and Paul did.

Confessing where we have collaborated in systemic violence will be a lifelong process, for we continue to live in this world. Our life will be redefined profoundly: to stop collaborating with the belittling or taking of life will render us new creations in Christ Jesus. A prayer attributed to St. Francis comes to mind as a counter to all collaboration with violent systems:

> Lord, make me an instrument of your peace.
>
> Where there is hatred, let me sow love;
>
> where there is injury, pardon;
>
> where there is doubt, faith;

where there is despair, hope;

where there is darkness, light;

where there is sadness, joy.

O Divine Master, grant that I may not so much seek

to be consoled as to console;

to be understood as to understand;

to be loved as to love.

For it is in giving that we receive;

it is in pardoning that we are pardoned;

and it is in dying that we are born to eternal life.

St. Francis, like the apostle Paul, sought to live in full collaboration, not with this world's powers, but with Jesus' life and teachings. This was an extreme position compared to how the powers of church and state have been wed since the fourth century (St. Francis lived during the twelfth). Yet, in God's love, we become new beings who celebrate the giving—never the taking—of life.

Legalism: From Confession to Celebration of God's Love

Love does not dictate right belief or action. Love has no need of a crutch such as these to bolster its journey through life. When love is real, it moves and has its being within life itself, and it *is* life itself. Love does not need something added to it to confirm its existence. Love's only rule is the rule of love itself.

Human efforts to understand God's love will fail, for we are woefully dependent on outside stimulants and grab-handles to provide assurance. But these are not love, and they provide only false comfort. Anything other than God's real love will eventually become another crutch. Throughout time—and supremely so in Jesus—God's love has been demonstrated, lived, taught, and commanded; yet many have chosen to rely on things other than oneness with this God of love. Many have made even Scripture an object of right belief, thus missing the experience of God's love living in and through us.

What a joy it is to throw away every crutch. This past year I spent six weeks in a walking boot to give my Achilles tendon a chance to heal from a tear. Shedding that boot was a moment of great relief. In the months since, I have appreciated the gradual strengthening and healing of my body. Simply being able to walk without pain has been wonderful. I learned from my physical therapist just how much the boot gave the tendon a chance to heal. I also learned how much damage the boot did to other parts of my ankle and calf by restricting their natural function.

Imagine shedding the restrictive boot of religious legalism. Imagine taking off any restrictive dependence on rules other than love. Imagine taking time to slowly heal and strengthen your relationship with God and people. Imagine nothing but love growing and healing and freeing you to love even more.

The Outcome of God's Real Love

In place of violent resistance, withdrawal, collaboration, and legalism, God's real love offers formerly unimaginable ways to redefine our broken and hurting relationships. What remains is the celebration of God's love shared in community with all. To know God's unconditional love is to live this same love and watch as it transforms the world around us.

To transform the world around us is not always easy. We must pay the price of our former self-centered lives. We must be willing to give up many things in order to discover the unimaginable love of God. "Those who agree to carry and love what God loves, both the good and the bad of history, and to pay the price for its reconciliation within themselves—these are the followers of Jesus (Philippians 3:10-12)."[3]

3. Rohr, "Solidarity with the World."

10

God's Judgment Is Love's Tough Side

In the previous chapter, we stated that God's love is real, complete, consistent, unconditional, and always available to everyone; otherwise, it would not be God's love and it would not be real love. Common rebuttals to this assertion are reminders of scriptures about God's wrath, warnings about hell, and Jesus' stern rebukes of his opponents. What are we to make of the seeming contrasts and inconsistencies of scripture? On the one hand, we have amazing descriptions of God's love. On the other hand, we have words and phrases describing a seemingly scary, even vindictive God who ordered genocide and who will torture sinners forever in the fires of hell.

Biblical interpreters who claim to read the Bible literally try to reconcile the loving God and the scary God because in a literal view of scripture, somehow all passages have pretty much equal authority. On the other end of the biblical-interpretation continuum is a seeming abandonment of the understanding of scripture as given by God. Here there is little consideration of divine inspiration, and scripture is understood just like any other ancient text. The biblical account can be picked apart, examined under the microscope of critical thinking, and placed back together like a lab specimen to await later re-analysis.

The two descriptions above are caricatures and not intended to fully describe the careful process and thought that go into these very different ways of understanding the Bible. In no way do I mean to belittle or devalue any genuine attempt to come to terms with the Bible's message. My point is to note the very different approaches to the text. The examples above illustrate the myriad ways Christians and non-Christians have tried to explain the Bible's meaning.

I am not a biblical literalist, and I am not a scriptural lab technician. What I bring to the study of the texts is the following: First and foremost, I am a follower of Jesus. In my own meager ways, I attempt to live the life Jesus taught and lived. I will put no other voice or example above his. This is one of the ways I give my heart, soul, and mind to loving God, and this is how I experience God's love transforming my life from the inside out.

Second, I look to Jesus as the Word of God (John 1:1). In practical terms, this means Jesus is the living voice and image of God with authority over all religious writings, religious practice, and the whole Bible. As I approach all scripture through Jesus, the voices of many texts become one voice, one story, illuminated and illustrated by every other "word" (message, communication) of God in the Old and New Testaments, forming a rich texture together. I also hold a deep respect for both biblical lab technicians and biblical literalists, although I follow neither pathway.

From my view of scripture, the complete and uncompromising love of God is most fully described and lived by Jesus. In the Gospel of Matthew, Jesus repeatedly warns us of God's judgment in some of the gravest terms. But this chapter aims to show how God's love includes God's judgment, how God's judgment expresses God's love, and how Jesus' words of judgment illustrate in profound ways the nature of God's love. This may come as a shock. Yet, God's love must be the key to unlock the meaning of judgment. Otherwise we are back to disbelieving Jesus.

If we are serious about following Jesus, we must come to terms with God's judgment. Jesus gave us much to think about when it comes to love's confrontation with evil. Let's consider his sayings about the serious consequences of not living a life of love. But first we need to confront a few serious misunderstandings that have plagued the Christian church and the world for many generations.

SCRIPTURAL WORDS WE HAVE TRANSLATED AS "HELL"

There is no direct translation of the English word *hell* in the Greek or Hebrew Bible. This statement blasts apart a whole genre of Christian literature and challenges much of Christian thought back to St. Augustine in the fourth century. If you do an internet search on what the Bible says about hell, you will find answers opposite to what I am saying here. If you look up the word *hell* in your English Bible, you will find it among Jesus' own words in Matthew. There is obviously a great disconnect between what the biblical text does *not* say about hell and what most of us have thought it said about hell.

Old Testament

There is one Hebrew word used in the Old Testament and several Greek words used in the New Testament that have led generations of Christians to a misunderstanding of the afterlife. The Old Testament word is *Sheol*. This word simply means "the place of the dead" or "the grave." Of the sixty-five places in the Old Testament where the word *Sheol* is used, the King James Version of the Bible translates thirty-one of them "hell,"[1]

---

1. Klassen, *What Does the Bible Really Say*, 37.

but that translation is misplaced. Old Testament writers understood the concept of death and called it *Sheol*—the final resting place for all people.

Sometimes in the Old Testament *Sheol* is used within the context of poetry depicting, or at least hinting at, God's judgment. Deuteronomy 32:22 is a good example. Within a harsh rebuke to those who made idols of other gods (vv. 15–43), this song of Moses seems to lend itself to a Christian view of eternally punishing fire. "For a fire is kindled by my anger, and burns to the depths of *Sheol*; it devours the earth and its increase, and sets on fire the foundations of the mountains." If we read this text as a reference to hell as a place of eternal punishment, we misunderstand its meaning. This text is a poetic way of emphasizing how seriously God takes the sin of idol worship.

Again, *Sheol* simply means "the place of the dead." Various biblical psalms and proverbs attest to this meaning. At times God is praised for saving someone from *Sheol*. Psalm 86:13 reads, "For great is your steadfast love toward me; you have delivered my soul from the depths of *Sheol*." Psalm 139:8 even claims God's presence everywhere includes even *Sheol*: "If I ascend to heaven, you are there; if I make my bed in *Sheol*, you are there."

In some of the books of Psalms and Proverbs, death (*Sheol*) is clearly seen as a warning against loose living or as a fate to be avoided. Speaking about children, Proverbs 23:14 says, "If you beat them with the rod, you will save their lives from *Sheol*." It does not say "save their lives from hell." In fact, the previous verse (v. 13) is a parallel saying: "Do not withhold discipline from your children; if you beat them with a rod, they will not die." This idea of death is used in a similar way to how we might today say that some things lead to life and some things lead to death. Some things are life-giving and some things death-dealing. Our speech today is filled with metaphoric language that points beyond literal meaning. In the same way, we must carefully read the language in the Bible with recognition that much is said dramatically and not intended literally. How could beating a child with a rod literally save them from dying? The writer of Proverbs would have known better than to think this way.

All in all, the Old Testament never uses a word equating our English understanding of hell as a place of God's eternal punishment in the afterlife. It is important to be clear about this and to stop using Old Testament texts to bolster our understanding or our defense of hell.

> KJV translates *Sheol* as *hell* whenever they want to convey it as the particular destination of the wicked. However, when portraying the fate of the righteous, they translate it *grave*. Hmmm. Obviously, the translators would have had a major problem if they had consistently translated *Sheol* as hell in all these verses. [Psalm 89:48] would convey that every person would go to hell, and [Job 14:13] that Job asked to go to hell!

In the rest of the popular modern versions, the literal translations, and the Hebrew and Greek texts, there are NO references to hell in the OT, or of the concept of everlasting tormenting flames—not one.[2]

New Testament

There are three Greek words, *Gehenna, Hades*, and *Tartarus*, which occur in the New Testament and often are translated with the English word *hell*. As with the Old Testament word *Sheol*, these three words do not describe an eternal fire as punishment from God. These three words, especially *Gehenna*, have been misused by Christians for centuries to further the cause of a supposedly fearsome and angry God who is the opposite of what Jesus taught and showed us. It has become nearly impossible to extract our thinking from the images of demons with pitchforks, at the behest of God, roasting sinners eternally, or of the defeated evil people of this world literally burning in a lake of fire designed by God as their afterlife punishment forever.

To use these three Greek words to bolster our notions of hell is unconscionable. It is time to stop, carefully examine these words, and place them where they belong in our understanding of God as complete and real love. We can then move forward without a schizophrenic and unbelievably cruel notion of God.

Gehenna is used seven times in the Gospel of Matthew, three times in Mark, once in Luke, and once in James. All references from Matthew, Mark, and Luke come from Jesus. It seems Jesus is the one we must credit for introducing us to the idea of *Gehenna*. Later in this chapter we will look at the context of Jesus' sayings on judgment, which at times include the use of *Gehenna*. For now, let's focus on understanding the literal meaning of the word.

Gehenna was literally the garbage dump of Jerusalem. Randolph Klassen writes:

> *Gehenna*, the name of the Valley of Hinnom, the ever-burning garbage dump southwest of Jerusalem . . . had an evil history. Under the depraved leadership of King Ahaz, Israel was encouraged to worship the god Molech and burn little children there as an offering to this pagan god. King Josiah put a stop to that practice and labeled the area accursed. Thereafter *Gehenna* became a sort of public incinerator. Always the fire smoldered in it, a pall of thick smoke lay over it, and it bred a loathsome kind of worm that was hard to kill. Often the bodies of the worst criminals would be deposited here.[3]

Similarly, Jon Sweeney states the following:

> By the time of Jesus in the early first century, the Valley of Hinnom was well-established as a cursed place just outside Jerusalem with a constant fire burning. By then, people mostly disposed of their trash there, but Roman soldiers

2. Ferwerda, *Raising Hell*, 41.
3. Klassen, *What Does the Bible Say*, 46–47.

would also throw the bodies of criminals executed by crucifixion in the infamous pit. There was no other use for such a pitiful location with a sinister history that backed right up to the Old City, close to the Holy Temple.[4]

In addition, Julie Ferwerda explains:

> It has been suggested that Jesus referred to the impending Roman siege against Jerusalem in 70 AD, about forty years later. In this siege more than a million Jews were killed inside the city (either starved or put to the sword) and their dead bodies were reportedly taken outside the city and burned in the garbage dump of *Gehenna* ("hell"), where the worms and maggots infested any remains.[5]

It is easy to see why Jesus would use the image of *Gehenna* to warn his hearers of the dire consequences of their unloving words, thoughts, and actions (Matt 5:22, 29, 30; 10:28; 18:9; 23:15, 33; Mark 9:43, 45, 47; Luke 12:5). Those in first-century Palestine listening to Jesus speak of *Gehenna* would have known this to be a terrible place of death and decay. They would have also understood Jesus to be talking of a literal place on the then-present landscape just outside the city of Jerusalem. They would not have thought he was threatening to literally send them there. They would have taken his *Gehenna* sayings as emphatic warnings against living lives that hurt others, hurt oneself, and led people astray from God (note his use of *Gehenna* in Matthew 23). They could not have imagined he was warning them of an eternal punishment of fire by God's hand. Indeed, they had little, if any, concept of either eternity or eternal punishment because the only related concept in their scripture was simply *Sheol*.

The torturous route that so many have taken through the centuries to the current understanding of hell draws primarily from sources outside of biblical texts.[6] Certainly, Jesus is not the source of our hellish imaginings, just as he is not literally telling us to cut off our hands or feet or to gouge out our eyes (Matthew 5:29, 30; 18:9; Mark 9:43, 45, 47).

The word *Hades* was used by Jesus in Matthew 11:23; 16:18; Luke 10:15; and 16:23. *Hades* also occurs in Acts 2:27 and 31 (quoting and referencing, respectively, Psalm 16:10). Finally, it is used in Revelation 1:18; 6:8; 20:13; and 20:14 (*Death and Hades* are used in tandem in Revelation). *Hades* is the New Testament counterpart to *Sheol* in the Old Testament, literally meaning "the place of the dead" or "death" itself.

The story of Lazarus and the rich man in Luke 16 includes an imaginative use of the word *Hades*. Taken literally, this parable of Jesus might lead us to think of *Hades* as a place of torment. But to take the story this way ignores the meaning of the word *Hades* and all the uses of *Sheol* in the scriptures Jesus knew. Also, if taken literally, this story becomes the nearly ridiculous description of a fantasized afterlife, and we soon

---

4. Sweeney, *Inventing Hell*, 99–100.

5. Ferwerda, *Raising Hell*, 46.

6. Sweeney goes into great detail to back up this statement in *Inventing Hell*.

lose the impact and intent of the tale. It is intriguing—and sad—that many Christians find it easier to imagine literal torment in hell (for others, that is) than to realize the extreme emphasis Jesus places on compassion for people who are suffering and in need in this present life. Jesus is a master of storytelling, using vivid imagery to make his point. Over and over in the gospels, he teaches authoritatively, giving dramatic depictions of both good and bad consequences for the lives we live. The whole point of Jesus' story of Lazarus and the rich man is not to describe hell or heaven but to emphasize the steadfast witness of scripture ("Moses [the law] and the prophets"—verses 29–31) and of Jesus himself when it comes to seeing the suffering of others and responding with mercy.

Hades occurs in Revelation four times. In each instance, it is a companion word to *Death*. Revelation 1:17–18 quotes Christ saying, "Do not be afraid; I am the first and the last, and the living one. I was dead, and see, I am alive forever and ever; and I have the keys of Death and of *Hades*." True to Jesus' claim to having the keys to Death, in Revelation 6:7–8, the Lamb opens the fourth seal and out comes the pale green horse ridden by Death and *Hades*. These two frightening figures were granted terrible power to inflict death upon one-fourth of the earth. Finally, in Revelation 20:13–14, these two symbols of death are defeated—"thrown into the lake of fire." Along with them, in verse 15, those unnamed in the "book of life" are also thrown into the "lake of fire."

Throughout Revelation is a tremendous struggle between the forces of good and evil. The forces of evil are generally understood to represent the Roman Empire.[7] The force for good is God in Christ Jesus, who, in the end, conquers death and destruction through the faithful witness of the Lamb that was slain. Throughout Revelation, all faithful witness and worship are directed to God and the Lamb, opposing Rome's demand for obedience and worship. The outcome of the struggle is never in doubt, even during times of great suffering and death. This assurance is given at critical junctures, such as Revelation 11:15, which reads: "The kingdom of the world has become the kingdom of our Lord and of his Messiah, and he will reign forever and ever."

The symbolism throughout Revelation cannot be taken literally or we will lose the meaning and the good news of John's vision. Strange horses, seals, riders, killings, tragedies, stars, angels, a dragon, a whore, plagues, trumpets, mouth swords, a pregnant woman giving birth, war in heaven, a beast with multiple horns and diadems—all these symbols were used by John to communicate hope to his readers at the end of the first century. John was saying, in effect, "God in Christ Jesus reigns supreme, no matter what terrible things we may experience in this life under the earthly power of Rome. Though we suffer torture and death, we must remain faithful, for in the end, God in Christ Jesus will come down to us, gather us, and live among us forever. Death (*Hades*) itself will be destroyed."

7. Kraybill, *Apocalypse*, 37.

Finally, the word *Tartarus* is used only once in the Bible, in 2 Peter 2:4. If we follow the text closely, we find that Peter is describing a temporary place for sinful angels and, if we read through the end of the chapter, possibly for the worst of sinners among people. *Tartarus* is described as a place of punishment until the final judgment of God. This passage is also an assurance of God's mercy for people who are faithful and righteous.

Note that in Peter's mind, *Tartarus* is temporary. He only describes it as a place of temporary punishment (v. 9) and says nothing about torment, fire, or eternal torture. In Peter's view, there is a separate place and experience after death for the righteous and the unrighteous. This is a "holding place" until God's justice is finally brought to bear on all.

Note also that Peter describes the unrighteous in the most terrible terms. They are people involved in "depraved lust" and "who despise authority" (v. 10). They are slanderous, "irrational animals," "born to be caught and killed," "blots and blemishes," with "eyes full of adultery, insatiable for sin"; they "have hearts trained in greed," and are "accursed children" (vv. 12–14). This severe condemnation continues through the end of chapter 2.

I don't know that I have ever encountered someone who met the qualifications of Peter's unrighteous. Yet many Christians have allotted a place of eternal punishment for anyone who does not acknowledge Jesus as their Savior. I personally know many people who, while not acknowledging Jesus, live lives every bit as righteous as those of most Christians. These people would come nowhere close to Peter's description of those who might find themselves, albeit temporarily, in a place called *Tartarus*.

My point is not to try to assess who would go to *Tartarus* or even to figure out exactly what Peter means by *Tartarus*. My point is that *Tartarus* is not the *hell* we have tried to make it. We do not get our traditional view of hell from Peter. And remember, this is one word used only one time in all of scripture, with specific reference to fallen angels.

THE ABSENCE OF REFERENCES TO HELL IN OTHER NEW TESTAMENT WRITINGS

You might think the sermons and teachings in the book of Acts would be full of so-called hellfire and brimstone. Nothing could be further from the truth. Hell is never mentioned in Acts.

Peter was especially close to Jesus and all Jesus taught and lived. Jesus named Peter "the rock" upon which he would build his church and said that "the gates of Hades will not prevail against it" (Matt 16:18). Yet Peter's first two sermons in Acts 2 and 3 illustrate how his approach to sinners was opposite that of threatening eternal punishment. In both these sermons, Peter confronts the people as responsible for killing Jesus ("this man . . . you crucified and killed," 2:23, and "you killed the Author of life,"

3:15). What greater sin could there be? Surely those responsible for the crucifixion of Jesus would deserve a place in hell. I can hear the condemnation to eternal punishment thundering from Christian pulpits.

As proof that Acts is a continuation of the gospel story of Jesus, Peter simply named the horror of what people did, then called them to repentance just as Jesus had done. This repentance is not so they can escape hell. It is about how they can turn toward life and experience God's forgiveness, the gift of the Holy Spirit, and the "refreshing . . . presence of the Lord" (Acts 2:38; 3:19-20). Here Acts bears witness to Jesus and his salvation with a wonderful message of good news. Throughout the book of Acts, this message of good news was brought by Peter, John, Phillip, Paul, and others to the crowds of people who, in some sense, participated in Jesus' death, to the authorities who conspired together to kill Jesus, and even to the Roman emperor.

Klassen states:

> It is noteworthy to observe that nowhere [in Acts] is the church enjoined to rescue people from hell. The motive in their evangelism is to proclaim Good News precisely because it is such "good news"! To be forgiven. To be welcomed by the Creator as Savior. To find direction for life and what follows through allegiance to Jesus Christ as Lord. To become fully free and alive in the family where love predominates and God is now called "Father." These are the blessings that prompt the sharing of the gospel. The threat of hell seems to play little part.[8]

Not insignificantly, in Acts we also find the witness of martyrdom. The message Peter, Paul, and the others brought to their peers and authorities alike was good news of repentance and forgiveness offered even to those who were executing them. The message of Jesus was brought to bear on humanity's worst sinfulness in positive, noncoercive, nonthreatening, and nonretaliatory ways. This was the way of both Jesus and the early church. This is not the way of many Christians today. The wrongful application of our view of hell has contributed greatly to the Christian justification of state-sponsored violence, personally vindictive acts and attitudes, and the divisive ways we treat one another. All the while, we have strayed from Jesus, the early church's witness, and virtually all of the New Testament. A correction to our present-day understanding of God, hell, and judgment is enormously important if we are to return to the message of Jesus, the church he sponsored through Peter, and other New Testament writers.

Consider the absence of hell in Paul's letters—nowhere does Paul speak of hell. The greatest evangelist and church planter of his day, Paul had no use for our modern concept of hell. Amazing! Even in the throes of a passionate discourse on God's judgment (Romans 1:18–2:16), Paul stops short of a description of hell. The absence of hell is also significant in the Gospel of John and the three epistles of John.

8. Klassen, *What Does the Bible Really Say*, 55.

All these omissions of any mention of hell make for a strong indication that the gospel of Jesus Christ does not depend on a present-day Christian idea of hell. The gospel of Jesus did fine for several hundred years before theologians began to formulate a doctrine of hell.

ORIGINS OF THE CONCEPT OF HELL

It is not within the scope of this chapter to thoroughly examine the origins of the concept of hell as eternal punishment. That said, we need to gather enough information to direct those who either question what has been stated above or desire more information on why so many Christians have believed and still believe in an unbiblical view of hell.

Pre-Christian sources of hell as eternal punishment including torture, demons, and fire go back as far as early Mesopotamian religion, predating even our Old Testament patriarchal history. There were Egyptian writings about hell. Hell also occurs in Buddhism and Hinduism. Zoroastrian stories about people being judged and sent to hell predate the birth of Christ. Greek thought would have also contributed via Plato and others.[9] Plato's writings predate Christ by more than four hundred years. *Tartarus* is a name used by the Greek poet Hesiod around 700 BC.

For the purposes of our discussion, consider two important points: First of all, despite the influences around them, the Old Testament writers did not pick up on this view of God and the afterlife. We don't get "hellish" images from the stories of our ancient scriptures. The monotheism of the Hebrew people, the emphasis on Yahweh as the one and only God, would preclude any serious consideration of the mess of gods and goddesses, and of any battles of good versus bad gods. Furthermore, Israelite writers were not concerned with the need for an afterlife in order to somehow come to terms with the injustices of earthly life. They remained steadfast in their emphasis on this life and on the importance of holiness through obedience to God *now*. Our Old Testament scriptures had the option of including the influences of "hellish" thought, and they chose against it.

Second, it is important to understand that the thought of hell became pervasive among people in various regions and out of different religious roots quite early in the scope of known history. This widespread belief in hell from earliest times says two things: (1) There seems to be something we humans feel we need that has to do with a longing for justice, a sense of incompleteness, perhaps our own desire for revenge or self-affirmation. Whatever it is, we seem to have unfinished business with life and God—a primordial need to which hell speaks. (2) This need, so pervasive in the human psyche, was rejected by the Hebrews. Not only did they not choose a "hellish"

---

9. Klassen, *What Does the Bible Really Say*, 63; Sweeney, *Inventing Hell*. Again, Sweeney goes into great detail on this point.

option available to them; they resisted a very deep sense of human need and instead trusted Yahweh to be enough for them.

Emphasis here is on *Yahweh being enough*! Where faith fully shines from Hebrew scriptures, the writers bask, totally content, in their present relationship with God. (Job 42:1–6 is an excellent example.) We Christians could learn a lot from this degree of contentment. Maybe then we would not need to try to control life after death. And just maybe, we would not need the promise of a future reward to goad us into loving God.

By New Testament times, the Pharisees believed in an afterlife, including hell. This view had its roots in the years between the Old and New Testament writings (consider 2 Esdras 7). Others in New Testament times, such as the Sadducees, rejected the idea of an afterlife.

Hell, in the sense of eternal punishment, was not a part of the earliest writings of the church fathers; in fact, the majority were on the side of some form of universal and eventual salvation.[10]

The first lonely voice on hell comes to us from Tertullian. Tertullian was the only believer in hell we hear from until later in the fourth century.

In *Raising Hell*, Julie Ferwerda quotes Ken Vincent regarding Tertullian:

> The first person to write about "eternal hell" was the Latin (West) North African Tertullian (160–220 AD), who is considered the Father of the Latin church. As most people reason, hell is a place for people you don't like! Tertullian fantasized that not only the wicked would be in hell but also every philosopher and theologian who ever argued with him! He envisioned a time when he would look down from heaven at those people in hell and laugh with glee![11]

I suspect Tertullian should not be judged too harshly based on his misconception of hell. That said, and if Dr. Vincent is correct, we already see in Tertullian the hurtful seeds of vengeful thinking, leading to the problem of a long, long span of church history involving some of the worst vindictiveness the world has ever seen. It all starts somewhere, and my contention is that it starts in the human heart. From the darkness of the human heart comes our reading of biblical texts in ways the writers and the first centuries of commentators would not have supported.

Much is at stake if we start to think differently about God, God's judgment, and the afterlife. Many Christians' approach to the world, sinners, and unbelievers—with judgment, division, and war—would need to change. Many find the absence of hell in the witness of the Bible and early Christian thought too uncomfortable a truth. Is it any wonder some do not want this change?

10. Ferwerda, *Raising Hell*, 54–55.
11. Ferwerda, *Raising Hell*, 54.

From Tertullian we jump a couple centuries to what may be the saddest chapter in church history regarding the concept of hell. In the fourth century (the time period of the "marriage" of church and state following Emperor Constantine's conversion to Christianity), we encounter St. Augustine. Again, I quote Vincent:

> By far, the main person responsible for making hell eternal in the Western church was St. Augustine (354–430 [AD]). Augustine . . . was made Bishop of Hippo in North Africa. He did not know Greek, had tried to study it, but stated that he hated it. Sadly, it is his misunderstanding of Greek that cemented the concept of eternal hell in the Western church. Augustine not only said that hell was eternal for the wicked, but also for anyone who wasn't a Christian. So complete was his concept of God's exclusion of non-Christians that he considered un-baptized babies as damned. When these babies died, Augustine softened slightly to declare that they would be sent to the "upper level" of hell. Augustine is also the inventor of the concept of "hell Lite," also known as Purgatory, which he developed to accommodate some of the universalist verses in the Bible. Augustine acknowledged the Universalists, whom he called "tender-hearted," and included them among the orthodox."[12]

It has been claimed that the root of horrors like the Spanish Inquisition and countless other acts of torture and death over the centuries can be linked to Augustine's advocacy of the right of Christians to persecute others—not only non-Christians, but also Christians who had the courage to stand up to those in power. Remember that Augustine lived and wrote during the era of the co-opting of Christianity by the Roman Empire, and this becomes more and more frightening over the years. As a Christian in the Anabaptist tradition, I have many spiritual ancestors who fell victim to church-sanctioned torture and murder during the sixteenth century.

From Augustine we can link to Jerome's translation of the Bible, known as the Latin Vulgate, which "was heavily influenced by Latin hell-inventing theologians like Tertullian and Augustine."[13]

From Jerome's Latin Vulgate we can link to the horrors of Dante's *Inferno*. Sweeney explains:

> An Italian poet named Dante Alighieri changed everything with his famous *Inferno*, which he began writing in about 1306 [AD]. But to read the *Inferno* today is to realize how little it has to do with the Bible. There is far more Greek and Roman mythology—adapted by Dante from classics such as Hesiod's *Theogony*, Virgil's *Aeneid*, and Ovid's *Metamorphoses*—than there is scripture in Dante's nine circles of hell. . . . Cleverly using Virgil and lots of funky myth,

---

12. Ferwerda, *Raising Hell*, 55.
13. Ferwerda, *Raising Hell*, 56.

Dante is the one who made eternal punishment exotic and real, as well as Christian.[14]

Then we progress to twentieth- and twenty-first-century Christian writers and commentators, which leads us to an entire genre of popular Christian writing today. As recently as a year ago, I purchased a copy of one of the more respected Christian commentaries on Revelation, only to discover the now centuries-old, automatic assumption of eternally torturous hell. It seems as if careful biblical scholarship took a vacation when it came to promoting the concept of punishment in the afterlife. This is further proof of how Christian thought has been co-opted not just in Augustine's day, but for the centuries since.

RETHINKING HELL

I'm painfully aware of how lightly I have touched on the historical development of the concept of hell. If you are doubtful of or intrigued by what I have presented, please follow up by studying the texts listed in the footnotes and bibliography at the end of this book.

At this late date in the history of Christianity, we might ask if it is even possible to approach the Bible with unbiased thoughts concerning hell, the afterlife, and God's judgment. If you grew up in the folds of Christianity, consider both the sum of all the teachings on hell and the absence of alternate readings you have encountered. My guess is that most who are reading this chapter have never been exposed to the history I've just presented. I'm sixty-six years old, have been in the Christian church all my life, have pastored in the church for thirty years, and have never heard a sermon explaining the origins of the idea of hell. I am ashamed to admit that until now, I also have never preached or taught on this topic.

Some may find it impossible to approach the teachings of Jesus through any lens but that of "hellfire and brimstone." Yet, the call to hear and believe Jesus rings loud and clear.

In order to hear and believe Jesus, we must first step back and examine our own hearts on the topics of hell and God's judgment. The primordial need of humans for revenge, punishing justice, and self-justification comes from *our* hearts and not God's. Our insistence on the reality of eternal torture in some sort of hell speaks first of our own unresolved pain and suffering in this life.

Where has this need come from? What or who has formed your thoughts and actions that depend on the notion of a god that tortures people forever? Why would you not rejoice in the possibility that God's love is eternal and for all? Would you think anyone else's suffering relieves your own? Does your understanding of God depend on your heart's longing for vengeance-based justice? Can you begin to imagine God's power in the form of love and forgiveness, God's sovereign justice/righteousness, and

14. Sweeney, *Inventing Hell*, 3.

God's essential mercy filling your heart and mind as, together, we approach the teachings of Jesus?

Can we back out of Dante's hell, described in his *Inferno*, published in 1321? Many will not be ready to question the belief system of dominant Christian teachings on hell. But for anyone wishing for release from a fearsome God, letting go of hell will be great news. Let us begin to imagine a world where God is totally safe for all, where the millions of people the church has condemned to hell's permanent torture are instead recognized as still loved by God and still offered forgiveness by God, no matter what.

WITH EYES AND EARS OF LOVE

There are many ways to approach scripture. What we bring to our study of the text often determines what we take away from the text. If we bring an unquestioning view of a torturing God, an unwavering commitment to the necessity of violence in this life, and a long-standing satisfaction with the church's traditional teaching on hell, then we will easily find multiple verses from the Old and New Testaments in support of what we already believe. Many Christians have been doing exactly this for centuries.

Jesus often challenged his listeners to see and hear with eyes and ears of faith. He both challenged and fulfilled first-century understanding and application of scripture. He infused scriptural understanding with his essential oneness with God. He went to the heart of every matter of faith and life with God's heart. Complete and perfect love is God's love (Matt 5:48), and it is commanded of us as well (Matt 22:37–40).

The challenge to any follower of Jesus is to see and hear as he calls us to see and hear. In doing so, we must submit to his teachings and life example. We must learn from Jesus what is the heart and soul of God. We must experience God's heart and soul from within as God reshapes our very core. We cannot do this without first submitting to his kingdom come and will being done (Matt 6:10). The kingdom and will of God are to be lived within the justice and righteousness of God's kingdom now (Matt 6:33). If we are not going to believe Jesus in regard to these teachings, it is useless to believe his judgment sayings because we will misunderstand and misuse them.

We will also fail to see and hear Jesus if we try to interpret his judgment sayings using biblical references other than his own teachings and ministry. No Old or New Testament writer would want to stand before God and declare their understanding superior to God's. Even if you believe in a very literal understanding of scripture, how can you not look first to the words and example of Jesus our Lord? Isn't Jesus Christ Lord over any understanding of scripture we could bring?

The point is to emphasize the importance, first and foremost, of understanding Jesus' teaching on judgment within the context of his overall life and ministry. Let's be sure to take all of what has been said about God's love in chapter 9 and apply it to the texts below. Let's apply everything we have learned from Jesus in the beatitudes, his restatement of the law, his warning against judgment, his healing ministry, his parables, his total forgiveness, his absolute love, and his challenge to the religious leaders of his day. After we have thoroughly taken all of those aspects of Jesus, we are ready to hear his statements on judgment, because seeing and hearing Jesus brings us into the fold of God's love.

God's love trumps everything from the personal to the global, from inner struggles to distant war. Try to imagine the expansive and amazing possibilities that unfold when we allow God's love to be free from all our constraints, including our interpretations of scripture. Now it is safe to challenge a rigid and fear-based orthodoxy with love. We no longer need to fear the eternal pain and suffering of evil, for in one way or another it will be vanquished. That's how powerful God's love is! Now we are ready to hear and see Jesus as he confronts evil head on with God's searing, unconditional love.

Love's Tough Side

Love is not real if it is weak, and there is no weakness in God's love. If God's love is complete and unconditional, then anything unloving will run headlong into the "wrath" of love. Evil in any form will feel the weight of love's strong judgment. Have you ever turned quietly aside in the face of a dirty joke, an abusive situation, injustice for the poor, an unfair use of power, a violent outburst, a cruel lie, the resignation of cynicism, an intolerant spirit, a judgmental attitude, or violence in any form? You surely have, as have I. But God's love has not.

An alternative reading of Jesus' judgment teachings, one that does not include a torturous hell or a God to be feared, can provide Christians with a more powerful message of ministry and evangelism than does fire and brimstone. Becoming clear about what Jesus teaches about God's purpose and nature will free us to live and share fully in the image of God. We will have lost the false justification of violence based on the notion that God is violent. Once we retire our schizophrenic view of God (loving here, torturing there), there is great hope for our own schizophrenia to subside. Through this relearning, we will experience the confrontation of God's tough love ready to overcome any lack of love in us and our world.

Jesus' Teachings on God's Judgment

In *The Last Word and the Word After That,* Brian McLaren lays out the following sequence concerning how the Christian church has often thought and taught about hell:

> 1. Our contemporary modern Western conservative Protestant gospel would say this:
>
>> Behavior: Not accepting Jesus Christ as personal savior, not being saved or born again, not asking Jesus into your heart so your sins can be forgiven, etc. Consequence: Being sent to hell. Point: Accept Jesus as your personal Savior.

2. Not one passage from the Gospels says anything remotely like this.[15]

Using the following passages as examples, let's test the above ideas.

It should be noted that there are more than thirty places in Matthew where Jesus speaks of some type of serious consequences for not loving, for practicing injustice, for mistreating others, etc. Taken all together, these teachings amount to an emphatic pronouncement against anything that lacks or opposes God's love. We will look at four such teachings that represent some of his most explicit warnings and that use the word often translated "hell."

Lest some reading this chapter bring the accusation of proof-texting (using a few specific passages out of context to prove a point), it is important to emphasize that throughout this book we are studying the *entire* life and ministry of Jesus. All of Jesus' teachings and ministries in Matthew are ground zero for addressing the following texts. We are doing the opposite of proof-texting when we take all of Jesus together as one non-schizophrenic image of God. In regard to judgment, Matthew's Jesus speaks the most frequent and colorful warnings of all four gospel writers; thus, Matthew makes the ideal test case.

In the following interpretation of the texts, I purposely do not ascribe to God the traits of anger, revenge, or any sort of premeditated torture, whether temporary or eternal. Thus, I may be accused of bringing a bias to the text, which is exactly what I am doing. I want to be utterly clear that the bias I bring is, to the best of my knowledge, an accurate rendering of the whole life and ministry of Jesus. I would simply plead that any critics of this methodology would also do all they can to understand and believe Jesus in his entirety. I don't presume to have the final say on understanding all of Jesus, but I would love to shift the interpretive process of the Christian community to a goal of understanding and believing Jesus in all he said and did, and to be done with sound bites and theological assertations that skip over any aspect of his teaching and ministry.

The following pages offer several tests of whether our understanding of the text is acceptable: (1) Does our understanding of the text square with the God of love shown us in Jesus and explained in chapter 9 of this book? (2) Is this message free of the bias of a punitive church history, power politics, or a combination of these? (3) Is this good news to all people, not just those who feel justified by their own righteousness? And (4), given who Jesus was and the situation he was in, is this our best understanding of what he intended to communicate?

Let's begin by hearing the texts in the order they come in Matthew. There may be value in hearing the teachings back to back.

> *Matthew 5:29–30* [Jesus said,] "If your right eye causes you to sin, tear it out
> and throw it away; it is better for you to lose one of your members than for
> your whole body to be thrown into hell. And if your right hand causes you to

15. McLaren, *Last Word*, 115.

sin, cut it off and throw it away; it is better for you to lose one of your members than for your whole body to go into hell." (Matthew 18:8–9 is similar.)

Matthew 13:47–50 [Jesus said,] "Again, the kingdom of heaven is like a net that was thrown into the sea and caught fish of every kind; when it was full, they drew it ashore, sat down, and put the good into baskets but threw out the bad. So it will be at the end of the age. The angels will come out and separate the evil from the righteous and throw them into the furnace of fire, where there will be weeping and gnashing of teeth."

Matthew 23:33 [Jesus said to the scribes and Pharisees,] "You snakes, you brood of vipers! How can you escape being sentenced to hell?"

Matthew 25:41–46 [Jesus concluded the parable of the sheep and the goats,] "Then he will say to those at his left hand, 'You that are accursed, depart from me into the eternal fire prepared for the devil and his angels; for I was hungry and you gave me no food, I was thirsty and you gave me nothing to drink, I was a stranger and you did not welcome me, naked and you did not give me clothing, sick and in prison and you did not visit me.' Then they also will answer, 'Lord, when was it that we saw you hungry or thirsty or a stranger or naked or sick or in prison, and did not take care of you?' Then he will answer them, 'Truly I tell you, just as you did not do it to one of the least of these, you did not do it to me.' And these will go away into eternal punishment, but the righteous into eternal life."

"If your right eye causes you to sin . . ."—Matthew 5:29–30

This text comes as a dire warning against the dangers of lust (5:27–30). Jesus took one of the ten commandments and leveled it directly against the patriarchal system that in his day gave enormous advantage to men. For a scriptural example of this, read John 8:3–11 and consider all the ramifications of the "woman caught in adultery." Here in Matthew 5, Jesus directed the warning about lust to the male religious community of first-century Jews. He named the heart of the sin. He made clear that sexual sin starts in the mind and heart, coming through how we look at someone and then touch them. He went way beyond simple prohibition of adultery and directly challenged the dominant status of men. In no small way, Jesus took on the systemic sin of a society where male sexual sin hid behind a wall of privilege and destructive power.

To get a sense of the importance of this teaching, we must consider the ongoing and recent news of sexual sin inside and outside the Christian church. This is a huge problem for us today, and Jesus was saying it was a huge problem for his first-century listeners too.

Within the fuller context of Matthew 4 and 5, this warning on lust comes to us as instruction for a new community of people whose hearts are to be filled with the Holy Spirit (5:3), whose lives are turning toward kingdom living (4:17, 23), who truly seek justice and righteousness (5:6, 20), who turn their anger into reconciliation (5:23–25), who do not return hurt for hurt but turn it into good (5:38–41), and who love and pray for enemies just as God loves completely (5:43–48). In every part of this section of Matthew, Jesus was showing the nature of God's heart of love and calling all people to truly live this way. He was also warning them about the extreme danger of not living lives that follow God's heart of love.

Dallas Willard states it this way:

> In Matt. 5:20–48, then, we find out precisely what fulfillment of the law would look like in daily life. In this crucial passage, where the rightness of the kingdom heart is most fully displayed, there is a sequence of contrasts between the older teaching about what the good person would do—for example, not murder—and Jesus' picture of the kingdom heart. That heart would live with full tenderness toward everyone it deals with. This passage in Matthew 5 moves from the deepest roots of human evil, burning anger and obsessive desire, to the pinnacle of human fulfillment in *agape*, or divine love. In this way the entire edifice of human corruption is undermined by eliminating its foundations in human personality.[16]

The purpose of Jesus' teaching on lust, and the broader teachings of chapter 5, is to call us into a heart-to-heart relationship with the God of complete love, from which we will then live entirely different lives within a community of love. Jesus' teaching here is not a treatise on the afterlife, but on life as we are invited to live it now.

If we keep our focus on what Jesus has been calling us to become in love—think back through all that we have discussed in this book—we realize firsthand the exhilaration of love's power in our daily words, actions, attitudes, and relationships. And we do not suddenly lose this focus now when we hear him declare the dire warnings about living outside the heart of God, as if he were saying, "Now let's make God into a fearful being in order to turn our hearts in the right direction." Instead, the warnings become for us part and parcel of the message of love.

Let's suppose for the moment that you and I are best friends. We share a deep love for one another. We are hiking high in the mountains along a narrow path. At one point I turn around and see that you are heading toward a 1,000-foot drop-off. I immediately warn you. I want to get your attention and redirect you to safety. I fear for your safety. But you keep moving toward the drop, and I repeatedly call out my warning. As you get closer to an inevitable death, my warnings get more and more emphatic. By the time you are at the very edge, I am screaming. I am trembling with fear motivated by my intense love for you. At that moment of life or death, I will say and do just about anything to save you, and it is all because I love you.

Over many generations, God's people did not heed God's warnings. This is the sad part of the Old Testament story. Jesus' whole reason for being on earth was to be

---

16. Willard, *Divine Conspiracy*, 136–37.

God's love incarnate so that all humans would know the love of God and God's saving grace (John 3:16). Jesus was God's all-out means of doing anything necessary to save us from going off the 1,000-foot cliff. This is the really big context of the passage on lust.

But that's not all. Jesus, the supreme invite to God's mercy and love, faced the ultimate rejection of the religious guardians of God's people. In the face of Jesus' ministry, both the religious leaders and all who followed them were on the precipice of death. They were in fact dying this death daily! They were falling to their deaths as Jesus addressed them!

Is it any wonder Jesus used strong language? Is it any wonder he boldly confronted evil at both the personal (lust) and corporate (male privilege) levels? Is it any wonder he spoke of death as the way that led to the horrible garbage dump of Gehenna, for in his day there could be no more graphic way to depict it? In this passage, Jesus is not telling us God is a torturer. He is telling us that our lustful desires will only take us in the way that ends in death. It is a terrible, horrible thing, this death! The way of death (in this case, living with lust) is a terrible thing! The way of death (the systemic violence of sexism) is a horrible thing! Throughout the world and throughout history, millions of people's lives have been shattered by the failure to heed Jesus' warnings on sexism and sexual sin.

How could Jesus, our God of complete love, do anything *other than* all that he could possibly do and say to stop our fall from life into death? Just as I would scream at you or forcefully grab you from the edge of the 1,000-foot cliff because I love you dearly, Jesus, with more love than I could ever muster, shows us God's complete and unconditional love as he rebukes evil and those who live it and promote it.

The tragedy of using a passage like this one to bolster a view of hell is that we risk missing Jesus' point entirely. We are then left dangling from and falling over the side of a steep cliff. Which is exactly what we see when we take an honest look at the world around us.

"Throw them into the furnace of fire"—Matthew 13:47–50

The parable of the fish caught in the net is much like the longer parable of the weeds (Matt 13:24–30, 36–43). In Matthew 13, Jesus tells a total of seven parables, all about the kingdom of heaven, and all communicating the importance of Jesus' life and ministry for the new community of his followers.

If we hope to understand Jesus' stern warning about the evil ones who will be thrown into the furnace of fire, we'd better know what he means by "kingdom," and what he means by "righteous." Otherwise, anyone seeking to justify themselves will easily put themselves with the righteous in the kingdom and judge others to be the evil ones outside of it. This is what many Christians have done down through the generations since Augustine. Too many folks have followed the church's standard teaching on hell by using passages like this one to justify both their belief in the torture of hell and their own exclusion from it. At the same time, many of these same people have not followed Jesus and his teachings on the kingdom, along with the righteousness necessary to live a kingdom life.

The kingdom Jesus is teaching about in these seven parables is the reign of God—on earth as in heaven—in the lives of those who believe Jesus and live his teachings now. There is one kingdom of God, and it is both now and yet to come. This kingdom is made up of those who put God's kingdom and God's righteousness first, before anything else. All of Jesus' teachings and ministry are given for us to believe and to live. These teachings and ministry examples reveal God's redeeming love for all of humanity. If we forget this last part, how can we be counted with the righteous? Would we not ourselves be the evil ones, the very ones thrown into the fiery furnace? We should be extremely careful what kind of God we wish for.

Once again, we must resist temptation to divide Jesus or God into different beings with schizophrenic personalities. If we wish to understand what Jesus is saying about the evil and the righteous, their future, and their judgment by God, we cannot take this parable as anything separate from God's love taught and lived by Jesus, even while he endured the cross. In the early part of Matthew 13 Jesus repeatedly pleads for people to hear and see with understanding, knowing and living God's heart. Surely this is how we are to learn from all scripture, including this one.

In this text Jesus emphasizes the vast difference between those (using my metaphor) who walk the path safely up the mountain and those who step over the edge of the cliff. His focus here, and ever since he began his ministry (Matt 4:17), is on living in God's kingdom now. His purpose is to direct us safely up the mountain.

Let's also look at some specific wording of this passage—those words and phrases typically used to support the idea of a torturous hell at the behest of a vengeful God. In this passage the word *Gehenna* is not used, but in verses 49–50, Jesus says, "So it will be at the end of the age. The angels will come out and separate the evil from the righteous and throw them into the furnace of fire, where there will be weeping and gnashing of teeth."

What if we read these two verses without the preconception of eternal hell and a torturing God? It might be hard to step out of this interpretive history, but try to imagine a God of all love and mercy: A God in love with every human child who ever has been and ever will be born. A God willing to sacrifice everything to reach us with love; a God ready to run and embrace us like the father of the prodigal son (Luke 15:20). A God who will do anything, including calling out dire warnings, to keep us from falling to our death and destruction. A God of endless forgiveness who has called us to love and forgive in the same complete way.

Now apply this understanding of God to these two verses. This is the least we can do if we intend to believe Jesus and take him at his word—indeed, at *all* his words and actions. This then is an alternate reading:

> At the end of this present time, there will come a time of sorting out, a time of God's judgment, when those who live evil lives apart from the kingdom of God will be separated from those who live the righteousness of God in the kingdom. This is a time of justice when the love of God will sear the hearts of those who remain apart from the kingdom, those who have chosen not to believe Jesus and live as he has taught. These then will be thrown into the "furnace of fire" to be refined, to be melted and molded, to experience the anguish of all the suffering they have caused, and to endure the searing of God's love for them.

I ask you, Which interpretation of these two verses aligns with forgiving others so we can be open to receiving God's forgiveness? Forgiving seventy times seven? Loving enemies so that we will be children of God? Jesus dying on the cross and forgiving his torturers? Would it be the traditional view of God torturing the vast majority of humanity forever and ever? Or would it be the God of love who judges in the piercing power of love as described above?

Some may say the interpretation above is too soft, too easy on sin, or so bland as to render God's judgment insignificant. Sure, we can think of it in this way, but that illustrates our human view of love's ineffectiveness. How could God's love be ineffective? It seems that Jesus' warnings of judgment make it quite clear how serious this judgment is. Those who want an eternal torturing hell have chosen to find it in these warnings, but a careful reading of Jesus' warnings can just as easily be taken as love's tough side. With this "tough love" understanding, Jesus is saying two important things: (1) He is calling out in the most serious of ways those of us who are headed toward a terrible death, falling off that mountainside. And (2) he is saying that everyone, at the end of this time we now know, will face God's judgment, and that this will mean God's justice applied with the rigors of love's examination.

And wouldn't such an exam be a complete one, in the sense of laying bare anything unloving in our lives and judging its hurtful nature? Any masks or coverings we try to use to hide would be pulled back, and the dark side of our innermost being would be revealed. We would face the refiner's fire of Malachi 3:1–5, but its purpose is not to destroy, but to purify and make whole.

Think of God's judgment as a great light ready to illuminate all the darkness in us. We will be forced to face ourselves in contrast to the exacting, complete love of God. No more denial. No more self-justification. All our guilt for all our violence will be called to account. This is where any presupposition of our innocence is absurd. Think of the violence perpetrated by Christians for centuries, yet these same Christians enjoy the idea of other sinners—not themselves—going to God's judgment of hellfire. Talk about seeing a speck in someone else's eye when there is a log in our own (Matt 7:3)! If anyone is going to burn in hell for eternity, it will be those who do not believe Jesus and who disobey what he has taught us (Matt 7:21–27).

The last thing a violent person wants is to come face to face with a God of complete love, because that person would have to (perhaps for the first time in their life) truly look at their own cruelty and self-preservation. They would need to stare into the void where love should have been. They would be forced to see how they belittled God's love, how they did not take it seriously, how they proceeded through life choosing to believe that violence held a place of honor. They would be devastated, and maybe, just maybe, that devastation could be the place where God's searing love becomes God's healing and forgiving love. Think of how in the Old Testament God always sought the return of people to faith and obedience (e.g., Mal 3:6–7).

In the dire warnings of Jesus, he used imagery, metaphor, and hyperbole. He intentionally did not speak in literal terms because he was expanding the warning in exaggerated ways to get past our thick-brained complacency and misguided composure. He was in fact challenging the very people who in his day had it all together religiously. That same type of people today are most often the ones touting the hellfire doctrine, and they seem blind to this terrible mistake. Which leads us to the next text.

"You snakes, you brood of vipers!"—Matthew 23:33

Matthew 23 is a heart-rending accusation of religious hypocrisy wrongly focused outward on rule-keeping instead of inward on repentance and renewal. Jesus leveled this accusation against the very persons who had renounced him from almost the beginning of his ministry. They did not listen with ears to hear, nor did they see with eyes of faith. They opposed Jesus, and they chose not to follow him or do what he called people to do. It would behoove us to take this warning seriously and ask ourselves if we have truly seen and listened to Jesus, believed him, and followed him. If we are religious leaders and have not done so, this chapter is directed at us too.

It is important to not scapegoat the Pharisees of Jesus' time. Yes, they are the main protagonists in Matthew's gospel story, but rule-keepers are alive and well in any age. There are countless variations on this human theme. The basic trait of rule-keepers is a rigid adherence to an external measure of goodness applied to themselves and especially applied in judgment of others. The external measure of goodness is mostly (often subconsciously) used to bolster one's own rightness, but sometimes it can be twisted into a mental self-punishment. Regardless of how rule-keeping is applied, it acts like blinders on the otherwise seeing eyes and plugs up the otherwise hearing ears that Jesus so often talks about. Seeing and hearing as Jesus would have us do is impossible for those caught in a rigid orthodoxy of rule-keeping.

Recently, the small house church I belong to discussed Matthew 12:43–45, in which Jesus says:

> When the unclean spirit has gone out of a person, it wanders through waterless regions looking for a resting place, but it finds none. Then it says, "I will return to my house from which I came." When it comes, it finds it empty,

swept, and put in order. Then it goes and brings along seven other spirits more evil than itself, and they enter and live there; and the last state of that person is worse than the first. So will it be also with this evil generation.

While this seems like an odd saying of Jesus, it made perfect sense in the context. of Matthew 12. In this chapter, the resistance to Jesus has intensified greatly. Verse 14 reads, "But the Pharisees went out and conspired against him, how to destroy him." Then the Pharisees accused Jesus of casting out demons by the power of Beelzebul (the devil), essentially condemning him as satanic (12:24). These rule-keepers of Jesus' day were the religious leaders who not only remained silent as people walked off the cliff to their spiritual death, but defined and prescribed the very path that led to such destruction. They were, in Jesus' words, "blind guides of the blind" (Matt 15:14).

As our group wrestled with Matthew 12:43–45, it became apparent to us that Jesus was saying, loud and clear, "Don't focus your attention on cleaning the house!" In other words, cleaning your house is a fine activity, but don't let it become the *reason* you have a house! Taken literally, we can see the application. Taken spiritually, Jesus was saying you can clean your spiritual life all you want, but if that is your focus, you will become empty and vulnerable to the indwelling of ever worse spirits making an ever greater mess. The only reason to clean our spiritual house is so that the Holy Spirit will dwell in us and live through us. This can only be the spirit of love, grace, mercy, forgiveness, and reconciliation—nothing less.

Back to snakes and vipers. The rule-keepers of Jesus' day were striving to keep the "house" of their generation clean, no matter what. Earlier generations of rule-keepers killed the prophets (Matt 23:31), and this present generation continued that legacy (vv. 34–36). Anyone who challenged the rule-keepers and their clean house was subject to being murdered. That was a serious defense of their rigid cleanliness, and it comes down to this in every generation, even to this present day.

In Matthew 23:33, Jesus declared the certainty of judgment on the rule-keepers. They were snakes and vipers because they bit their victims and infected them with a deadly poison. They were not just guilty of going over the side of the cliff themselves; they were leading a whole generation of people to a horrible spiritual death. The destruction of *Gehenna* awaits these rule-keepers! Jesus emphatically claimed that rule-keepers must face the destructive horrors they have wrought against their followers. At the end of this age, God will face down the rule-keepers with a relentless adherence to love's demands. Consider the juxtaposition of rule-keeping devoid of God's love on the one hand and the expansively complete demands of God's love on the other.

This text is not about God's nature as a destructive and torturing force, though present-day rule-keepers will use it to defend their "house-cleaning" nature. This text is about the certainty of love's exacting judgment of rule-keepers of any generation. In the larger view of Matthew's gospel, the message is clear and consistent: rule-keepers kill spiritually, and they had Jesus killed physically. We could even argue that the main reason for Jesus' life and ministry was to fully confront spiritual rule-keeping. Let this passage serve as a stern warning for the very ones who claim a hard and fast hold on the torturing nature of God.

"And these will go away into eternal punishment"—Matthew 25:41–46

This passage is part of a larger passage (all of chapter 25) focusing us again on the kingdom of heaven (see v. 1) and, more specifically, part of Jesus' parable of the sheep and the goats (vv. 31–46). This may be the harshest warning about judgment Jesus ever offers. Essentially, he is saying that those who are not merciful, generous, kind, and loving to others in need will face eternal punishment, being thrown into the "fire prepared for the devil and his angels" (v. 41). How could Jesus have said it more strongly? If we are not living God's love by serving people in need, we are bound to a fiery punishment—our fate is equal to that of the devil.

Keep in mind, fire means a variety of things in both Old and New Testaments. Fire can mean refinement and purification. If we can let go of our historical under-standing of hell, then even this vivid depiction of judgment can hold the hope of redemption. In this passage, Jesus takes the sin of withholding mercy and service from others, and shows how it is the opposite of God's will and way in this world. Not show-ing mercy puts us into the same mess with the devil. Withholding mercy might just be the worst thing we can do in this life! Jesus is saying that punishment, the result of a self-centered life, is assured now and in the future. There is no escaping the ongoing reality of the horror our lack of love has wrought. The punishment is eternal, and we have brought it on ourselves. God does not cast us into the fire; we cast ourselves in. Jesus says, "Depart from me" (v. 41), and "These will go away" (v. 46), indicating the agency of the evildoers themselves. We can easily make the case that the people Jesus is accusing have in fact already removed themselves from living in the presence of Jesus.

Please consider the power of God's refining love. Surely, the purifying fire of a love as complete as God's love will persist until the devil is no longer the devil, until the unmerciful are cleansed of their evil hearts. Who is to say that God's fiery love is not applied to all who fail to live it? Who can say it does not extend from this present life into all eternity?

I am not suggesting we water down any of Jesus' judgment sayings. I am saying we must take them more seriously than ever before. Our unmerciful ways in this life lead to our self-inflicted, ongoing destruction, and it is inescapable. Rather than an assurance that right belief and some form of rule-keeping will save us, Jesus nails us with the truth about our unloving hearts. No one escapes this judgment. No longer can we push this unloving off on our notion of God. God is not and never has been the unloving one. God is the very definition of love. Our projections onto God of a punishing hell are simply a tragic way of hiding from the unmerciful evil in our own hearts. Jesus knew this and declared ultimate judgment upon it.

Consider the idea of hell as it has been defined by many forms of Christianity. If this hell is what Jesus was talking about, God would consign us to enduring the fires of hell forever because we did not visit the prisoner in this life. I cannot imagine being responsible for torturing someone with fire for even a second. The thought that *God* would do this to millions of people for eternity makes God into the epitome of what we often think of as the devil. If this were so, the world truly is "going to hell in a handbasket," and there is no God to save us from it.

Summing Up These Four Texts

In the passages above, we have examined four of the clearest and most direct sayings of Jesus on judgment in the book of Matthew. While there are other similar sayings, these four provide a representative sample from which point we can now think carefully about the others.

What has been said in this chapter will not answer all possible questions about the meaning of God's judgment, so let's suppose for a moment that a person still adheres to the traditional doctrine of hell. If we take Jesus at his word in these four passages while holding a traditional view of hell, let's be honest enough to face up to who is going to hell. If there is a torturing hell, it is reserved for those who treat women as sex objects (Matt 5:29–30), those who do not see and hear and believe Jesus (13:47–50), those who are rule-keepers (23:33), and those who ignore the needs of others (25:41–46). If there is a literal fiery hell, there are and will be many people experiencing eternal fire who did not and do not expect it. I wonder if all who do not fully follow Jesus' teachings and example against violence (those who do not see and hear him and do not do what he says) would really want to hold fast to their belief in eternal hellfire if they knew it was prepared for them. What about those without compassion for the poor and less fortunate? What about those who participate in sexual mistreatment of and injustice for women? What about all the rule-keepers (which might just include us all)?

If we were to study other judgment texts of Jesus in Matthew, we could then include the fires of hell for those who remain angry with and estranged from a brother or sister. (Do I hear someone pointing out the divisions in the church?) We could include all who do not repent (as Jesus defines repentance). It would include all who mistreat others and fail to forgive.

For centuries, these and other failings of people have not been the categories of behavior Christians have associated with a condemnation to hell, and this certainly displays a lack of taking Jesus at his word and believing him. In the traditional view, hell has been reserved for unbelievers, non-Christians, those whose doctrine does not match up with mainline authority, those who skip going to church, and, of course, all sorts of people we judge as evil. Meanwhile, we overlook the warnings Jesus levels directly at us!

Those of us who have defended the traditional view of hell have been guilty of hypocrisy. We have made up our own categories for sins deserving of hell and refused to believe Jesus. For centuries we have fallen into the same trap the Pharisees fell into. As Jesus described them, they demanded adherence to the law while not keeping it themselves (Matt 23:1–4). Furthermore, if we were to examine all the judgment passages of Jesus, even a very literal reading of the texts would not amount to the traditional Christian view of hell. These texts do not ascribe eternal punishment to God. They do describe the destructive outcome of our disbelieving Jesus, and they specifically describe the categories of sin deserving of this destruction.

ALL THE WRONG REASONS FOR HELL

If Christians throughout the centuries, from Augustine to today, had the will and the humbleness of spirit to lay their hearts bare before God, the need to have others tortured in hell would be exorcised and healed. If the human heart were released of its own pain, there would be no felt need for a punishing God to justify violence. Just as surely, for as long as we do not allow God to fully heal us, we will not know the true and expansive nature of God's love. To know God's complete love for us and the whole world would eliminate any dark space in our hearts. Instead of threatening people with hell, we would long to share God's complete love with everyone and in every circumstance.

For multiple reasons the traditional view of hell has been a terrible idea and a virally destructive force in human history.

Reason One

Likely the worst result of the traditional view of hell is what it says about God. The idea that hell even exists means, at the least, that God abandons millions of God's children to eternal torture by fire. The worst-case scenario is that God *sends* these millions to hell and tortures them endlessly. Either way, this would make God infinitely more terrible than Hitler! It would make God into our worst nightmare monster. This God becomes a worse devil than any other devil we have thought up.

For those who accept it, this horrific view of God negates just about everything Jesus said and did during his ministry years. It utterly contrasts the purpose and work of Christ's cross. It defeats the affirmation of Jesus we find in his resurrection. It destroys the meaning of Christianity from the inside out. Any reference to Jesus Christ's love and forgiveness must be overlooked or at least relegated to less than an accurate definition of God. We are left understanding God apart from the witness of Jesus; thus, anyone could justify war, division, resentment, and judgment based on Old Testament stories of conquest. The defense of this view often uses the line that God is unchanging, the same yesterday and today and forever. But this defense collapses if used to cobble together a God of love in Jesus with a God of eternal torture. And so our spiritual schizophrenia continues.

Reason Two

The traditional view of hell makes God unbelievable. If you adhere to this view, please think carefully about how this affects your spiritual journey. You have wedded your faith to a God less loving than you are. You have put your trust in a God who could torture you for eternity, and still might. Consider the role fear plays in your concept of God. Have you ever experienced a wholesome and intimate relationship with someone you feared? It's not possible. How can you believe God in any thorough way while keeping a safe distance from the wrathful part of God? Can you really *know* anyone—including God—whom you fear? Can you believe a God you do not know?

Reason Three

Anytime there is coercion—using a threat of punishment, suffering, or death to get one's way—free will fades. Think of how this plays out in this life. Now think of how threats of a fiery hell taint our ability to freely chose intimacy with God. If God uses fear to threaten sinners with hell, we are all threatened. No matter how much we convince ourselves of heaven's reward, somewhere down very deep inside, we know our own sinfulness and, in turn, the threatening displeasure of this God. To at least some extent, we have lost the assurance of love and forgiveness on the part of a truly loving God.

While the threat of hell hovers over us, no matter how distant we imagine it, we will come limping—not leaping—into the arms of God. Even as we prescribe hell to those we deem less worthy than us, we subconsciously acknowledge the threatening shadow of our own evil. Somewhere buried inside, we know the awful truth of this threat. We know it lurks within our need for retaliation, defense, and vengeance. We can't help but project this same threatening presence onto God. Grace has now forsaken us on an incredibly important subconscious level. Ephesians 2:1–10 states that God's love and grace saved us "when we were dead through our trespasses." If it is not free, it is not God's grace. If it is offered through threat, it is not free.

Reason Four

The God of hell is a lie. This is because we have projected our own hardness of heart onto God and created God in our image. This has been a long and complicated journey, full of power politics, acquiescence to religious authority, and a lack of courage to honestly hear and believe all of Jesus. The first Christian sources for hell come from Tertullian in the third century and Augustine in the fourth. We already noted how both harbored ill will toward the ones they consigned to hell. This is a warning signal about the projection of our need for vengeance, not God's.

Reason Five

God loses; the devil wins. If we had to guess, what percentage of all people ever will be Christians who qualify for heaven, according to the doctrine of hell? Would it be 10 percent, 20 percent, maybe 30 percent? I find it hard to imagine the figure being as high as 10 percent, but for the sake of this scenario, let's say it is 10 percent. If, then, 90 percent of all people are already in hell or will be soon, guess who is winning the war between good and evil. This idea proves false the concept of an all-powerful God. Though it may not be the intent of the folks who believe in hell, they have essentially given up the fight. They have given up all hope for billions of souls!

Reason Six

If we accept the doctrine of hell, think of all we would miss from Jesus' life, teachings, and ministry because it cannot be reconciled with the idea of a torturing God. To choose hell based on Jesus' warnings of judgment, while ignoring everything else he taught, limits how we understand his instructions on forgiveness, loving enemies, not staying angry, returning evil with good, his forgiveness from the cross, and his admonishments to live and do all that he has taught. Look out at the world today and see how many Christians continue to participate in the many forms of violence. There is an enormous disconnect between how many Christians live and believe, and how Jesus lived, taught, and died.

Was Jesus not God when he taught all the wonderful things about love, forgiveness, and reconciliation? If we have skipped over Jesus' sayings about love and forgiveness, we have missed some of the most important knowledge about who God is, who God wants to be in our lives, and how God wants to change the world with complete love. This changing of the world comes through life lived within God's kingdom, which Jesus has so thoroughly described for us. If we do not live as Jesus taught and lived, we miss out on the joy, grace, and love of being a part of the kingdom God. The false assurance of hell for sinners is a cheap substitute for life in God's kingdom.

Reason Seven

How we go about studying and interpreting the Bible says much about who we are and the life choices we have made. What informs how we approach scripture? If Jesus is not the key to our understanding of God and the Bible, what is? Why would we believe other voices over against Jesus? If we take seriously the history of the doctrine of hell, why align ourselves with this view? If we still support divisions, vengeance, judging others, or violence in any form, from where do we draw support for these things? Let's be honest about to whom and to what we have given our first allegiance.

The biblical view of God in general gives overwhelming witness to a God of love. Contrast that with one Hebrew word and three Greek words that translators have wrongly represented with our English word *hell*. Add to this the fact that these four words come nowhere close to our traditional view of hell. These words have been mistranslated for centuries. Why would anyone want to continue such an ill-informed and unloving way of interpreting scripture?

Reason Eight

For those who believe in hell, how much of this belief is about their own pain and hardness of heart? Are we like Tertullian, delighting in the hope that our enemies or any of the "Godless" will burn in hell? Would we want to look into hell and watch the suffering? Could we enjoy heaven knowing the hellish fate of most of humanity? How do we feel about a God who would allow our "unbelieving" friends and family members (people we love with all our heart) to endure burning in hell forever, and watch them do so?

Maybe we think these questions border on the ridiculous. Maybe we have not thought through all the implications of a belief in hell. Maybe we have not asked ourselves what really motivates our belief. Perhaps it is time to examine our hearts in light of Jesus' heart, while admitting that our focus on hell has been a diversion serving to mask our inner shame and fear.

Reason Nine

Hell allows Christians the excuse to torture and kill. Just look at history and at the world today. Where do we put our trust? Do we in the United States really believe our money is truthful when it says, "In God we trust"? Christians do torture and kill. Most of us go along with it and justify it in the name of self-defense, or "making the world safe for democracy," or whatever "right belief" we are defending. What US money should say is: "In our own power to mold the world in our image we trust," or "In our superior firepower we trust."

To be able to say, "In God we trust," while killing people, we must have a view of God that allows us to kill people. The traditional view of hell gives us the excuse we need.

Reason Ten

If we hold on to a view of hell, we greatly limit our spiritual development. Destruction is our own doing. For proof of this, reread all of Jesus' judgment warnings in Matthew. It is time we all grow up spiritually and take responsibility for our sin, whatever it is.

It is time we fully realize the real-world repercussions of the violence of our unloving words and deeds. It is time to heed Jesus' warnings and also realize the eternal repercussions.

Reason Eleven

We fool ourselves if we think believing in hell is a good thing. The non-Christian world sees the lie and knows our hypocrisy all too well. We are scoffed at for trying to come across with love that, in the end, turns to violence in this life and hell in the next. Most thinking non-Christians do not want anything to do with a faith so full of lies. They would tell us to take off our masks of love and be honest that we and our God are not genuinely loving.

Wherever we go, our hypocrisy has terrible implications for outreach and evangelism. Ask anyone sincerely attempting to reach out to the Muslim world today. Think of how Jews view Christians after enduring centuries of violence. Ask why Christians are sending soldiers with guns around the world and not more loving people with the gospel of Jesus Christ. Think about how the non-Christian world views our Christian-sponsored aggression.

Reason Twelve

We gain nothing good from our belief in hell. Christians throughout the centuries have used hell to scare people into becoming Christian. Some Christians still use this threat with children and adults whose fears are easily preyed upon. "Do you want to go to hell or heaven?" Who in their right mind would choose hell? Who would want to cross an angry and vengeful God (shades of Johnathon Edwards' sermon, "Sinners in the Hands of an Angry God")?

Pure and simple, this tactic teaches people to fear God, and not in the biblical sense of fear as reverence. What hope of intimacy with a God of pure love is left for these "believers"? Where do they go and what do they do with their own violent inclinations? Confess them to an angry God? To a God they are afraid of?

You might ask, then, Why become Christian? Why not live a sinful life with abandon if there is no hell to pay? Don't we need the fear of hell to get people to believe and behave?

Contrary to popular and conventional belief, becoming a Christian has nothing to do with avoiding a bad afterlife. Becoming a Christian has everything to do with experiencing and sharing the most profound and amazing love ever possible! If this is not the motivation to become a Christian, we are evangelizing for some other faith system. If we have not experienced and are not presently living this amazing love, we ought not share our version of God. The vast resource of God's love is and has always been the true motive for a life with God, and it is more than enough!

IT IS TIME TO TAKE ALL EVIL SERIOUSLY

Is torture in hell waiting for evil people? And who would these people be? The un-saved? The nonbelievers? Folks who have written off church and Christianity?

Evil, including violence, comes in many forms. I am purposely using a broad definition of *violence*, from emotional or spiritual abuse to any form of physical hurt. If we hurt anyone with the words we speak, the actions we take, or the inaction we choose, we participate in violence. How we treat each other matters. War is, of course, an extreme example of violence, but war does not start with battles and bombs. War starts with unreconciled hurt and anger as simple as an everyday insult or the scuf-fling of children on the playground. With time and experience, unresolved pain grows larger and larger in the human heart.

Because so much hurt goes unresolved, violence becomes systemic in society. Systemic violence has had great influence in the Christian church since the church's beginnings. No matter how vigilant you and I may be, we, too, suffer the effects of systemic violence, and we are subject to participation in it. Violence is the epitome of evil. We could look at each of Jesus' judgment warnings in Matthew and identify the specific form of violence he warns against. Where Jesus warns outright about judg-ment because of evil, it is a clear and terrible form of violence.

Everyone has at times treated violence in some form as insignificant. We all overlook certain kinds of evil. It would behoove us to pay greater attention to our own participation in violence and to our culpability in systemic evil. While we cannot completely avoid involvement with systemic evil, we can confess it and allow God to heal it within us and through us. But until we are willing to see all forms of violence as evil, we will skate through life ignoring much of the pain of others, some of which we have helped inflict.

Many who tout the doctrine of a torturing hell defend it in part by saying it must be this way so that evil is taken seriously and ultimately dealt with by God. I agree entirely with the part about evil being taken seriously and ultimately being dealt with by God. In fact, one message of this chapter is a strong admonishment that we all need to take evil *more* seriously than we previously have. To do this, we must stop it, name it, and confess it in ourselves first, before we define God's judgment and before we ever consign others to God's judgment. If we practiced this honest form of confession, any need we feel to define God's eternal judgment and pronounce it on others would wash away with our own tears.

IT IS TIME TO TAKE GOD'S TOUGH LOVE SERIOUSLY

Life in its fullest now and life after this life are defined by God's love. Likewise, evil can be defined as the absence of God's love. To not take evil seriously is to not take God's love seriously. God's love is neither a theory nor a distant ideal. God's love is the most real thing in the universe, and where it is absent, God's loving judgment will always be necessary.

To whatever extent anyone is complicit in evil, sooner or later they will experience the purifying fire of God's love. *That means all of us!* Whatever judgment awaits any of us after we die will be entirely administered by God's love. According to Jesus, God's loving judgment will not be based on whether we prayed the sinner's prayer, claimed to be born again, went to church, refused to kneel before a football game, held the right belief, or backed a particular political candidate. Rather, love's judgment will bring to bear the full requirements of God's love on all the places in our lives and hearts where it has been lacking. God's love does not tolerate violence. Violence—that is, evil—must be and will be destroyed, and it will be destroyed by God's love.

But love's destruction of evil is not just reserved for the afterlife. It is a horror to think that our present lack of love could be excused or dismissed. To pretend our present infliction of pain would go unnoticed by God shows we live in a world despairingly out of touch with God's purpose for us.

When I was a kid, my mother represented to me the most loving example of any human being I knew. All she had to do was look at me and I knew I was loved. When I was in high school, a young woman liked me and was looking for some positive attention from me. I don't remember what I said to her, but I know I hurt her feelings. It just so happened that this girl's mother and my mother were friends, and my cruel words returned to me via my mother's clear message of disapproval and disappointment. I was crushed by my mother's love. I knew, from the bottom of my heart, that I had been mean to and had hurt someone. I was instantly remorseful and prepared to do my best to apologize for the hurt I had caused. It was my mother's love, having nothing to do with a threat of punishment, that chastened me and rocked my young ego off its high horse.

This example might seem insignificant, but fifty years have passed, and I still remember the awful feeling of guilt as clearly as if it were yesterday. My mother would not have needed words; her look of disappointment was enough to burn my conscience. Her unconditional love seared my soul and imprinted this love in my heart for the past fifty years. I will take this love to my grave and beyond.

If one experience of a mother's love could wield fifty years of influence, think of what God's love can do for eternity. My mother's love was but a small portion of God's love diluted through the life of a frail human being and imparted to me. Fifty years later I am still reeling with this love's burning. We cannot imagine the power of God's love undiluted and directly focused on us like a laser piercing our minds and our souls. This is the love Jesus spoke of throughout his life. This is the love Jesus showed to others throughout his life. This is the love Jesus showed us as he suffered and died on the cross. This is the love by which God invites us and holds us accountable in this life and the next.

None of us alive have yet to take this tough love seriously enough.

WHAT DOES GOD'S ULTIMATE JUDGMENT LOOK LIKE?

We cannot pretend to know the specifics of the final outcome of God's love and its power over violence and evil. We can be sure about the biblical witness—God wins. Jesus repeatedly warned those who lived as if God's love would not win. Paul emphatically pronounced Jesus the winner in Philippians 2:9–11.

> Therefore God also highly exalted him and gave him the name that is above every name, so that at the name of Jesus every knee should bend, in heaven and on earth and under the earth, and every tongue should confess that Jesus Christ is Lord, to the glory of God the Father.

We can also know that God is not restricted by our human ideas about justice, judgment, and punishment. The English word *hell* and its traditional meaning are nothing but a cobbled-together dark-side view of the human heart. This view of our heart's dark side reveals the sins of judging we will need to abandon in search of God's love. It is silly for Christians to rely on some extrabiblical knowledge of just how God will finally bring all things to right. It goes beyond silliness and becomes dangerous when we attempt to know eternal things while ignoring what Jesus taught us about the here and now. My plea is that we believe Jesus and stop with the silliness conjured up out of human need.

HOW, THEN, DO WE LIVE IN THE FACE OF EVIL?

This is an enormously important question, and it may just be the core question of the following chapter. As a way of providing eternal hope and a bridge to the living of this hope discussed in chapter 11, let us hear these words about Jesus from Colossians 1:19–20.

> For in him all the fullness of God was pleased to dwell, and through him God was pleased to reconcile to himself all things, whether on earth or in heaven, by making peace through the blood of his cross.

This is where our hope lies, both now and forever.

11

SALVATION AND THE CROSS OF JESUS CHRIST

I t is in fact impossible to understand the meaning of Jesus' death if we do not know the meaning of his life. The centuries-old tendency to sever Jesus' death from his life has created a great disconnect between the cross and God's will and way in this world. While this chapter confronts and perhaps even confounds us with a new understanding, I hope it will also prove transformational.

If the cross is seen primarily as a symbol of Jesus dying for our sins, Christianity is a profoundly different religion than the movement Jesus began. This chapter calls us to examine some hard questions: Why has there been such a need to explain the meaning of Jesus' death? What is behind the seeming death-of-Jesus anxiety that Western Christians have felt for centuries? Why, for so many people, has Jesus' life taken a back seat to his death? What do we gain from having God responsible for Jesus' death and making it into a theological problem? What are we avoiding? We will provide at least some answers to questions such as these in the pages to come. We will also continue to look at Jesus' life and teachings, in order to rediscover the true meaning of his death.

THE HOPE KNOWN TO PAUL AND AVAILABLE TO US

Hope is about what happens next. Where is life taking us? Observing the world around us in order to gain hope is like visiting a clinically depressed reader of tea leaves—a sure and steady path to hopelessness. Every time we see a glimmer of hope on the horizon of this world, some form of violence snatches it away. Violence is a part of this world's DNA, and we cannot escape it. We must not pretend there is a way out, for denial will only end in frustration and our own spiritual and emotional depression. The conundrum we find ourselves in as human beings—having to live within systemic violence in its many forms—is why Christians for centuries have sought to make peace with the system. This has been a failed attempt to rise above hopelessness.

Over the years, most Christians have sought survival in the world of violence by accepting some limited form of violence. Hence, we have the "just war" theory, which allows for our violence under certain conditions. Christians are free and even encouraged to join the military and go to war. We have made our peace with violence, and we truly believe it is the only way to live in this "fallen" world.

In the face of hopelessness, Paul's words from Colossians 1:19–20, quoted at the end of chapter 10, sound a strange call to a hope all but forgotten:

> For in [Jesus] all the fullness of God was pleased to dwell, and through him
> God was pleased to reconcile to himself all things, whether on earth or in
> heaven, by making peace through the blood of his cross.

Paul is confident of the past, present, and future of "all things, whether on earth or in heaven" because he is fully confident of the meaning of Jesus' death on the cross. Paul is saying something extremely positive here, and it is part of a larger context (verses 15–20) where he essentially places "all things" under the complete authority of God in Jesus Christ. Everything gets reconciled and reconnected through Jesus as the full indwelling of God. The cross—the death of Jesus—is here a most powerful symbol of this reconciliation of "all things." In fact, the culminating work of the cross of Christ is to create peace out of the chaos of a violent world.

This is not a statement about personal salvation in any way related to traditional evangelical Christian dogma. This is a significantly more hopeful statement devoid of personal escape from this life of violence and death. This is an all-inclusive statement about the reconciliation of everything we know. According to Paul, we are part of a huge undertaking only God can accomplish. How can Paul be this hopeful? We look around at a deeply wounded past, present, and future, and we say Paul (or anyone this hopeful) is crazy. What could possibly be going on within Paul that he sees something we cannot?

We have dumbed down the work of the cross. We have made it into a personal spiritualized way out of the violence of this world, even as we remain complicit in this violence. We have not believed in the complete reconciliation work of God in Jesus Christ. We have lost our hope in the peace made by the blood of Jesus on the cross.

What follows in this chapter is a way back to divine hope for all of us. Christ did not just meet Paul on the road to Damascus (Acts 9); Christ meets us all, and he invites us into God's reconciliation of "all things." We have talked about God's complete forgiveness and God's complete love. Now we will talk about God's complete work of reconciliation (salvation) and the meaning of Jesus' death. It is time to take up the challenge to believe Jesus in his entirety—his life, his death, and his resurrection. This embrace of Jesus is the only way for us to join Paul in the hope he proclaimed. This miracle of hope restored is about God's way for us to boldly and confidently confront systemic violence in all its forms. In so doing, we will discover both an old way and a new way of understanding salvation.

THE SEVERING OF JESUS' DEATH FROM HIS LIFE

My interest is not to propose a new theory of atonement (salvation). I am interested in seeing Christians become less dependent on theory and more dialed into a relationship with the whole Jesus. I say this in part because of the trouble theories about God have brought upon the church and the world. I will make a broad statement here, and no one will be happier than I am if it is incorrect: Since the fourth century and the marriage of church and state, by and large Christian doctrine and theology have significantly ignored the life and ministry of Jesus. Perhaps *ignored* is too strong a word. It might be more accurate to say we have placed Jesus' life and teachings on a shelf somewhere to gather dust while we have focused (at least for the last 1,700 years) on theories about his death. Read the major creeds from the fourth century, and notice how they skip from Jesus' birth right to his death—no mention of his life and ministry. We have made Jesus' death instructional and his life mostly irrelevant. Admittedly, I'm generalizing a bit, but there is also truth to this claim.

Dominant Western Christian thought for centuries has held to understanding Jesus' death as a violent event in which God was more or less involved. Either there is a violent battle between good and evil, or God's justice is in need of satisfaction, or God needs to persuade humans of God's love. In all these, and the many variations of these theories, there is a cosmic need—and *God* need—for Jesus to die.[1] All these theories focus on Jesus' death without significant consideration of his life. They are negative approaches to what happened in Jesus' death and so, by their very nature, become a part of systemic violence and the hopelessness of our world. This conforms to the never-ending cycle of violence by which our world works. Any theory about the meaning of Jesus' death that ignores his life and places God in a violent role simply imitates and rotates within systemic violence.

To think of God as one who sends Jesus to his death and even needs Jesus to die, it is necessary to keep Jesus himself up on that dusty shelf far away from the practicalities of this life. In all of Jesus' life, his teachings, and especially his submission to a violent death, we have the living example of a God who loves beyond our capabilities to imagine. If this same God is also responsible for Jesus' death, no matter how we try to frame it in positive terms, this God is complicit in the most horrible kind of child abuse imaginable. Is it any wonder our Christian doctrine allows us the role of violent accomplice to the world's evil? Is it any wonder we remain so schizophrenic in our expressions of warm-fuzzy faith while participating in violence ourselves?

1. Weaver, *Nonviolent Atonement*, 1–19.

Three Theories of Atonement

Three major theories of atonement have captured the attention of the Western church in the years since the fourth century. There are also variations of these three, along with a few alternatives. J. Denny Weaver's book *The Nonviolent Atonement* is a must-read for anyone interested in digging deeper into these theories. For the purpose of this chapter, I offer an admittedly oversimplified look at the three theories in the order they came into use in Western Christian thought. (To my knowledge, the Eastern Church has shown relatively little interest in theories such as these.)

The first is referred to as the classic view and received special attention through the work of Gustaf Aulen (1879–1977). Aulen refers to it as *the Christus Victor theory*. It was a loosely held view, never officially formulated by the early church, which cast the world as a battle between good and evil. God wins the battle by giving Jesus over to the devil and the powers of sin. But the devil is fooled in that Jesus is then raised victorious by God.[2]

The second view did not come along until 1097. This was the first time a formal theory of atonement became widely accepted by the Western church. Anselm, who was archbishop of Canterbury from 1093 to 1109, developed what would become known as *the satisfaction theory of atonement*. This view recognized humanity's sinful nature as having offended God. Therefore, it was necessary for a serious rebalancing of the debt owed. Justice had to be restored. "Anselm's image posed the death of Christ as the means to satisfy the offended honor of God."[3]

The third major view, called *the moral influence theory*, was first suggested by Abelard (1079–1142). Abelard rejected Anselm's satisfaction theory and instead declared that Jesus had to die in order to convince humanity of God's great love for us. In this theory, there is not a change in how God perceives us but in how we perceive God. While this theory allows for God to have a more passive role in Jesus' death, it still implicates God.

J. Denny Weaver summarizes the three predominant theories:

> While these atonement images all talk about how Jesus' death saves, they differ significantly from each other. The motifs are easily distinguished by keeping in mind that each theory has a different object for the death of Jesus, or has the death of Jesus aimed at a different entity. For classic Christus Victor, in either the cosmic battle or the ransom versions, Satan is the object of Jesus' death; Jesus' death is directed toward the devil. In Anselm's version of the satisfaction theory, the offended honor of God is the object of Jesus' death. In Protestant Orthodoxy's version, God's law stands as the object of Jesus' death. For the

---

2. Yoder, *Shalom*, 61.

3. Weaver, *Nonviolent Atonement*, 16.

moral influence theory, sinful humankind—that is, us—is the target of Jesus' death.[4]

It is important to state that there are things we can learn from these theories, including the biblical and historical contexts from which they arose. Each of the views offers partial good news and should be evaluated carefully lest we lose some of the depth perception needed to go beyond them.

However, the major theories of atonement have also greatly misguided the church and the world in the following (and perhaps other) ways: (1) These theories do not adequately account for the ministry and the teachings of Jesus—they are focused on the meaning of his death apart from any full account of his life. (2) All three theories and their variations credit God in some way with the killing of Jesus. (3) A violent understanding of God opens the door to justifying our own violence. (4) Dependence on these theories has led us away from any real look at the systemic violence we participate in daily and have for centuries.

While there are exceptions, general Christian thought in the Western world, especially as we experience it in the United States, continues its dependence on these three theories. Some form of the satisfaction theory is perhaps most prevalent while some form of the moral influence theory offers more liberal-minded Christians a way to see God in more loving terms. Following Aulen's work, the classic view gained more attention in the latter half of the twentieth century.

Throughout this book I have stressed the importance of believing Jesus, taking him at his word, learning from his loving ministry, and applying his life and teachings to our present life in this world. Nowhere is this focus on Jesus' life and teachings more important than now, as we reconsider the meaning of his death. After ten chapters, all closely attuned to Jesus' ministry and its scandalous implications for the church and the world, we should find striking the church's almost complete lack of attention to Jesus' life within the context of the meaning of his death. Indeed, it is the prime example of scandal. There is no better example of short-sighted thinking and tunnel vision in all of church history. We have misunderstood God; lost sight of the evil of present-day violence; practiced a hypocritical, limited love; and spread a sanctimonious and false gospel to the world.

WHEN THE CROSS IS ROOTED IN THE LIFE OF JESUS

As stated above, if the cross is primarily a symbol of Jesus dying for our sins, Christianity is a very different religion than the movement Jesus began. It does not have to be this way. We are not left to the devices of theories about Jesus' death, and we are not captives to those unwilling to follow the life Jesus lived. When we keep Jesus' entire ministry in focus while committing ourselves to emulating his life the best that we can, many things can change about our approach to his cross. Just consider for the

4. Weaver, *Nonviolent Atonement*, 18.

moment how much will change about our understanding of Jesus' death if we forgo the hypotheses of past theologians. Now we can concentrate on all the wonders of Jesus' life and ministry. Now we can allow all Jesus' teachings to sink into us and inform our understanding of how he was perceived by both his followers and his antagonists. Now we can let the story of Jesus unfold naturally as it does in the gospels without some preconceived theory over-focused on why he "had" to die.

It is of utmost importance to take the story of Jesus' life and ministry as a whole from start to finish. This approach takes each event, teaching, and confrontation within the story seriously. This approach also concludes that the reason for Jesus' violent death is found in the story leading up to it. *The death of Jesus was a historical event cemented in the circumstances of his life.*

When we see the cross as rooted in the life of Jesus, we discover two essential truths: (1) The cross lays bare the evil of the violent human system then and now. Those responsible for Jesus' death are credited accordingly, and systemic violence is taken seriously. (2) The cross stands for God's total commitment to love and nonviolence. God's nonviolent kingdom come is thus seen throughout all of Jesus' life, with the final act of his life and death being an exclamation point when Jesus' kingdom life is celebrated in the most astonishing way: through God's resurrection of Jesus. Indeed, God does not kill; God raises to life.

Let's examine both truths.

Violence Exposed as Evil

> Now the earth was corrupt in God's sight, and the earth was filled with violence. And God saw that the earth was corrupt; for all flesh had corrupted its ways upon the earth. (Gen 6:11–12)

It would be accurate to say that some form of violence has always dominated human culture. I am referring to all forms of violence, physical, emotional, spiritual, and psychological. Humans are immersed in systemic violence, and we often unconsciously participate in it. Our immersion in systemic violence, at least in part, explains why for centuries the Christian church has focused on Jesus' death more than on his life. We seem stuck in the cycle of violence, while seeking a death-defying circus act to release us from this prison. We cannot imagine any way out of it without ascribing a violent solution perpetrated by God. We have not been able or willing to consider a truly nonviolent God, for this view would not fit our pact with violence.

The suffering and death of Jesus is not the focal point of his life, though many have tried to make it so. Rather, the cross is the focal point of *evil* violently executed in an effort to stop *the message of his life.* Jesus' death was foreseen throughout his life of ministry—the opposition to him was cruel, intense, and calculated from the start. Meanwhile, he taught love and peace and mercy. He healed and made people whole while confronting and confounding the systemic violence of his day. A rational reading of the story of Jesus' life recognizes it as the epitome of love. Why, then, was he hounded, persecuted, and killed?

Systemic violence is not rational. Systemic violence responds to threat with any violent means it has at its disposal. The story of Jesus, start to finish, is a story of God's unfailing love regardless of the evil that confronts it. Within all four gospel accounts of Jesus' life, it is utterly clear who killed Jesus, and these accounts are gruesome. These accounts beg us to take them seriously.

Violence is systemic because it is the means of protecting and defending human control and stability. Unless we are willing to confess our own role in the ongoing violence of our world, we will not be free from believing we need a violent version of God. We mistreat one another in various ways and at all levels of human interaction. As I have said earlier, war is terribly violent, but it does not start with war—it starts with unresolved hurts spawned by mistreatment and fear. It is spawned by a broad systemic reliance on *power over.*[5]

Our basic human response is denial, which protects and bolsters our violent system. Denial looks away from violence, pretends either that it is necessary or that it is not really there. Denial does nothing to end violence, to challenge it, or to provide alternatives. Denial keeps us locked in the system of violence. In claiming the cross as God's violent saving act, Christians have pretended not to notice the real cause of Jesus' death. Sure, we ascribe his death, in part, to the cruelty of the Roman system, but we do not acknowledge the much-too-similar cruelty of our own system. In the death of Jesus, we blame the Romans, the Jewish leaders, and even God. And with the accumulation of centuries, we have formulated our denial into theories about Jesus' death instead of accepting our role in death and destruction today.

What of the Evil in Us?

Earlier in this book we discussed the failings of right belief, arguments, and divisions among Christians. We gave witness to how these things have led to violence toward both Christians and non-Christians. It is time to look at how this same violent nature within us has gone unaddressed by our theories about Jesus' death.

1. *Nothing in our traditional theories about Jesus' death has delivered us from being embroiled in religious controversy and other forms of violence.* On the contrary, these theories have often contributed to our controversies. The atonement theories do not help us live in God's kingdom of love now—if anything, they divert us from doing so by keeping us focused on the wrong end of life. Theories are only helpful if they propel us to better living, if they lead us back to God's will and way within real-life circumstances. If the theories described above are truly about atonement—a process of making us "at one" with God—they have failed miserably. How can we be at one with God and not with all our neighbors (Matt 22:39)?

5. Boyd, *Myth of a Christian Nation,* 18.

How are we better, because of our understanding of Jesus' death, at loving and being one with non-Christians? How about our being at one with immigrants, with the poor, with people of a race or sexual orientation or gender identity different from ours, with all who suffer injustice, with all babies born and unborn, with our personal enemies, with our country's enemies, and with the whole world? Remember Paul's reference in Colossians 1:19–20 to "all things." That includes everyone!

We have found it convenient to focus on Jesus' death and, in a convoluted way, to use it to bolster our self-centered desire for vindication if not in this life, then in the next. In so doing, we make the death of Jesus about *us* and our selfish desires. If we could be objective and look closely at violent God-theories, we would recognize this as a house of cards. In the end, it is self-serving rhetoric lacking spiritual depth, devoid of the power to heal us, and vacant of salvation.

2. *Our theories of atonement have justified our belief in a God of violence and therefore our own ongoing violence.* In one way or another, these theories attribute Jesus' death to God and therefore absolve the world of its systemic violence.[6] This is a highly deceptive shell game in which we have faked out almost everyone, including ourselves. We have taken the focus off Jesus, off his teachings, off the controversies and the atrocities inflicted upon him by the ways of this world. We have then placed the shell firmly over God, our designated evil one. We have made the very author of complete love culpable for the most violent act in history! How is this possible?

When we live our own forms of violence, we join the very forces of evil that nailed Jesus to the cross. We become the perpetrators of God's death while claiming to be the beneficiaries of it. There can be no greater twisting of the truth than to say we are going to heaven while we perpetuate the same sort of murderous violence that killed Jesus two thousand years ago. Remember Jesus' words to Saul on the road to Damascus—"Saul, Saul, why do you persecute *me*?" (Acts 9:4; italics added)—indicating how personally he identifies with all who suffer violence.

We find the truth of this last paragraph too heavy to bear. We cannot live with it, so we hide behind theological falsehoods—even going so far as to twist the death of Jesus onto God in order to deflect it from ourselves. We have enabled centuries of our own violence and baptized it by placing blame on God.

3. *To pretend that our focus on the event of the cross can magically change our relationship with God is absurd.* If we pretend to be at one with God while disobeying, instead of obeying, everything Jesus commanded us (Matt 28:20), we place our need for violence above obedience toward God. We have also claimed union with God while living in a way opposite to that of God. Remember the dire warnings of Jesus throughout his ministry. The judgment of God's love is awaiting all of us who live in disobedience, and if anyone were going to a supposed hell, would it not be those who disobey Jesus?

---

6. Weaver, *Nonviolent Atonement*, 17, 19, 44.

The traditional Christian formula for salvation goes something like this: Confess your sins, accept Jesus as your Savior, and go to heaven when you die. Who makes this stuff up? Try: the religious folks who want heaven while continuing to distribute hell on earth in the form of self-righteous beliefs, divisions, merciless living, and war.

We must take the magic act out of our theories about Jesus' death. A magic act is just that—an act. It is a falsehood intended to fool the eye and the mind. The traditional Christian teaching about being saved from our sins is a magic act intended to fool our hearts. Some will say that the traditional formula is *not* just a magic act, in that it intends to truly allow God to change how we live. I appreciate this emphasis, but this hoped-for result is often not realized, and it certainly is not realized fully and consistently in most Christian lives. Furthermore, the magic-act formula is both vague and often meaningless, applied to whatever way of life so-called Christians choose to live. This comes from a focus on Jesus' death and not on his life. The magic act not only allows for a violent understanding of God; it once again supports just about any kind of violent way of life we choose. It has greatly contributed to keeping the real Jesus up on the dusty shelf, and it has obscured the real-life meaning of sin and salvation. More on this to come.

4. *Our theological mind games have served our own purposes and our own forms of retributive justice.*

We do not have space here to adequately discuss the vast difference between our world's way of punishing justice (called "retributive" justice, from the word *retribution*) and the biblical view of God's justice as providing people what they need ("distributive" or "redemptive" justice). Suffice it to say that to model God's justice after our own, which focuses on violence and punishment, is blasphemous (*blasphemy* being the biblical word for bowing to our self-made image of God). We have been blinded by the surrounding culture and the world's way of dealing with pain. We have succumbed to returning violence for violence and justifying it with a God-blaming formula.

Our views of reward and punishment are our own unless we learn them from Jesus. To leap over Jesus' life to get to his death means, in part, that we have no interest in learning from him. We are stuck in retributive justice and a punishment mindset. Once again, our theories of atonement have blinded us to our own violent ways of thinking and living while we think we are playing out the justice of God. Instead, we remain captives amid the world's violence. The theories have not saved us.

5. *If we take away our own need for violent, punishing justice, we are free to see God's way in this world and the next in terms of love and reconciliation, just as Jesus lived it.* Who needed the death of Jesus? Who needs it now? If we apply these questions to the gospel story of Jesus, some interesting conclusions inform our thinking in what might be new ways. We will not discover evidence that God needed Jesus to die, though some try to manufacture it. From within the story itself, we can release our hold on violent understandings of God.

Who Really Needed Jesus to Die?

One can say, of course, that sinners needed and still need the death of Jesus. But why? Where is the logic in this? What does Jesus' death accomplish for sinners if we take away the magic-act formula, if we take away our blame on God for Jesus' death? While we surely witness God's love shown to us in Jesus' death, this does not mean we *needed* him to die to somehow save us. We will explore the wonders of his saving life along with the meaning of his death in a bit. Keep in mind for now that Jesus' death can only be understood within the context of his life. *What sinners, and all violent people, have always needed is the life and love Jesus taught and lived.* To make his death our need obscures the real salvation event of all—Jesus' life!

To somehow credit the devil, or God's need for punishing justice, with Jesus' death borders on the insane. How can God owe the devil anything? Isn't God supreme? Does God need to pay evil with evil, or pay off a legal balance sheet with evil? These theories credit the devil with the power to hold us ransom, or a legal balance sheet with power over God. Meanwhile, these theories seem to absolve us of our own responsibility for the mess we have made of our lives. How convenient for us! Once again, some magic formula has come to our rescue in the actions of God that kill Jesus, miraculously pay off the devil or the debt, and leave us without any responsibility for our failure to live as Jesus taught.

What, then, is left when we ask, Who needed Jesus to die? Staying true to the story of Jesus, it was the power brokers of state and religion who used violence to impose their own will and way on the people of the first century and, of course, onto Jesus. Weaver explains how his own theory of atonement, which he calls *narrative Christus Victor*, differs from the satisfaction theory:

> Asking who needs the death of Jesus or what the death of Jesus accomplishes for narrative Christus Victor brings a revealing point to the foreground. *For this image, the closest thing to a need for Jesus' death is that powers of evil need his death in order to remove his challenge to their power. And if this is the need, it accomplishes nothing for the salvation of sinners, nor does it accomplish anything for the divine economy* [emphasis mine]. Since Jesus' mission was not to die but to make visible the reign of God, it is quite explicit that neither God nor the reign of God *need* Jesus' death in the way that his death is irreducibly *needed* in satisfaction atonement.[7]

Within all four gospel stories of Jesus' life, a combination of religious and state power brokers kill Jesus. As Weaver explains, in order to protect their own power, they had to remove Jesus' challenge to it. This appears to be the simple fact of the matter. But let's go a bit deeper into this truth since the major atonement theories have avoided it, and they had their reasons.

---

7. Weaver, *Nonviolent Atonement*, 72.

Throughout history, power brokers have used violent means to ensure their desired outcomes. This was as true in Jesus' day as it is today. Anytime a power broker is at work in this world, violent means are used, and violence-defending versions of so-called truth are announced. Justifications are found for violence, and scapegoats are always named. For power brokers to flourish, there must be a dominant narrative explaining their right to use violence. Once the church of Jesus Christ was wed to power-broker state government in the fourth century, the church itself needed a dominant narrative to explain its right to the use of violence. Suddenly, it became exceedingly convenient to transfer the focus of Jesus' suffering and death off the systemic violence always used by power brokers. The major theories of atonement provided the needed scapegoat.

Rather than admitting any culpability on the part of the powerful in the death of Jesus, the dominant Western church of the fourth century formed a narrative counter to Jesus and in defense of their need to wield power and to justify their violence. The actual life and teachings of Jesus were placed on that dusty shelf while theories of hell and atonement wedded violence to a state-sanctioned image of God. *The shocking truth of power-over violence, indeed systemic violence throughout human history, was hushed right out of the Jesus story.* For the most part, the church found ways to continue being a violent power broker while idealizing the image of Jesus dying on the cross.

Through the centuries voices have decried the tragedy of falsely absolved violence. This book and this chapter add my voice to that outcry. While power brokers need Jesus to die so as to end the challenge he mounts against their defense of violence, we desperately need voices to say it is not okay to scapegoat the devil, God, or sinners in general. *The cause of Jesus' death was systemic violence, and most of the world is still entrenched in it.*

A Bridge to Real Salvation

Did Jesus die for our sins? Not in any sort of traditionally held understanding. In fact, the traditionally held understanding of his death has come from participation in the sinful nature of humanity. Jesus died because people killed him to protect their system against God's amazing love, which Jesus brought through his message and his life. Jesus died because of the sin of the *system*, and the system remains alive and well among us today. The system of violent justification that needed Jesus to die and, indeed, killed him may look different today, but its essential nature is the same. Our society's system, within the church and outside the church, is just as dependent on violence as were the people who killed Jesus in the first century.

If we can accept the truth of this last paragraph, then Jesus' death can be a witness to his life and ministry, and a revelation unmasking the nature of evil and violence. We might have to actually catch a glimpse of systemic violence and our own involvement in it in order to gain hope of the true repentance to which Jesus has repeatedly called us.

In this, then, his death does bring the hope of that peace which Paul named in Colossians 1:20. If Jesus' death can be for us a capstone to his life of love, revealing the evil we have lived and the terrible truth of all violence, it becomes a part of the salvation God offers us. In a very specific sense, then, the old formula of salvation from our sins can still apply. We just need to be very careful to understand sin as the violence it is; to know who is culpable, including ourselves; and to acknowledge how Jesus has shown us the way out of sin through his life and his death.

Finally, everything changes when we treat the cross within the context of the whole story of Jesus, making a whole narrative of salvation, start to finish. When we keep Jesus whole, among other things we see him offering a life in God's love apart from any violence, and we see this consistently from the beginning of his ministry to the end and beyond. We see how the forces of violence confronted him from the beginning and how he offered the fulfillment of God's intent for humanity as a distinct alternative to violence. He offered us God's heart of unfathomable love. This becomes a pathway of deliverance, if we accept it as such. Salvation becomes a way of life, not death.

Salvation as God's Total Commitment to Love and Nonviolence

The Meaning of Salvation in the Bible

Salvation has become a vague religious term Christians tend to toss around as they prescribe ways to attain it or ways to deny it to others. For many, salvation has been the result of the magic formula of the sinner's prayer. The idea is that we are saved from our sins by, in some precise way, receiving Jesus into our lives or being received by him. Too often, *salvation* is used as a synonym for the reward of heaven now that all the bad stuff in us has been washed away, with no serious application of salvation to this life on earth. This is not the biblical understanding. Nor should it be ours.

Jesus gives us a wonderful phrase that illustrates God's salvation in a practical way. Christians know this phrase well from the traditional version of the Lord's Prayer: "Deliver us from evil" (the NRSV reads "rescue us from the evil one," Matt 6:13, or "from evil," in a note for that verse). It is set in the context of "Your kingdom come. Your will be done, on earth as it is in heaven" (Matt 6:10). *Salvation*, in its general biblical understanding, finds its synonym in the word *deliverance*, and for the most part in the Bible, it is applied to the present life on earth. This may come as a shock to many who have only thought of God's salvation in terms of future reward.

In *Shalom: The Bible's Word for Salvation, Justice, and Peace*, Perry Yoder examines the words used in Old and New Testaments for the English word *save*. He writes:

> Thus we can sum up our study of the Hebrew material regarding God's saving actions by stressing that the words for *save* used in the Hebrew scriptures

refer to salvation from real historical, political, and material distress. These words point to the deliverance or liberation of the needy, the disadvantaged, the poor, and helpless from their oppressors.[8]

The best example of what Yoder is saying, and the seminal salvation act of God in the Hebrew scriptures, is God's act of delivering the Israelites from oppression in Egypt.

In the New Testament, the word meaning *to save* is the Greek word *sodzo*. Regarding the usage and meaning of *sodzo* in the gospels of Matthew, Mark, and Luke, Yoder makes this important point:

> It is striking that only in one case out of almost fifty is *sodzo* used with sin as its stated object. That usage is found in Matthew 1:21, in a comment explaining the name of Jesus—which in Hebrew means savior. Another reference where sin seems implied, though not used as the object of the verb "to save," is Luke 7:50. In the synoptic Gospels, the meaning of salvation is quite similar to what we have seen in the Hebrew Scriptures: *salvation occurs mainly as a matter of dealing with physical, material problems. Rarely does it refer to internal, spiritual, moral defects or faults, like sin.*[9]

Yoder goes on to discuss the use of the term *to save* in the book of Acts, Paul's letters, and other New Testament writings. His point, and the point of application for this chapter, is that the biblical concept of salvation almost exclusively concerns physical and material deliverance from human need in the here-and-now. In Acts and in Paul's letters, salvation also looks to the future, yet even in these writings, the object of salvation is almost never our interior sinful nature.

This does not mean the scriptures are unconcerned with what lies within the human heart. Jesus himself constantly pointed to the need for God's love and compassion to flow from our hearts. But biblical salvation is not focused primarily on the future, and is not centered solely on our internal condition. It is not so much personal salvation after death as deliverance from what oppresses us—and the world—now.

We could list countless examples of oppression in the world, and all need God's salvation-deliverance. We are called to pray for and act toward this deliverance *now*. The sad irony of the magic-formula version of salvation is that it directly conflicts with the biblical understanding of salvation. While we think we are being saved to go to heaven, we are very often the perpetrators of violence and the reason for others' need of salvation, according to the biblical understanding of it.

---

8. Yoder, *Shalom*, 43.

9. Yoder, *Shalom*, 47.

The Role of the Cross in Salvation

So, according to the biblical witness, what is sufficient to address the historical accumulation of human violence? What can save us from ourselves? The answer is not a magic formula pretending to absolve us of the mess we are in. It is not the lone event of Jesus' suffering and death. It is not an act of God that clears us once and for all of our wrongdoing even as we continue to do wrong. The only thing that can save us—that can "deliver us from evil"—is a complete rebuttal of the rationalization of evil, the denial of it, continued complicity with it, apathy toward it, diversion from it, and excuses made for it. The evil is within us, surrounds us, and has engulfed us. We have condoned it and even welcomed it, and God in Christ Jesus has said that enough is enough! *Jesus' nonviolent life, his teachings, his compassionate ministry, and his confrontation with violence and evil have commanded a way out, a way of salvation.* We are all in great need of this salvation-deliverance from the evil within us and around us.

The cross does have an important role to play in God's saving work through Jesus. The violent death of Jesus on the cross achieves two essential moves toward God's salvation of humankind: (1) The cross unmasks forever the powers of violence.

> From a position of apparent weakness, the reign of God as present in Jesus confronted and submitted to power. His nonviolent death was not a departure from the activist pattern of confronting the social order and making the reign of God visible. In the face of active or direct evil or violence, the refusal to respond in kind is a powerful, chosen act, not a mere passive submission. Refusing to return evil for evil unmasks the violence of the evil acts, and demonstrates that the evil which killed Jesus originated with humankind and not with God.[10]

(2) The cross provides the capstone for the life God lived in Jesus even to the bitter end. Jesus willingly endured suffering and death at the hands of violent men and a violent system. In the face of the worst evil, Jesus lived out the same love he had taught throughout his life; rather than return violence for violence, he offered peace; instead of acting in retaliation or self-defense, he offered forgiveness and compassion.

HOW, THEN, ARE WE SAVED?

The essential biblical meaning of salvation is deliverance from evil in any form. This is what Jesus accomplished in his life on earth, including in his death. God does not force our acceptance of salvation-deliverance. We can choose our own way through life, which is what so many, including many Christians, have done. Whenever we choose our own salvation, God's salvation is denied us by virtue of our own choice. Most of us want both our type of salvation and God's. We want free rein with the use of violence, and we also want God to save us, so we invented a magic formula. The

---

10. Weaver, *Nonviolent Atonement*, 40.

problem with this conjoined "salvation" is that our salvation attempts wield violence, undermining our chance to experience God's deliverance, because God's salvation is nonviolent, entirely without evil. God's salvation is never our own. Nor is it a watered-down version that accommodates violence. This is why it is so important that Jesus went to his death without any violence on his part. It shows beyond a doubt that God's salvation does not include violence.

This brings us to the heart of God's good news in Jesus Christ. The very reason for God to become incarnate was to show us a way out of our own failed and failing attempts at saving ourselves. We seem to have an unlimited ability to force ourselves back into the salvation process. Especially since the fourth century, Christians have been some of the worst violators of the hope of salvation in Jesus Christ. We have rejected the totally nonviolent God found in the life and death of Jesus. Even so, God's good news in Jesus remains the only real salvation we will ever know. God's salvation is available, and it looks something like this:

God's salvation is available to us immediately and always.

Jesus taught, lived, and died to give us the hope of peace and love. In Jesus, "hope" based on any kind of violence (which is not real hope anyway) is extinguished. This is a practical and helpful shift for the sake of living life today. We can be free of anger, bitterness, woundedness, fear, anxiety, or any forms of retaliation that have held us captive. We can be free from the belief that we need to use violence to protect ourselves.

When we hold the cross of Jesus in tandem with his life, it becomes a symbol of all he taught and lived, and of a way of life that is realistic and possible for us too. The meaning of the cross and God's salvation applies to every aspect of our relationships with God and others, so it transforms our daily life. Instead of Christ's cross being disconnected from how we live in the present by means of a theory that it somehow saves us when we die, the cross of Jesus is connected to each moment of our here-and-now. We have chosen to accept God's salvation instead of pursuing our own.

God's salvation is a miracle!

Only God can free us from the evil and violence in our hearts. Only God can end the reign of systemic violence in us and in our world. Absolutely nothing else can end systemic violence; it has held us captive since the beginning of time.

A few years back, at a worship service I was attending, toward the end of the sermon, the pastor made a plea for donations to an organization that sent Bibles to military service-members. He also showed a video that included troops descending from helicopters to deploy in battle. I became physically sick, not for lack of compassion for people serving in our military, but because the biblical message of hope was being profoundly misused to support the world's attempt to save us through violence. The subtleties of how our violent salvation and God's nonviolent salvation are intertwined surround us. We are both victims and perpetrators of this deep misconception. Every attempt at self-salvation denies the hope of God's true salvation—the miracle of miracles—and returns us to hopelessness.

Jesus does everything imaginable in his life and in his death to draw us completely into God's salvation miracle, but it seems the would-be followers of Jesus do everything imaginable to deny it. We ought to just admit we don't believe him because we don't *want* to believe him. We'd rather save ourselves. But it's the very definition of insanity to claim God's salvation for ourselves while denying the miracle of salvation in Jesus day by day.

How can violent people know the salvation miracle of God? We must submit to God's heart of total love shown us in Christ.

Redefining salvation is a necessary beginning.

If we will allow Jesus to define our sins and instruct us in the ways of complete love, God's salvation will be able to grow in our heads and hearts. Rather than a nebulous understanding of sin, or a specific definition crafted by self-righteous people, we will begin to see sin simply in each unloving act. Salvation will be for us deliverance from unloving speech or violent acts. This new understanding will change us at a fundamental level. Says Weaver:

> This sacrifice of Jesus' life revealed the full character of the powers that enslave sinful humankind and that oppose the rule of God. Through the resurrection, God in Christ has in fact defeated these powers "for us." And it is only when we acknowledge our complicity with and bondage to these powers—that is, confess our sin—in their opposition to the reign of God that we can start to envision liberation (salvation) from them.[11]

All violence, without exception, opposes the reign of God. This we learn by believing Jesus. If we take Jesus' whole life, death, and resurrection seriously, we will come into the presence of God's judging love, which will reveal any violence remaining in us. God's salvation delivers us from the evil within us and opens our eyes to the evil of violence in the world.

God's salvation requires us to give up our own salvation attempts.

This is the only way it can work. Throughout scripture, God is the faithful one and humans are unfaithful. We in the twenty-first century can choose to continue this pattern of human unfaithfulness, or to rely on God's faithfulness. Which is not to say we can put an end to our evil and violent ways ourselves. We must realize that we have

---

11. Weaver, *Nonviolent Atonement*, 76.

no means to remove ourselves from systemic violence. Whatever we attempt will only fool us into thinking we have saved ourselves, while it cements us further into the system of violence and makes our next attempt even harder.

Imagine a person who is drowning, flailing about but only managing to waste their remaining strength. That would be us trying our best to live nonviolently. Rather than rely on our own efforts, we must submit to the Spirit of Jesus, the will and way of God in the world. In so doing, we will discover the miracle of God's salvation from evil.

At the end of all human hope is the hope of God. When we grieve our utter hopelessness, we become vulnerable to the miracle of God's salvation. To an extent, this has been the Christian teaching all along, but the difference is in recognizing the real sin in and around us. This sin is not a vague moral decay defined as not living by certain religious rules; it is the reality of our drowning within systemic violence and our violent attempts to save ourselves.

We simply must stop. Granted, it is a huge undertaking to submit fully to Jesus, but there is no way to experience God's salvation but through the way of Jesus' challenging love and of his suffering and death. Anything else is the way of other gods we have created.

Only God's salvation is the real thing.

Love in all its life-transforming power and glory swells the human heart to bursting. No suffering or death, no insult or injury, no fear or anxiety can stem the flow of God's saving love in action. All that Jesus taught, lived, and suffered was and is the real work of God's salvation. Anything opposed to this complete Jesus is the work of those who would snatch salvation from us. God's salvation is the righteous reign of God in clear relief, understood and acknowledged as totally separate from evil. Violence is a destructive force. Jesus' life and death together are a spiritual united front opposed to any violence or evil in our hearts. No longer can we pretend that some baptized form of violence is a part of God's salvation, for it just does not fit with true salvation. The masquerade is over.

The cross and the life of Jesus, combined, restore us to life in God's pure love.

The cross is our symbol of *life*, not death! How can death ever be a symbol of God's salvation? Death is no longer the focus of our Christian message to the world.

To take the focus off of Jesus' death on the cross and place it on his ministry does not reduce the meaning of the cross. It actually *adds* tremendous meaning. The cross now stands for God's way of living the beatitudes, righting the wrongs of our angry outbursts, infusing a violent world with the challenge of love and reconciliation. In the terms set forth in Jesus' life and death, our lives now exude the real salvation of

God, and it is life-transforming for all of our daily living. The cross now symbolizes lives of love—Jesus' life and ours—that have the power to transform death into life all around us.

Jesus' purpose on this earth was not to die for our sins.

Jesus' purpose was to live and proclaim the reign of God's kingdom come and will being done. Weaver states:

> In carrying out his mission, Jesus was ready to die and he was willing to die. It was not a death, however, that was required as compensatory retribution for the sins of his enemies and his friends. It was a death that resulted from fulfillment of his mission about the reign of God.[12]

It is incredible that for hundreds of years the church could miss the importance of this point. God's reign of love, forgiveness, reconciliation, and peace on this earth, if taken seriously by our faith and action, reveals a salvation profoundly more dramatic, practical, and wonderful than any news of a violent transaction with the devil, death, or God that would secure our nebulous future. The truth is that the life of Jesus is our life too. God intends to confound the systemic violence of this world with its opposite—love and justice and life on earth embodying God's life and bringing God's salvation.

The capstone that the cross places on Jesus' life confirms that every awful event, angry and bitter discourse, and atrocious violence imposed by humanity is redeemable through nonviolent love. The death of Jesus resounds with the echo of his life living the reign of God on earth. His death is a clarion call for us to live his life too, even in the face of the worst that the world can deal us. God's salvation lived as God's reign on earth provides floodlights to reveal the truth of love and the lie of violence. God's salvation defines our reality now.

Suffering is a part of salvation.

Most of us do not want to hear this truth, but what we learn from suffering is dramatically different than what we learn from privilege and comfortable living. Suffering is part of life in this world. If we try to avoid suffering at all cost (which we often give as our excuse for using violence), we miss the lessons suffering can teach us.

Our own suffering can teach us solidarity with others who are suffering. From suffering, we learn not just an easy emotional response, but mercy, as identifying and uniting with those in need. In suffering, we have opportunity to lose our sense of status above others. We no longer live expecting comfort and wealth, but in expectation of intimacy with all people. In suffering, we experience the falsehood of our privileged way of life and, just maybe, start to understand how our privilege plays

12. Weaver, *Nonviolent Atonement*, 42.

into the suffering of others. Our worldview expands to include caring for all people regardless of race, religion, nationality, or any other factor, while our dependence on a comfortable lifestyle lessens.

Rather than nursing our woundedness and seeking to punish someone who has hurt us, we can learn from our suffering. Instead of projecting our pain outside ourselves onto others, we can allow the pure love of God to heal us because it needs no scapegoats of any kind. We may just also find freedom from self-accusation and shame, from our inner need to use punishment to right the world's and our wrongs.

Suffering puts us within reach of God's compassion. Our ego boundaries are down. Our easy solutions to the world's problems are unmasked. We venture into a humbleness born of the emptying process of experiencing pain. We may just find the depth of God's compassion for us and in turn learn the joy of this shared compassion as we reach out to help others.

The cross, perhaps our most meaningful icon of someone suffering on behalf of the world, is an example of God's amazing redemptive power to transform any evil into good! God can and does use suffering to shift the balance of power in this world. This is not victory *over evil*; it is winning *evil over*!

Suffering that submits to the hands of evil will always have a redemptive effect on evil itself. Though we may not see this in the short run, evil's power to influence and rule by force is diminished. Evil is revealed and dethroned in our minds and hearts, and to the world. As a result of our suffering, we are better able to identify with Christ and with God's compassionate will and way in this world. We are better able to become one with God—the essence of salvation!

We now learn to truly be forgiven.

Having learned through our suffering a pathway to salvation, every darkness in us is revealed as a place where God can touch us and remake us. We are not saved from our sins by Jesus' death on the cross. We are shown by Jesus' life and death that we are forgiven of our sins within the new life of the kingdom of God. This is an ongoing living and reliving of the truth of being forgiven and forgiving others. God uses us to dispense salvation to the world, and we spread God's forgiveness all around us. Now perhaps we can love everyone and forgive everything.

Salvation is not an event; it is a process.

As we discover the wonders of God's goodness and grace in and through Jesus, all the lessons of his life and death, we realize that salvation is an ongoing experience of Jesus' life becoming more and more our own. In the process of God saving us, we come ever closer to knowing for ourselves a total commitment to love and reconciliation. We come closer and closer to experiencing a oneness with God's love and reconciliation. We edge our way into a wholistic love and reconciliation with the world. We begin to realize more every day just how this total love and reconciliation destroy the system of violence by truly making peace from within it.

Matthew's Story of Jesus' Suffering and Death—Chapters 26–27

> While [Jesus] was still speaking, Judas, one of the twelve, arrived; with him was a large crowd with swords and clubs, from the chief priests and the elders of the people. Now the betrayer had given them a sign, saying, "The one I will kiss is the man; arrest him." At once he came up to Jesus and said, "Greetings, Rabbi!" and kissed him. Jesus said to him, "Friend, do what you are here to do." Then they came and laid hands on Jesus and arrested him. Suddenly, one of those with Jesus put his hand on his sword, drew it, and struck the slave of the high priest, cutting off his ear. Then Jesus said to him, "Put your sword back into its place; for all who take the sword will perish by the sword. Do you think that I cannot appeal to my Father, and he will at once send me more than twelve legions of angels? But how then would the scriptures be fulfilled, which say it must happen this way?" At that hour Jesus said to the crowds, "Have you come out with swords and clubs to arrest me as though I were a bandit? Day after day I sat in the temple teaching, and you did not arrest me. But all this has taken place, so that the scriptures of the prophets may be fulfilled." Then all the disciples deserted him and fled. (Matt 26:47–56)

While the full story of the torture and death of Jesus is told in Matthew 26–27, the passage quoted above fully illustrates the clash between God's kingdom and those of the world. Our human kingdoms wield power by the sword. God's kingdom clearly chooses other means to reach its objectives. Jesus declares that he could have called on God to rescue him with twelve legions of angels. He had a choice. He submitted to his death and suffering willingly. He knew there was purpose in his life's mission, and he knew this mission must be completed in the cross. He knew his and God's commitment to love and peace and reconciliation was an uncompromising and complete commitment. Scriptures needed to be fulfilled; in other words, God's kingdom of love and reconciliation as shown in scripture must be fully revealed for all the world to see.

The clash of the two kingdoms is real. The differences between the two kingdoms are irrefutable and irreconcilable, though we humans try every trick in the book to refute or reconcile the differences. If only we would open our eyes and ears, the full revealing of God's kingdom of love and reconciliation would reveal the stark contrast represented by all our violent alternatives.

It is interesting that in this text Jesus references his time of teaching in the temple. Daily, in full view, he had been teaching about the kingdom of God, but our kingdom powers came at night, avoiding the light of day. This contrast should not go unnoticed.

At least one of the disciples had a sword and used it to defend Jesus. The Gospel of John identifies him as Peter. The disciples were still straddling the two kingdoms.

Later, in the post-resurrection stories and the book of Acts, swords are no longer a part of the disciples' stories. But for now, only Jesus draws a clear line where one kingdom ends and the other begins. Jesus chastises the use of violence, heals the wound caused by the sword, and challenges the crowd that came for him by letting them know how badly they have misunderstood his mission.

The actions and words of Jesus in this garden scene present us with a strong witness to God's will and way in this world. Fully realizing what lay ahead, Jesus stood firm on the will and way of God's kingdom. How could he have done this without the ultimate power of God's love and reconciliation coursing through him? We too readily dismiss Jesus' ultimate sacrifice as *not* a total contrast to our will and way in this world, and continue to miss the clear and great divide between the two kingdoms.

As the story of the false accusation, torture, and death of Jesus unfolds, each agonizing scene plays out as further confirmation of Jesus' resolve to live the way of God's love. Each scene also confirms the terrors of systemic violence, the same force that is at work in our world today. With this in mind, we see the real work of God in and through Jesus during his suffering and death. Every ploy and plot twist, every vicious word and action, all the mocking and glee of the torturers mark the kingdoms of this world for what they are. While Jesus loves and forgives even while he suffers, the world imposes rage and rejection. While our violent nature exposes its demonic character, even so, God's living love is revealed.

Solving the Problem of Sin through Life instead of Death

Our traditional atonement theories have attempted to solve the problem of sinful humanity by coming to terms with Jesus' death. This is entirely misguided. We must change our focus from death to life. Traditionally, Christians have claimed the resurrection of Jesus was the answer to the death problem, and they were correct with one huge exception. If the death of Jesus is credited as *the* event of salvation, resurrection carries an anemic meaning—God killed Jesus and then raised him back to life? Why? How does this save us? If Jesus had to die, why "cancel out" that death? We see again how we must then create a magic formula and convince ourselves to believe it. We can theorize all we want about heaven and our eventual escape from this present life, but salvation for the afterlife doesn't truly solve the problem of death and its violent minions in the present world.

If all we want is a spiritualized and theoretical creed to absolve us from sin in the end, then the traditional atonement theories provide this. In this formulaic thinking, the practicalities of this present life are easily overlooked. We have the assurance we want; our sense of guilt and shame is tempered enough for us to plow on through this life. We are freed to celebrate formulaic salvation in our worship songs. We are convinced hell is not waiting for us (only for others). We are glad to escape questions about our complicity with violence because our present accommodation and use of violence have been separated from our future salvation.

Yet, one of the tests for any understanding of salvation should be whether it applies to daily life. To examine that question, we need to immerse ourselves in Jesus' life and teachings, to believe Jesus as he tells us to lose our life so we can truly find it. We must be willing to let go of our grasp on the life we have known, because in one way or another, this life has been a prison of power and violence. We must walk away from this prison, realizing we have been our own jailers.

To walk away from the life of death and violence we have known is to welcome the full understanding of salvation that Jesus taught and lived. When all we have left is our dependence on God's salvation, then and only then will it be real to us. Then and only then will Jesus' life in God be *our* life in God. Then and only then will we experience reunion with God—reconciliation with God at the core of our *daily lives*. Then and only then will we know a reality bigger than death—the reality of life in Jesus, not only in the future but in the present. To look fully to Jesus, his teachings, his life's mission, and the kingdom of God he announced for this life is to experience the only real salvation.

What are we saved from? We are saved from every form of violence and death ever invented by human beings. We are saved from all the accumulated centuries of systemic violence and death. Within this salvation, we are freed to love as completely as God loves because we are now "at one" with God—the true meaning of atonement.

The Cross as God's Total Commitment to Life

There is nothing halfway about God's salvation. The cross demonstrates and symbolizes the complete solidarity of God with Jesus' life and with the life God intends us to live on this planet. Let's take this one step further. The cross shows us the epitome of God's nonviolent love for all to witness. The cross is God's will and way in this world.

We have been tricked into thinking this present life is separate from life eternal, that somehow death meant something important, something to fear, something to flee from, something to ruthlessly defend ourselves against. We forgot, or maybe we never knew, that all God has ever been about is life! How, then, could the cross be an exception to the very nature of God? God is love. This is the simplest and most profound thing we can ever say or realize. Love does not die, it does not fail, and it does not ever leave us. The cross shouts the truth of this love to the mountaintops, to the bottom of the sea, and to the beginning and end of all history. Paul's version of this truth is in Romans 8:35–39.

> Who will separate us from the love of Christ? Will hardship, or distress, or persecution, or famine, or nakedness, or peril, or sword? As it is written, "For your sake we are being killed all day long; we are accounted as sheep to be slaughtered." No, in all these things we are more than conquerors through

him who loved us. For I am convinced that neither death, nor life, nor angels, nor rulers, nor things present, nor things to come, nor powers, nor height, nor depth, nor anything else in all creation, will be able to separate us from the love of God in Christ Jesus our Lord.

The cross has never been about death. The cross is all about the love of Christ proclaimed by Paul. Death is a smokescreen, a false shadow of our fear. The sword and those who wield it? Persecution? Peril? Rulers? Powers? These are all nothing in the face of God's love in Christ Jesus! When we know this, we can live God's salvation, removed from any focus on death.

The Litmus Test of Theology

The litmus test of any theory of theology must be how it measures up to the message of Jesus, his description of God's kingdom, and his supreme depiction of God's love in action. Because of centuries of confusion, any understanding of Christ's cross must especially meet these same criteria. The reason this test of theology is so important is because without Jesus guiding our thinking and doing, we will invariably dumb down God. Without Jesus teaching us, we become the teachers and, like the Pharisees of any age, the makers of the rules. We become gods unto ourselves using God to bolster our own way of thinking and, therefore, our own way of living.

The ideas in these pages, too, must be submitted to the litmus test of Jesus himself. If you find that anything here does not align with Jesus' life and teachings, discard it. Review and test the ideas presented here. Try them under the microscope of God's complete love. But don't stop with these pages; continue with the "pages" of your own life. This, finally, is where the real test of Jesus' life and teachings takes place. It is in our lives that death must meet its end.

Resurrection as God's Great "Amen!"

Death itself has been destroyed! This is the truth of truths discovered on the morning of the third day after Jesus' death. Why do we look for the living in the place of the dead? Was there ever any doubt that the tomb was empty, is empty, and always will be empty? Doubt is just human thinking. It surely is not God's thinking. God has always been thinking life.

Amen does not mean the final turn of events. *Amen* means "So be it!" *Amen* is "used to express solemn ratification (as of an expression of faith) or hearty approval (as of an assertion)."[13] God's resurrection amen asserts hearty approval and solemn ratification of all that Jesus taught and lived, even while going through the portal of death. The resurrection is not so much a celebration of *victory over death* as a celebration of *life* as it was always intended to be celebrated. Jesus' life is God's life told and

13. *Merriam Webster Online*, s.v. "amen."

shown to us in glorious love. What unbounded joy when we, in the midst of our present lives, realize our own resurrection within the life and resurrection of Jesus! Then we too, like Paul, can honestly declare, "Death, where is your sting?" As we comprehend what Jesus was saying and doing in his life here on earth, our celebration begins; it continues as we grasp more deeply his suffering and death; and it culminates in the ongoing celebration of God's never-ending work of resurrection.

Death in this present life will still often bring us sadness, but it never again needs to be a lasting sadness. It is now only a passing shadow of fear that ends in the welcome embrace of God's love. As the final word on suffering and violence, death and dying, God gives us the template of Jesus—*all* of Jesus.

Let the celebration begin! This is the real work of the church of Jesus Christ in this present life. Let's celebrate the reign of God's complete love, grace, and forgiveness with every thought and hope and dream and deed. This celebration of the church announces to the world an end to the powers of violence and death as God's salvation transforms the world.

Heaven as the Continuation of Reconciliation and Hope for All

One more time, read Paul's words in Colossians 1:19–20.

> For in [Jesus] all the fullness of God was pleased to dwell, and through him God was pleased to reconcile to himself all things, whether on earth or in heaven, by making peace through the blood of his cross.

Heaven does not get much emphasis in the Gospel of Matthew. I believe this is because Jesus was all about showing the way of salvation for the here-and-now of life on earth. By no means does this preclude the assurance of life everlasting. It simply means that heaven is the *continuation* of God's reconciliation, which has already been available to us in this life. The hope of heaven for all things makes perfect sense, flowing seamlessly from the witness of Jesus' life, death, and resurrection.

All things, as Paul makes clear—on earth and in heaven. *All* things, brought together, reconciled, reconnected by the peace made through Jesus' cross which bears witness to the salvation brought by the good news of Jesus' life. Do we think Paul excluded suffering and death from "all things"? Do we think Jesus forgot about the violence our hearts lust after when he went about reconciling "all things"? Do we think the peace brought by his blood on the cross did not cover the reunion of people divided from one another or the loving embrace of former enemies?

In the economy of God's salvation as taught and lived by Jesus, "all things" means *all* things. Whatever work of reconciliation goes unfinished in this life will be accomplished in heaven. *God's kingdom come, God's will be done, on earth as it is in heaven.*

Christians, of all people, have no reason to believe in—to place trust in, to give credence to—death and the world's systems of violence. We, of all people, know the reason for the celebration of both life eternal and our present life in Jesus Christ. The hope of heaven simply prompts us to also find hope here and now because the God of heaven is the God we learn to know in Jesus, the God of our salvation!

12

The Amazing Last Words

HEALING FROM THE WOUND OF CHRISTIANITY

Some hurts and injuries are too great, too terrible, and too debilitating for us to imagine they will ever heal easily or completely. I partially tore my Achilles tendon about eight months ago. I tried to self-heal for two weeks and that failed. I then sought medical help. I spent six weeks in a walking boot, and mistakenly thought that would be the worst of it. Alas, I am still recovering. The recovery process takes daily care. I am aware of every little ache or twitch that tells me my right Achilles tendon is not the same as my left uninjured one. I have never had an injury that lasted this long or demanded so much of my attention. Until this injury, I took healing for granted; I had come to believe my body would always heal itself naturally with little effort on my part. Now I know I was wrong.

Christianity has been wounded too, to a degree greater than what we have understood. This wound has been inflicted by millions of people and for many hundreds of years. This wound is now embedded in the soul of humanity; it is written on the world like permanent marker on white pants. The stain can't simply be washed out; the pants cannot be returned to an unblemished state. In this present day, many have come to believe the stain is just the way the pants were meant to be, that the wound is the reality, and that nothing more can or should be expected.

Mass shootings at schools and places of worship still shock us, but they do not motivate us to change. Truth in public discourse seems lost and barely missed. Prejudices of all sorts are nursed and often used to bolster an appearance of strength and self-confidence. Our anger, resentment, bitterness, and fears are catered to by those in power. We are used as pawns for political gain. Every day brings us a fresh feeling of conflict, like the shadow of storm clouds blocking the sunrise. The conflict resides in our marriages, our families, our friendships, our neighborhoods, our schools, our workplaces, and our places of worship. The truth is that our conflict resides first in us, and we carry it through our day like a nagging animal aggressively straining at its leash. Our conflict wants to be set free to pounce on the world around us.

The wound of Christianity comes from a very great fall. I once hiked and climbed up Long's Peak in Colorado. The last part of the climb involved careful hand and foot placement in small rock cracks and on nubs of granite that jutted out. Below me was only air for 1,000 feet. Had I fallen, I would have had plenty of time to think about my coming death. It is one thing to fall out of bed, and a whole other thing to fall for 1,000 feet and out of life.

In the early part of the fourth century, the Christian church began to fall out of life from an unmeasurable height. One thousand feet would not begin to cover this distance. The fall was not sudden, but it was sure. To use a biblical analogy from Peter's life (Matt 14:28–33), the church in general took its eyes and ears off Jesus and succumbed to its fears while sinking below the angry waves of the world. At least Peter, attempting to walk on the angry sea, cried out to Jesus for salvation; the church, by and large, has not. Instead, much of Christian leadership and laity have sought salvation from within the angry waves. The salvation Jesus brought to this world says, "Don't hide in the boat; walk on the water, and come to me." Many have climbed out of the boat only to find their fears too great. While sinking amid the angry waves of this life, most people end up trying to save themselves.

It is the little unattended pains that grow into open, lasting wounds. Living as wounded animals appears to be our fate. While many Christians over the centuries forgot their calling from Christ, he still says, "Come to me." Instead, Christians normally lick their wounds and lean on their own defenses, like most other human beings on the planet.

We talk of the fall of Christianity as having begun in the fourth century when the emperor Constantine claimed faith in Jesus in support of his military power. This was a decisive time period in the great fall, but fear and woundedness have been around from the beginning of human existence. To combat this woundedness, the church, by and large, has fallen into the bed of politics. This church, while sleeping with the enemy, will not and cannot save us, and it cannot save itself no matter how wedded it remains to the violence and powers of this life. We witness this wedded attempt at salvation constantly, and it seems to be a stain never to be removed. The white pants of our faith and faithfulness might never be the same again.

But wait! In the final chapter of Matthew we discover again the call of Jesus. Jesus says seven amazing things to his disciples. They are simple and straightforward, not difficult to understand. In a real sense, these simple statements sum up his life and teachings, and they project all he has said and done onto the wall of future life in the kingdom of God. For those who would be committed to following Jesus today, these seven final instructions are priceless. These are don't-miss words for us to live by.

The world only changes as you and I first change. Once real change takes place inside us, God's heart flows into our hearts and minds. From the depths of our own heart we now live the love of God's heart. Our lives become all about knowing and showing God's love. This is not an agenda, a cause, a program, a belief system, a goal, or anything to accomplish. It is who we are becoming, and it is enough to be full of this overflowing love!

With God's love filling and flowing within and from the depths of our hearts, what does it now matter if we are Christian, Jew, Muslim, Hindu, atheist, or agnostic? These are just labels on the outer casings of our lives, like the branding for the right kind of kidney beans. I don't mean to say our labels are without value, but when God's complete love engulfs us, our labels lose their significance.

If you are holding tight to a label, think for a minute about Jesus' purpose in the life he showed us. Jesus was not orthodox anything but himself. He did not tell us to be Christian or to claim any other form of religion. He told us and showed us God's love, period. He invited us, even commanded us, into God's loving way of living. Human beings like you and I built up the religious structures and placed the labels on them. When our labels become our focus, then our walk over the angry waves to Jesus ends in desperate attempts at our own salvation.

To make all of this practical, we turn to the seven final instructions Jesus gave us in Matthew, which call us to repent from anything added to or subtracted from God's love. We will immerse ourselves in Jesus' final words through stories that claim the joy, the truth, and the ultimate triumph of God's love—present and available in our lives every moment of every day. These last words of Jesus are truly amazing!

THE INCREDIBLY HOPEFUL LAST WORDS

"Do Not Be Afraid"

Two women are fleeing the empty tomb of Jesus. An angel has just told them not to be afraid, yet how can they not be fearful of this new turn of events, on top of all the horror they have witnessed in the previous days? Suddenly Jesus himself appears to them and repeats the message: "Do not be afraid" (Matt 28:10). Jesus knows we humans are a fearful lot. What day goes by without concern, worry, anxiety, uncertainty, indecision, and outright fear crossing our minds and hearts? The results of this inner turmoil spill out of us and too often rule our lives.

Even—especially—in our moments of great anxiety, Jesus confronts our fear and commands its end. Above all, God is not to be feared! And God's world need no longer be a scary and uncertain place for us. An empty tomb means life is safe and assured for the first followers of Jesus and for those throughout all the years to come. We are now saved from our fear and our addiction to it. While everything in life has the potential to become our personal nightmare—people and things we depend on, like friends, family, wealth, power, popularity, political influence, military defense—God in Christ

Jesus is the only one with whom we have nothing to fear. In him, fear itself has been conquered. Imagine!

When God is not scary, and resurrection is certain, our dependency on all other things fades. While the world around us plays on our fears to use us and control us, God offers a safe haven where we only experience real love and true security. Yet the people of Jesus' day could not accept God's desire to gather them into loving safety and peace, so Jesus wept (Luke 19:41–42). Then like now, people were addicted, paradoxically, both to fear and to defending themselves against it.

The quandary facing the two Marys as they ran from Jesus' tomb was a confusing mix of hope and dread. Death and all its terror still held sway over their hope for life. How could they have known the full significance of the empty tomb? Death seems so real to us too, so sure, so threatening of our existence, imposing such significant losses throughout our life.

What if death is actually our awakening to life without falsehood? What if our fear can be transformed into the joy of the empty tomb as we are fully united with God?

Big John in the Juvenile Detention Center

When I was a pastor in Bellefontaine, Ohio, one Sunday a month I visited the juvenile detention center. First, I spoke to the girls for half an hour, and then I spent half an hour with the boys.

When I first began this routine, two guards always led the youth into the classroom where we met. The guards took seats at the back of the room where they could observe and intervene if necessary—if I lost control of the group. They were a welcome security blanket for me, though I never actually needed them. After several months without incident, one Sunday afternoon I was surprised when the guards led the youth into the classroom and then left. For a full half-hour with the girls and a half-hour with the boys, I was the lone adult in the room with about two dozen teenage offenders.

I decided if the guards could relax, it meant they trusted me to keep control of the situation. As the months went by, I found strength in knowing my time with the youth would be positive. I especially looked forward to times of dialogue with them. I found that when I invited their responses, it opened a fresh amount of risk, since they were not always polite or above acting out. But it was in the risk that we found the greatest potential for connection. When I allowed them to be real, I too became more real.

One day, about two years into this ministry, the half-hour with the girls went as usual, but my time with the boys did not. This Sunday I opened the entire time for dialogue. I purposely did not choose a topic or plan out anything I would say. I simply opened our time by asking them what they wanted to talk about.

Every bed in the boys' side of the detention center must have been filled that day because as the youth filed in, every chair in the classroom was taken. There were three officers this time, and they brought in more chairs. Normally I had plenty of room in the front of the classroom, but with the additional chairs, I ended up with my back literally against the cinder-block wall at the front of the room with no more than three feet between me and the first row of boys. That day the officers did not leave the room, and I soon found out why.

Since I had no other plan, I proceeded with asking my opening question: What did they want to talk about? I got an immediate answer from a boy in the middle of the front row. I don't know his real name, but I call him Big John because he was twice my size. He was the reason the officers were in greater number and stayed in the room. I could only imagine the vast differences in life experiences between Big John and me, and all the reasons he might have to distrust me and challenge me.

Big John wanted to talk about suicide and hell, and he said so in a clearly con-frontational way. A young man known to many in the room had recently committed suicide. John was asking a relevant question, while challenging me, the preacher, to come up with an adequate answer. I knew he and I were now in a contest for control of the classroom. I knew he expected me to give a pat answer he could scoff at, and perhaps scoff at me, and at God. I watched the guards in the back as they shifted in their seats and readied themselves for action.

Fortunately, suicide was a topic familiar to me. I decided to tell John and the other boys my personal story. I told them how approximately five years before, I had lost my marriage, my family, my job, my home, and for several years my career, all in one short span of time. I could only tell this true story with my heart and soul. The room had been buzzing from the boys' anticipation of a conflict; now it became totally quiet. The guards settled back in their seats.

I explained to the boys how in the aftermath of my losses, I became severely depressed. My heart was broken in so many ways, and I was suicidal for many months. I had a daily walking circuit that took me across a bridge over the Mississippi River. It was the heart of winter in Minnesota, and the cold waters of the river called my name every day. While on the bridge, I would pause and think about the plunge I could take to my death. It was like living on a knife's edge between jumping or not. With almost all my heart I wanted to die. But one piece of me would not let me jump. I had a sixteen-year-old daughter whom I loved dearly, and I could not bring myself to say goodbye to her.

After telling this story, I turned directly to John and asked him to be God for the moment. He sat up straight and swelled with the thought. I then asked him, "If I had committed suicide, would you, as God, have sent me to hell or would you have welcomed me home with loving arms?" Without any hesitation, John said that as God, he would have welcomed me home in love.

I simply told him he had answered correctly.

For the remainder of the half-hour, John and I were partners in leading a discussion about a God so safe and so full of love for us that no kind of death could stop the love, could separate us from God. Of all the times I spoke at the juvenile detention center, that half-hour was the most significant and rewarding. It became a holy time, and that center became holy ground.

A Future without Fear

Life's meaning can only be truly discovered when we stop believing our fears and start believing Jesus. At age seventeen, Big John was already a hardened offender with great resentment brewing in his heart. He was ready to rumble in response to a world of hurt and a hurting world. He was prepared to fight the way the world fights, and I'm sure he was good at it. Yet even he knew Jesus' answer to violence. Even he knew something about a love beyond measure. The seed of hope and of a future without fear resided in his heart. Some diminished but real part of John still held desperately to the message of Jesus and the complete love of God. For at least some moments in John's life, he was able to participate in the future life of fearlessness to which Jesus has called us.

I would guess that most human beings fear death, and we often project this fear onto God. Meanwhile, throughout the biblical narrative, God repeatedly tells us not to be afraid.

Think of Jesus in Matthew 28:10, having recently undergone a horrific death himself, telling his followers not to be afraid. He is living proof of life, not death! He is saying in effect, "Let them torture and murder you, defile you, curse you, and shame you. That is all they can do. That is all death can ever do. And though these are terrible things, they are fleeting within the expanse of an eternity of God's and our life of loving."

The things Jesus taught and lived are the only eternal things. They are the will and way of God, who loves completely. Therefore, Jesus can look death and destruction in the eye and, out of his own experience, instruct us to not fear anything in this life or the next. He is casting aside any fleeting, fearful thought regarding our future because we are in God's loving care.

Think of the women and men who had followed Jesus. Think of the horror they had witnessed and how fearful and hopeless they must have been. Think of the sad future they envisioned. It must have been a lightning-bolt kind of shock to hear him say, "Do not be afraid." In this extreme context of death turned to life, all that has gone before gets projected onto the future screen of life. "Do not be afraid" is the absolute declaration of life over any sort of death. All that Jesus taught and lived is now our destiny, and there is nothing outside our own choices that can stop it. Even in a world where weapons of mass destruction threaten, life is forever assured, while fear is challenged and dismissed.

Simply put, we humans have nothing more to fear, period. Life's victory over death is accomplished. Death has been proved to be a shadow dispelled and a doorway opened. Any act of violent control, any self-salvation attempt, any excuses for participating in the world's acts of destruction are pathetic dependencies on things that are passing away. These are not our future! In Jesus, our future leapfrogs past our fear, especially fears of death or of God. In Jesus, we now see and hear and know life's true meaning forever.

"Go to Galilee"

In the same verse, after Jesus tells the women not to be afraid, he then says, "Go and tell my brothers to go to Galilee; there they will see me" (Matt 28:10). Likewise, in the shortest and most credible ending of the Gospel of Mark, the angel declares, "But go, tell his disciples and Peter that he is going ahead of you to Galilee; there you will see him, just as he told you" (Mark 16:7). This idea of returning to Galilee and seeing Jesus again is like a totally unexpected plot twist at the end of a great mystery novel. Up until this moment in the story, who could have guessed that beyond all hopelessness, new expectations, new information, and a new beginning would bring back hope?

Let's not miss the significance of returning to Galilee to see Jesus. Galilee was where discipleship began. It was where Jesus called his disciples, started the movement that would change the world, and taught and lived the kingdom of God. Galilee is the symbolic location of ministry, healings, and the fulfillment of scripture. It is where the will and the way of God in this world first came into focus and into life itself through Jesus. Galilee was the caldron of both amazement and bitter conflict. It was where Jesus and his disciples faced off against the powers of their world even as what was brewing finally bubbled over into the terrible events in Jerusalem. Galilee was where God came directly into contact with a desperate and hurting world, and where real people, with all their warts, found themselves face to face with love embodied.

To return to Galilee and see Jesus is to embrace the movement of God all over again! It is to acknowledge that the powers of death have no lasting meaning, cannot stop the movement, and in fact only serve to relaunch the movement. What is the result of the death and destruction dealt by the world? What can the powers of evil claim for their efforts? What emanates from torture and murder? The answer will astound you! God simply leads the movement to a new phase where more and more people experience and champion complete love. Ministry and mission spread out, reach more people, and further change the world.

Talk about a reason not to fear—the only thing that torture and death have been capable of doing is increasing hope, renewing joy, and producing a greater harvest of love! And all this will happen through the lives of the ones who so recently deserted Jesus in fear and hopelessness. This can only be a God thing as powerful and full of resurrection as the empty tomb. Our own tombs can now become empty too.

The meaning of life everlasting is realized in the phenomenon of ever-new beginnings. We think there is just hopelessness. We think death is an ending. We think we must use death to try to conquer death. All the while, Galilee awaits us. Our job is to return there and see God again, to see and hear God again just as Jesus called his disciples to do in the first "act" of life everlasting—Matthew 5–27. Seeing and hearing Jesus continue to be our main tasks as each new beginning affords us the opportunities. We are to drop our own nets and boats immediately and follow Jesus (Matt 4:20, 22). Our ministry is to be modeled after Jesus' ministry and no other.

Galilee always awaits our return. We humans have the perennial necessity to repent and begin again. To some extent we will always mess up, just as the first disciples did. We will never fully and perfectly follow Jesus. The point here is to always return to the basics, to start over again and again with Jesus as our guide instead of turning in some other direction, relying on other powers. Galilee is always there for us, no matter how seriously we have lost our way. We will always need to return to the beatitudes and everything Jesus taught us from the beginning.

Galilee is not the center of power, the center of religious devotion, or the symbolic, exclusive place to meet God. Galilee, not Jerusalem, is where we meet God every day, where sins are forgiven and lives are restored. Consider the significance of Galilee as symbol of reconciliation with God at potentially every level of our hearts and every moment of our day!

Whereas in Jesus' day, reconciliation with God was to take the form of official, sacred observance officiated by the temple professionals, now in everyday Galilee, in the wake of death's carnage, God's overpowering love for us waits like an avalanche poised above our heads. Wherever we have been, wherever we have failed, wherever we have hopelessly relied on forces of violence and death for our salvation . . . these places are mirages of our past. Seeing Jesus again in Galilee, we can know a completely new beginning within God's full embrace. Even those of us most deeply hurt and most hurtful toward others can also now know the experience of following Jesus for real and ministering to others as he ministers to us.

Some of what I have written in this book is likely a challenge to a certain understanding of Christianity. I have asked readers to think about radical concepts poised to change how they live in this world. If, by any chance, you are wondering or troubled about your previous life's dependence on violent solutions or are feeling overwhelmed by new possibilities for living violence-free, you have come to the right place. Here, where Jesus calls all disciples back to Galilee, is your opportunity to start over with fresh insight and new commitment to see and hear him. Please do not use this book to set a new course for your life; instead, go back to Galilee—in Matthew and the other three gospels—and learn all you can from Jesus himself.

Consider also the book of Acts as a means of returning to Galilee and seeing Jesus. For anyone to think Jesus' movement died when he did, they would have to ignore the book of Acts, along with much of human history. The stories of returning to Galilee are all around us, filling and refilling the annals of history. One such story is that of the Meserete Kristos Church in Ethiopia.

Resurrection from Persecution

The Meserete Kristos Church in Ethiopia grew out of the efforts of Mennonite missionaries, Mennonite Central Committee work, and Mennonite Relief Committee work back in 1945. Gradually over the years, the relief and mission work transferred to Ethiopian leadership. This also brought about the church's name, which means "Christ is the foundation." In 1974, Haile Selassie I, the long-term emperor of Ethiopia, was dethroned in a coup that resulted in Marxist rule. Over time, the Christian church in Ethiopia, including the Meserete Kristos Church, came under intense persecution.

Meserete Kristos Church leaders were arrested. Church meetings were forbidden, and physical violence against MKC members was encouraged.

> In January 1982, the Marxist government confiscated all of Meserete Kristos' offices, worship buildings, bank accounts and physical property. In addition to the confiscation of property, six of MKC's leaders were arrested and held in detention for 50 months. They were kept in cramped conditions, knowing that at any moment they could be executed. These six MKC leaders included: Kelifa Ali, Kiros Bihon, Shamsudin Abdo, Negash Kebede, Abebe Gorfe and Tilahun Beyene. While these church leaders were in jail and with no buildings to congregate in, church members took it upon themselves to hold church services in private. A law was in place at the time stating that nobody could meet in groups larger than five people except on holidays. Recognizing the magnitude of this law, MKC members organized a network of "cells" in which members would meet at each other's houses in groups of five. A majority of these cells did not include any form of leaders or trained pastors because there weren't enough leaders to go around, but rather were comprised of ordinary church-goers. There was always the constant risk of police raids, so members communicated by word of mouth and attendees entered and left the house individually. This cell organization allowed the underground MKC to flourish as people intimately shared their personal faith in small groups of trusted friends. Attendance grew exponentially as people became disillusioned with the communist system and were searching for meaning in life other than Marxist doctrine. The Meserete Kristos Church officially ceased to exist; however, the democratization process in 1992 initiated by the newly founded government allowed the church to reemerge and obtain some of its lost property. This ten-year period of underground activity didn't serve the communist government's intended purpose of decreasing church attendance. Rather, it signified a drastic explosion in church membership as numbers rose from 5,000 to 34,000 members.[1]

1. Jacob Swartzentruber, "Meserete Kristos Church, Ethiopia."

In the face of severe persecution, the Meserete Kristos Church in Ethiopia grew nearly seven times over in the span of ten years. As of 2014, the MKC had multiplied much further and was a worship community of over 471,000 people (members and others) across 756 congregations and 875 church planting locations.[2] As of 2017, MKC continued to grow and included 310,877 baptized members.[3]

From 5,000 members in 1982 to almost 311,000 in 2017, plus many more worshiping together! This is phenomenal growth, and proof of what "returning to Galilee" can be and accomplish in the face of persecution. We need to fear nothing once we experience our return to Galilee, for this is where we truly learn our dependence on Jesus, the source and author of our return to being God's images in this world.

"All Authority . . . Has Been Given to Me"

> And Jesus came and said to them, "All authority in heaven and on earth has been given to me." (Matt 28:18)

Verses 18–20 of Matthew 28 are commonly called "The Great Commission." These are the parting words of Jesus to his disciples, according to Matthew, from which the church has taken its sense of mission for centuries. Much has been said and written concerning what Jesus intended to communicate here. I wish to emphasize the importance of this address in light of what we have covered in the previous eleven chapters.

First in the Great Commission is Jesus' claim to authority. Jesus clears up any question about the scope—*all*—of this authority, and then about its source: it comes directly from God, for no other source could possibly provide it. Consider these words from Jesus in Matthew 11:

> All things have been handed over to me by my Father; and no one knows the Son except the Father, and no one knows the Father except the Son and anyone to whom the Son chooses to reveal him. (Matt 11:27)

God's complete authority is given to Jesus, and it reigns over everything in heaven and on earth. We should also note how his all-inclusive authority infuses everything else he says in his commission. A form of the word *all* occurs four different times in these few verses, and in each instance it lends great emphasis to everything Jesus is saying.

We have emphasized previously that "all" really means *all*! But if Jesus possesses full authority over everything, what does that mean to us today in a world full of other authorities? What does this complete authority mean for the sake of our return to Galilee—our return to all Jesus taught and lived as recounted in Matthew?

---

2. Wikipedia, s.v. "Meserete Kristos Church."

3. Barb Draper, "Ethiopian Meserete Kristos Church."

Over the generations, most Christians have struggled mightily with this concept of "all authority." It is nearly impossible for humans to submit completely to the authority of God, and Christians often seem no better at it than anyone else. A whole variety of authorities in our lives want to supersede the authority of Jesus. Throughout this book we have looked at examples of how people, including Christians, have dismissed and disbelieved what Jesus taught and lived. In all the ways we allow other powers to rule us, be they governments or personal addictions, we fail to take these last words of Jesus, the Great Commission, seriously enough.

But "all" does mean *all*—Jesus is the complete authority over the universe, not just in a future heaven but here and now. All the hurt and torment in this present world, including our participation in it, comes from lives not fully submitted to the one and only real authority that has created and even now sustains heaven and earth. In the chapters of Matthew, this one real authority has taught and shown us how to live. Where we have fallen short, it comes down to a crisis of authority.

One final time in the book of Matthew, Jesus says he is the only one. The only authority. There can be no other. Anyone willing to believe him has no need for my words. The real and only authoritative book is the one Jesus writes through his words and his actions. To sum up the pages in this book: Believe Jesus; take his authoritative words and actions as your own completely and always.

You and I will never submit perfectly to the complete authority of Jesus, but what we can absolutely accomplish is to end all pretense. Because of the overall witness of Jesus, we can recognize the times we miss the mark, fail to love fully, fail to trust his salvation completely, and try to serve other authorities. We can and must honestly name all the false powers and false gods we have allowed to supplant the authority of Jesus. We can become fully aware of our need for repentance and turning back to the authority of Jesus. Though we will never be perfect, we no longer have an excuse not to turn back, take Jesus at his word, and then live our lives and allegiances differently.

War is not inevitable, not for those who recognize the full authority of Jesus. Our participation in any kind of violence, hurt, or painful interchange is not the prescribed script of our lives. In reading and understanding the words and actions of Jesus, we now have the choice to live our lives according to his. In every real sense, our lives can become recognition points whereby we and all the world see Jesus as the only real author of life and authority over life.

The authority of Jesus over our lives takes on very practical meaning in the real-world politics of our day. Recognizing the total authority of Jesus means other authorities must be set aside. This, in part, means that we who wish to follow him need to place his teachings and living example above all other influences in our lives. One thing this surely means in our confusing and politically charged world is that any political alliance we may want to make must meet the standard set by Jesus himself. Otherwise, we compromise our loyalties and undermine our ability to live within the kingdom of God now. This is a stringent and difficult requirement for many

Christians, especially here in the United States. In this country, it has become nearly impossible for Christians to distinguish between "country politics" and "God politics." When these very different politics become fused, Christians lose their ability to place Jesus' authority above allegiance to country and personal political leanings.

A simple rule in politics for Christians today is to always ask, "Whose authority am I placing above all others?" If the answer is Jesus' authority, then who we vote for and which policies we support must follow the rule of God's complete love for all people everywhere, for this beautiful and wonderful planet God has created, and for need-based justice and peace at all levels of society. To follow Jesus allows us no other choice. Take his words and deeds—not mine—as confirmation of this.

Politics or Friendship?

In the throes of partisan politics leading up to the 2008 US presidential election, the men's Bible study I attended became a bit fractured as we talked about how to vote. Jason was particularly concerned with how I was planning to vote. We decided to get together, just the two of us, so we could talk faith and politics privately. At that time Jason was a casual friend, and we only knew each other through the Bible study. I was pastoring a local congregation, while Jason was a member of a different church and a different denomination. There were many reasons for us to disagree. However, we both loved the church and claimed Jesus as Lord of our lives. In our private conversations, we never reached agreement on how to vote in that national election. Instead, we became dear friends.

Some years later, Jason died in a motorcycle accident. Attending his funeral was difficult, and I struggled with deep sadness over his life cut so short. Following the service, Jason's parents sought me out. Though they were surely grieving more deeply than I was, they took the time to speak glowingly of Jason's and my friendship and of the respect he had for me. I felt a partial release from my sadness, and great humility. Not until that moment had I realized how important our friendship had been to both Jason and me. No partisan politics had held sway over Jesus' love flowing in us and through us. God's love held the authority over our relationship, not the lure of country or the divisive nature of our political system.

Since 2008, division has only increased among us. This division will continue and likely worsen in the years to come. Most of us are arguing about all the wrong things because we are pushed and pulled by allegiance to multiple authorities. Having multiple authorities will always divide us and draw us away from Jesus. My friendship with Jason taught me that I have no control over anyone else's allegiances. I am not responsible for past, current, or future politics in my country. Any positive influence we might have in politics comes only from our undivided allegiance to Jesus as we accept his sole claim to authority in heaven and on earth. When you or I bow only to

Jesus and his way of total love, divisions will fade from our view. This is the way God's universe of love works. This is the only way heaven and earth become one!

"Go . . . and Make Disciples"

> "Go therefore and make disciples of all nations." (Matt 28:19)

Following Jesus' claim of total authority, and considering this claim's life-altering significance, Jesus commands, "Go therefore and make disciples." In the proverbial nutshell, this captures the meaning and purpose of Jesus' time on earth. His mission was not simply to change first-century history, but to change *all* human history. He showed us how to make disciples. That is what he lived and died for.

Just as he has been given all authority by God, Jesus now imparts this authority, in certain respects, to all who would take up his command. While we could enumerate all the ways the church has messed this up, let's instead focus on the powerful and wonderful possibilities found in this command.

In the Greek, there are three participles in verses 19 and 20: *going, baptizing*, and *teaching*. Let's focus first on the word *going*. Our English translations try to smooth out how the passage reads, so they substitute the word *go*. I get frustrated with translations that change the meaning of a text. A worthy English translation of this wording would be "As you now are going." The tense implies an action that is ongoing and is a foregone conclusion. Jesus is saying, in effect, "As your life has unfolded and is unfolding, your continuing mission is to make disciples. Make disciples as you continue to journey through life." In other words, making disciples is not a separate activity from ongoing life; it *is* ongoing life.

Don't miss the implication that Jesus is acknowledging his disciples' continuous mission in life: past, present, and future. Even though the disciples had bungled things and misunderstood Jesus during their apprenticeship, he recognizes their past efforts and encourages them onward. Remember the call to Galilee. There is always a new day for following Jesus. Put your stumbles behind you and move on; reconnect with Jesus and his mission. Nothing in your past can stand in your way. You can immediately, right now, drop your nets (your personal agenda) and take up your cross (God's agenda). You can immediately recommit to the full authority of Jesus and live fully according to God's will and way in this world. You can get on with making disciples regardless of your former alliances or allegiances.

When We Lose Our Way

I clearly remember a time in my pastoral ministry when I stumbled and, at least temporarily, lost my way. If it had been up to me, I would have left the pastoral ministry altogether. I found myself desperately wanting a way out of my present life.

It came when I realized my ministry track was moving in a different direction than the church where I was serving and indeed much, if not most, of the Christian church as a whole (at least as I knew it at the time). This realization caused me quite a crisis. I remember spending at least one sleepless night lying on our living room floor imploring God to get me out of the mess I was in. I had become overwhelmed with the sense that my present ministry was over, while I had no clue where God might want me next. I felt defeated, a failure, and rather useless to my friends, family, and the church.

Early on the morning after my night on the floor, I opened my email and found an advertisement for a camp director job. Under the duress of my circumstances, the job sounded perfect for me. I concluded that God had answered my nightlong prayer in a timely fashion. I became exuberant. I lost no time in applying for the job. Soon I interviewed for the job and became convinced I would be hired. Eventually I was invited to the camp itself for a tour of the grounds and a second interview with the board of directors. My wife accompanied me. Despite a growing list of nagging doubts, I was sure I was going to get that job and escape my life of pastoral ministry.

That evening on the six-hour drive home, I experienced the closest thing to a Jonah-and-the-fish story I have ever known. As we left the camp, a bank of very angry clouds overtook us. We almost lost the canoe strapped to the roof of our car, due to the wind that hit us. In a small town, I pulled behind a large brick building to wait out the storm. I'm not sure our car would have stayed upright otherwise. Once the wind died down, we continued our drive, only to be pounded repeatedly by some of the heaviest rains I have ever driven through. Then came such flooding that we had to drive slowly through standing water on a major highway.

Fortunately, no one drowned that night, and we eventually made it home safely. Emotionally, though, I was thoroughly shaken. The nagging doubts I had been feeling began to shape up into a sense of depression. Not long after that night, I found out the camp director job I "knew" I had secured had gone to someone else. My world crashed in on me with more force than I had previously known. I tendered my resignation to the church and spent the next few months without any sense of my future work, where we would live, how we could afford to live, and just what I would do with my life. I felt washed up on shore, not so much by a vomiting fish, but just as washed up, nonetheless.

After what seemed an eternity, but was actually just three months, a job offer came. It was nothing I had expected or sought. It was a total surprise and became a redirection of my ministry like no other. The offer was to become a transitional pastor, a role in which my ministry gifts could match the needs of struggling and hurting congregations. It became the perfect job for me, and it was how I finished out my career as a pastor.

I look back now on my "Jonah experience" and can see the mistakes I made, the wrong assumptions, and my lack of faith. What truly stands out, though, is how steadfast God was in leading and guiding me through that troubled time. God sternly, and then gently, directed me to keep going along my life's journey making disciples, even when I had lost my way. It was Jesus again saying, "While on your life's way, make disciples."

One of the best things about this command of Jesus is that it is not separate from the living of our lives. Though I was called to many years of pastoral ministry, your calling might be at a car dealership, a grocery store, a factory, or a house full of growing children. Regardless of what station of life we find ourselves in, Jesus calls us to make disciples. If we are disciples of Jesus, then we are to also be disciple-makers right there in the circumstances of our lives.

What Jesus Did Not Call Us to Make

We might be surprised if we take time to think about what Jesus did *not* call us to make. He did not call us to make Christians, or church members, or believers. He did not call us to make saved people, or Sunday school teachers, or committee members. He did not call us to make people believe correctly or behave better. He did not call us to make the right political alliances. He did not call us to hold evangelistic meetings. He did not call us to trust him to get us to heaven when we die. He did not call us to say the sinner's prayer. He did not call us to make ourselves safe in this world. He did not call us to make the world safe for democracy. He did not call us to take sides, support conflict, or make war.

Jesus simply called us to make disciples. What about this calling is so difficult to understand? The question is, can we focus clearly on this one calling? This one overarching commandment? Many other things may be very good things, but if we miss Jesus' main calling to make disciples, these other things will fail and move us away from Jesus himself.

Making Disciples Naturally

You will probably think I am crazy for saying this, but here goes: Making disciples is just about the most natural thing we will ever do. Let me explain.

First, forget all the churchy expectations anyone has ever lobbed your way. Forget elaborate theologies and debated orthodoxies. Shut down all your tendencies to live up to certain standards. Put your brain on hold and open your heart to the utter and total sense that God is all love and only love, God's love is yours to receive and give away, and the time for this love is *now*. The absolute love of God is the source and sustenance of the universe. This same love of God is what Jesus taught and lived. To know and live this love is why you and I have been created. If love is not the truth within God's created universe, Jesus is a lie, and the God Jesus revealed is an illusion. To be human is to be created for love and loving, to be connected to God at heart and soul depth, and to live forever within God's will and way of love and loving.

When we are engaged, connected, enlivened, and fully directed by God's love, God flows in and through us normally, naturally, and automatically. We don't need to pretend to be good or loving, or to live rightly. We just need to stay in that space where God flows; then love will flow in us in turn. So much in this life and in our minds can draw us away from our place in God, but none of these change the reality of God's created order and God's will and way in the world. God's constant desire is for creation (especially humanity) to turn and return to the loving heart from which we came. God is always calling us to turn and return to this place where we will be reformed in total love.

To be a disciple of Jesus and go through life making disciples is the most natural way to live. We were created for this. This is the beginning and the end for us. It is precisely this that Jesus came to teach and show us. Nothing could be truer about life in God's creation. This is exactly what is at stake in whether we choose to believe Jesus, accept his life as our own, and make disciples of all around us. If we are to see, hear, and accept Jesus' command to make disciples, three things are essential. Though seemingly obvious, they easily become veiled by our desires for other things this world offers.

We must fully know to whom we belong. Jesus did not call us to be someone else's disciples. He clearly did not intend for us to follow those in this world who had power, wealth, influence, or human control. In fact, we have already made the argument that the powers of this world were aligned against, tortured, and killed Jesus; surely these same powers continue to resist him with all their might. We could easily make the point that these powers, the very ones that say wonderful things and lure us with their glitter and their gold, call us to the very opposite of following Jesus.

We must be utterly sure of our allegiance to Jesus and his authority over our life. We cannot be sure of anything if we do not intimately know what he taught and how he lived. The previous chapters have been dedicated to such knowledge. This becomes then a clarion call to all people, especially Christians, to let go of everything else they have assumed or been taught in order to study, learn, and live the life of Jesus.

Belonging to Jesus makes all the difference between (1) simply calling ourselves his followers and (2) allowing him to live in us. The first amounts to a constant struggle with the world as we fail to resist its influence. The second means we stop the struggle and welcome God's full embrace. The first is all about what *we* try to do. The second is about what *God* does by loving us. The first pits us against people and ideologies. The second frees us to love all and everyone—even those the world would call our enemies. The first invariably draws down our energies and depletes our inner strength. The second renews us and enlivens us with the courage and power to face all situations, no matter how evil or horrible.

A wonderful place to begin again with learning the life of Jesus is his teachings on the beatitudes in Matthew 5:3–12. I will say again that in these blessings we discover our true identity as images of God. The sum of these is who we have been created to be. In Jesus, we discover ourselves in the very image of God. Osborne states:

> Jesus mandates that all mission activity emulate his pattern of discipling followers as exemplified in this gospel. They must be brought to understanding and to that deep ethical commitment patterned in the Sermon on the Mount and the Community Discourse; then they will become "trained as disciples in the kingdom" (13:52 [Today's New International Version).[4]

We must be committed to remain in our place of belonging. In Christ we have a lifelong place of belonging. If we are not willing to let go of the constant securities life around us offers, or if we allow life's securities to retake us, we will lose what we have gained. God's abiding love will wait for us, but love's flow to and from us will constrict and perhaps even cease entirely. We will find ourselves back in the struggle to resist, and failing to resist, the world's influence. The life of Jesus will no longer be our life.

Belonging to Jesus and living the life he shares with us is a moment-to-moment, everyday relationship. This belonging becomes our identity. Knowing God's love is an ongoing process. The source of our belonging is eternal, as is the intended oneness of the relationship.

We must allow God's love to guide our learning from and following of Jesus. It is one thing to carefully read the teachings and examples of Jesus. This is a good place to start our journey with him. But head knowledge will only take us so far and will always be vulnerable to the myriad interpretations in which Jesus is picked apart and his power of love is defused. We have so many past examples of interpretations that deflated the power of Jesus' love.

So, we read and learn all we can from the gospel stories of Jesus. Then we combine those with the love of God moving in and through us at its deepest level. We take our identity in God's love, and from that place of knowing, we see and hear everything in Jesus through the eyes and ears of God's complete love. With the assurance of God's love, we then can hear and see Jesus for who he truly was and is. What makes everything real is belonging to Jesus, being committed to him, and knowing him in and through love.

Trusting the Natural Flow of God's Love

When we belong moment to moment in God's love, when we know Jesus in our heads and our hearts, then making disciples is just plain fun—more than fun, it is challenging, invigorating, and abundantly satisfying. Making disciples of Jesus is all about loving people. We make disciples by forgiving everyone, accepting and loving everyone, speaking in love, and acting in love. We are both compassionate and bold. We are naturally able to love and confront the world around us simultaneously. Because we

---

4. Osborne, *Matthew*, 1080.

now know beyond a doubt that we are forgiven fully, we can offer love with no strings attached. Our love is not dependent in any way on the way we are treated, or the way circumstances play out around us. We have a much deeper source of love—we have life in the source of all love.

Just because it is natural, that doesn't mean making disciples is always easy. I have found that it is always a learning experience. Some years back I was sitting in my comfortable pastor's office. It was a lazy afternoon and I was probably about half asleep. The church secretary had gone home, and I was alone in the building when the phone rang. The call was from a young woman named Jeanie, inquiring about the use of our church building for her upcoming wedding. She was from the community and I guess had heard we had a nice facility for a wedding. I asked her for more information and told her I would check out our church policy on the use of the building (I was still new there and wasn't sure of all such matters) and get back to her.

As it turned out, I discovered, to my relief, that there were no rules restricting unchurched community members from renting our building. The fees were moderate and the guidelines, pretty simple. The real question I faced was my own personal policy about performing a wedding where neither the bride nor the groom had any Christian affiliation or beliefs.

When I called the young woman back, I explained the building use policy. I also explained that I was a Christian minister and that if they wanted me to officiate the wedding, it would need to be a Christian wedding and my role would clearly be as a Christian minister. She was interested in having me do the wedding, so I explained further that whenever I officiated a wedding, I also required the couple to go through about ten hours of pre-marriage counseling with me. This, too, seemed to suit her just fine. I still had doubts as to how serious she really was; plus, I had no idea what the groom would think about all this. But we set a time when she and her fiancé, Robert, would come by the church to meet me, tour the building, and discuss the possibilities of coordinating a wedding together. I was not confident they would even show for the appointment.

They did show, and we spent about an hour together. They both continued to express interest in having the wedding in our building and having me officiate. I had given careful thought to how I would navigate this arrangement. So, during our conversation, I handed them a covenant I had written to guide us and keep some important things clear. I had outlined the pre-marriage counseling process: ten hours counseling at $30 an hour; we would meet weekly, and they would pay me for each session at the time of the session.

It was the money that caught Robert up short. It seemed they did not have a lot of financial resources. I directed Robert to the part of the covenant that said at the end of the ten hours of counseling, if they followed through with attending and paying for all the sessions, I would gladly return the full $300 to them. I was not interested in their money. I was interested in their commitment. It took a while for the return-of-the-money idea to sink in and for Robert to believe me. Before they left that day, we had a signed covenant and a plan to work together. I was still not sure what I was getting myself into.

For years, in my pre-marriage counseling of couples, I had used a program that includes an intensive questionnaire filled out separately by both the bride and the groom. My first counseling session was spent having Jeanie and Robert fill out the questionnaire. I sent in their answers to be compiled into a compatibility report. What I received back was a shock. In all my years of pre-marriage counseling, I had never seen such a terrible score from the questionnaires. The materials from the company diagnosed Jeanie and Robert's potential marriage as a total train wreck and clearly outlined that I should by no means proceed with the counseling and wedding. Much of what was at stake concerned abuse, but there were other important issues as well.

I carefully prepared for our second counseling session. Once Jeanie and Robert arrived and settled in, I laid everything on the table. I showed them the results and explained that, although I had entered our covenant in good faith, at this time I would not be able to continue guiding them toward marriage. I apologized profusely for how things had turned out. I fully expected them to stand up in anger and stomp out of my office.

Instead, they stayed seated and tearfully told me the honest story of their relationship. By the end of the session, I had swung back 180 degrees on my decision to not continue with them. After hearing them out, I knew I could not abandon them. In the weeks following, they came to all ten counseling sessions and faithfully paid each time. In thirty years of pastoring, I never witnessed hard work, honesty, and redemption with any couple that even came close to what Jeanie and Robert demonstrated. I was thrilled to give their money back. In fact, I was tempted to pay *them* for the time we spent together! I could hardly believe the miracle of healing God accomplished in those ten sessions.

At the wedding ceremony, our church sanctuary was about half full of their friends and family members. I knew that few of those in attendance had spent much time learning anything about the Christian faith. I also knew everyone was aware that I was a Christian minister officiating the marriage of two people who had not professed any Christian faith.

When I officiate a wedding, all the pomp and circumstance means nothing to me. The part I find so important is when I spend about ten minutes speaking from my heart to the couple themselves. I don't care how many people are in attendance—I speak only to the couple. Others get to listen, but they are not who I address.

As part of my message to Jeanie and Robert, I spoke about their background and how they both came to their marriage without the resources of faith and a community of faith. I talked about the beauty of the relationship the three of us had developed. I said that they had so much to look forward to in their life together. I also said that at some point in their lives, trouble would come, they would be shaken, and they would need more than just themselves and their families. I told them that when that time of trial came along, I hoped and prayed they would find a faith community to journey with them. I said that my great desire for them in their time of need was for them to find a church home like this one, and I quoted Colossians:

> As God's chosen ones, holy and beloved, clothe yourselves with compassion, kindness, humility, meekness, and patience. Bear with one another and, if anyone has a complaint against another, forgive each other; just as the Lord has forgiven you, so you also must forgive. Above all, clothe yourselves with love, which binds everything together in perfect harmony. And let the peace of Christ rule in your hearts, to which indeed you were called in the one body. And be thankful. Let the word of Christ dwell in you richly; teach and admonish one another in all wisdom; and with gratitude in your hearts sing psalms, hymns, and spiritual songs to God. And whatever you do, in word or deed, do everything in the name of the Lord Jesus, giving thanks to God the Father through him. (Col 3:12–17)

While I remained in that community, Jeanie and Robert became my good friends. Together with my wife, the four of us ate out together. They gave us Christmas gifts. Nothing in our relationship had turned out the way I thought it would. It is now clear to me just how important is the task of making disciples. It is a task waiting for us every day and in every relationship we experience. In each moment we share with others, we are given by God the opportunity to give away the love of Christ. There are so many formal and informal times with people of any persuasion when what we say and do can introduce the potential for them to know and follow Jesus. If we are disciples of Jesus, making disciples happens as we journey through life. Let's remember the entire breadth of this command: "all nations" means everyone—no exceptions. Our work is worldwide, and not restricted to any category of people.

"Baptizing Them"

> ". . . baptizing them in the name of the Father and of the Son and of the Holy Spirit." (Matt 28:19)

It seems many Christians think of baptism as an event to publicly symbolize their decision to follow Jesus, and in part, this is true. Yet, if this is all it is, baptism would carry little transformational meaning; it would potentially function like a magic formula for instituting people into the folds of the church and heaven's future reward. This can hardly be Jesus' intent. None of Jesus' teachings in the Gospel of Matthew leads us to a shallow, symbolic, or temporary (albeit heartfelt at the time) commitment to present kingdom living. Jesus was all about teaching and demonstrating undivided and ongoing loyalties to God's will and way in this world.

It is interesting to note that the only previous references to baptism in the Gospel of Matthew refer to the baptism of John the Baptist. Even these seem to garner little emphasis beyond the actual ministry of John in chapter 3. Jesus and his disciples did not baptize others, at least not in Matthew's version of the story. In chapter 10 Jesus sends out the twelve disciples with explicit instructions, but he says nothing about baptizing anyone. Yet, here in his last commandment, Jesus institutes baptism as an important aspect of making disciples. Why here? Why now?

Let's remember, the overarching command is to make disciples. To be a follower of Jesus means you are not following someone or something else. Throughout this study of Matthew, we have emphasized how Jesus spoke to the heart of the matter, how Jesus required a change of heart, and how his instructions called for complete renewal of our hearts. There is no way for us to become disciples of Jesus or make disciples of others without this change of heart. It seems that the only way to follow him is from the depth of our hearts. If we follow Jesus' way of centering on the heart, we can surmise he is now including the act of baptism as confirmation that our heart is now fully aligned with him, that we accept his life as the pattern for our own at such a deep level as to transform all we think, do, and say.

Furthermore, Jesus makes clear that baptism engages a full relationship with God: baptism is "in the name of the Father and of the Son and of the Holy Spirit." No aspect of God is left out. This is not just about the walk Jesus took through time and human history. This is total alignment with all aspects of God. In other words, the full authority of Jesus is assumed within the completeness of God. Jesus was no mere mortal who pointed us toward God, said important things, and called us to listen to him. Jesus has all authority because he—the Son—is an essential part of God.

Being baptized and baptizing others call us to bring ourselves, heart in hand, into submission to all of God on an intimate level. Jesus is telling us to give our heart completely not to an idea or an ideal, but to the very being of God. In our baptism, we open ourselves fully to God's heart and to its influence on ours. Imagine the power of God's loving heart fully fused with yours. Now imagine accepting Jesus' call to make disciples with this same level of God-infused loving relationship.

Possibly the most powerful New Testament description of the baptism to which Jesus calls us comes from Paul in Romans:

> What then are we to say? Should we continue in sin in order that grace may abound? By no means! How can we who died to sin go on living in it? Do you not know that all of us who have been baptized into Christ Jesus were baptized into his death? Therefore we have been buried with him by baptism into death, so that, just as Christ was raised from the dead by the glory of the Father, so we too might walk in newness of life. (Rom 6:1–4)

What Paul explains in these verses is a complete identification with Jesus: his death is ours and his life is ours. In baptism, we undergo the same degree of transformation as Jesus did when he relinquished his life completely on behalf of the world and allowed God to raise him up. We are "all in"! Jesus' death and life are everything to us now. If we are to baptize others as Jesus would have us do, we first must undergo his death and experience his life as our own. Only then will we be qualified to baptize others.

Dying to self is essentially grief work written across the whole expanse of our lives. Grief work isn't easy, but it is essential. When we avoid it, all sorts of mental and emotional troubles prohibit our spiritual growth. When the grief work of dying to self is incomplete, we know only a limited version of God's love. We remain vulnerable to the lure of the world's powers. Anything less than God's love is not a part of the intimacy God intends for us and our world. To the extent that we try to deny death and its hold on our world, we deny God's intimate care for us and the world. This place we call reality, then, is an alternate universe from the one in which God created us to live.

Baptism is a powerful symbol in the moment of its enactment. But real baptism takes place every day! We are to remember our death and experience life in Christ always.

Baptism for a Lifetime

When Hurricane Katrina hit in 2005, I received a call from a friend who had already headed to the Gulf region to help. They needed more workers to cut up trees that had fallen on houses and to cover roofs with tarp to keep homes from being damaged further. Three of us arrived a few days later and went to work. I soon discovered that it was very hot in southern Mississippi in September. By 9:00 in the morning, after about an hour's work, our clothes were soaked through with sweat.

People volunteered in all aspects of the effort. Some cooked and fed us excellent meals. A church opened its doors so the volunteers would have a place to eat and sleep. I particularly remember the hard-as-rocks army cot I slept on and the children's bathroom with the short little toilet!

The entire operation was done with volunteers from around the state and country. Most of the homes in the small city where we worked were damaged, some nearly destroyed. Before the effort was finished, over half the houses had sections of roof covered with blue tarp. Drinking water was a precious commodity. Whole pallets of bottled water sat waiting for us to load up our packs and coolers each morning. People opened their homes for us to take showers. In a community still living in de facto segregation, lines between races were blurred.

For one week of my life, there in southern Mississippi, I got to watch people selflessly helping others. A part of every volunteer's life had to die so they could give time and effort to serve people they had never met. I don't want to romanticize the Katrina cleanup effort; neither do I want to miss its significance. But what does this have to do with baptism and baptizing? The Katrina volunteer effort is evidence of hearts molded to the heart of God. This was a spiritual act. When our hearts are submitted to God for dying and then living, we live out our baptism into Jesus and his life of loving service.

I purposely use this story to illustrate the potentially all-invasive nature of baptism. Though the Katrina cleanup effort was temporary, it points to a permanent state of serving instead of being served, of dying daily in order to live what Jesus taught. Through serving others, our moment of baptism becomes a lifetime of baptism. No more theory, no more magic formula. We now find our identity in Christ, who served us in the most complete way possible.

"Teaching Them to Obey Everything"

> "... and teaching them to obey everything that I have commanded you." (Matt 28:20)

Remember, "all" means *all*. Jesus did not say "teach them my commandments that are comfortable to you." He did not say "pick and choose between the things I have taught you." He did not say "teach them to obey in part or until they think they know better." Jesus seems oblivious to the problems of our world that seem insurmountable to us—like how we deal with people like Hitler or when we cannot bring ourselves to turn the other cheek.

Jesus makes clear that God expects obedience in *everything*. He did not say we had to do everything perfectly, but clearly, he intends for us to commit to it all, nonetheless. When we most want an escape hatch is probably the time we most need his heart to guide our hearts. If we take this part of Jesus' last command seriously, we get back to the basics of life in his life. By "basics," I mean his words and actions alone and ahead of other words and actions we live or see in others.

We will not be capable of teaching others to obey everything Jesus has commanded unless we ourselves are obeying him at this level. We need to go back to the definitive understanding of how we are to live as followers of Jesus. Nothing else comes first. Not family, marriage, church, country, self-preservation—nothing else by which we define ourselves or over which we formerly compromised. I quote Richard Rohr:

> Either we learn how to live in communion with others, or, quite simply, we're not ready for heaven and are already in hell. We have been invited—even now, even today, even this moment—to live in the Communion of Saints, in the Presence, in the Body, in the Life of the eternal and eternally Risen Christ.[5]

Hell is not the place God sends bad people to be tortured for eternity. Hell is when and where people live out their anger, pain, resentments, fears, and false depictions of

---

5. Rohr, "Returning Home."

God. *It is so essential that we hear, see, and obey Jesus in everything because life in Christ frees us from hell on earth.*

Jesus commands every part of us and our lives here on earth. We can choose to disobey part or all of him, but we will never alter the truth of God's love. It is the truth of the universe. This truth carries on with or without us. We can choose to be a part of God's love or not. Hell is what we choose when we turn from obedience to Jesus.

Think for a moment what it would be like to teach something we do not know and live ourselves. We would be faking it. We would be misleading others. Reread Matthew 23, where Jesus condemns the Pharisees for this sort of false teaching. Think about how important it is to Jesus that we today hear his command to teach people to obey *everything* he has commanded. If we ourselves are not obeying *everything* he commanded, yet try to teach others, we will fail miserably. We will actually be teaching them *not to obey everything* he has commanded. Indeed, much of Christian teaching has done this, opposing the teaching of Jesus' Great Commission.

The present participle *teaching* is intended to indicate ongoing instruction. Our total obedience to Jesus, and teaching this obedience to others, is an essential element of making disciples as we go *all* through life in this world. Without knowing and teaching *everything* from Jesus as we journey through life, we will not fulfill the Great Commission. This Commission is the culminating commandment of Jesus in Matthew, and it returns us to Galilee, where we discover how to follow Jesus all over again.

Looking for Pennies

I met Danny when he was walking the streets looking for pennies. Dimes would be okay too, he said, but pennies were his main goal. Danny was homeless. He said he had been a successful race car driver, and I did not believe him. After I got over thinking he was using me, we struck up a friendship. Over a year or so, with help from others, we found Danny a place to live and eventually a job. Last I heard, Danny was driving race cars again, which is still hard for me to believe, but apparently, it's true!

I can't begin to tell you all the ups and downs of our friendship, my personal failings and Danny's as well. We slowly learned from each other, actually. Danny came to the church where I pastored, but it did not stick for him. I think he did not feel he fit in, and he saw through some of the hypocrisy. One thing I learned from Danny was to better see through hypocrisy, my own included. While Danny had his own issues, he also saw through mine. He did not allow me to manipulate him; he stood his ground and I am grateful.

Some would say that in the end, my efforts to disciple and teach Danny failed. I don't think so. I think the give-and-take in our relationship was a valuable part of teaching discipleship. It was not up to Danny to save me, or for me to save Danny. As far as my part in our friendship was concerned, I was responsible to love him honestly and serve him when and where I understood how to do so. Every moment of our time together was a chance for one of us to pass on the loving teachings of Jesus. I hope I did my part. There were surely times when Danny did his.

The stories I have shared in this chapter demonstrate that everyday "stuff" is where making disciples happens. We all have access to everyday "stuff." I suppose big miracles happen now and then, but it is best not to wait for them. Jesus gave us practical, doable, livable, everyday teachings and life examples of loving and serving others. He told us the practical, everyday truth, and I will go to my grave declaring it loudly, especially to those who teach it halfway. To teach "everything" means *everything*.

"I Am with You Always"

"And remember, I am with you always, to the end of the age." (Matt 28:20)

With his last words, Jesus once more addresses our doubts and fears. To fulfill the commission he has just given us is an awesome task and one for which we are not prepared. In our fear and doubt, we might ask what it really means when Jesus says he is with us always. Consider these words his parting gift, his lasting promise, his guarantee that his life is truly ours to the end of the age.

Also, consider the present-tense affirmation that he *is* with us. There is no distance between him and us at any point of our life on earth. His life, teachings, and ministry were, are, and always will be with us. What he taught in the Sermon on the Mount is with us daily. The law of love he called us to is an everyday guide. His loving ministry is fully directed to and through us now. His death and resurrection give definition to how we live and die in all the glory of life in the present.

I really love chocolate cake. The more chocolate in it, the better. But it is the rich chocolate icing that seals my love for the cake. It is especially the icing that calls to me insistently: "Eat the cake!" It might be a stretch to use this food metaphor, but I find in it a compelling truth about Jesus, his life, and his calling on our lives. If Jesus' life of teaching, leading, loving, healing, serving in and through death, and his resurrection can all be represented by the cake, then this final promise is the icing. This final promise says, loud and clear, "Eat this cake!" Don't settle for anything less!

If only we believed that the icing is real, the cake might also become real to us. The continual presence of Jesus with us throughout every day of our lives—if we realized the awesome implications—would surely prompt us to partake of all the life he taught us. Jesus declares his presence with us, enabling us to live the commission he gave. Whatever violence remains in our lives, Jesus is with us, teaching and leading us back to God's complete love. This is not some saying in an old book written 2,000 years ago. This is Emmanuel, God with us, teaching and guiding us through life with each new day.

God is with us. Fear and doubt are no longer our masters.

Stories of Jesus' Presence

Back when I was the Resident Director of a men's college dorm, I was called from my apartment one evening into the midst of an angry mob of very large football players. These guys were seething. I was frightened to my core for the safety of the students and my family, not to mention myself. I managed to get them settled enough to tell me their story. It started with a young white man racially slurring several African American men. The football players had responded in anger and threatened the white man. The white man became frightened and returned to his room where he had a hunting rifle hidden. He brandished the gun in the faces of the football players. This lit up the entire dorm. As the men told me this story, their anger piqued all over again.

I was one person amid dozens of angry voices threatening violence like I had not heard before. Yet it seemed the angrier they became, the calmer I became. This calm had nothing to do with me, because I was terrified. No training had prepared me to be calm in this situation. The calm simply took over in me. I knew we were on the verge of a race riot, and something more than my presence was needed. The calm prompted me to offer the assurance of justice. The calm said to get additional help to do this. The calm in me (not me myself) was enough to stave off an immediate riot. The calm convinced them justice would be done. The calm convinced them help was on the way.

I placed an urgent call to the Director of Students. He came immediately. He, too, shared a sense of calm that was living in him. Together, slowly, we all began to talk about a way through the crisis. All voices were heard. The outrage was acknowledged, and a series of steps were outlined to begin to ease the pain that now filled the eyes of all the young men in the room.

Nothing but the presence of Jesus himself, his love, and his assurance could have been the winning force that night. This was beyond all human capabilities, but not beyond the one who taught us to love our enemies and pray for them so that we would become God's children on an everyday basis.

Another evening, many years later, while I relaxed at home after closing down my pastoral duties for the day, I received a tragic phone call. A relatively young man had had a massive heart attack and died in the presence of his family. He had a wife and five children, the oldest being teenagers. The caller was an elder in our church asking me to come to the local emergency room. I was not relaxed anymore. I was filled with great sadness for the family and an overwhelming sense of inadequacy. How could I bring anything meaningful or helpful to this family's grief-stricken hearts?

As I entered the hospital, I was met by the elder and his wife. They ushered me into a back room where the family and a few close friends had gathered. I am ashamed to admit that while walking toward that room, what I mostly felt was dread. I had no idea what to do or say. At that moment I wanted to be anywhere in the world but there. So much for the pastoral heart I thought I had.

In a very real sense, it was not me who entered that room. My body was there, but it was as if I were somewhere else looking in. It was the first hug and all the tears that followed. It was the overpowering moment of grief reflected in everyone's eyes. It was the strength and courage of the family themselves. It was God absolutely taking over where I could not emotionally go. And it was all these things together that brought pure holiness to earth in that room.

All fear was vanquished for that night in that hospital room. Jesus was not only present; he was living his life in us. We finally ended our time together in a circle of prayer, holding hands around the perimeter of the room. I still remember the unbelievable words I heard prayed by the man's two teenage daughters. Through their tears, in the midst of their agony, they thanked God for the life of their father. They were not pretending. They were not merely mouthing words they "should" say. They were laying out their hearts to God in a profound trust perhaps only seen in children. But this last thought reveals my own unbelief, for the absolute truth of that night is contained in Jesus' words: "And remember, I am with you always, to the end of the age."

Always a New Beginning

The timeframe Jesus names in his final words covers all of human history up until the consummation of time as we know it: "to the end of the age." Following that time, we will know only the joy of living in the presence of God. The stories above are only two among the myriad stories we could tell together—stories of grace and salvation as we sometimes stumble headlong into the presence of Jesus living God's will and way in us.

If God is with us, who can be against us? Some will say that a lot of the world's worst can be against us. The question is, can the world's worst truly stand in the face of God who stands with us? But will we ever know what it is like for God to stand completely with us if we duck and run in the face of the world's evil? Will we ever know full reliance on God? The full presence of Jesus? The true outcome at the end of the age?

Nothing will significantly change for us and our world apart from a true crisis of identity. I ever hope for that crisis to surprise us. As we witness the apparent dying of the church today, at least in the United States, I sense the crisis coming. What I hope will emerge is the living of the life of Jesus in every moment and every imaginable way without the trappings of religious ideology. What a gift to the world that would be! What an end to hypocrisy! What a way to say no to evil and yes to God's love in every circumstance!

Any authentic resurrection of the church will need to be fully patterned after the life of Jesus, not in part but in whole. His authority must reign supreme! There will be no resurrection apart from his. There is no life apart from his. Apart from him there really is no church. I am pretty certain that if the resurrection of the church is to happen, it will be—at least at the beginning—unrecognizable to us. That will be its greatest gift. Ones we least expect might be those who lead us back to Jesus.

Once again, hear Jesus' amazing last words:

> Do not be afraid . . .
>
> Go to Galilee . . .
>
> All authority . . . has been given to me . . .
>
> Go . . . and make disciples . . .
>
> baptizing them . . .
>
> teaching them to obey everything . . .
>
> I am with you always.

These amazing last words conclude the Gospel of Matthew. But with these words of promise, our life in Jesus Christ begins anew.

BIBLIOGRAPHY

Barclay, William. *The Gospel of Matthew*. Vol 1. Revised edition. Daily Study Bible. Louisville: Westminster John Knox, 1975.

Bauer, Walter, William F. Arndt, and F. Wilbur Gingrich. *A Greek-English Lexicon of the New Testament, and Other Early Christian Literature*. 4th ed. Chicago: University of Chicago Press, 1952.

Bauman, Clarence. *The Sermon on the Mount: The Modern Quest for Its Meaning*. Macon, GA: Mercer University Press, 1990.

Beatty, Warren, Elaine May, and Robert Towne. *Heaven Can Wait* (feature-length film). Directed by Warren Beatty and Buck Henry. Paramount, 1978.

Boyd, Gregory A. *The Myth of a Christian Nation: How the Quest for Political Power Is Destroying the Church*. Grand Rapids: Zondervan, 2005.

Buber, Martin. *I and Thou*. Edinburgh, T. & T. Clark, 1937.

Clemens, Philip K. *Beyond the Law: Living the Sermon on the Mount*. Scottdale, PA: Herald, 2007.

Damon, Matt, and Ben Affleck. *Good Will Hunting* (feature-length film). Directed by Gus Van Sant. Miramax, 1997.

Draper, Barb. "Ethiopian Meserete Kristos Church Continues to Grow," *The Mennonite* (December 19, 2017). https://themennonite.org/daily-news/ethiopian-meserete-kristos-church-continues-grow/.

Ferwerda, Julie. *Raising Hell: Christianity's Most Controversial Doctrine Put Under Fire*. Kindle ebook. Sandpoint, ID: Vagabond Group, 2011.

Finley, James. "Dreaming Compassion." *Daily Meditations*. Center for Action and Contemplation, February 24, 2017. https://cac.org/dreaming-compassion-2017-02-24/.

Gushee, David P., Glen Harold Stassen. *Kingdom Ethics: Following Jesus in Contemporary Context*. 2nd ed. Grand Rapids: Eerdmans, 2016.

King, Martin Luther, Jr. *A Gift of Love: Sermons from Strength to Love and Other Preachings*. Boston: Beacon, 2012.

Kittel, Gerhard, and Gerhard Friedrich, eds. *Theological Dictionary of the New Testament*. Vol. 6. Translated by Geoffrey W. Bromiley. Grand Rapids: Eerdmans, 1968.

Klassen, Randolph J. *What Does the Bible Really Say about Hell?* Telford, PA: Pandora, 2001.

Kraybill, J. Nelson. *Apocalypse and Allegiance: Worship, Politics, and Devotion in the Book of Revelation*. Grand Rapids: Brazos, 2010.

Krueger, William Kent. *Vermillion Drift*. Cork O'Connor series. New York: Atria, 2010.

Lehman, Tim. *Seeking the Wilderness: A Spiritual Journey.* Newton, KS: Faith and Life, 1993.

Lewis, C. S. *Surprised by Joy.* London: Collins, 1955.

Luz, Ulrich. *Matthew: A Commentary*, Vol. 2. Translated by James E. Crouch. Edited by Helmut Koester. Hermeneia. Minneapolis: Fortress, 2001.

———. *Matthew: A Commentary*, Vol. 3. Translated by James E. Crouch. Edited by Helmut Koester. Hermeneia. Minneapolis: Fortress, 2005.

McLaren, Brian D. *The Great Spiritual Migration: How the World's Largest Religion Is Seeking a Better Way to Be Christian.* New York: Convergent, 2016.

———. *The Last Word and the Word After That: A Tale of Faith, Doubt, and a New Kind of Christianity.* San Francisco: Jossey-Bass, 2005.

Merriam Webster Online, s.v. "amen." Accessed September 27, 2019, https://www.merriam-webster.com/dictionary/amen.

Osborne, Grant R. *Matthew.* Exegetical Commentary on the New Testament. Grand Rapids: Zondervan, 2010.

Rohr, Richard. "Returning Home," *Daily Meditations.* Center for Action and Contemplation, November 20, 2018. https://cac.org/returning-home-2018-11-20/

———. "Solidarity with the World," *Daily Meditations.* Center for Action and Contemplation, June 1, 2018. https://cac.org/solidarity-with-the-world-2018-06-01/.

Rohr, Richard, and John Feister. *Jesus' Plan for a New World: The Sermon on the Mount.* Cincinnati: St. Anthony Messenger, 1996.

Senior, Donald. *Matthew.* Abingdon New Testament Commentaries. Nashville: Abingdon, 1998.

Stassen, Glen Harold. *Living the Sermon on the Mount: A Practical Hope for Grace and Deliverance.* San Francisco: Jossey-Bass, 2006.

Swartzentruber, Jacob. "Meserete Kristos Church, Ethiopia." Last modified October 10, 2016. https://anabaptistwiki.org/mediawiki/index.php?title=Meserete_Kristos_Church,_Ethiopia&oldid=16497.

Sweeney, Jon M. *Inventing Hell: Dante, the Bible, and Eternal Torment.* New York: Jericho, 2014.

Weaver, J. Denny. *The Nonviolent Atonement.* Revised and expanded. Grand Rapids: Eerdmans, 2001.

Wikipedia, s.v. "Meserete Kristos Church." Last modified February 20, 2019. https://en.wikipedia.org/wiki/Meserete_Kristos_Church.

Willard, Dallas. *The Divine Conspiracy: Rediscovering Our Hidden Life in God.* San Francisco: HarperSanFrancisco, 1998.

Wright, N. T. *How God Became King: The Forgotten Story of the Gospels.* New York: HarperOne, 2012.

———. *Simply Jesus: A New Vision of Who He Was and Why He Matters.* New York: HarperOne, 2011.

Yoder, Perry B. *Leviticus.* Believers Church Bible Commentary. Harrisonburg, VA: Herald, 2017.

———. *Shalom: The Bible's Word for Salvation, Justice, and Peace.* Newton, KS: Faith and Life, 1987.

Young, William P. *The Shack.* Los Angeles: Windblown, 2007.

Zschech, Darlene. "Potter's Hand." Performed by Hillsong. Sony Music Entertainment. Video posted August 25, 2010. https://www.youtube.com/watch?v=bgXL3y9RIbI

CPSIA information can be obtained
at www.ICGtesting.com
Printed in the USA
FSHW020434131219
64733FS